THE
PORTSMOUTH
REGION

The Portsmouth Region

THE
PORTSMOUTH
REGION

Edited by
Barry Stapleton and James H. Thomas

ALAN SUTTON
1989

ALAN SUTTON PUBLISHING
BRUNSWICK ROAD · GLOUCESTER

First published 1989

British Library Cataloguing in Publication Data

Stapleton, Barry
The Portsmouth region.
1. Portsmouth Region (Hampshire —
History
I. Title
942.2'792 DA 690. P8

ISBN 0-86299-374-1

Jacket illustration: Part of Johan Blaeu's *Atlas Novus*, 1648.

Typesetting and origination by
Alan Sutton Publishing Limited.
Printed in Great Britain by
Dotesios Printers Limited.

CONTENTS

Part One THE ARCHAEOLOGICAL BACKGROUND

Part Two THE HISTORICAL BACKGROUND

Part Three THE NATURAL ENVIRONMENT

Part Four TWENTIETH-CENTURY PORTSMOUTH

LIST OF ILLUSTRATIONS

PLATES Page

FIGURES
Page

MAPS
Page

LIST OF ILLUSTRATIONS   ix

TABLES   Page

CONTRIBUTORS

David Carter — Department of Geography, Portsmouth Polytechnic.

John Chapman — Department of Geography, Portsmouth Polytechnic.

Brian Daley — Department of Geology, Portsmouth Polytechnic.

Nicholas Fox — Hampshire County Library, Winchester.

Fred Haynes — Formerly School of Biological Sciences, Portsmouth Polytechnic.

Margaret Hoad — Portsmouth City Records Office.

David E. Johnston — Department of Adult Education, Southampton University.

Hugh Mason — Department of Geography, Portsmouth Polytechnic.

R.C. Riley — Department of Geography, Portsmouth Polytechnic.

David J. Rudkin — Director, Fishbourne Roman Palace and Museum.

Barry Stapleton — School of Economics, Portsmouth Polytechnic.

Fay Stranack — Formerly School of Biological Sciences, Portsmouth Polytechnic.

James H. Thomas — School of Social and Historical Studies, Portsmouth Polytechnic.

John Webb — Formerly Faculty of Educational Studies, Portsmouth Polytechnic.

Ron Windle — Formerly Department of Social Studies, Portsmouth Polytechnic.

PREFACE

This volume of essays has been long in the making – seven years to be precise. During that time there have been changes in both direction and contributors. What started with a meeting in the Lord Mayor's Parlour at Portsmouth as a projected series of ten or eleven volumes, covering Hampshire in its entirety under the auspices of the Hampshire Field Club and Archaeological Society, has become, instead, one volume of essays dealing with Portsmouth and its immediate region. That said, however, the volume, intended to be the first of the series, aims to provide a comprehensive survey of Portsmouth and its region, an area of growing national and international importance over the centuries. Furthermore, it is the first such broad survey of the region that has been undertaken since before 1914 and, as such, incorporates the findings of much more recent research.

The book considers four main themes – the archaeological background from prehistoric times to the industrial archaeology of the modern era; the historical background from the Norman conquest to the First World War; the natural environment dealing with the flora and fauna of both land and water; and twentieth-century Portsmouth. Much is revealed about the impact of man on the environment of the region from his beginnings and the associated patterns of early settlement, through the varying uses of land and sea over time as the population increased, to the impact of the expanding conurbation of the twentieth century. This conurbation is centred on Portsmouth which, though non-existent in Domesday times and founded only in the late twelfth century, grew to dominate the region by the end of the nineteenth. Hence the emphasis in the last section of the work is placed squarely on the emerging city of Portsmouth. The region, for the purposes of the book, is defined as including the city of Portsmouth, the area eastwards to the borders of West Sussex, northwards to the slopes of Butser Hill and westwards to the Hamble river. It therefore includes reference to the following communities – Bedhampton, Blendworth, Boarhunt, Catherington, Chalton, Clanfield, Cowplain, Droxford, Emsworth, Fareham, Farlington, Gosport, Horndean, Hambledon, Havant, Hayling Island, Meonstoke, Portchester, Purbrook, Rowner, Soberton, Southwick, Titchfield, Waterlooville, Wickham, Widley and Wymering.

In any publication which contains the work of fifteen different and differing contributors the position of the editors is not likely to be an easy one. We are only too aware that, in endeavouring to produce a cohesive whole, especially in those areas in which our expertise does not lie, we may well have inadvertently offended the sensibilities of some of our fellow writers. If so, we regret it. It has to be said, however, that any modifications which have been made were undertaken in order that the final product would form a satisfactory and satisfying total volume for the benefit of readers, and not remain some fourteen independent chapters. In the case of Chapter 4 the Medieval section was written by Margaret Hoad and the remainder by John Webb. To those contributors who have borne our requests with patience and understanding, we are grateful.

Barry Stapleton
James H. Thomas

ACKNOWLEDGEMENTS

Numerous debts in terms of human kindness were incurred by the editors while the volume was in preparation. For research support and facilities we are obliged to Dr Harry Law, President, and Peter Mills, Vice-President of the Polytechnic, Professors T. Podolski and G.M. Martin, Deans of our respective Faculties, and Mike Dunn and Malcolm McVicar, our two Heads of School. To the numerous archivists and librarians whose materials were worked upon, a special debt of gratitude is warmly extended, especially to Sarah Quail, Portsmouth City Records Officer, Rosemary Dunhill, County Archivist of Hampshire, and the Portsmouth Central Library for allowing access to the local history collection for the illustrations used in Chapter 12. In the Geographical Information Services Unit of the Department of Geography of Portsmouth Polytechnic we are indebted to Alastair Pearson, Bill Johnson and Roger Homer for the production of maps and photographs. For providing a grant which ensured publication of this volume we are pleased to acknowledge the generosity of the Hampshire Field Club and Archaeological Society. To three members of the Polytechnic staff we are indebted for typing and clerical assistance. Our gratitude goes first to Lorraine Shaw and Jan Martin, but most particularly to Jan Kirton whose invaluable contribution was beyond the normal call of duty.

Finally, for endeavouring to cope with the strains imposed upon us by our contributors and others, we are deeply indebted to Alexandra and Suzanne. For any errors that remain we plead guilty.

ABBREVIATIONS

A.N.L.	*Archaeological News Letter.*
A.R.	*Annual Register.*
B.I.H.R.	*Bulletin of the Institute of Historical Research.*
B.L.	British Library.
CBA	Council of British Archaeology.
C.H.O.P.	*Calendar of Home Office Papers.*
C.S.P.D.	*Calendar of State Papers Domestic.*
C.T.B.P.	*Calendar of Treasury Books and Papers.*
C.U.L.	Cambridge University Library.
Ec.H.R.	*Economic History Review.*
G.L.	Guildhall Library
G.M.	*Gentleman's Magazine*
H.R.O.	Hampshire Record Office.
J.P.C.T.I.A.S.	*Journal of the Portsmouth College of Technology Industrial Archaeology Society.*
L.G.	*London Gazette.*
P.C.L.	Portsmouth Central Library.
P.C.R.O.	Portsmouth City Record Office.
P.P.	The Portsmouth Papers.
P.R.O.	Public Record Office.
Proc.H.F.C.	*Proceedings of the Hampshire Field Club and Archaeological Society.*
Proc.P.S.	*Proceedings of the Prehistoric Society.*
P.R.S.	*Portsmouth Record Series.*
R.A.H.	*Rescue Archaeology in Hampshire.*
S.P.R.	Southwick Priory Registers.
V.C.H.	*The Victoria History of the Counties of England.*

PART ONE
THE ARCHAEOLOGICAL BACKGROUND

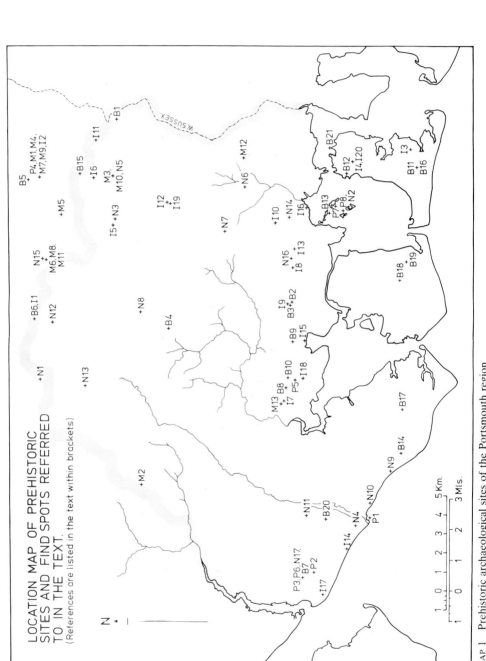

MAP 1   Prehistoric archaeological sites of the Portsmouth region

1
PREHISTORIC

David J. Rudkin

The prehistory of an area as small as the Portsmouth region has to be viewed in a wider context. Consequently, the evidence will be examined within the general framework of the prehistory of southern Britain as a whole.[1] It will also be considered within the traditional technological periods of Stone Age, Bronze Age and Iron Age. Although this is now recognised to be a less than perfect system when comparing large areas, it is nevertheless very convenient for a region of this size.[2]

Men are first thought to have reached southern Britain at a time of dramatic climatic changes. For many thousands of years there were fluctuations between glacial periods of intense cold and warmer interglacial eras. Warmer spells also occurred within the periods of glaciation, thereby permitting some human occupation. It is possible that one of modern man's predecessors, *Homo erectus*, arrived during a warm spell in the antepenultimate or Anglian glaciation perhaps as long ago as 350,000 BC, although the evidence for this is very tenuous. More positive evidence comes from the succeeding Hoxnian interglacial between perhaps 250,000 and 200,000 BC, by which time bands of *Homo erectus* were crossing the land bridge from the Continent following the herds of game, upon which, as hunter-gatherers, they were largely dependent. These incomers practised a crude flint technology resulting in chopping tools and coarse thick flakes. These tools have been found at sites such as Clacton, Essex, Swanscombe, Kent and Kent's Cavern, Devon. Similar implements have been found at Rainbow Bar, Hill Head, Titchfield[3] (P.1) and may represent human activity from this period. The similarity, however, could be due purely to the crudity of the flint working, and the tools may well have been produced many thousands of years later.[4] At a later date within the Hoxnian interglacial, other groups were producing very distinctive hand axes and, to a lesser extent, flake tools. Known as the Acheulean industries they appear throughout the Hoxnian interglacial and preceding Wolstonion glaciation (*c.* 200,000–125,000 BC) and Ipswichian interglacial (*c.* 125,000–70,000 BC) They may even have survived in Hampshire until the early phases of the final Devensian glaciation (*c.* 70,000–8,300 BC).[5] Vast quantities of these Acheulean hand axes (see Plate 1) occur in Hampshire, many coming from the gravel workings near Hook (P.2) and Warsash (P.3). There is no doubt that many were derived from elsewhere, having been

3

PLATE 1   Lower Palaeolithic hand axes from the Hook-Warsash area

swept up and redeposited by the Old Solent River. These are recognisable by their
blunted, rolled condition. However, some remained in their original place of
deposition, such as those from the 17m raised beach at Warsash.[6] Other stray finds
from further inland, such as those from the top of Butser Hill (P.4), presumably
represent accidental loss such as may have occurred on hunting expeditions. By far
the most significant discovery, however, is a flint-working site at Red Barns,
Portchester (P.5), on the southern slopes of Portsdown.[7] Here a small excavation
revealed a working floor covered in waste flakes, broken or unfinished hand axes,
scrapers and hammer stones in a grey soil matrix. The sharpness of the artefacts
indicated that they had not been disturbed since they had been discarded by their
makers who were presumably exploiting the nearby outcrops of flint nodules. The
remarkable state of preservation resulted from a layer of calcareous mud which had
engulfed the site during the Wolstonian glaciation. In that period a major
innovation in flint technology, the Levallois technique, introduced the concept of a
prepared core produced by radial flaking. From this core it was possible to produce
a flake of controlled shape, one that was large, quite thin and of a regular form. The
result was a shape reminiscent of the carapace of a tortoise, hence the name
'tortoise core'. This technique was almost certainly developed by the same groups
that had been producing Acheulean tools and both Levallois flakes and tortoise
cores have been found in gravel deposits on the north shore of the Solent,
especially in the Warsash gravel pits (P.6).

Possibly in the late Ipswichian interglacial, or more probably in the succeeding early phase of the Devensian glaciation, a new form of hand axe appeared. It was carefully worked and heart-shaped and is typical of one of the several known Mousterian flint industries: the Mousterian of Acheulean Tradition (MTA). The evidence suggests that at least some of these Mousterian industries were the work of *Homo sapiens neanderthalensis*. However, it was *Homo sapiens sapiens* who was producing the Upper Palaeolithic flint industries in Britain by the end of the last glaciation. Evidence in the Portsmouth region is very sparse, almost all coming from the islands in the north-west corner of Langstone Harbour, where the tools found were all based on flint blades. They included a burin or graver, scrapers, shouldered points and backed blades from Long Island (P.7)[8] and an exceptionally fine end scraper from Bakers Island (P.8), all bearing a marked similarity to those found at another open-air site at Hengistbury Head. The tools from the islands were not found *in situ* but had been eroded out on to the shore, indicating that the area at least was exploited, if not occupied, by a band of hunter-gatherers some time during a late phase of the final glaciation, probably between 12,000 and 10,000 BC.

The boundary between the Palaeolithic and the Mesolithic (Middle Stone Age) periods coincides with the end of the last glaciation and the onset of neothermal conditions, fixed by radiocarbon dating to *c.* 8300 bc. Inevitably, the increasing temperature and rainfall led to vegetational changes from a tundra flora to birch and pine forests and finally to an oak-mixed forest cover. This resulted in the development of a forest-loving fauna such as red and roe deer, elk, wild pig and wild oxen, which, in turn, required man to employ different hunting techniques. Changes in the size of hunting groups may well have followed, but archaeological evidence for this assumption is lacking. However, microliths manufactured from small flint blades which occur widely on Mesolithic sites were certainly used for tipping arrows, indicating that hunting by bow and arrow had been adopted. The large migratory herds of the open tundra had disappeared, but the reduction in the animal population available for hunting does not appear to have adversely affected population growth. At least 5,000 Mesolithic sites are known to have existed in southern Britain.[9] However, it seems most likely that the occupants were exploiting additional food resources, such as shellfish in coastal regions, for which much evidence survives in northern Britain, and plant food which, unfortunately, leaves little trace in the archaeological record. In fact, scant organic material of any kind survives, leaving the flint industries as almost the sole evidence for an understanding of the period. It is upon these flint industries that the chronological framework of the period has been constructed. It has been divided into earlier and later Mesolithic in Britain as a whole, but with a third component, a Horsham or Wealden industry, in south-east England. In the Portsmouth region approximately 80 areas of Mesolithic flint scatter have been recorded. As hardly any of these have been excavated, it is difficult to say what they represent in human terms. Possibly they were just isolated flint-working floors located near convenient flint outcrops. Nevertheless, sites tend to cluster into groups often of an apparently similar age,[10] such as the twelve on Butser Hill (M.1),[11] although the flint scatters do not contain enough characteristic tool types to assign them to a particular chronological context. However, earlier Mesolithic material has been recognised on one or two sites in the Portsmouth region, the most important being at Sandy Lane, Shedfield (M.2).[12] Many flints, including eight microliths, were recovered from the topsoil and selective sectioning of the underlying sand surface produced many more. The sectioning also indicated the limits of the flint scatter, suggesting an area approximately 73m across which may have represented a group of smaller sites. Two artefacts from the site are worthy of special consideration. The first is a remarkable double-ended flint pick, some 31cm long, strongly resembling the head of a modern pick and presumably used in the same way. The pick would have been mounted in a hole in the haft, whereas the reverse is the case with the modern implement. The second artefact was an axe resharpening flake: a waste flake of characteristic form which was struck off the cutting edge of a blunted axe or adze. Axe resharpening flakes are not uncommon, but this particular example was made of a material from outside the Portsmouth area and was presumably brought in by trade or long-distance movement. Such a view is supported by a Portland chert microburin, the waste from the production of a microlith, found on Windmill Hill, Chalton (M.3).[13] In addition, assorted pebbles of Palaeozoic rock from south-west England have been found on Butser Hill (M.4), Tegdown Hill (M.5) and Salt Hill (M.6).[14] Although natural processes may have been responsible for this long-distance movement, it seems most likely that human activity was involved.

It is difficult to say if Horsham sites are present in the Portsmouth region. The hollow-based points which are typical of this industry appear on both Butser Hill (M.7) and Salt Hill (M.8), but were found with both earlier and later Mesolithic material so their significance is difficult to evaluate.

Material from the later Mesolithic period has been found on several sites such as Butser Hill (M.9), Windmill Hill (M.10), Salt Hill (M.11) and the islands off Farlington Marshes. Two sites are worthy of special consideration. First, Wakefords Copse, Havant (M.12), where the levelling of a hillside revealed a group of approximately twenty pits on the summit and a group of seven more on the eastern slope. The latter clustered around a working floor on which two core axes, a pebble rubber and flint waste flakes were found. Four of the pits showed traces of stake holes round the southern and western perimeters suggesting some form of wind-break. It is surmised that these depressions were a group of 'huts' possibly for summer usage. Although the Wakefords Copse 'huts' were very small, the largest being approximately 2m by 1m, there was one larger depression near the top of the hill which bore no traces of stake holes around it. This depression contained a hearth which gave a radiocarbon date of 3730±20 bc (c. 4540 BC).[15] Secondly, the discovery of a later Mesolithic flint-working site near Fort Wallington, Fareham (M13), produced large quantities of axes and axe roughouts, microliths and microburins, cores, picks, groovers, scrapers, borers and a saw. It would appear that the local high-grade flint was being exploited possibly for supplying finished tools to the surrounding flintless areas.[16] This was a small-scale precursor of the axe factories of the succeeding Neolithic, or New Stone Age.

The Neolithic heralded a complete change in the economy of man in Britain. During the second half of the fifth millennium BC, the first farmers arrived from mainland Europe bringing with them domesticated cattle, sheep and pigs and cereals such as emmer, einkorn and six-row barley. Unfortunately, evidence for these innovations is largely lacking in the Portsmouth region, mainly due to the very few known Neolithic sites and the limited amount of their investigation. In terms of animal husbandry, horn cores of aurochs from a pit at Corhampton (N.1) may represent the remains of a domesticated specimen, although they could have been the result of hunting as must have been the red deer bones found with them. No carbonised grain or grain impressions on pottery have been recovered, but a saddle quern found in Langstone Harbour (N.2) indicated that some types of grain were being ground, although not necessarily domesticated cereals. Equally tenuous evidence is provided by the flint sickles from Clanfield (N.3) and Titchfield (N.4) which were probably used for harvesting cereal crops, but could have been used for reed cutting. The development of cereal cultivation on the chalk downs, which were probably lightly wooded, would have necessitated extensive clearance around settlement sites and this is borne out by limited evidence from Sussex.[17] Any large-scale clearance would have required axes and these have been commonly found both of flint and stone. The former appear to have come from the Sussex flint mines, in operation as early as 4300 BC, and also from sources within the region. Several flint axe roughouts have been found on Windmill Hill, Chalton (N.5), suggesting the presence of a small axe 'factory', utilising surface outcrops of flint as no mine shafts have been found in the vicinity.

Soon after the opening up of the Sussex flint mines, axe 'factories' were established in the west and north of Britain exploiting outcrops of igneous and metamorphic rock. Although axe-producing sites presumably began for the purpose of supplying local markets, an impressive trade network eventually evolved with stone axes being transported over remarkable distances. Of the stone axes from the Portsmouth region, three from Leigh Park (N.6), Waterlooville (N.7) and Hambledon (N.8) originated in Cornwall, one from Lee-on-the-Solent (N.9) came from North Wales, whilst two jadeite axes from Hill Head (N.10) and Titchfield (N.11) originated in Brittany.[18] Such trade was both necessitated by, and resulted from, the practice of agriculture which permitted a settled way of life, a potential food surplus and a greater element of social organisation. This was also manifested in the construction of very large monuments such as causewayed camps and henges. None of these has been recorded in the Portsmouth region, although causewayed camps occur just inside West Sussex. However, one form of Neolithic communal work found in the Portsmouth region is the earthen long barrow. In essence this is a long earthen mound, constructed from the spoil of two flanking ditches, normally with one or more burials at the eastern end. The size of the mound is out of all proportion to the burial area and it seems likely that the mound itself was constructed for some social, ceremonial or religious use in addition to its basic mortuary function.[19]

At least three earthen long barrows exist in the region – Giant's Grave, Meonstoke (N.12), Droxford (N.13) and Bevis' Grave, Bedhampton (N 14) – and it is probable that a fourth barrow which has been totally destroyed by chalk quarrying existed near the George Inn, Portsdown. Another long barrow, largely denuded, is located on Salt Hill (N.15) at the northern limit of the region. Of the surviving three, by far the best preserved is Giant's Grave (see Plate 2), measuring approximately 60m long by 20m wide and up to 2m high. Unfortunately, it has been damaged by quarrying along its length and by ploughing at its ends. The Droxford barrow is difficult to interpret as it seems to have been included in a later land boundary and has had soil built up along one side. Nevertheless, it appears to be approximately 30m long by 15m wide and up to 3m high. The third example, Bevis' Grave, can now only be seen as a crop or soil mark from the air. This is the only barrow to have been excavated systematically, revealing that the mound had been

PLATE 2   The Neolithic long barrow, Giant's Grave, Meonstoke

totally removed to a level below the old land surface.[20] The southern flanking ditch was partially excavated, proving to be 100m long, 6m wide and 2m deep. Part of an antler pick was recovered from the primary silting. Such picks and scapulae shovels would have been used in digging the ditches.

Although the monumental structures of the dead are located with relative ease, the houses of the living are an entirely different matter. Indeed, no actual houses have been located in the Portsmouth region. It is possible, but by no means certain, that the pit at Corhampton containing the remains of aurochs and red deer referred to above, as well as simple early Neolithic pottery, represents an occupation site. Although there must have been many such sites in the area they have yet to be found. Some are possibly represented by the scattering of Neolithic flint-working waste on Portsdown, for example, though these may just have been knapping sites. Unfortunately, the best clue, pottery, does not survive well when exposed to the elements, owing to its low-temperature firing. Only a mere handful of pottery has survived from the region, all of it recovered from excavations.

From about 2600 BC there appears to have been an influx into Britain of new people, traditionally referred to as the 'Beaker folk' due to the distinctive vessels found in their graves. Such interments normally contain inhumations and are frequently under round barrows as opposed to the long barrows of the indigenous Neolithic population. Occasionally, the graves contain copper artefacts indicating that the Beaker people were familiar with simple metalworking. That they were pastoralists is an assumption based mainly on the small number of Beaker houses found. Certainly none is known from the Portsmouth region; the only evidence of their presence is from burials. An oval barrow 400m east of the George Inn, Portsdown (N.16), was partially excavated in 1926[21] and revealed two cremations under flint cairns with the crouched skeleton of a 'young man' accompanied by a flint dagger, a jet bead and fragments of a single beaker. Unfortunately, it is difficult to interpret this rather complex barrow burial as no adequate excavation report was written and the finds have since disappeared. The only other recorded Beaker evidence from the area was an undecorated biconical beaker, found in a gravel pit at Warsash (N.17), but this was an accidental find and no details of its original archaeological context survive.

The chronology of the Bronze Age has been based largely on pottery and metal types and it is often difficult to appreciate what was happening in human terms. In the Early Bronze Age, from around 2200 BC onwards, there appear to have been various groups of people distinguished by their differing funerary traditions. Some groups are recognised by the urns in which their cremated bodies were buried. The collared urn was one type, so named because of its deep overhanging rim. A single example has been found in the Portsmouth region, buried inverted in a lynchet at Barnet Copse, Chalton (B.1). It contained, in addition to the cremated bones, an annular jet pendant, five amber beads, an amber spacer plate, used for separating strands of a necklace, and seven faïence, or glass paste, beads. The presence of such items is reminiscent of the very rich burials seen in the Wessex area which have been collectively grouped under the title of the 'Wessex Culture'. Such burials may have represented a wealthy and dominant aristocracy practising a pastoral economy.[22] Alternatively, they could have been merely the burials of wealthier members of the local Early Bronze Age community. Whichever is the case, two Wessex-type burials have been discovered in the Portsmouth region. A cremation was found at Southwick Hill Cross Roads, Portsdown (B.2),[23] at the bottom of a pit 0.3m deep. Incorporated with the calcined bones were 107 discoidal shale beads, 16 amber beads and a 'V'-perforated shale button with a gold cover. Also in the pit, but separate from the cremation, were the crushed remains of a slotted incense cup of Wessex form. A second Wessex burial, this time an inhumation, was discovered subsequently in the same area (B.3). The burial was that of a female between fifteen and seventeen years old and approximately 1.7m (5ft. 8in.) tall. The skeleton was lying on its right side in a semi-flexed position, facing east. In front of its forehead were two vessels. One was a simple bucket-shaped pot just over 60mm high and the other was a double-ended vessel of hour-glass shape, 65mm high with a 65mm diameter, having an external decoration of alternating bands of pointillé and whipped thong impressions (Plate 3). The latter's function is unknown, but four similar vessels have been found from other Wessex contexts. A radiocarbon date of 1059 bc (*c.* 1325 BC) was obtained from the skeletal material, a date which is 200 years more recent that the latest previously recorded radiocarbon date for Wessex material and may be a reflection of conservatism in the peripheral areas of the Wessex culture.[24] It is probable that both Wessex burials were originally beneath round barrows, which were removed at the time of the building of the Palmerston forts in the late nineteenth century. Other round barrows on Portsdown survived a little longer,[25] but none are visible today. The best examples of such burial mounds in the Portsmouth region are a group of three bowl barrows at Great Ervills Farm, Denmead (B.4), although damaged examples survive on Butser Hill (B.5) and on and around Old Winchester Hill (B.6).

PLATE 3   Vessels accompanying an Early Bronze Age burial, Southwick Hill Cross Roads, Portsdown

In this part of England barrow cemeteries seem to disappear at the end of the Early Bronze Age, to be replaced by cremation burials mainly in flat cemeteries. The groups of people practising this burial rite have been loosely classified under the umbrella title of 'Deverel-Rimbury Culture', although significant differences can be seen among its component parts. The Deverel-Rimbury Culture was originally thought to have been a late Bronze Age phenomenon, but it now seems likely that it originated in the Early Bronze Age with a radiocarbon date as early as 1740 bc (*c.* 2100 BC). A number of Deverel-Rimbury urns have been discovered in' the Portsmouth region. Gravel extraction in the Warsash area (B7) led to the discovery of some for which there are only inadequate records.[26] More recently, three urns were found during construction of the M27 motorway which intersects Portsdown. The top of an inverted bucket urn was discovered near Downend Lane, Fareham (B8),[27] the body and base of a bucket urn, buried upright in a pit, was unearthed near Falmouth Road, Paulsgrove (B9),[28] and the base of a third bucket urn was revealed west of Nelson Lane, Fareham (B10).[29] Further urns have been found on Hayling Island (B11 and B12), Farlington Marshes (B13) and Lee-on-the-Solent (B14).[30]

In the Portsmouth region only one settlement site is known, at Gravel Hill Bottom, Chalton (B15).[31] This was of Middle Bronze Age date and a carbon 14 determination produced a date of 1243±69 bc (*c.* 1540 BC). It appears to have been a small farmstead consisting of two circular huts measuring 6m and 4.5m in diameter, two working floors and three pits. Amongst the finds was a loom weight, indicating that the inhabitants may have been weaving during their short occupancy of the site. The abandonment of several useful bronze items suggested that the site may have been vacated hurriedly. Interestingly, traces of Celtic field systems, which may well date back to the Middle Bronze Age, still survive on nearby Butser Hill and in the Chalton area. Such systems almost certainly continued in use through the succeeding Iron Age and into the Roman period.

Technologically, the most important innovation of the Bronze Age was the development of bronze founding, an activity which became most significant in the Portsmouth region during the Middle Bronze Age when the area appears to have been important for metalworking. A number of hoards containing both new and broken axes, or palstaves, and other, decorative, objects, provide supporting evidence for this view.[32] The largest hoard was found at Gable Head, Hayling Island (B.16) and consisted of twenty-seven looped and unlooped palstaves, one plain and one decorated arm ring, and the remains of a quoit-headed pin, so-called because it was topped by a large flat ring. A smaller hoard of nineteen palstaves and a plain arm ring was found beneath a concrete floor at HMS *Sultan* (B.17), Gosport. A further group of at least four palstaves was uncovered during building works at St Mary's Hospital, Fratton (B.18), but as their significance was not recognised only two were retained. At St James' Hospital, Milton (B.19), one palstave and four bracelets, two plain and two decorated, were found during the last century but were destroyed in the Second World War. Fortunately, drawings survive and interestingly the decoration on one of the arm rings was almost identical to that from Gable Head. Another nineteenth-century find, at Titchfield, was a hoard of six whole and three fragmentary palstaves (B.20). Although these hoards contain a wide range of palstave types, there are nevertheless similarities between all of them and northern French examples. These hoards probably represented the stock of an itinerant smith or group of smiths from a regional centre considerably influenced by northern French traditions. That none of the hoards was located more than two miles from the shore strongly indicates that the centre was concerned with maritime trade. A spiral twisted bronze torc or neck ring found at an undisclosed location in Langstone Harbour may have been part of a disturbed hoard.

The beginning of the Late Bronze Age was marked by the introduction of a lead-bronze alloy. The addition of lead to the bronze increased the fluidity of the molten metal permitting the manufacture of thin-walled castings. However, by this time the zenith of bronze production in the Portsmouth region seems to have passed, since only the fragments of three Late Bronze Age socketed axes from Northney, Hayling Island (B.21)[33] have so far been discovered.

In recent years interpretations of the Iron Age in southern Britain have been undergoing considerable change. The traditional view of the Iron Age as a period of successive waves of continental invaders has now been largely replaced by one favouring local development by indigenous Bronze Age communities. It has also become clear that certain features once assumed to be purely of Iron Age date originated in the Bronze Age. One such development is the hill-fort. There is no reason to suppose that the Portsmouth region's sole example of a hill-fort, Old Winchester Hill (I.1) (Plate 4), has such early origins. In its present form it consists of a pear-shaped area of approximately 5.6 hectares enclosed by a bank and ditch, with an outer counterscarp bank. There are two inturned entrances to the west and

PLATE 4 The Iron Age Hill-Fort, Old Winchester Hill

east, with further outworks attached to the eastern one. It is possible that in the later part of the first millennium BC Old Winchester Hill was one of a line of 'developed' hill-forts running across the chalk downs of Hampshire and West Sussex.[34] One of these was the extensively excavated Danebury Hill. If Old Winchester Hill was at all comparable, then it may well have been an important centre of population with related industries, commerce and an extensive sphere of influence. It is possible that Butser Hill (I.2), where there are cross dykes of probable Iron Age date, was a forerunner of Old Winchester Hill.

A somewhat enigmatic site is to be found on the eastern side of Hayling Island. Tournerbury (I.3) has a single bank and ditch enclosing some 2.6 hectares with a single original entrance to the west. Only a minimal amount of exploratory work has been done on the site and its function is far from clear.[35] A fortified site would not be out of place since the Iron Age shrine found there suggests that Hayling Island was of some importance in the later Iron Age. The shrine in Towncil Field, North Hayling (I.4), lay beneath a later Romano-Celtic temple and consisted of a rectangular enclosure surrounding a central circular timber structure which may have been roofed. During excavation the latter appeared as a series of three concentric V-shaped gullies, the innermost containing post holes. Two large post holes flanked an entrance on the eastern side. The central area contained post holes and a pit in the middle, perhaps used for libations. Exactly how the shrine operated is difficult to say, but the majority of the dedicatory offerings were found within the outer enclosure to the east of the central structure. They consisted of brooches, bracelets, rings, horse and cart trappings, weapons, often ritually bent, and local coins, as well as some from Armorica and Central and Belgic Gaul. The shrine appears to have been built about the middle of the first century BC and survived until shortly after the Roman Invasion of AD 43.[36]

Approximately a dozen Iron Age settlement sites, mostly farmsteads, have been excavated in the Portsmouth region, none extensively and almost all under rescue conditions. Bones from two or three sites indicate that oxen, horses, pigs and sheep were being reared and that deer were being hunted. An iron reaping sickle from one site and quern stones from another show the harvesting and grinding of grain. Iron harness, cart fittings, or both, suggest the use of horses or oxen as draught animals, although either was probably kept for meat. Spindle whorls, loom weights, a weaving comb and a thread-picker demonstrate that weaving took place. Further indication of the expansion of economic activity and trade is provided by the production of salt which appears to have been an important and probably seasonal activity in the coastal zone of the Portsmouth region. Traces of such activity exist at the heads of Portsmouth, Langstone and Chichester harbours and elsewhere along the region's coast. They range in date from the middle to the end of the Iron Age (see Table 1).

Until the later Iron Age a barter system for the exchange of goods must have been the norm, though during that period of prehistory the currency bar's development as a unit of exchange took place. Iron bars of various forms were used, some appearing to be sword blanks, which could be readily converted into weapons if necessary.

TABLE 1

EXCAVATED IRON AGE SITES IN THE PORTSMOUTH REGION

Location	Map Reference	Date of Occupation or Activity*
Farmsteads:		
Clanfield Reservoir[37]	(I.5)	7th–6th century BC & 3rd–1st century BC
Chalton Site 50[38]	(I.6)	6th–5th century BC
Wallington Military Road[39]	(I.7)	5th–3rd & 3rd–1st century BC
George Inn, Portsdown[40]	(I.8)	4th–3rd century BC
Southwick Hill Cross Roads[41]	(I.9)	4th–3rd century BC
Crookhorn Lane[42]	(I.10)	3rd–1st century BC & 1st century AD
Chalton Site 15[43]	(I.11)	Late 2nd–early 1st century BC
The Causeway, Horndean[44]	(I.12)	1st century AD
Stock Enclosure:		
Hoylake Road, Portsdown[45]	(I.13)	
Salt Production Sites:		
Brownwich Farm, Titchfield[46]	(I.14)	1st century AD
Paulsgrove[47]	(I.15)	3rd–1st century BC
Bedhampton foreshore[48]	(I.16)	3rd–1st century BC
Hook[49]	(I.17)	1st century BC–1st century AD

* Based on pottery evidence.

Currency bars of this type have been found at the shrine site on Hayling Island. However, by about 150 BC coinage proper, entering Britain from Belgic Gaul, was soon to be copied and developed in the south. One particular type, the British D type or 'Cheriton' gold stater, appears to have had a special affinity with the Portsmouth region as three of the five known examples definitely came from the area.[50] Two were found near Portchester (I.18) and one at Horndean (I.19). A fourth, of uncertain provenance, may well have come from the region. It would seem likely that these staters were struck locally. Unfortunately, all were casual finds providing little indication of their cultural and social significance.

By the second half of the first millennium BC the rulers of the tribe of the southern Atrebates, commencing with Commius, included their names on the coins they produced. Inscribed gold coins of Commius's sons, Tincommius and Verica, have been found at Fareham and Portsmouth respectively. Others have been discovered at the Hayling Island shrine (I.20). Since prehistory is the study of man before the survival of written records, the production of inscribed coins heralded the end of Britain's prehistoric past. The Claudian Invasion in AD 43 and the consequent arrival of more literate and cultured Romans, marked the dawning of a new historical era.

2
ROMAN TO SAXON

David E. Johnston

The appearance of a Roman legion in AD 43 brought the Portsmouth region into the historic period with a jolt. It is hard to believe, however, that it came as a surprise. In the ninety-odd years since Caesar's encounter with the tribes of Kent and the south-east Midlands, an invasion must have been accepted as inevitable; traders' gossip and the more occasional sight of reconnoitring warships may well have prompted more than one invasion scare.[1] With the exception of Old Winchester Hill, the region contained no hill-forts to serve as refuges and strong-points, and the invasion forces could have passed through unopposed.

The legion was the II Augusta, commanded by the future emperor, Vespasian. Taking advantage of friendly tribes at Chichester, the invaders had established a temporary supply-base on the site shortly to be occupied by the Roman palace at Fishbourne. Here the fleet and the land forces met. The next verifiable base is near Wimborne, in Dorset, close to a suspected store-base in Poole Harbour. There may well have been an intermediate base also existing at Bitterne, near Southampton. Excavations have shown that within thirty years or so a small settlement and probably a harbour existed there. By then, it is believed[2] that the $27\frac{1}{2}$ miles between Chichester and Bitterne were marked by a direct main road.

This major road – number 421 in modern classification and Iter VII in the Roman – took its first straight alignment westwards through Southbourne, Emsworth and Warblington to Havant; the modern A27 preserves its course fairly accurately. The next alignment was probably sighted from high ground to the west of Havant and extended to meet the first. This new line passes through Purbrook, where it is picked up by a short stretch of modern secondary road. It then passes to the north of HMS *Dryad* to join the A333 at Walton Heath. From North Boarhunt it parts company with the modern road and heads for the south of Wickham, passing through the allotments of Fullimore's Field where it has been traced archaeologically. To the west of Wickham, near Park Place, the road forked, one branch continuing to Bitterne, the other taking the main traffic north-westwards to Winchester.[3]

During the next three centuries of Roman rule this road served a number of small settlements, farms and villas in the fertile coastal strip. No other Roman roads have

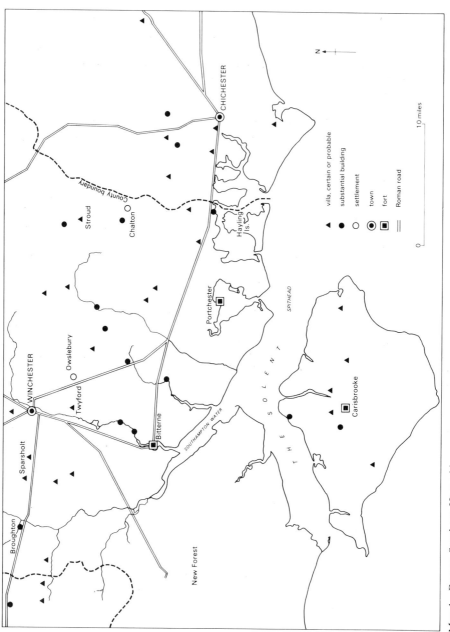

MAP 1   Roman Southern Hampshire

been positively identified and a developing network of minor, unmetalled tracks for cross-country communication remains a matter of conjecture. Many of the settlements would have remained similar to those of the Iron Age. Such is the tenuous nature of most archaeological discoveries in the region, however, that surviving Roman pottery is often the best clue to the new way of life. In this way both Havant and Fareham can claim Romano-British origins.[4] At Fareham, pottery ranging from the beginning to the end of the Roman period has been found by excavation in a silted-up ditch. More significantly, the finds also included roof tiles and other building debris, showing that structures of a fully Roman type had also existed. The river, still tidal to the old bridge east of the church, would, in Roman times, have had a silt-free channel accessible from Portsmouth harbour and Portchester. At Havant, the pottery evidence includes two categories of higher-class wares – the red-gloss samian imported from Roman Gaul as tableware and amphorae that once contained wine or olive oil. Oyster shells, so distinctive a feature of Romano-British sites, provided an example of everyday food. In the second century, a well was dug at Havant. Wells were virtually an innovation in Roman times. Havant would have been a market, conceivably an official staging-post on the main road to the west, and a community where the acceptance of Roman values would have been officially encouraged. Even in the most conservatively British of rural settlements, the Roman influence can be detected. For example, in the excavation of a settlement at Paradise Lane, Fareham, now sealed by the M27,[5] it was clear that the wooden buildings were rectangular and that the timbers had been secured with nails of Roman type.

By contrast with these nucleated settlements of Iron Age type, the region is fortunate in having an example of a much rarer type of 'village', where both Roman influence and tighter social organisation seem to be indicated by the dwellings as excavated.[6] Occupation of this downland site near Chalton began in the early years of Roman rule and continued well towards its end. From the early phase of settlement, only parts of two ditches have been excavated, though there were certainly dwellings nearby. Field banks, dating from the second century, indicated intensive cultivation inside the settlement, probably in private gardens belonging to individual households – in other words, the Romano-British equivalent of the medieval toft. The plan of the surviving earthworks looks almost medieval, an orderly pattern of rectangular house-platforms arranged to follow the contours. The houses were evidently timber-framed, with some of the main posts set into the ground and the others placed on stone pads or sill-beams. One house, and there were doubtless others, had flint foundations that probably carried a timber-framed superstructure. Such 'villages' are rare, though comparable examples have been found in Sussex, Wiltshire and elsewhere. This rarity, however, might be an illusion and one day the type will probably be recognised as a consistent part of the rural scene. One final point should be noted: although Chalton's neat rectangularity looks very Roman, it was a purely native community, for the finds included very few exotic objects (a brooch, some glassware and a coin) and the pottery was largely devoid of samian and fine ware, being predominantly from the Rowlands Castle kilns a few miles away. Chalton's inhabitants appear to have been both physically and culturally isolated.

Isolated or not, these peasant households will have paid their taxes to the authorities. This is important, for although the countryside of southern Hampshire may have looked relatively unaffected by the arrival of the Romans, the framework of everyday life had changed fundamentally. Everyone, without exception, was registered in the appropriate administrative centre, or *civitas* capital. In the case of south-east Hampshire, the region was part of the *civitas* of the Belgae, whose capital *Venta Belgarum* is now Winchester, although the nearest large settlement was actually Chichester.

Taxation, in both kind and cash, was a burden that lay heavily upon the peasant farmer, who was obliged to adjust his skills to the production of a huge surplus. This factor more than any other was responsible for the appearance of villas in the region, as indeed throughout Britain. As it happens, this important aspect of Romanisation is not particularly well represented in south-east Hampshire as little more than hints of several substantial buildings of unknown status survive. 'Villa' may be too grand a term for what were very much working farms; one such, at Scratchface Lane, Bedhampton, is known to have been a masonry and brick house built in the second century AD during what is recognised as the first wave of villa building. Its associated field systems have been detected by fieldwork.[7] Others seem to belong to the second wave in the later third and fourth centuries, such as that at Bury Lodge, Hambledon.[8] Here the house faced a slope falling to the west on which three strip lynchets can be discerned. These are cultivation terraces formed, or at least enhanced, by contour ploughing and are a type that began in prehistoric times and continued throughout the Roman period. Two buildings, the owners of which were evidently prosperous, have been found near Rowlands Castle.[9] One residence had a red and white tessellated floor (a coarse mosaic of large cubes of brick and limestone), while the other boasted not only red tessellation but also painted wallplaster. They may, in fact, be two buildings on the same 'estate', for the intensive farming then required was most effective in large, professionally-managed units. The best documented of local villas is that lying between Havant and Langstone,[10] being well placed for access both by sea and route 421. Even so, it is very inadequately known from excavation, but seems to have been a house with rooms connected by a corridor and to have had its own bath-suite. This apparently followed the usual Roman practice of having a centrally-heated *tepidarium*, an apsidal room that must have contained the hot bath, and a cold room (*frigidarium*) to complete the bathing sequence with the equivalent of a cold shower and a rub down. Waste water from the baths and perhaps from a latrine was carried away by a fine drain lined with reused roof tiles. The villa may represent early development on this part of the coast, as the coin series ranged from Vespasian (AD 69–79) to Constans (AD 337–350), indicating a long life. Small objects illustrated the everyday life in the house, including spoons, knives, a *stylus* for writing on wax tablets and a variety of personal ornaments.

Such prosperity may have been connected with the extensive, but imperfectly known, salt-workings in Langstone Harbour and elsewhere along the coast.[11] Evaporation of sea water for salt production was one of several rural industries practised in the region. Another was the pottery manufacture at Rowlands Castle producing handsome grey domestic wares of a type made at several other kiln sites on the south coast. The clay deposits were further exploited in making bricks and tiles, for which the demand was almost inexhaustible. This industry was well developed in the Botley–Fareham area where the products were fired both in clamps and in permanent kilns. One site that could justly be called a 'factory' has been thoroughly excavated at Crookhorn Lane.[12] Large clay pits were accompanied by brick-built kilns designed to allow the heat to be distributed by regularly spaced flues into the stack of bricks under a large wooden superstructure. Brick-making and drying were apparently carried out in a large aisled building nearby.

The coastal strip, however, was vulnerable to sea-borne raids and piracy. These activities reached a peak in the third century AD and it has been suggested that a raid put an end to the prosperity of the Havant villa.[13] A glimpse of these troubled times was provided by recent excavations on a small earthwork at Tournerbury, on Hayling Island,[14] where a prehistoric ring-work was certainly reoccupied, possibly even refurbished, in the later Roman period. Imprecise pottery evidence suggests a date of between AD 250 and 400. The contemporary insecurity may well have spelled the earlier end of the nearby Roman temple, the history of which went back at least to the early days of the Province. Long thought, on the evidence of inadequate excavation,[15] to be a villa of highly peculiar form, it has now been recognised as a temple of a type best paralleled in Gaul.[16] The first building was an Iron Age shrine of wood, resembling a native round-house, but set in a roughly square enclosure. In the first century AD it was completely rebuilt in masonry in the same circular form with a porch and a colonnaded ambulatory enclosing a square court. Dedicatory offerings in both phases were copious and often unusual. They show that the shrine was a place of pilgrimage for visitors from Gaul and they emphasise a close connection with the presumed royal family of Verica and Cogidubnus at Fishbourne. Indeed, it is believed that the same architects and masons were responsible for both remarkable buildings. The end of the temple, early in the third century, matches that of the palace, though a link with the coastal insecurity of the time is no more than a reasonable deduction.

The third century threat to southern and eastern Britain came principally from southern Scandinavia and the Low Countries and included the ancestors of the later Saxon settlers. As a result, in AD 283, Rome appointed Carausius, himself of barbarian origins, to the command of the Channel fleet with a commission to clear the sea of pirates. To Carausius can be ascribed the systematic beginnings of the chain of great 'Saxon Shore forts' from Portsmouth Harbour to the Wash. Portchester Castle was one of the first to be constructed.[17] The great defensive wall is 3.04m thick, was originally 6.08m or more in height and used about 18,349 cubic metres of flint and mortar. A new design feature was the semicircular projecting bastions, each carrying heavy artillery in the form of a *ballista* or catapult with a clear 'killing area' in front of the walls. The design of the gates was also innovatory with inturned walls enclosing a small courtyard overlooked by the rampart walk. Using these new forts as a power-base, Carausius successfully challenged the Emperor of the west and established an independent Empire of Britain and the nearer part of Gaul – a usurpation that lasted for ten years until its suppression in AD 296. Immediately after the Carausian episode, the military buildings inside Portchester were carefully dismantled – a sign both that the revolt was over and that the seas were, for a while, safer. The occupants, who now included women and children, may well have formed a peasant militia and caretaker garrison. However, about AD 340 the fort was recommissioned with a regular military garrison that survived for some thirty years before being withdrawn. This was succeeded by the establishment of a non-Roman garrison of mercenary troops, apparently of

Germanic origin as evidenced by their sunken-floored huts (*Grubenhäuser*), their grass-tempered pottery and other significant pieces of equipment.

Such are the links, both in Portchester and its neighbourhood, to the next identifiable settlers, the Anglo-Saxons of the fifth and sixth centuries. Some groups – by a gradual, piecemeal process – came through invitation, while others were uninvited. The picture is certainly not one of violent conquest everywhere, but rather of coexistence. Cunliffe has argued that the south coast around Portchester was settled by these newcomers in the early fifth century and that it was a 'treaty-area' in which they were reluctantly tolerated by their British neighbours who did not wish for closer contact.[18]

What was to become Wessex was now the land of the West Saxons – the *Gewissae* as Bede recounted. A picture of peaceful assimilation is provided by the archaeological material. However, a different and more traditional picture is furnished by written sources, in particular the Anglo-Saxon Chronicle. Although written much later, during Alfred's reign, it used earlier genealogies and stories of landings, battles and deaths of kings. The entry for AD 495 states that 'Two chieftains, Cerdic and his son Cynric, came to Britain with five ships at the place called *Cerdicesora*, and they fought against the Britons on the same day.' This, and further battles recorded in the Chronicle, probably took place to the west of Southampton. The chieftains' success supposedly marked the beginning of the royal house of Wessex, whose territory included the Isle of Wight, captured in AD 530 and bequeathed by Cynric to his nephews, Stuf and Witgar, four years later. The Chronicle, however, records another landing, in AD 501: 'Port and his two sons Bieda and Maegla came to Britain with two ships at the place called Portsmouth; and there they killed a young British man of very high rank.'[19] Here at least is a recognisable place-name, even if the account actually refers to Portchester.

Who were these settlers? Bede answers succinctly. They came, he wrote, 'from the three most formidable races of Germany, the Saxons, Angles and Jutes. From the Jutes are descended the people of Kent and the Isle of Wight, and those in the province of Wessex opposite the Isle of Wight are called Jutes to this day.'[20] To the native Celts they were all 'Saxons', but to the archaeologist certain distinct groups and even territories are identifiable. One such is the *Meonwara*, the settlers along the River Meon, whom Bede knew to be Jutish in origin.[21] The extent of their territory is not clear. However, Port and his sons were evidently Saxon not Jutish, so their territory around Portchester and Portsmouth should, perhaps, be excluded. The northern limit of the *Meonwara* depends on our understanding of the enigmatic earthworks at Froxfield and East Tisted.[22] The autonomy of the *Meonwara* did not last long; in the seventh century their territory was 'given', with the Isle of Wight, by the powerful King Wulfhere of Mercia to King Aethelwalh of the South Saxons. In *c.* AD 686, however, the kingdom of the South Saxons fell to Caedwalla of Wessex and so both the Meon valley and the coastal belt became part of the kingdom of the West Saxons. Identifying the *Meonwara* archaeologically has been difficult as, until the recent work at Meonstoke, there were no excavated settlements from this early phase. For example, a single grave discovered accidentally at Meonstoke is now known to be part of a cemetery;[23] and one detail, a square buckle with two horseshoe-shaped fittings, indicates links with the Jutish graves of Kent and the Isle of Wight. Not far away, at Droxford, the construction of the railway in 1900 disturbed a substantial cemetery; however, it was not until 1974 that the station's disuse allowed careful excavation of the site.[24] Forty-one graves out of an estimated three hundred or more were found. The settlement must lie under modern Droxford and its cemetery was in use for at least one hundred and fifty years, from the mid-fifth century and throughout the sixth. Nearly half of its occupants seem to have died between the ages of twenty and thirty and many were warriors buried with their spears, shields and swords. This was a pagan cemetery and the continental affinities of many of the objects point to connections with the Low Countries and the Frankish kingdoms of the Rhineland.

The settlement pattern and the system of land tenure were, inevitably, connected and both are today the subject of much speculation. Roman land-units or estates may possibly be recognisable in Saxon and later units and one hypothesis is that, singly or in groups, these formed the basis of large Saxon ones, each dominated by a central *llys*, a court or chief place of the district.[25] Alternatively, the Saxon reorganisation of land-units may have obliterated their Roman, or even pre-Roman, outlines. A shifting settlement pattern has been identified at Meonstoke,[26] from post-Roman occupation of a Roman building at Shavard Farm, to early Saxon settlement nearby and finally in a move to a site or sites in the river valley – Meonstoke, Exton or Corhampton where there is a late Saxon church. A similar shifting pattern, from prehistoric to medieval times, has long been recognised at Chalton.

The early date of some Saxon settlements is revealed by their names. Wickham, for instance, is a combination of the Old English –*hām* and the Latin *vicus* or village – a Roman origin that can be substantiated archaeologically.[27] The same can be said of Havant, although here there was royal property; land in the settlement was leased by King Athelstan to his minister, Wihtgar, and the street named The Pallant preserves more than an echo of the Latin *palatium*, or palace. The name Havant combines *hāma*, a personal name, and *funta*, a spring. The 'ham' element, whether derived from *hām*, homestead, or *hamm*, meadow or water-meadow, appears once more in Fareham where it indicates a very early Saxon settlement. Again, as at Wickham, the presence of both a Roman road and Romano-British occupation marks continuity from Roman into Saxon times. A second group of place-names, those ending in 'ing' and 'worth', is believed to indicate secondary settlement in the middle and late Saxon periods. This would fit in with the archaeological evidence for Blendworth and Idsworth being middle Saxon and secondary to the older settlements at Chalton.[28]

The remarkable Saxon village on the hilltop of Church Down, Chalton was recognised during an intensive field survey of the area and was completely excavated between 1970 and 1976.[29] Sixty-one structures were recovered and, although this was perhaps not quite the earliest settlement here, the artefacts combine to place its main occupation in the seventh century. Only four of the houses were of the *Grubenhaus* type noted already at Portchester. In one, the sunken floor, which had definitely not been boarded over, contained a rich harvest of artefacts and charred remains of its superstructure. The buildings, rectangular and constructed of timber presumably with thatched roofs, were of three distinct types. The first group contained the longest, 9m or more in length, with a doorway in the middle of each long side and internal divisions cutting off about one fifth of the interior. The second group had opposed doorways but no internal partitions, while the third group comprised the smallest, with one doorway only. These types must reflect functions. Perhaps some were the 'halls' and 'bower houses' recorded a century or so later in *Beowulf*, as well as smaller outhouses. Some of these houses, or groups of buildings, were separated from their neighbours by fences, but no streets were detected and the whole plan seems to have had a tidy, if unsystematic, layout. Few of the buildings replaced earlier houses and it is quite possible that most, if not all, were standing at one time. No single building stands out as a great man's hall, though there was one curious structure, long and narrow with the unusual feature of a central line of posts forming two aisles. Most oddly, it was made up of four unequal sections, each slightly out of alignment with the next.

Chalton is justly celebrated as the typical pre-Domesday village in Hampshire, as few Saxon villages in Britain have been excavated in anything like their entirety, although only extensive excavation elsewhere will reveal how typical it was. Portchester at this time, however, presents a contrast, with only a few families farming the area within the walls and probably erecting their less than substantial buildings in different places at different times.[30] Not until the end of the seventh century was a complex of more substantial dwellings created.

Heathen gods were generally worshipped in this period, but Wessex was converted to Christianity by Bishop Birinus, who arrived in AD 634. Thus was established an enduring religious faith and, in the form of new churches, the most durable buildings for some centuries to come. According to Bede, Bishop Birinus was commissioned by Pope Honorius I to preach the Gospel 'in the distant lands beyond the English dominions where no other teacher had been before him.'[31] He is believed to have landed at Portchester where, Bede stated, he found the Gewissae or West Saxons so 'completely heathen' that he decided to start his mission here. His first major convert was Cynegils, King of the West Saxons, an achievement which led to the conversion of the Isle of Wight by a missionary priest, to the building of the New Minster in Winchester and to the creation of a vast diocese that had its centre first at Dorchester-on-Thames and only later, after a subdivision, at Winchester. However, the credit for the rather later conversion of the *Meonwara*, it has been argued,[32] should go to Wilfred who was campaigning in Sussex in the 680s. Notwithstanding these conversions, paganism lingered on in the Isle of Wight, in spite of its nominal conversion earlier, and also in some parts of southern Hampshire. The recently excavated pagan cemetery at Bedhampton[33] may be chronologically the very latest. Its use certainly began earlier in the seventh century, but two artefacts – an antique escutcheon and a decorated strap – might well show that burials continued into the eighth century. Eventually, interment in heathen burial-places was ended summarily by Church decree.

Parish churches were not built immediately, as open-air preaching was carried out by priests from the new 'Minsters', such as that at Winchester, and from the new religious community at Titchfield. Fortunately, five Anglo-Saxon churches survive in the region.[34] At Fareham, the clue to early work is the long-and-short masonry in the north wall of the church of St Peter and St Paul; at Warblington the central tower is partly Saxon and was the core of an interesting and unusual church; and at Hambledon, the twelfth-century nave has clear Saxon origins. The simple church at Boarhunt is substantially as it was built in late Saxon times, though a recent re-examination has suggested[35] that the western part of the nave is a subsequent addition. The most important and interesting of these early churches, however, is undoubtedly St Peter's, Titchfield, identified as a 'minster church'[36] in what was, by the time of Domesday in 1086, a large royal estate. The original Anglo-Saxon west porch survives and forms the lower part of the tower; the west wall of the nave is Anglo-Saxon throughout its height and the nave may preserve the original plan. Its importance lies partly in its exceptionally early date, for it may go back to the late seventh century, and partly in its close parallels to a group of early churches in Northumbria. There is every reason to see in this church the influence of Wilfred and his masons. The recent study[37] of the Saxon parish of Titchfield shows it to have been large and to have included at least the later parishes of Wickham and Fareham.

Although the origins of many Hampshire parishes are still uncertain, it is clear that the beginnings of the present parochial system can be identified in the mid-Saxon period. In turn, late Saxon estates would have influenced the shape of medieval parishes and hundreds.

Finally, the sequence at Portchester will take the story up to the Norman Conquest. An architectural link with Titchfield has often been suggested for the Watergate archway, the similarity and date of which have long been a source of speculation. It has been argued that Portchester was given to Bishop Wilfred as a 'mission station' in the seventh century,[38] and furthermore that he demolished the crumbling masonry, using it to build or rebuild both arches.[39] This has now been challenged by the view that there is no connection.[40] As stated above (p. 21), the eighth- and ninth-century structures within the walls at Portchester were reasonably substantial and life in them was well above peasant level. Nevertheless, by the early 900s they, too, had been swept away and their site covered by a stinking refuse-heap. Dramatic changes were evidently taking place at Portchester, as the refuse was the food-waste from numerous refugees or a garrison quartered elsewhere in the fort. In AD 904, Portchester was acquired by King Alfred as one of the *burhs* or strong-points in the defence of Wessex against the Danes and as a place of refuge for the inhabitants of a wide area. Moreover, the fort is listed in the document of *c.* AD 920, the *Burghal Hidage*, which gives the dimensions in hides of the new burhs. As in nearby Chichester, the Roman walls were serving their purpose once again.

In the eleventh century, the fort was still owned by the king, but was divided into three separately held manors. The excavations[41] revealed what must have been the large aisled hall and three subsidiary buildings belonging to the freedmen who held this part of the manor. To this complex was added, in the early eleventh century, a masonry tower, perhaps for a bell.

By the middle of the century, these buildings were disused and part of the site had been taken for a small cemetery. Not long afterwards, the tower, now isolated, was rebuilt. With the Conquest of 1066, the three manors of Portchester were brought together by William and assigned to the Mauduit family. A strongly fortified residence was being created in the north-west corner of the old Roman enclosure. Only those grim Roman walls, the Watergate archway and the lonely tower then stood to remind the new owners of some six centuries of occupation by their Roman and Anglo-Saxon forebears.

3

INDUSTRIAL

ARCHAEOLOGY

R.C. Riley

The early economic development of south-east Hampshire was in a large part the result of the decision by Richard I in 1194 to create a naval and military base at Portsmouth from which he could attack France. Much of the area in the vicinity became increasingly tributary to the town as it grew fitfully according to the caprices of monarchs and their foreign policy. At the core of events was the dockyard, separated from Portsmouth by a tidal creek and, after 1667, by De Gomme's ramparts. The accession of William of Orange after the Glorious Revolution of 1688 caused England and the United Provinces (now the Nether-lands) to unite against France. Substantial naval losses in the ensuing Nine Years' War (1689–97) led to the decision to develop, in place of Chatham, the strategically valuable harbour of Portsmouth as the prime base for the royal navy. A building programme was commenced in 1691 and during the eighteenth century the dockyard emerged as one of the largest, if not the largest, industrial enterprises in the country. Between 1750 and 1814 dockyard employment grew unevenly from 1,600 to 3,900. As a result, its one other competitor, Chatham, was narrowly outpaced.[1] That so much remains of this period is both a tribute to the quality of the workmanship and a fortunate result of the navy's continuing requirement for small vessel facilities.

The 1691 scheme called for the construction of two basins and two dry docks to supplement the existing complement of three dry docks.[2] The work, a major feat of engineering at that time, was directed by Edward Dummer, surveyor to the Navy Board, and was completed by 1698. Remarkably one of the docks, the Great Stone Dock, and parts of the basins survive, the dock being among the oldest in the world still in operation. The North Dock, now No. 6 (see Fig. 1), was originally made of wood and doubled both as a dry dock and as a means of access to one of the new basins, being much smaller than the Great Stone Dock, now No. 5. However, the Desmaretz map of 1743[3] indicates that the North Dock had already been separated from the basin and completely rebuilt to dimensions similar to those of the Great

24

1   Steam Basin
2   No. 2 Ship Shop
3   Smithery
4   No. 3/4 Ship Shop
5   Block Mills
6   Iron and Brass Foundry
7   Store
8   No. 1 Dock
9   No. 2 Dock
10 No. 3 Dock
11 No. 4 Dock
12 No. 5 Dock
13 No. 6 Dock
14 Great Ship Basin
15 No. 24 Store
16 No. 25 Store
17 The Parade
18 Water Tank
19 Hatchelling House
20 Short Row
21 Great Ropery
22 No. 15 Store
23 No. 16 Store
24 No. 17 Store
25 South Office Block
26 Tarring House
27 No. 9 Store
28 No. 10 Store
29 No. 11 Store
30 Chain Test House
31 Royal Shelter
32 No. 5 Boathouse
33 No. 6 Boathouse
34 No. 7 Boathouse
35 Dockyard Wall
36 Main Gate
37 Ice House
38 Pay Office
39 No. 2 Slip
40 No. 5 Slip
41 No. 1 Ship Shop
42 Admiralty House
43 Academy
44 Fleet Offices

FIGURE 1   The Georgian and early Victorian dockyard at Portsmouth, 1980

Stone Dock. At the beginning of the twentieth century, the latter dock was lengthened at its head to accommodate the sharp bows of metal-hulled vessels. North Dock was not rebuilt and thus closely represents the original dimensions of the Great Stone Dock, which were 69.4m by 26m.[4] Both docks are notable for their Portland stone stepped sides, for sets of stone slides set in each side wall for the movement of materials to and from the floor of the dock, and for graceful, shaped stonework at their heads tracing the line of the bows of wooden sailing ships. Water was removed by horse-powered capstans driving continuous chain bucket pumps and it is likely that the culverts linking the docks to the base of the pumps, clearly marked on contemporary plans, are still in use. Of the two basins, much remains of that to the landward of the North Dock, which had lost its initial function by 1743 and, reduced in size, had become a reservoir within the dock pumping system. Samuel Bentham, Inspector General of Naval Works 1796–1807 and ever conscious of the need to economise, later built two tiers of brick vaulting, one above the other, in the reservoir, retaining the lower level for water circulation, creating storage space above and building the Block Mills at ground level. The north wall of the second Great Ship Basin was incorporated in Bentham's much enlarged basin of 1801, making it difficult to identify the earlier structures. In addition, South Dock built in 1703, fell victim to Bentham's reorganisation of a century later.

Associated with this dock construction was a range of building slips, seasoning sheds, working sheds and storehouses, none of which has survived, partly because they were of timber construction and partly because they were swept away during subsequent expansion. However, an exception is the English bond-brick boundary wall of 1704–11, which replaced De Gomme's 'pallisadoes', still to be seen by following the line of Admiralty Road and Bonfire Corner to Marlborough Gate. The date '1711' is set into the brickwork at Bonfire Corner. In the light of the deficiencies that became apparent in the early years of the Seven Years' War (1756–63), the Admiralty projected further extensions to the yard in 1761, including another dock, now No.4, which was opened in 1772. Identical to the Great Stone Dock, it was built on the site of a former slipway in the south-east corner of the Great Ship Basin; the dock was lengthened and its head squared off in 1858.

Fortunately, the majority of other structures built after 1761 were of brick rather than wood, thus ensuring the survival of one of the finest collections of Georgian industrial premises in Britain. All are of rich red brick with attractive fenestration and all but one have wooden interiors. Most numerous are the storehouses, nine of which survive in three clusters. The three most distinctive are Nos. 9, 10 and 11, of 1782, 1776 and 1763 respectively. Each has a central pediment and three storeys, with arches framed in stone on the ground floor; the metal base-plates of cranes added later may be seen at the extremities of each storehouse. Brick walls 0.91m thick and massive wooden joists supported by stone corbels at each end emphasise the solidity of the buildings.

Adjacent to the ropery are the slimmer structures of storehouses Nos. 15 (1771), 16 (1771) and 17 (1781), No. 16 being distinguished by the inscription '1771 GR III' worked in blue brick in the eastern gable end; No. 17 merely has its date set in the brickwork. The remaining three stores, built between 1786 and 1790, lie to the east of the Great Stone Dock and of No. 4 dock. They were originally two storied buildings with both an open courtyard in the centre and especially attractive pediments. Store No. 24 alone remains as it was constructed, the others having had additional floors added, losing much of their architectural merit. Though the manufacturing premises have now lost their original function, the 333.75m long Great Ropehouse of 1776, which spanned almost the entire width of the yard at that time, is patently the most evident survivor. It inhibited movement until, on losing its ropemaking function in the 1860s, it was pierced by three arches. This great structure is nothing more than an excellently preserved shell, for the interior flooring is carried on steel columns separate from the walls. Linked to the eastern end of the ropehouse by a covered passageway carried on arches is the hatchelling house of 1771, where fibres were prepared for rope spinning. Adjacent to the north-western corner of the ropery is the 1771 tarring house, now boiler shop west.[5] The location of docks and buildings in the Georgian and early Victorian dockyard is illustrated in Fig. 1. Growing naval demands were reflected not only in the extension of dockyard facilities, but also in the development of specialised premises outside the yard. The Victualling Board was responsible for building the extensive cooperage at their Weevil Lane, Gosport, yard (617005) between 1778 and 1780.[6] The single-storey, wooden-clad, large windowed buildings have lain empty since the demise of the daily rum ration in 1970.

Although the dockyard was an outstanding industrial complex, the surrounding area of south-east Hampshire very much reflected traditional rural life. Evidence of continuing agricultural activity is represented in the fine fifteenth-century tithe barn at Titchfield (539065), its timber framework carrying a tiled roof. The barn's western wall was made of flint to keep out the weather, in contrast to the wooden-clad east wall which had two doors, until recently surmounted by elegant awnings. More muted examples of barns, usually of flint with brick quoins and forming integral parts of the rectangular homestead typical of the eighteenth century, are common, as can be seen in one at Clanfield (698169). However, the four-bay red-brick thatched barn at Meonstoke (613199) is exceptional. A further variation is provided by the five-bay, tile-roofed, brick barn at Brownwich Farm, Titchfield (519036) where, in the nineteenth century, power was drawn from a small stream to drive a water wheel for chaff-cutting and kindred operations. Granaries, mounted on their characteristic staddle stones, are much rarer and, unlike so many in the rest of the county, those in the Portsmouth region are seldom of timber-framed brick but are wooden-clad, though that at Catherington (693139) is an exception. Those at Blendworth (710135), Hambledon (645150 and 655160) and Soberton (604153) have horizontal timbering, but the two at Brownwich Farm are unusual in having vertical planking. In the era before the introduction of forage and root crops allowed an increased number of cattle to be kept in the winter, dovecotes were sometimes employed to provide a supply of fresh meat. A fine example is that at Manor Farm, Hayling Island (721008), thought to date from 1325 and containing 600 nests in two rectangular stone buildings. A less grand survivor is the flint and brick, tile-roofed dovecote at St Clair's Farm, Soberton (604153).

Closely associated with agriculture was corn-milling, an important local activity consequent upon the demand for flour in both Portsmouth and London, the latter being served by coastal vessels. It is frequently difficult to offer precise dates for the fifteen water-mills, six windmills and four tide-mills of which visible traces remain. The majority of these were in operation in the eighteenth century, though some mills known to be of a later date, such as Chesapeake Mill (1820), Wickham, (574115) and Town Mill (1897), Emsworth, (751058), replaced earlier mills and used their predecessors' leats.[7] In most cases, the surviving artefacts of the water- and tide-mills are restricted to the outline of a mill-pond. Occasionally, however, a wheel-pit and overflow channels also survive, as at Havant Mill (715059), Bedhampton Springs Mill (703061) and Lumley Mill (752064) where the site is more remarkable for the curious extravaganza which was the miller's house than for industrial relics.[8] All that remains of the 1735 Slipper Mill at Emsworth (754054) are the tidal pond gates which, at critical states of the tide, operated apparently unaided.

Fortunately, the region contains some mills which have survived intact, probably the oldest of these being Emsworth's Quay Mill (748055), the land for which was conveyed in 1759. Here the tidal gates were constructed so as to permit the entry of small vessels into the tide pond. Neither Quay Mill nor the tiny Lymbourn Springs Mill, Langstone (720049) are architecturally outstanding. However, Chesapeake Mill, Wickham, with its large windows and steeply-pitched roof, and the tall elegant red-brick Titchfield Mill of 1830 (541061) with its double mansard roof, are arguably the finest ones remaining. Chesapeake Mill, the timbering of which was derived from a captured American man-of-war of this name, continues to draw power from the River Meon, although its machinery is driven by an Armfield turbine installed in 1913, with supplementary electric motors.[9] Titchfield Mill lacks substantial interior machinery, but possesses a pair of metal water-wheels featuring

PLATE 1   Remains of the pentrough and rim of the waterwheel at Boarhunt Mill

curved paddles. Less striking architecturally is Boarhunt Mill (606091), but in compensation it contains virtually a full set of machinery, including two pairs of Derbyshire millstones made by Hughes and Sons of London, and, with the exception of one of the stone nuts, all the largely wooden drive mechanism is intact. Outside the mill remain the metal rims of the overshot wheel manufactured by C. Sutton of Shirley, Hants.

Wind-milling, once important on Portsea Island where water power, other than tides, was absent, was less favoured elsewhere. Two brick tower windmills survive at Chalton (716160) and Langstone (720049), having been converted into residences. The former now sports non-functional sails while the latter, which has a two-pitched tower, is unusual in being on the same site as a water-mill – Lymbourn Springs Mill. The miller ensured that flour could be loaded directly into sailing barges by building adjacent premises on piles in the harbour. The remains of another coastal windmill may be seen at Portchester (619044).

Brewing was a further activity based on agriculture, but until the eighteenth century was carried out by individual inns on the premises. Large-scale brewing developed in urban centres, leading to the decline and virtual disappearance of smaller units of production. However, a remarkable early nineteenth-century survival is the minute Emsworth brewery (754057) serving a single adjacent inn, whilst at Southwick an early nineteenth-century brewhouse (626085), housing a complete set of equipment and a small horizontal steam engine, was added to an earlier eighteenth-century brick structure. Both the Emsworth and Southwick

PLATE 2   The millstones and their casings at Boarhunt Mill

PLATE 3   One of the stone nuts (the smaller cog) which turned a runner millstone at Boarhunt Mill

PLATE 4   Langstone windmill. Lymbourn Springs Mill is just visible on the left of the picture

breweries employed wooden venting to allow the circulation of air, a solution also adopted in tanneries and exemplified by the now greatly modified eighteenth-century tannery at Titchfield (541058).

While milling and brewing were industries supported by agriculture so too, in part, was the provision of basic raw materials for the dockyard, local estates providing timber, grain and horses, frequently through contractors. An additional raw material provided for a short period was wrought iron furnished by a local enterprise. Henry Cort's claim that he could supply iron at half the current price from his little water-powered works at Funtley (550081) was quickly taken up by the Victualling Board. The contract encouraged Cort to take out patents in 1783 for a grooved roller as a means of shaping hot metal speedily and accurately and, in 1784 in a less innovatory fashion, for the production of wrought iron in a reverbatory furnace. His downfall five years later was brought about not so much by the site's severe power limitations and the difficulty of bringing in coal from Fareham Creek, but by bankruptcy consequent upon litigation involving his partner's father. The premises were burnt down in 1878, but the outline of the pond, the head-race tunnel beneath a road, the wheel-pit indicating that the wheel was no more than 3.8m in diameter and 1.2m wide and the earthworks, conducting water from a spring to the pond, survive. In addition, part of the outline of the works including a bricked-up arch to a second water-wheel, and adjacent walls and paths liberally sprinkled with slag, can also be seen.[10] That such a minute enterprise could supply most of the iron needs of the dockyard is eloquent testimony to the nature of shipbuilding at the time.

The growth of industry and urbanisation in the region was assisted by, and was simultaneously the cause of, developments in transport. However, the first important transport innovation in south-east Hampshire had little impact, largely because it was ahead of its time and did not serve an important town. The Titchfield Canal of 1611 was one of several ventures undertaken by the enterprising Henry, second Earl of Southampton, and was constructed on his own estates so that no private Act of Parliament was required. This was over a century and a half before the recognised beginning of the Canal Age in Britain. A brick twin-arched bridge remains at Great Posbrook (539048), the widest of the arches being such that only very narrow punts could have passed beneath, while the masonry of one of the lock gates, now cut off from the sea as a result of the sea defence works at the mouth of Titchfield Haven, may be viewed from a convenient road bridge a quarter of a mile inland (531027). Early attempts at road improvement were largely restricted to the construction of bridges, such as the fine, if tiny, Stony Bridge (543065), thought to date from 1625, over the River Meon near Titchfield Abbey. It was not until a century later, however, that road transport provided evidence of rationalisation in the shape of the Portsmouth and Sheet Bridge Turnpike of 1711. The Gosport, Bishop's Waltham, Wickham and Chawton Turnpike followed in 1758, Portsmouth and Gosport thus achieving improved road links with London but not with each other. The Turnpike Acts required milestones to be erected, of which a number have survived. Weathering caused the original inscriptions in the stonework to become indistinct and iron plates were therefore often added. In some instances, it is still possible to discern the lettering in the stone and a comparison with the information on the plate indicates that not all milestones are located at their original sites. Several milestones survive on the A3 north of Horndean and on the

A32 north of Wickham, while the remaining stone on Portsea Island near the Market House Tavern (644014) has an unusual curved top to its face which bears no plate at all. In the centre of Fareham a further milestone with a plate is set into the wall of the Bugle Hotel in Quay Street (581061). Coaching inns associated with the turnpikes abound in the region.[11]

However important land transport might have been, the coastal location of so many of the towns in the Portsmouth region caused sea-borne communications to play a vital role in their development. Portsmouth, Fareham and Emsworth were thriving commercial ports, yet surprisingly little remains of their eighteenth-century activities. Only at Fareham (579055) does an eighteenth-century warehouse survive, complete with half-hipped roof, S-shaped tie plates and, in the upper storey, wooden-framed, unglazed windows with seven closely-set wooden mullions. Adjacent is a ropery, possibly of seventeenth-century origin, known to have been used as a hospital in the Napoleonic Wars, and showing evidence of having been subsequently widened and heightened.

In the eighteenth century, as has been shown, water and wind were the dominant energy sources, the activities of smithies, brickworks, breweries and bakeries providing the main exceptions. In the early nineteenth century, however, led inevitably by the dockyard, steam power made its appearance in the region. Although its diffusion was slow, by 1850 it had wrought, almost alone, fundamental changes upon the economy and society. One critical change was the speed of the urbanisation process so that, as the period progressed, industrial archaeological remains are found increasingly in the towns rather than in the rural areas.

The Napoleonic Wars initiated a fresh round of dockyard expansion, Samuel Bentham being appointed to take charge of the work. A man of outstanding ability, he introduced the age of iron and steam into the dockyard and, fortunately, much of his work remains to be seen.[12] The Great Ship Basin was doubled in size in 1801 to its present limits, incorporating a wooden caisson at its entrance to allow the passage of vehicles from one side to the other. When the wood rotted in the 1840s, the existing iron caisson, of the same dimensions as the original, was installed. Within the basin, two dry docks, No. 2, which now houses HMS *Victory*, and No. 3, in which the *Mary Rose* rests, were added in 1802 and 1803 respectively and, outside the basin, No. 1 dock was completed in 1801. Apart from their greater length and depth, they were similar in design and materials to the earlier docks.[13]

Perhaps Bentham's best-known achievement is his role in the establishment of the Block Mills in 1802. Five years earlier he had installed his own patented circular saws, driven by a steam engine. In addition, he recognised immediately the potential savings inherent in the designs, submitted to him by Marc Brunel, for the mass production of pulley blocks. Consequently, he persuaded the Navy Board of the scheme's validity and engaged Henry Maudslay to make the first forty-five machines which, when completed in 1808, represented the world's first example of machine tools made in metal for mass-production purposes.[14] Nothing remains of the steam engine that provided the power, but the layshafts and belt-wheels are *in situ* on the ground floor and there are two fixed hoists operated by endless chains. On the first storey, bolted to both the floor and roof, is the swing-arm circular saw used to cut *lignum vitae* for the pulley-wheels, a scoring machine, a trenail lathe for the manufacture of dowels and a corner saw. Two outstandingly ingenious machines, now in Southsea Castle Museum, are the automatic mortising engine that worked at 400 strokes per minute without attention and the shaping engine in which ten block shells revolved and were cut by a gouge simultaneously. Small wonder that Brunel's creations were nothing if not sparing with labour, even if the Block Mills Muster Book of 1807–8 lists forty workers in receipt of wages.[15] The machinery paid for itself within four years and was still working over a century later. By comparison with such a display of technological excellence, the fabric of the mills is pedestrian, though mention should be made of the interior wooden columns bearing a distinctly classical Tuscan appearance, in some instances further embellished by the addition of crude early angle-poise lights. The wooden interior structure of this and other buildings constituted a considerable fire risk, to which Bentham reacted by erecting a ring main system fed from an elevated water tank. The original was replaced in 1843 by a structure of two tiers of arched girders above circular columns, considered to be 'a landmark in constructional history'.[16] Bentham had earlier, in 1798, seen fit to render the pay office fireproof by the construction of a vaulted brick roof carried on cast-iron pillars.

Bentham's shameful dismissal in 1812 and the cessation of hostilities three years later ushered in a period of dockyard retrenchment. Not until the 1840s, with the growing acceptance and reliability of steam engines, did the Admiralty begin to make provision for steamships in Portsmouth. A powerful objection to the use of steam power was the vulnerability of paddle wheels to attack, but the evidence provided in 1840 by HMS *Rattler* of the efficiency of the propeller dispelled most doubts.[17] The age of steam was also the age of iron-framed buildings of which the yard had six, four striking examples still surviving. The first, designed as a mast house, was No. 6 Boathouse built in 1843, facing the Mast Pond. Since, however, the intention was for work to be carried out on the ground, first and second floors, the building required great integral strength. The upper floors were carried on cast-iron columns and on girders bearing the instruction 'the load on this girder should not exceed 40 tons equally distributed over its length'. The girders were given added strength by a system of underslung trusses, thought to be one of the first examples of the use of stressed cast-iron. Smaller girders linking the columns were lettered to facilitate assembly and secured by slots rather than bolts. Until 1980, when they were demolished, the yard possessed two of the earliest large single-span roofs fabricated in iron. Built in 1843 and covering No. 3 and No. 4 Building Slips, the spans were 27.4m between the columns and 18.3m above ground level at the height of the roof, and very much precursors of similar structures to be built by railway companies. The distinctiveness of No. 2 Ship Shop, constructed in 1848, is however external, although the use of iron beams avoided the need for obstructive interior columns. It was built of deep-red brick offset by the Portland stone framing to the tall round-headed windows, with both gable ends taking the form of elegant Portland stone pediments. The building was 182.9m long and was used for the assembly of engines and boilers. Immediately to the west is the large Smithery of 1852 where work such as the forging of anchors was undertaken. South of the Steam Basin, opened in 1848, lies the Iron and Brass Foundry of 1854 which, with its large round-headed windows, deep-red brick and contrasting Portland stonework, very much reflect No. 2 Ship Shop. The upper floor incorporates a water sprinkler system fed from a tank on the roof, a logical extension of Bentham's approach to combating fire. Separate from these structures, but nevertheless an integral part of the 1843 development plan, is the Chain Test House in the south-western corner of the yard. Unobtrusive from without, its interior includes cast-iron columns linked by socketed tie bars, light iron roof trusses incorporating decorative flourishes and a floor partly consisting of ballast castings marked 'Po', an abbreviation for Portsmouth, where they were made.[18]

However, on the other side of the harbour, the era of major expansion in the Gosport Victualling Yard[19] took place, curiously enough, when there was little activity in Portsmouth and was consequent upon the decision in 1827 to transfer victualling from Portsmouth to Gosport. The vast bakery, the steam-powered flour mill and the engine house designed by Sir John Rennie and, most impressive of all, the three-storey wooden-framed granary mounted on cast-iron Tuscan columns, its front flush with the water's edge, all date from 1828–30. Devised by G.L. Taylor, architect to the Navy Board, and constructed by Hugh McIntosh, the building is a monument of national significance.[20] Installed there was Thomas Grant's biscuit-making machinery, invented in 1828 and capable of producing 10,000 hexagonal hard tack biscuits per hour, nothing of which, unfortunately, remains. To the south of this complex are the Rum Store of 1830 and the Tank Store, built by Grant when he introduced metal water-storage tanks to the fleet in 1838. Plans were made in 1829 for a 119.4m deep well and the pumphouse on the site has every appearance of dating from the 1830s.[21]

Since steam industrialisation was essentially an urban phenomenon, it is hardly surprising that small early nineteenth-century industrial premises should have been swept away with the process of urbanisation. Consequently, in this period, the industrial archaeology outside both the dockyard and Gosport's Royal Clarence Yard is restricted to a few interesting survivals and to evidence of the growing sophistication of transport. One such survival is Treadgold's foundry and shop in Portsea (633003) dating from the 1830s. The foundry has not worked since the early 1960s, but two hand-operated bellows and associated hearths remain, together with a host of tools. The shop is Dickensian, full of clutter, including a pair of counter scales by Barwood of Middle Street, Southsea, and is notably lacking in light. Mouldings in the beams, which are entirely visible, suggest they are of maritime origin. The building is of red brick with 'Portsmouth grey' headers, some of which are glazed, a style now rapidly disappearing from the city. The adjacent office retains its high stand-up desks and, more remarkably, its speaking tubes used to communicate with other parts of the premises.[22] A second notable survival is the flour mill at Fareham Quay (579056). This substantial two-storey, flat-roofed structure of 1830 appears to have been steam-driven from the outset and is most notable for the interior use of cruciform-plan iron columns.[23] Of the other surviving evidence, street furniture sometimes indicates former industrial activity; one instance is the series of manhole covers in King's Terrace, Southsea (638994), manufactured by Garnett and Co., at their Ferrumite Works, Portsmouth in the 1820s.

Transport improvements were one of the central features of economic develop-ment during the first half of the nineteenth century, strengthening the links between south-east Hampshire and the rest of the country. The Titchfield–Cosham Turnpike of 1810 and its east–west extensions facilitated both coastal links and those between Portsmouth and Gosport, by virtue of intersecting with the existing turnpikes running north from Gosport and from Portsmouth at Fareham and Cosham respectively. The evidence may be seen in milestones at Drayton (673056) and Farlington (688058), where the metal plates are only marginally smaller than the stones themselves, and at Wymering (640056), where there is a small plate on a large stone. Since the information is also presented differently, the Wymering milestone may be a replacement. The small milestones with carved inscriptions on the additional turnpike between Waterlooville and Droxford, such as that at Denmead (656120), are indicative of the growing complexity of the road network. Frequently where rivers were encountered, bridges were required, but the terrain and width of the rivers did not inspire structures of especial merit. The bridges were of brick with occasional Portland capstones: Wallington Bridge (583067) used five small arches, Titchfield Bridge (542059) carried the road over the River Meon on two taller arches and Brock Bridge (611198) had three very small semi-circular ones. Not all bridges were elements of turnpikes and some, such as Cut Bridge (607170) over the Meon at Soberton, were erected to facilitate movement in rural areas. On this bridge, a plaque declares that it was 'Built by Subscription 1823'. Rook's Bridge (627084) at Southwick is unusual in that it has a single brick arch lined with strong voussoir stones.

Although having benefited from road improvements, the region was nevertheless advantageously placed for seaborne transport. Despite the potential for coastal shipping, however, the section of the Portsmouth and Arun Canal between Langstone Harbour and Landport was opened in 1822. Inevitably, traffic was slight and the canal company reacted by constructing a quay near Portsbridge and a cut giving direct access to Portsmouth Harbour, allowing the closure of their 'white elephant' in 1831. The western section was sold to the Brighton and Chichester Railway in 1845 and the central section became Goldsmith Avenue in the 1890s, but east from the White House (665995) in Milton Road to the sea lock (678999) the towpaths and the canal bed may be traced easily. Built to handle 150-ton sailing barges, the sea lock is of generous proportions and, although the gates have gone, the brickwork is in good condition even though most of the Portland capstones have been removed. Remains of a second lock are just discernible inland of the first in a small boatyard (676998), while the unmistakable tall, slim outline of a beam engine pumping house, used to maintain the water-level in the canal, is clearly evident amid more conventional houses in Waterlock Gardens (675998). As though to underline the irrelevance of the Portsmouth Canal, and to emphasise the expansion of commercial shipping, a dry dock, complete with Portland stone stepped sides and a caisson gate, was opened in the Camber at Old Portsmouth in 1863 (631996). The construction of a lighthouse at Southsea Castle in 1823 further assisted maritime navigation.

Without doubt, however, it was the railway that provided the most far-reaching social and economic effects of transport improvements, permitting the speedy dispatch of farm produce, the development of specialisation in manufacturing and, not least, the growth of tourism. The new form of transport made an impressive arrival in the region with the London and Southampton Railway's line to Fareham and Gosport, opened in 1841. Sir William Tite was engaged as architect and his magnificent fourteen-bay Tuscan-colonnaded station in Portland stone at Gosport (614002) is one of the outstanding structures of the early railway period in Britain. Neither the overall roof, nor that above the colonnade, has survived. Still remaining are the matching gate pillars and the iron railings added when the line was extended, at Prince Albert's suggestion, into Clarence Yard in 1845 for the convenience of Queen Victoria.[24]

The royal station within the yard (618004), which has been incorporated almost entirely within another more recent structure, is a simple curved building in brick, distinguished only by window mullions bearing the royal crown and sceptre. Fareham station (569062), opened in 1841, was a more modest affair, as the original small stone building to the left of the entrance indicates. Although clearly of some antiquity, the five slender iron columns carrying the platform canopy may not date from 1841, but were certainly incorporated long before the general extension work of 1889. Much of the Cosham station building of 1848 (658051) is original and the entrance through a narrow, arched wood-panelled passage may still be seen.

From the east came the London, Brighton and South Coast Railway, opening a station in Portsmouth (641002) in 1847, though rebuilding in 1866 has removed virtually all traces of the original, the entrance of which was, like Gosport's, on the south side of the line. The fabric of Emsworth station (748064) dates from a later period, as does that of Havant (718065), and the most notable original remains are a series of level crossing keepers' houses, such as that at Copnor (660014), and a delightfully sinuous twenty-one-arch, humpbacked brick bridge (702062) carrying the road to Bedhampton Springs Mill, whose owner insisted on a high quality structure in compensation for the loss of amenity.[25] The London and South Western Railway extended its service to Portsmouth in 1848 and in the process

PLATE 5   Part of the royal station at Royal Clarence Yard

constructed the thirteen-arch brick Quay Viaduct at Fareham (580059) and the even more powerful seventeen-arch Cams Viaduct (587062) over the Wallington, a feature of which is the false arches flanking the skew arch taking the road.

The age of iron and steam, which had arrived in the dockyard during the 1840s, spread throughout the region during the second half of the nineteenth century, providing a rich legacy of artefacts. The dockyard underwent a dramatic extension which more than trebled its area between 1864 and 1881. An almost continuous building programme of dockyard facilities was maintained until 1914, as vessels became larger and more sophisticated and as the nation became wedded to a policy of rearmament. The majority of the new facilities were grouped around the enormous No. 3 Basin, completed in stages between 1876 and 1912, the excavated material being used to create Whale Island via a specially constructed rail link. Docks Nos. 12–15, to the south of the Basin, though the largest in the yard, were still incapable of accommodating the Dreadnoughts and, consequently, were extended between 1903 and 1914. The wooden No. 5 Building Slip was doubled in size and No. 2 Slip, a traditional patent slip with two rail-mounted cradles, was provided with a steam winch manufactured and dated in 1896 by Cowans Sheldon, which is still *in situ* although not in use. Water-levels in the new dock system were controlled by No. 1 Pumping Station completed in 1878, which is notable for its high-level circular windows above the internal gantry crane and for the fluted iron columns within the building. The strength of its beams suggests that beam engines may have been installed initially. Three other buildings deserve consideration. First, the Combined Workshops, with elegant pedimented coat of arms, were built in 1886. Secondly, No. 1 Ship Shop was constructed in 1867 with its fenestration and juxtaposition of red brick and Portland stone making it very similar to the Iron and Brass Foundry. Thirdly, the Factory, with two adjacent 182.9m by 45.7m main sections was reputed to be among the largest in the world when completed in 1907.

Minor modifications were effected in the older part of the yard. The form of No. 7 and No. 5 Boathouses, completed in 1875 and 1882 respectively, is especially interesting. To minimise the weight carried on piles driven into the Mast Pond, they were given wooden frames and cladding after the early eighteenth-century fashion. To add to their authenticity, the window frames protrude beyond the cladding and, typical of the Georgian era, the windows consist of a large number of small panes. The components of this vast industrial enterprise, which employed 10,400 people in 1911, were linked by a comprehensive railway network. Much of the track remains, as do some of the turntables, for instance that in Murray's Lane. In addition, on South Railway Jetty, the Royal Shelter built in 1893 still survives, resplendently painted, with decorative smoke vents and canopies on the seaward side and elaborate finials at the gable ends. There was once a single-line track with a swing bridge connecting the yard with the Harbour Station and two of the bridge's pontoons may be seen against the jetty wall. Outside the yard, the level crossing gates over Alfred Road (639006) and Edinburgh Road (640005) are still in position and, remarkably, a double-armed wooden semaphore signal survives at the latter crossing.[26]

Across Portsmouth Harbour, the Admiralty Marine Technology Establishment at Gosport (613986) houses R.E. Froude's ship model test tank constructed in 1886 and subsequently used to test all naval vessel designs until 1945. The original tank, measuring 145m by 6m,[27] remains and a section of the original carriage, a model of the steam engine employed to draw it, a ruling machine for the production of graph paper and a propeller dynamometer are housed in an adjacent museum.[28] Though the importance of naval shipbuilding is undoubted, commercial shipbuilding, with the exception of Vosper's yard in the Camber, which itself closed in 1985, was never as significant in the region. Elsewhere evidence, such as the remnants of a patent slip at Emsworth (752055), is limited.

After shipbuilding and ship repairing, the major activity in Portsmouth throughout the century was the clothing industry, with corset-making very much its leading sector.[29] The Marina Factory in Southsea (662989) erected in 1897, the Kingston Factory (650017) in 1904 and the Goldsmith Avenue works (657998) in 1921 remain. All possess three floors, large windows and, in the case of the Marina Factory, a clerestory at the apex of the roof. Only in the case of the Goldsmith Avenue works has any attempt been made to brighten otherwise purely functional brickwork. In Fratton Road (650015) the firm of Voller represents the survival of a small business still operating in its original premises opened in 1899. While the clothing industry might have employed more workers, the largest industrial premises outside the yard were concerned with brewing[30] and, possibly because of their sound construction, a surprising number have survived although seldom as breweries. The exceptions are Brickwoods brewery, Portsea (632005), an amalgam of buildings and building styles lacking in cohesion, and Gale's brewery at Horndean (707133), largely dating from 1869 and complete with brick tower, wooden-clad cooler, cooperage, barrel-rolling track and two small vertical steam engines, one thought to have come from a Gosport ferry. Other interesting survivals include Young's Victory Brewery at Landport (641008) and the brewery at Wickham (574114), its tower dated 1887. The now-derelict Wallington brewery (585069), dating from 1888, is unusual in that it incorporates a malting.[31]

Remnants of the once-important brick industry are preserved in the form of the brickworks' office at Rowlands Castle (733104), itself made of a selection of bricks and tiles once produced on site.[32] Shells of two Berry down-draught kilns, subsequently converted to oil firing, are to be found at Denmead Pottery (656112).

The nineteenth-century development of urbanisation created problems of heating, lighting, sanitation, drainage and water supply and increased the likelihood of epidemic diseases. Attempts to solve these problems occasioned the emergence of public utilities. Gas manufacture began in Portsmouth as early as 1821, but only a few original buildings remain of the most recent gasworks, that at Hilsea (664029), opened in 1904.[33] Otherwise, the legacy of the coal-gas industry is restricted to spiral-guided holders at Fareham (585059), Gosport (615994), Havant (726075) and Emsworth (749061). In 1868, following a series of severe cholera epidemics, a sewage pumping system was installed in Portsmouth and a small engine house, enclosing a pair of Clayton beam engines, was built at Eastney (673992), the original fluted columns of which are still visible. Continued population growth necessitated the building of a second engine house in 1887, containing two compound beam engines by James Watt and Co.[34] The architecture of both engine houses reflects the contemporary civic style which became undeniably more functional by the Edwardian period. Thus the gas-engine house of 1904 is entirely unobtrusive, although its huge Crossley engines and centrifugal pumps represent a major advance from steam technology. The gas-engine house also contains an interesting working collection of smaller gas and oil engines.

In tandem with drainage improvements were those in water supply. The oldest surviving artefact, long since disused, is the brick-walled Drayton Basin (678058), opened in 1812 by the Portsmouth, Portsea and Farlington Water Works Company. Of the 1860 pumping station at Havant (710063) only the gatehouse remains, but adjacent is the impressively large, terracotta brick pump house of 1927, no longer housing its triple expansion steam engines. At Bedhampton (706063), the 1889 and 1902 engine houses are intact, while the slim storehouse at the Bury Cross pumping station at Gosport (598996) is the former beam engine house of 1884. The Soberton station (596142) began to supply Gosport in 1907, employing horizontal steam engines, with the consequence that the building is of modest height and merges well with its rural setting. There are a number of smaller pumping and booster stations in the region, such as those at Portsbridge (655047) and Maindell, Fareham (588070).[35] Further progress in heating and lighting came in 1894, when a public electricity supply was first generated in Portsmouth at the Camber Dock (632996). The site was converted to residential use in 1985. The tiny electricity generating station at Fareham, operating between 1897 and 1932, may be seen on the quayside (578057).

The second half of the nineteenth century was also the period in which much of the present day railway system was established, providing a valuable insight into both contemporary building styles and Victorian travelling conditions. Undoubt-

PLATE 6   Portsmouth and Southsea station, a good example of high Victorian architectural style

edly, the *pièce de résistance* is the rebuilt Portsmouth and Southsea station (641002) completed in 1866, full of French-Italianate flourishes, coloured brickwork, a decorated parapet and clock, keystones with a figurehead resembling Neptune and intricately-wrought ironwork in the entrance canopy.

More subdued is the 1876 High Level station which, unusually, has the lettering 'PER', representing Portsmouth Extension Railway, worked into the roof brackets. Portsmouth Harbour station (629000) also dates from 1876, though the entrance was rebuilt during the inter-war period. Portchester station (616058), incorporating attractive flintwork, has a platform canopy, a feature of which is the large circles in the spandrels of the brackets. A delightful cottage station of 1859 is that at Rowlands Castle (734108), and Droxford (612185), now converted into a residence, has pleasing neo-Elizabethan overtones. Conversely, Fratton station (653000), opened in 1885, is overwhelmingly functional. Surprisingly, the essential features of Portsmouth's second terminus, the short-lived East Southsea station, operating between 1885 and 1914, are well preserved (650984).[36] Fast disappearing are level crossing keepers' houses, though one remains at Havant (720065) and another at Copnor (660014). Between Hayling Island and the mainland are the metal pontoons of the 1867 manually operated swing bridge linking two sections of a wooden viaduct across Langstone harbour (718042). Indicative of the relative cost of iron and brick by the end of the century is the substantial metal bridge, comprising four sets of braced tubular piers, erected in 1903 to carry the Meon valley railway line over the railway at Wickham (595116).

An essential part of the urban transport network, linking with the railway stations, was the tramway which, by allowing people to reside further from their place of work, contributed substantially to the spread of housing in the early twentieth century. Tramways ran in Portsmouth between 1865 and 1936, being electrified in 1900. For a network of such eventual complexity, surprisingly little remains, for virtually all the track has been removed, but residual elements include a section of interlaced track in Rugby Road, Fratton (651998), a short section at the Broad Street terminus in Old Portsmouth (6296). More obvious remains lie in the former tram sheds at Highland Road, Southsea (665990), and at the Hoeford Depot (579046) of the former Gosport and Fareham company which operated between 1905 and 1929. The abutments of a bridge over Southwick Hill Road (658058) and a traction pole near the George Inn (669067) are the principal relics of the Horndean Light Railway, an electric tramway that operated between 1903 and 1935.[37] In Portsmouth many traction poles have survived, having been used subsequently for trolleybuses and then as lampposts, and some tram shelters are still in existence, the most remarkable of which, once located in Guildhall Square, is now to be found at Cosham (656050). Other items of street furniture which reflect the gradual improvement in public services during the Victorian period include pillar boxes, fine examples of which can be found at World's End (633123), dated 1859, and at Gosport station (614002); former gas lampposts, above all those in the old village of Bedhampton, and electric lamp-standards, those in Fareham High Street, dated between 1897 and 1903, and those on Southsea sea front being the most decorative. Water supply manhole covers and drainage gratings bearing the local makers' name abound and represent a mundane if very necessary element in the progress of urban society.

It would be surprising if industrial societies were not to leave evidence of at least

PLATE 7   The 'Penfold' pillar box at Gosport railway station

some of their activities, but the richness of such legacies is not always fully appreciated. This chapter has demonstrated not only the range of existing industrial artefacts in the Portsmouth region, but also the way in which these artefacts result from the interaction between politics, economics and technology. Strategic political decisions concerning foreign policy gave rise to the dockyard, which lay at the very centre of the regional economy. The docks, basins and buildings of the yard reflected the most cost-effective method of shipbuilding and repair at particular periods. A prerequisite of such developments was technological innovation and, in large part, this may be traced through a study of the artefacts remaining in the yard. Elsewhere, interaction may not have been so complex, but the decline of rural industry and the rise of urban activity were encouraged by both economic and technological change. Thus the rural, water-powered corn mill and the turnpike milestone are symbols of an earlier era than that epitomised by the essentially nineteenth-century urban foundry, corset factory and railway station. Within the towns, street lighting, gasholders and pumping stations testify to the link between the move to improve social conditions and technological means of achieving such progress. By highlighting such interrelationships, the study of the artefacts of industrial change represents an important element of local history.

PART TWO
THE HISTORICAL
BACKGROUND

4

FROM THE NORMAN CONQUEST TO CIVIL WAR

Margaret Hoad and John Webb

By the time of the Norman conquest in 1066 most of the main areas of settlement in south-east Hampshire had already been established. In the next two or three centuries some of these settlements, such as Applestede (Southwick), were to vanish and other new ones, for example Portsmouth, were to be formed. In this region of Hampshire there were three main areas of occupation. One was in the Meon valley from Titchfield northwards, following the line of the original Jutish settlement. The second was along the coast south of Portsdown Hill to the Sussex borders and the third was between the South Downs and the Forest of Bere. In the south of the region there were numerous communities; in the north they were far more widely scattered, except where the River Meon made easier access possible. The Domesday Survey of 1086, designed to enable William I to assess with greater accuracy the valuation for taxation purposes of the lands he had but recently won, is considered today to be an inadequate record, but with all its imperfections it does provide the best surviving evidence as to the nature and extent of land utilisation in the late eleventh century.[1] Although the survey of manors was made hundred by hundred, the final arrangement was by overlords within each county. This rearrangement scattered the manors of any one hundred, creating doubt in some cases, for instance Alverstoke, as to which hundred a manor belonged.

Of the hundreds, that of Titchfield largely comprised one of the pre-Danish *parochia* or mother parishes of Hampshire,[2] though by 1086 Fareham had become separated from it and Alverstoke may or may not have belonged to it. Titchfield itself was a royal manor and was said to be a 'berewick' of another royal manor, that of Meonstoke. This is believed to have been for administrative convenience,[3] but Titchfield did not remain in royal hands for long as by 1100 it had been granted to Paganus de Gisors, ancestor of John de Gisors, the founder of Portsmouth.[4] Although Titchfield was not the largest manor in terms of population, it was the only one in this part of Hampshire which had a market at that time. Droxford and Fareham were both ecclesiastical manors of the Bishop of Winchester and hundreds in their own right, though the latter's population was almost twice as large as the former's. Indeed, throughout the Meon valley the manors with the highest working populations belonged either to the Bishop or to the monks of the Cathedral Abbey of St Swithun and St Peter at Winchester.[5] Only the southern half of Meonstoke Hundred is included in this region of Hampshire, although the hundred stretched as far north as West Meon. Hugh de Port was an important lay overlord here but, even so, nearly half the manors were in ecclesiastical hands.[6] Furthermore, the region included only the southern half of Finchdean Hundred,[7] which contained the extensive manor of *Ceptune*. This manor's working population was only about a third of that in the Meon valley and the southern coastal strip, an indication of its difficulties of access, generally less favourable farming conditions and smaller total population. An enormous manor, it was held by Earl Roger of Shrewsbury, who also had other landholdings on the eastern edge of Hampshire.[8] However, after his son's rebellion against Henry I in 1102, the earl's lands were forfeited and *Ceptune* manor was divided into areas approximating to the modern settlements of Chalton, Clanfield, Catherington, Idsworth and Blendworth. The remaining two hundreds of Bosmere and Portsdown, which lay along the south coast, were held among a number of overlords and undertenants with Hugh de Port holding most. Neither hundred appears to have had a dominant manor, a fact reinforced by their names, which represented geographical areas. The most surprising point that Domesday Book reveals, however, is the very small population to be found in the three manors of Copnor, Buckland and Fratton on Portsea Island. The total number of people indicated was only one-third of that of Hayling Island.[9] Both islands were dependent on a tidal causeway for access, but why Portsea Island should appear to be so little utilised cannot, as yet, be explained.

Of the other features mentioned in Domesday, churches were only irregularly recorded in some manors[10] and not at all in others, such as Titchfield, which nevertheless was known to have had one. Woods for the pannage of pigs, mills and meadows were regularly included, but only four of the region's manors, all on the coast, were specifically stated to have had fisheries.[11] Perhaps the most interesting economic feature was the reference to salterns, especially in Langstone and Portsmouth harbours. The salt industry was to remain important for many centuries, but the fact that two of the most valuable salterns were stated to be in Boarhunt suggests that, at the time of Domesday, Boarhunt manor may have stretched down to the sea, possibly in the area of Wicor or Cams Hall estate near Fareham. This would seem to indicate that modern parish boundaries are not necessarily those of the Domesday manors.

Of the religious houses in south-east Hampshire, the only one in existence by Domesday was the Benedictine settlement on Hayling Island, granted by William I to the Abbey of Jumièges in 1067. Though the Benedictine priory may not have been built until the thirteenth century, a cell may have existed from shortly after its foundation.[12] Problems constantly beset this priory. Being an alien foundation, it was seized by Edward I in 1294 and again by Edward II in 1325, both events being occasioned by war with France. In addition, throughout the fourteenth century, the priory suffered much from encroachment by the sea, especially in 1324–25 when it lost 206 acres of arable land and eighty acres of pasture. Even the priory church and buildings did not escape damage. Eventually in 1413, during the general dissolution

TABLE 1

DOMESDAY MANORS OF THE PORTSMOUTH REGION

- arranged in clockwise order from Titchfield Hundred
round to Portsdown Hundred

Key: * = Hundred specified in text   A = In demesne
       + = Hundred assumed   B = In hands of villeins and bordars
                                          TRE = Time of Edward the Confessor

Manor	Overlord	Tenant	Tenant Prior to 1066	Hides		Ploughlands		Inhabitants	Other Features	Value		
				1066	1086	A	B			TRE	1066	1086
TITCHFIELD (Ticefelle) HUNDRED								Villeins 5 Bordars 11 Serf 1 Total 17		£4	£4	£4
Brownwich* (Burnewic)	Bishop of Winchester	Ansgot	Edric	1	1	1½	3					
Crofton* (Croftune)	Count Alan of Brittany	–	Ulward	7	3	1	4½	Villeins 11 Bordars 2 Serfs 4 Total 17	Church Mill worth 12s 6d Fishery 2 salterns worth 100d 24 acres meadow Woods for 5 pigs	£8	£5	£4
Funtley + (Funtelei)	Count Alan of Brittany	–	Ulward under Earl Godwin	1	1		2½	Villeins 7 Serfs 2	Mill worth 10s 3 acres meadow	40s	40s	30s
*	Rannulf Flamme	–	Turi under Earl Godwin	1	1	1	2½	Villeins 4 Bordars 5 Serf 1	Mill worth 12s 6d 5 acres meadow Woods for 10 pigs	£4	£3	£3
*	Robert son of Gerold	–	Tovi	½	½		1	Bordars 3 Total 22	6 acres meadow Woods for 3 pigs	20s	20s	20s
Hook + (Houch)	Hugh de Port	German	Norman	1	1	1	1	Villeins 2 Bordars 3 Serfs 3 Total 8	1 acre meadow Woods for 1 pig	–	–	25s
Meon * (Mene)	Bishop of Winchester	–	Tovi	1	1		1	Villeins 2	2 acres coppice	20s	20s	20s
Rowner * (Ruenore)	William Mauduit	–	Coleman	5	2½	1½	2½	Villeins 10 Bordars 2 Serfs 2 Total 14	1 acre meadow Woods for 4 pigs	70s	30s	70s
Sigeons- + worth (Sugion)	Hugh de Port	Herle-bald	Ulvric	1	1	1	2	Villeins 5 Bordars 2 Serfs 3 Total 10	Mill worth 20s 5 acres meadow Woods for 5 pigs	60s	30s	60s
Stubbington + (Stubitone)	Hugh de Port	–	Godwin	3	3	1	2	Villeins 5 Bordars 4 Total 9	2 acres meadow	50s	60s	60s
Titchfield* (Ticefelle) "berewick of Meonstoke"	William I	–	Edward the Conf-essor	2	2	2	9	Villeins 16 Bordars 13 Serfs 4 Total 33	Mill worth 20s Market & toll worth 20s		Not Given	
Wickham * (Wicheham)	Hugh de Port	–	4 brot-hers held it as 2 manors	12	12	2	7	Villeins 15 Bordars 6 Serfs 5 Total 26	2 mills worth 20s 8 acres meadow Woods for 5 pigs	£10	£4	£7

Manor	Overlord	Tenant	Tenant Prior to 1066	Hides		Ploughlands		Inhabitants	Other Features	Value		
				1066	1086	A	B			TRE	1066	1086
FAREHAM (Ferneham) HUNDRED												
Fareham * (Ferneham)	Bishop of Winchester	–	Bishop of Winchester	20	20	2	14	Villeins 30 Bordars 16 Serfs 6	Church 2 mills worth 25s 25 acres meadow Woods for 10 pigs Pasturage worth 30d	£18	£10	£16
	"	Rolf Geoffrey	Hercus	7½) 4)	7½) 4)	4	5½	Villeins 24 Bordars 10 Serfs 4	3 mills worth 16s 16 acres meadow Woods for 3 pigs	–	–	£7
	"	William	Godwin	1)	1)			Total 90				
DROXFORD (Drocheneford) HUNDRED												
Droxford + (Drocheneford)	Bishop of Winchester for his monks	–	Bishop of Winchester for his monks	16	14	2	14	Villeins 32 Bordars 13 Serfs 6 Total 51	Church worth 20s 2 mills worth 15s 2d Pasture worth 12s 10 acres meadow Woods for 40 pigs	£26	£20	£26
MEONSTOKE (Menestoch) HUNDRED												
Alverstoke + (Alwarestoch)	Bishop of Winchester for his monks	–	Bishop of Winchester for his monks	16	10		15	Villeins 48	Woods for 2 pigs	£6	£6	£6
	"	Sawin a Knight		½	½	1		Bordars 2 Total 50				
+ Corhampton (Quedementure)	Hugh de Port	–	Alwin	3	1	2	1	Villeins 2 Bordars 6 Serfs 4 Total 12	Church 2 mills worth 22s 1 acre meadow	£8	5s	£8
+ East Hoe in Soberton (Hou)	Hugh de Port	–	Ulward	1½	1	1	2	Villeins 3 Bordars 2 Serfs 4 Total 9	1 acre meadow Woods for 4 pigs	40s	30s	60s
Hambledon * (Hamledune)	Earl Roger of Shrewsbury	Edward	Earl Godwin	1	1	1		Bordars 2	Woods for 6 pigs	20s	20s	20s
(Ambledune)*	William de Perci (thro' his wife Emma de Port)	–	Alwin	1	1	1	2	Villeins 6 Bordars 6 Serfs 2 Total 14	Mill worth 12d Woods for 4 pigs	£4	£3	£4
Meonstoke+ (Menestoche)	William I	–	Edward the Confessor	1½	0	1½	1½	Villeins 3 Bordars 16 Serfs 4	Mill worth 10s 3 acres meadow Woods for 10 pigs Pasture worth 10s	Not Given		
+	Bishop of Winchester	–	Bishop of Winchester	½	½	½		Villein 1 Total 24	Mill Church worth 20s	25s	25s	25s
Soberton * (Sudbertune)	William I	–	Leman under Earl Godwin	4	0	½	2	Villeins 6 Bordars 3	2 mills worth 15s 1 acre meadow	£3	£3	£3
+	"	–	Godwin	3	0	½	1	Villeins 3 Bordars 2	Mill worth 5s 3 acres meadow	40s	40s	40s
*	"	Henry the Treasurer	Andrac	2	1	1	1	Villeins 4 Bordars 5 Serfs 2 Total 25	2 acres meadow	30s	20s	60s

Manor	Overlord	Tenant	Tenant Prior to 1066	Hides		Ploughlands		Inhabitants	Other Features	Value		
				1066	1086	A	B			TRE	1066	1086
FINCHDEAN (Ceptune) HUNDRED												
'Ceptune' * ie Chalton, Clanfield, Catherington Idsworth & Blendworth	Earl Roger of Salis- bury	–	Earl Godwin	60	27	10	27	Villeins 55 Bordars 27 Serfs 22 Total 104	Churches (no number) 1 acre meadow Woods for 50 pigs Pasturage worth 10s	£56	£35	£80
BOSMERE (Boseburg) HUNDRED												
Brockhamp- ton * (Brochema- tune)	Bishop of Winchester for his monks	–	Bishop of Win- chester for his monks	6	4		4	Villeins 14	Mill worth 15s 4 acres meadow Woods for 20 pigs	£5	£5	£5
*	Hugh de Port	Herbert the Chamb- erlain	Sired under Earl Harold	2	2	1	½	Villeins 1 Bordars 4 Total 19				
Havant + (Havehunte)	Bishop of Winchester for his monks	–	Bishop of Win- chester for his monks	10	7		6	Villeins 20	2 mills worth 15s 3 salterns worth 15d Woods for 10 pigs	£8	£8	£8
Hayling Island (Halingei)*	William I	–	Leman under King Edward	2½	0	1	½	Villein 1 Bordars 8	1½ acres meadow	40s	20s	70s
(Helinghei)*	Bishop of Winchester for his monks	–	Bishop of Win- chester for his monks	5	4		3½	Villeins 11	1 acre meadow Woods for 1 pig	£5	£4	£4.10s
(Helingey)*	Abbey of Jumièges	–	Ulward under Queen Edith	12	7	2	17	Villeins 23 Bordars 37 Serfs 3	Saltern worth 6s 8d 2 fisheries worth 20d 1 acre meadow Woods for 20 pigs	£15	£10	£12
*	Earl Roger of Shrews- bury	Abbey of Troarn	Alward under King Edward	5	3		4	Villeins 11 Total 94	1 acre meadow Coppice woods	£4	£3	£4
Nytimber + (Neutibrige)	Earl Roger of Shrews- bury	Sired	Sired under Earl Harold	3	3	1	½	Villeins 2 Bordars 4 Total 6	Mill worth 5s 3 acres meadow Fishery	30s	30s	30s
Warblington (Warblite- tone)	Earl Roger of Shrews- bury	–	Earl Godwin	12	4	2	5	Villeins 17 Bordars 12 Serfs 6 Total 35	2 churches 1 mill worth 10s	Not Given		
(Note: this entry in Domesday found under Westbourne, Sussex. Only later was it included in Bosmere Hundred)												
PORTSDOWN HUNDRED												
'Apple- stede'+ ie. Southwick	Hugh de Port	Tezelin	Goding under King Edward	1½	1½	1	½	Bordars 13	Mill worth 15d ½ acre meadow Woods for 3 pigs	30s	30s	40s
"		A vassal		½	½	½		Bordars 3 Total 16				
Bedhampton* (Betametone)	Abbey of St Peter Winchester	Hugh de Port	Alsi under the Abbot	10	10	1	7	Villeins 12 Bordars 7 Serfs 7 Total 26	Church 2 mills for use of hall 2 salterns worth 37s 8d 3 acres meadow Woods for 30 pigs	£12	£10	£12

Manor	Overlord	Tenant	Tenant Prior to 1066	Hides 1066	Hides 1086	Ploughlands A	Ploughlands B	Inhabitants	Other Features	Value TRE	Value 1066	Value 1086
Boarhunt + (Borehunte)	Hugh de Port	Tezelin	Lefsi and Meruen as 2 manors under King Edward	1	1	1	½	Villeins 2 Bordars 2	Mill worth 5s ½ acre meadow	-	-	20s
*	Bishop of Winchester for his monks			½	½			Villein 1		-	-	6s 6d
*	Earl Roger of Shrews-bury		3 free-men under King Edward	11½	4	2	3	Villeins 10 Bordars 6 Serfs 6 Total 27	Church Mill worth 42d Mill for use of hall 2 salterns worth 22s 4d	£11	£11	£14
	"	1 knight		1	1	1						
Buckland * (Bocheland)	Hugh de Port	Held-red	Alward under Earl Godwin	3½	3½	2	2	Villeins 6 Bordars 2 Serfs 2 Total 10		60s	40s	60s
Copnor * (Copenore)	Robert son of Gerold	Held-red	Tovi under Earl Godwin	3	3	1	2	Villeins 5 Bordars 2 Serfs 2 Total 9	Saltern worth 8d	60s	30s	60s
Cosham * (Cosseham)	Hugh de Port under Bishop of Bayeux	Geoff-rey	Bricsmar under King Edward	2	2	1	½	Villeins 2 Bordars 2 Serfs 4		40s	-	30s
*	Anschitil son of Osmund	-	"	2	½	1	1	Bordars 6 Serf 1	Saltern worth 14d	40s	30s	50s
	"	-	Norman under King Edward	½	½	1	1	Villeins 2 Bordars 3 Serfs 3 23	½ acre meadow	40s	30s	40s
Fratton * (Frodintone)	William de Waren	Dis-melin	Chetel under King Edward	4	4	1	2	Villeins 4 Bordars 4 Serfs 4 Total 12		60s	30s	40s
Portchester * (Porcestre)	William Mauduit	-	3 free-men as 3 manors under King Edward	5	2½	2	1½	Villeins 5 Bordars 4 Serfs 4	Fishery for use of hall Woods for 5 pigs	£4.10s	£5	£6
	"	Durand		1	1	1			Mill worth 30d			
	"	Fulc-old	Alward under King Edward	1	1	½	½	Villeins 2 Serfs 2				14s
	"		Alvric under King Edward	2	2	1	½	Villeins 3 Bordars 4 Serfs 2 26	2 mills worth 5s 2 acres meadow Coppice woods	25s	25s	30s
Wymering * (Wimeringes)	William 1		Edward the Con-fessor	Never Assessed		2	4	Villeins 16 Bordars 6 Serfs 2	Woods for 5 pigs	Not Given		
Portion in Cosham	"		"	4	4		4 5	Freed men 8 Villeins 8 Bordars 8 Serfs 2	paying 49s 4d Saltern			
Portion in Portchester	"		"	Never Assessed		1	1	Villein 1 Bordars 6 Total 57	1 acre meadow Woods for 10 pigs			

of alien priories, the lands of Hayling were given to the recently-established Carthusian monastery at Sheen in Surrey.[13]

The next religious house to be founded in the region was the Augustinian priory established originally in the grounds of Portchester Castle by William Pontdelarche about 1128.[14] Until recently, it was believed to have been founded in 1133 by Henry I when he confirmed Pontdelarche's grant of lands including single hides in both Southwick and Applestede.[15] Pontdelarche had obtained Portchester when he acquired from Henry I the office of chamberlain, held by sergeanty of the castle there, after Robert Mauduit's tragic death in 1120 in the *White Ship*. However, in the troubled times of Stephen's reign, Pontdelarche constantly changed sides, even suffering temporary imprisonment in his own castle, and consequently created instability for the canons. Therefore, on Pontdelarche's death in about 1149, the canons moved to the land they held at Southwick and Applestede, where they were to remain until the Dissolution of the monasteries in the 1530s.[16] Applestede disappeared as a name in the thirteenth century and only recently has it been proved that it was sited in the modern village of Southwick which had taken its name from the adjacent priory.[17] Over the years, the priory added to its estates,[18] though at times the prior was reproved for poor standards and bad management.[19] Even so, the priory seems to have maintained a steady number of thirteen canons[20] and, indeed, the wedding of Henry VI and Margaret of Anjou took place there in 1445.[21]

A third religious house, of somewhat larger size with fifteen canons,[22] was the Premonstratensian abbey at Titchfield founded by Peter des Roches, Bishop of Winchester, in 1232 when it was endowed with a number of local estates.[23] An important feature of this house was its very fine library of which next to nothing now survives apart from its catalogue.[24] As with other monastic houses, further estates were acquired, including the manors of Portsea and Copnor,[25] and the Abbey's records suggest that these estates were efficiently run in spite of occasional disputes with tenants when both sides were seeking to gain advantage.[26]

The only other religious house in this part of Hampshire was of a different type. This was the hospital of St Nicholas, in Portsmouth, generally known as *Domus Dei*, and also founded by Peter des Roches in the first decade of the thirteenth century.[27] It was intended to give relief to pilgrims and travellers and to provide a home for six poor men and six poor women. Not a great deal is known about the history of this hospital, but it seems that not only were the poor men and women often neglected,[28] but also that the master or warden was frequently absent, for the post was often held in plurality by men favoured by the Bishop of Winchester, in whom the advowson was vested.[29]

It is fortunate that for both Titchfield Abbey and Southwick Priory a number of records survive which can be used to create a reasonable picture of the development of local communities.[30] On the Titchfield Abbey estates throughout the thirteenth and early fourteenth centuries, land transactions were increasingly numerous. A tendency to break up the larger tenants' holdings into smaller ones indicates a steadily rising population, probably the result of natural growth, as in England generally in the thirteenth century, or possibly due to a certain amount of immigration from the interior of Hampshire to the more prosperous areas of the coast. Even within the Titchfield estates there was a steady movement of people on business within a twenty-mile radius of the abbey. As for its arable land, there was a variety of field systems and not all were composed of open-field strips. In some fields enclosure had already taken place; in others, still open, no clear rotation of crops was possible as the fields were of uneven size, as in Portchester. Most of the tenants farmed on a subsistence basis and only on the demesne was a proportion of the agricultural produce sold. Thus the general famine of 1315–17 seriously reduced the population of the estates and numbers had not long been restored when the Black Death struck in 1348–49, killing a very large proportion of the population, possibly as much as eighty per cent. After this, the plague became endemic, as in most of the country, and outbreaks of greater or lesser severity regularly occurred. By about 1390, and as a result of firm management, the Titchfield estates had recovered somewhat after the Black Death and there was little immediate change in the area farmed until the fifteenth century. Rents remained fairly static, but labour services, additionally provided by the peasantry, were increasingly commuted for money payments.[31]

By the thirteenth century a number of growing urban communities existed in south-east Hampshire and there is evidence to suggest that many were sufficiently important to hold markets, practise a diversity of trades and have burgesses and burgage tenures.[32] Titchfield was one such community. Fareham, even though apparently never having been granted market rights, was nevertheless, by 1086, already a place of some size and importance (see Table 1) and had its liability to tax reduced because 'being on the coast it was exposed to the incursions of northern pirates'.[33] Havant, Emsworth, Wickham and Portchester all obtained the right to hold a market[34] and there is evidence of their developing borough status, though being boroughs under the Bishop of Winchester or some other local lord they never acquired the same independence as a royal borough. Gosport, which was part of Alverstoke, developed later. Even so, separate courts were held for Gosport and Alverstoke from the mid-thirteenth century onwards and though, like Fareham, Gosport had no grant of a market, burgage tenements existed by the fifteenth century.[35] By contrast, between the South Downs and Portsdown, there does not appear to have been any recognisable borough, though Hambledon and Boarhunt did obtain markets[36] and Chalton and Southwick were granted the same right, provided their markets were not a nuisance to other neighbouring ones.[37]

Distinctive among these communities was Portsmouth, a new town founded about 1180 by John de Gisors, believed to have been a merchant of Norman origin and already holding other estates in this area, including the manor of Buckland on Portsea Island, which he acquired in about 1170 from the de Port family. He may well have early appreciated that this manor's south-west corner then called Sudewede, though with limited access because of the surrounding marshland and water, contained an excellent natural harbour in the Camber. He therefore laid out streets, gave land and endowments for St Thomas' Church and let out 'places' for what was thereafter called Portsmouth.[38] Yet within a few years de Gisors forfeited all his estates, including his new town of Portsmouth, for supporting the rebellion of Prince John while Richard I was away on the Third Crusade. On Richard's return to England in 1194, the king seized and retained this new borough to which he granted its first charter. Certainly, Richard I did much to put Portsmouth on a firmer footing, even building a royal residence, but in size the town remained small for many centuries. His successor, King John, does not seem at first to have regarded Portsmouth with much favour even though he was regularly at Portchester. By 1212, however, it would appear that he had changed his view, ordering 'our docks at Portsmouth to be enclosed with a good and strong wall'.[39] Eventually, in Henry III's reign, the borough's unusual boundaries were finally established and the grant of a Gild Merchant made.[40] Though the origins and early development of Portsmouth's town council are hard to determine, the first mentions of a *prepositus* and of bailiffs are to be found in 1201 and 1207 respectively.[41] The Southwick Priory registers indicate on a number of occasions the names of those holding office and it is possible that in fact the *prepositus* was the senior of two bailiffs who was, in time, to be called a mayor. References to a 'burgemote' or *curia* and to town seals, still in use today, also exist.[42] The list of customs and usages which dates from the late thirteenth century mentions that the borough officers were to be elected annually at Michaelmas, together with twelve 'jurats' who formed the 'burgemote'. Included in this are many by-laws regulating life in the town and referring to the Courts of Record and of Piepowder, both dealing with cases of debt.[43] From 1295 onwards, Portsmouth regularly sent to Parliament two members elected by the mayor and burgesses, with the electoral returns being made by the bailiffs after 1447. At that time it was customary to pay the expenses of members of Parliament for boroughs at the rate of 2*s*. a day. This remained so until the early seventeenth century when it was expected that members would be gentlemen of private means.[44] Whether this sum was always paid to Portsmouth's members cannot be ascertained, but there is evidence, at least in the fifteenth century, that both Titchfield Abbey[45] and Southwick Priory[46] contributed towards such expenses on behalf of their estates on Portsea Island.

That Portsmouth was represented in English medieval parliaments may well have been the result of central government's recognition of the military and naval value of the town's location. While the good natural harbour had been used by shipping to a greater or lesser extent from Roman times onwards, it was primarily as a military centre that the area round the harbour, and later Portsmouth in particular, became important. Initially, a military base had been established by the Romans at Portchester, where in about 1100 William Mauduit built the Norman castle inside the Saxon Shore fort.[47] When Henry II came to the throne in 1154, he decided to keep this castle in his own hands as he recognised its strategic position. Subsequently, two monarchs, Edward II and Richard II, made considerable extensions to the building. Throughout the Middle Ages many kings set sail for France from either Portchester or Portsmouth and in the early thirteenth century Portsbridge was built to provide easier military access to Portsea Island. However, little was done to protect Portsmouth itself which, during the Hundred Years War, was burnt at least three times by the French in 1338, 1369, 1377 and possibly 1380 as well.[48]

The first step towards military organisation in the town was the specific appointment, in about 1369, of a separate Portsmouth military governor, with full powers to punish not only soldiers but all the men of the town and neighbourhood, and to hold an array for resisting an enemy.[49] These powers continued to be reserved to him in all subsequent charters and consequently created problems of concurrent and conflicting jurisdiction with the civil authorities over the townsfolk for many centuries. Despite the increased military jurisdiction, the work of physically enclosing the town with a simple earthwork and moat was not begun until 1386, following yet another burning of Portsmouth. Only later were more substantial fortifications constructed, with the erection of the Round Tower between 1417 and 1422 and of the Square Tower and bulwark in 1494.[50] Almost another fifty years were to pass before anything further was done to protect the town.

Portsmouth and its defences were first described in detail by John Leland, the indefatigable Tudor antiquary who, in about 1540, visited south-east Hampshire on one of his fact-finding missions.[51] At that time the town was in a state of modest prosperity, having been favoured by Henry VII, and more especially by his son, Henry VIII, who was eager to counter the growing French menace by establishing a strong, permanent naval base on the Channel coast.[52]

Travelling from Southampton by way of Hamble, 'a good fisschar toun', Leland passed through Titchfield. It was then a minor port near the mouth of the Meon, with an ancient market,[53] a grammar school, and Place House, the 'right stately' home of Thomas Wriothesley, later first Earl of Southampton, who had recently converted it from the Premonstratensian abbey suppressed in 1537. The new mansion was the centre of an estate of some 5,000 acres which, with other monastic pickings, made Wriothesley one of the two largest landowners in Hampshire at his death in 1550.[54] Leland dismissed Fareham and Gosport briefly as fishing villages and Portchester Castle, gradually falling into disuse as a royal fortress, also received little attention. No doubt he paid the one-halfpenny single fare and crossed the harbour to Portsea Island by the Gosport ferry which, so it was said in 1602, had been operated by the local longshoremen for 'divers years past'.[55]

Prominent on each side of the harbour entrance, when Leland arrived, was a round tower. These twin structures had originally been built in the early fifteenth century and on the sea-bed between them lay 'a mighty chaine of yren' which could be drawn up in an emergency to provide a defensive boom. Leland noted Portsmouth's 'mudde waulle armid with tymbre', on which were mounted 'great peaces both of yren and brasen ordinauns', and beyond which lay a ditch which almost encircled the town, but he failed to describe the imposing square tower, built by Richard Shirborne[56] on Henry VII's orders at the seaward end of the High Street. To the north-east, the ramparts were breached by 'a gate of tymbre . . . and by it', Leland observed, 'is cast up an hille of erth dichid, wherin be gunnes to defende entre into the toun by land.' Bisecting Portsmouth was 'one fair streate' (the modern High Street) in the middle of which, close by the parish church, stood the town house, centre of local government, which had been built 'of late tyme' at the expense of 'one Carpenter, a riche man'. Leland noted, too, the recently-closed medieval hospital, *Domus Dei*, and 'a chapelle in a vacant ground'. This was probably the building Portmuthians had been required to erect, in 1508, as part of the price paid to escape the effects of the decree of Greater Excommunication, by which all ecclesiastical functions and privileges had been withdrawn from the town. This savage penalty had been imposed soon after the barbarous murder of Bishop Adam Moleyns of Chichester outside the *Domus Dei* in 1450.[57] Not far away were Henry VIII's 'great bruing houses . . . to serve his shippes at such tyme as they shaul go to the se in tyme of warre.' Leland also referred to the 'great dok for shippes' which lay outside the town on the harbour shore. Built by Henry VII on a site near where HMS *Victory* now lies, this dry dock, unique in England, though an amateurish construction, had been a fundamental part of the king's plan. With its storehouses and workshops, it was the nucleus around which grew the great industrial complex which was the dynamic force in Portsmouth's later expansion and prosperity.[58]

Leland's description of Portsmouth is confirmed pictorially by the vivid, if slightly fanciful, mural painted at Cowdray House in the sixteenth century to record the abortive French attack on the town in 1545, an episode now best remembered for the sinking of the *Mary Rose*. Several notable maps also give valuable information about Portsmouth's layout in the Tudor period.[59] Yet, although the town's physical appearance is well recorded, it is virtually impossible to establish with any degree of accuracy the size and wealth of the population before the later seventeenth century. The church registers for the period have long since disappeared and the extant tax returns provide little information. Examination of the few fragments of evidence which do survive suggests that at the end of the Tudor period there were not more than about 800 people permanently domiciled, and a small population with a paucity of corporate resources is reflected in the unsophisticated character of the town records.[60] Demographic study of Tudor and early Stuart Portsmouth is made even more difficult by the dramatic fluctuations which occurred in the size of the population in times of peace and war. 'There is much vacant ground within the toun waulle', Leland wrote. '[It] is bare and little occupied in time of peace.' Camden, a generation later, similarly commented: 'In war time it is much frequented, at other times scarce at all; the inhabitants being more attentive to war and navigation than to trade.'[61]

Portsmouth town lay in the south-western corner of Portsea Island, in the centre and east of which were dotted several rural settlements which were served spiritually by St Mary's, the mother church of the island, to which Leland makes no reference, although he must have been aware of it as he journeyed towards Portsbridge, with its '2 arches of stone'. Travelling over Ports Down, 'a playn ground, partely by woodde', he reached Southwick, a village with 'a good bigge thoroughfare', but no market. 'The fame of it', he added, 'stoode by the priory of the Blake Chanons there and a pilgrimage to Our Lady.' The dissolved house had gone to one of Wriothesley's minions, John White, who made his home in the old prior's lodging and soon found himself in conflict with the workers on the estate, not one of whom, it was claimed, would remain, 'though they knew in what need he stood of them for the sowing of barley'.[62] From Southwick, Leland journeyed to Wickham, 'a praty townlet', which was 'welle occupied' and had 'a large thoroughfare'. Thence to Bishop's Waltham, where he inspected the Bishop of Winchester's medieval palace, 'a right ample and goodly maner place motid aboute and a praty brooke renning hard by it'. From here he was able to follow the road back to Winchester, the base from which he had set out on his tour of south-east Hampshire.

Leland's interests were mainly topographical and antiquarian and, except for agriculture, he revealed little about the economy of the area. References to farming practice were vague, but it is clear that a good deal of the cultivated land in the Southampton–Portsmouth–Bishop's Waltham triangle had already been enclosed.[63] Portsea Island was described as 'partely enclosid, fruteful of corn and hath sum wood'. A century later, at the time of the Civil War siege, an observer, probably exaggerating, spoke of the island as having '2,000 acres of corn now standing upon it'.[64] Portsmouth town itself had a semi-rural atmosphere, with hogs wandering the streets, extensive common fields and a hayward, a cowherd and a pound-keeper among its officials.[65] No doubt the salterns, a feature of the island in Elizabethan times,[66] were in evidence along the Langstone Harbour shore in Leland's day, although he failed to mention them. From at least the eleventh century, salt-making, like fishing, had been a source of employment for the inhabitants of the coastal villages.[67]

Much of Leland's Hampshire journey lay through well-wooded countryside, for across the area to the north-west of Ports Down stretched the Forest of Bere, 'welle replenishid with deere', and its outlier, Waltham Chase, both of which are clearly delineated on Saxton's 1575 map of the county. It was from these and other Hampshire forests that large supplies of timber were increasingly obtained, especially from the mid-seventeenth century, for use by the shipwrights of Portsmouth and of other royal dockyards.[68] In the sixteenth century, however, Portsmouth-built ships were still a rarity and the town's future uncertain. From being under the early Tudors the pre-eminent English naval port – its dockyard extended in the 1520s and its flank protected by the construction of Southsea Castle in the 1540s – Portsmouth by the time of the *Mary Rose* episode in 1545 was already entering a period of decline. With the development of Deptford, Woolwich and Chatham, which were closer to London, which was the centre of power and influence, plus the growing menace of Spain, with its bridgehead in the Low Countries, in place of the traditional rival, France, Portsmouth was relegated to a secondary role.[69] To add to the town's troubles, a serious outbreak of plague in 1563 killed more than 200 of its residents, and two fires in 1557 and 1576 devastated the royal storehouses near the Camber. In the second conflagration, inhabitants who had recently suffered 'great losses' at sea were said to have had merchandise and goods worth £2,200 destroyed. Not surprisingly, the ruling body in 1585 lamented 'the great ruin and decay of the town'.[70] Even so, the harbour continued to be used extensively as a rendezvous and refuge for shipping and, throughout Elizabeth I's reign, and particularly during the post-Armada years, Portsmouth was one of the places from which privateering was undertaken. Many servants from the inland towns and villages forsook their masters, so it was said, to participate in these ventures because of the rich rewards that were possible.[71]

It was to the wharfs of the Camber that Drake returned in 1586 from his Caribbean expedition, bringing with him the disillusioned settlers from Ralegh's first Virginia colony.[72] In January 1588, Drake was at Portsmouth again, calling in *en route* to Plymouth from the Thames. His men took the opportunity to practise their gunnery, but 'a piece broke and killed a man, with some other hurt'.[73] Ever since Elizabeth's accession, work on the fortifications had continued intermittently, but, despite a fever of activity in the 1580s[74] and Camden's assertion that 'nothing is wanting to make it a place of the greatest strength',[75] much remained to be done when the Spanish Armada entered the Channel. Fortunately, the events of 1545 were not repeated; in 1588 Portsmouth was never in serious danger of assault by the ships of Catholic Spain.

Among the leading families living on or near the coast were several whose espousal of the Catholic faith and doubtful loyalty made them a cause of great concern to the authorities. At Titchfield, Place House, under the second Earl of Southampton, had been a centre of the old religion and, although his son was brought up as a Protestant in Lord Burghley's household, he numbered several influential and defiant local recusants among his kinsfolk, including the Brownes of Cowdray and the Poundes of Belmont, near Bedhampton. In addition, there were lesser Catholic families like the Brunings of the large and important parish of Wymering, the Ludlows of Cams Hall, near Fareham, and the Henslows of

Boarhunt, whose houses were all within a short distance of the sea. Close to the Sussex border lived the Cottons who, of all the local recusant families, were the most intractable. Sir Richard Cotton, an official of Henry VIII's household, had been granted the manor and castle of Warblington, formerly the home of Margaret Pole, Countess of Salisbury, whom Henry VIII had sent to the block in 1541. Sir Richard's heir, George Cotton, who died in 1609, was a steadfast Catholic, in contrast with his Anglican brother Henry, Queen Elizabeth's godson, who became Rector of Havant and later Bishop of Salisbury. There is little doubt that Warblington Castle became a refuge for many adherents of the old faith. Near the end of Elizabeth's reign, there were no less than nineteen recusant households in the immediate vicinity of the castle. George Cotton seems to have been harassed more than most religious dissidents. Besides suffering spells in prison, he was required to pay over £6,000 in fines during the last twenty-eight years of his life. Nevertheless, he was able to avoid ruin and his son inherited the family's Hampshire estates, including Warblington Castle, which in Charles I's time was described as 'a very fair place, well moated about', with a central courtyard and many fine rooms.[76]

Although her father, half-sister and half-brother had all stayed at the castle, and she herself had apparently been there in 1586, Elizabeth I seems to have ignored it on her summer progress of 1591, when she journeyed from Chichester to the Portsmouth area. Little is known about the Portmuthians' reactions to the royal presence, but, as has been suggested, the town's first charter of incorporation in 1600 may well have been granted in response to their petition on that occasion.[77] Even if Portsmouth became constitutionally more secure, its economic fortunes were still at a low ebb. Throughout the reign of James I, its dockyard was of slight importance compared with those at Deptford and Chatham. In 1623 even the dry dock was filled in.[78] However, Portsmouth was stirred into activity from 1626–8 by the king's new aggressive policy towards France. The victualling and fitting out of the two La Rochelle expeditions seemed at first to mean a spell of prosperity for the business community, but in fact the government's financial shortcomings, the administrative chaos and the reluctant recruits' indiscipline made it a mixed blessing. In the neighbouring towns and villages, the evils of billeting and the general disorder brought a wave of indignation. Amid all the confusion, while Charles I held court at Southwick House, the home of Sir Daniel Norton, to complete the problems the Duke of Buckingham was assassinated in the Portsmouth mansion of John Mason, one of his principal aides and a leading figure in the town's small community of merchants, craftsmen and seafarers.[79]

Although he was a prominent resident and frequently busied himself with Portsmouth affairs, Mason took little direct part in town government which was in the hands of the mayor and his twelve assistants (called aldermen after 1627).[80] The garrison and fortifications were commanded by the governor, whose official residence was the former *Domus Dei*. In Tudor times, quarrels frequently broke out over the respective rights of these two powers and one leading burgess, Henry Bickley, was moved to preface his will with the statement that he was 'in fear of my life from Sir Adrian Poynings, Captain of Portsmouth and his servants'. More trouble erupted in the early seventeenth century and at the time of Charles I's ship money tax there were further quarrels over the mayor's efforts to assess the garrison.[81]

Portsmouth, it was said in the early seventeenth century, was 'a poor beggarly place'; even so, some of its leading inhabitants were well connected and prosperous. Victuallers like William Haberley, Henry Holt and William Winter, a kinsman of the Elizabethan surveyor of the Navy, and also Vice-Admiral William Towerson, MP, four times mayor and a member of the famous London merchant family of that name, were apparently content with the rewards that residence brought.[82] It is significant that today Portsmouth owns a remarkable collection of town plate, 'second only to that of Norwich', fourteen major pieces of which were acquired during the half-century preceding the Civil War.[83] The donors were mainly burgesses such as Haberley and his contemporary, Robert Bold, whose gift of a silver salt cellar was particularly appropriate since he had bought the manors of Portsea and Copnor in 1598 and consequently was lord of the salterns.[84]

Bold obtained his estates from Shakespeare's patron, the third Earl of Southampton, who was then heavily in debt. In the years that followed, Wriotheseley made efforts to exploit more fully the natural resources of his land. Timber was felled, iron-ore and fuel were used at the ironworks he set up at Titchfield and Beaulieu and, more remarkably, he and two partners harnessed the power of the River Meon to a mill which they built at Wickham to produce tin-plate, an enterprise which was 'far and away the earliest' of its kind in England. About this time, he also started, but apparently failed to develop successfully, a woollen-cloth industry at Titchfield. Moreover, he reclaimed large stretches of marshland near the mouth of the Meon by causing a sea-wall to be built, an event which was described in the parish register as the 'shutting out of Titchfield haven by one Richard Talbotte's industrie under God's permissione.'[85]

With the outbreak of civil war, the Wriothesleys and the Cottons aligned themselves with the king, while Richard Norton of Southwick, who in 1643 seized Warblington Castle, later 'slighted', was a stalwart Parliamentarian.[86] At Portsmouth, the governor from 1639 was Colonel George Goring, who gave both sides to believe that they had his support. In the event, it was for Charles I that he declared in 1642, although the townspeople seem to have been lukewarm in their allegiance. The siege by Parliament's forces was short, successful and virtually bloodless.[87] In the ensuing years, Portsmouth and its region entered a new, more significant period of its history.

5

FROM CIVIL WAR TO WATERLOO[1]

James H. Thomas

Between 1640 and 1815 the Portsmouth region underwent many profound changes. More than any other similarly-sized area in the British Isles, the region enjoyed fortunes that fluctuated wildly according to whether England was at war or not. The close relationship between regional development and the presence of the armed forces became increasingly evident, especially after 1690. Complex relationships developed between Portsmouth Corporation, the armed forces and the local inhabitants. Though none of the parties had a great liking for each other, each was indispensable to an efficient, effective and profitable relationship. In November 1781, Portsmouth's Recorder, John Missing, described the relationship: 'in all our Disputes, we have never lost sight of that Connection which so long subsisted to mutual advantage between the Board of the Admiralty . . . and the Corporation.'[2] Furthermore, the relationship extended well beyond the town as many landowners and farmers in the region were busy growing rich from contracting with the armed forces. During the 1660s, for example, Richard Norton at Southwick and Thomas Neale at Widley were producing timber and food respectively for naval needs.[3] While of major significance, the region's relationship with the armed forces has tended to overshadow other aspects of local development. In both national and international affairs, for instance, the Portsmouth region played a role of considerable significance. Regional commercial patterns and the consequent importance attached to inns were also noteworthy. Business successes and failures abounded in the region, deserving some comment. Finally, it should be remembered that the area had various links with London. With consideration of these elements, the region can perhaps be seen in a more rounded historical perspective.

In terms of national significance, the most important of the local conflicts with which the Civil War of 1642–1646 began was the siege of Portsmouth in 1642. The Navy's declaration for Parliament, depriving Charles I of London, made Portsmouth and its possession that much more important, while also ensuring that the conflict would be fought out in a closed arena. While Sir William Waller assembled on Portsdown Hill strong Parliamentarian forces, with which to besiege Portsmouth, the town's dissolute governor, Lord George Goring, made few preparations beyond ensuring that many women and children were carried to the safety of Hayling Island. The easy capture of Southsea Castle, of which the Parliamentarian leader John Pym was informed by letter from Stubbington,[4] lowered Portsmouth's morale considerably. Goring capitulated and for the remainder of the war the town remained firmly in Parliament's grip, though strong Royalist feeling persisted locally. Anthony Haberley of Portsmouth and Sir Thomas Badd of Fareham were both described as 'very active' against Parliament, explaining the latter's heavy contribution to the Decimation Tax of the 1650s.[5] While local communities grew inured to troop movements, skirmishes, property depredations and requisitioning, more than a few clergymen were ejected from their livings and replaced by 'intruders'. Michael Bold, previously incumbent of Portsea, acquired the combined living of Widley and Wymering in 1642, only to be ejected. Returning at the Restoration, he was vicar of Wickham from 1667 to his death in 1676.[6] Dr George Gillingham, *quondam* chaplain to Charles I, was persecuted 'from Place to Place' during the Civil War before becoming Chalton's incumbent.[7] Ejections consequent upon the Act of Uniformity (1662) were widespread in the region, affecting Portsmouth, Portsea, Farlington, Warblington, Hayling Island, Rowner, Titchfield and Clanfield.[8] It was small wonder, given the manifold changes, eventual disillusionment and near-anarchy that beset the country, that the Restoration was heralded with such overwhelming relief.

While Portsmouth and her region were important during Charles II's reign, it was after his brother's accession to the throne that the town became nationally prominent. By the mid-1680s the town was the country's most heavily fortified community, a fact which James II appreciated greatly, and in his policy of granting Catholics key positions Portsmouth played a role of major significance. Subtle changes were afoot, the import of which did not become apparent to local residents until it was almost too late. Sir John Biggs, Recorder since 1673, 'resigned' within six weeks of James II's accession, to make way for George Jeffreys.[9] Shrewder residents noted that the king's fascination for Portsmouth was almost obsessive, contrasting sharply with his aversion for Winchester which his brother had loved so dearly. Royal visits were made to Portsmouth in August 1686 and again twelve months later 'to view the new Fortifications'. One rather perceptive French observer was dumbfounded by the fact that the bulk of the defence strengthening had taken place on the *landward* side, facing the king's subjects.[10]

It was not until January 1688, however, that James II's true aims and fears were revealed with the appointment of James, Duke of Berwick, as governor. Replacing Edward, Earl of Gainsborough, owner of extensive estates at Titchfield and elsewhere in the region, Berwick also assumed the earl's offices of New Forest ranger and lord lieutenant. An uncompromising Catholic and an experienced professional soldier, Berwick was also James II's natural son. Should royal policies founder, the king felt, as a result of this appointment, that he could at least count on Portsmouth as a bolt-hole and potential escape route for himself and his immediate family. William of Orange's arrival at Torbay that November charged the local atmosphere. With his position as monarch and his own physical and mental health deteriorating continually, James II replaced Berwick with Lord Dover, an equally staunch Catholic. Dover arrived with a message for Lord

Dartmouth, the king's Protestant admiral who had failed so conspicuously to intercept William of Orange, regarding the safety of the Prince of Wales who had been brought to Portsmouth. 'I thinke my sonne is not safe, (as things are now,) where he is, and think it necessary to have him removed', wrote the frantic monarch. Though Dartmouth baulked, preparations went ahead for the infant prince's removal via Portsmouth. Sir Richard Beach warned Dartmouth percep-tively that it was

> intended to put the prince on board the yacht this night, and to be gone with him, . . . knowing very well what trouble and misery this kingdom may sustain for the future if his escape be not prevented, for he'll prove a second 'Perkin Warbeck'.[11]

In the event Lady Powis, one of the prince's aged guardians, beat a hasty retreat to London with her infant charge.[12] Despite William of Orange's inexorable progress towards London, the Portsmouth garrison remained resolute for James II. On 14 December 1688 Dartmouth outlined its condition:

> . . . The calamities threatening the Roman Catholic officers and soldiers still in garrison at Portsmouth, have much altered them . . . they seem very penitent for their former miscarriages, being . . . desirous to submit. . . .

A few days later the 'garrison of Portsmouth quietly submitted to the order of the prince, and drew thereout. . . .'[13] The townspeople's sufferings at this time were indicated clearly in a petition submitted to William of Orange early in 1689, which referred to an Irish and Popish garrison:

> who have Committed divers lamentable Murthers and grievous outrages upon us they have made themselves absolute Masters of our houses and goods and by free quartering upon us have utterly impoverisht o[u]r Towne and places adjacent and threatned to blow up the magazeene and extirpate us which they were resolved on.[14]

In retrospect, James II clearly blundered twice in his thinking on Portsmouth. Court martialling the five army captains who opposed the assimilation of Irish Catholic troops into the garrison harmed his cause while turning the officers into heroes. Ordering Berwick away from Portsmouth was also a grave mistake. Such miscalculations cost the king dearly.

Though William and Mary now occupied the throne, the exiled James II was not friendless. Talk of a second Stuart restoration was heard in both London and Winchester; at least two Portsmouth residents were brought to justice for offering toasts in 1693 and 1694 to King James's health.[15] In 1715, and again in 1745, the spectre of Jacobitism was to rear its head. The first upheaval threatened the new Hanoverian dynasty. A rising in the south west was planned, the exiled Prince of Wales being proclaimed James III at St Columb in Cornwall. Only the Earl of Mar's ineptitude and Sir George Byng's Channel squadron prevented French assistance and the rising was suppressed speedily. Given Portsmouth's proximity to France, it was thought prudent that the authorities should take no chances. On 26 July 1715 the recent Act for preventing tumults and riotous assemblies was read publicly and constables were exhorted to be particularly watchful. That September local customs officials were ordered to search ships coming from France for 'suspected passengers'.[16] In October 1,204 dockyard employees took the oaths of allegiance, supremacy and abjuration set out in an Act 'for Extinguishing the hopes of the Pretended Prince of Wales and his Open and Secrett Abetters'. By December a special dockyard foot regiment had been raised under Commissioner Isaac Townshend.[17] That such fears were amply justified was seen in the dispersal of a Hambledon gathering in 1716 on suspicion that Jacobite sympathisers and activists were at work.[18] When, thirty years later, fears were again roused, with the assembling of a French invasion flotilla, only a few Lancashire Catholics made any pro-Jacobite moves. Even so, home defence was below par and local associations, sponsored by lords lieutenant and financed by local subscriptions, were formed to offer some measure of resistance. Many of the Portsmouth region's wealthier inhabitants provided monetary assistance. William Rickman, merchant and contractor *par excellence*, with estates at Posbrooke near Fareham, contributed £50. His brother-in-law, Thomas Missing, MP for Poole, gave £100. Samuel Chandler and Thomas Stanyford, two Portsmouth attorneys, contributed £12 12s. and £30 respectively. Fourteen Portsmouth inhabitants subscribed £136 16s. between them.[19] A special dockyard regiment was again raised to provide an extra check against Jacobite incursions, though it was felt unwise by the Ordnance authorities to 'Arm the Inhabitants of Portsmouth'.[20]

While the Jacobite threat may have been only temporary, it is an inescapable fact that the region was affected considerably throughout the period of 1640–1815 by a European presence. Taking many forms, it resulted in some of the inhabitants of the region being better acquainted with Europeans than residents in other parts of the country, and also in a number of noticeable spin-offs on local life.

The presence of privateers at Dunkirk and Ostend encouraged an increased use of Portsmouth by arriving and departing diplomats. In June 1669, for example, inclement weather prevented Count de Molina, Spain's ambassador to England, from leaving. Ahmed ben Ahmed Cardenas, Morocco's ambassador, arrived in 1733 and was conveyed by coach to London. Outgoing ambassadors from Morocco and Tripoli left Portsmouth in July 1774. European diplomats kept themselves abreast of developments in the area even if they did not visit it themselves.[21] European dignitaries and monarchs visited the region, chiefly as a result of Portsmouth's attractions, thereby ensuring that local inhabitants had a better idea of what European royalty looked like than did people elsewhere in the kingdom. The London–Portsmouth road was awash with travellers in 1662 as they made their way to the port to be there when Catherine of Braganza arrived.[22] In 1698 Peter the Great, Tsar of Muscovy, journeyed down by road from London to witness a specially arranged mock sea battle off the Isle of Wight. The King of Spain, Prince George of Denmark, Portuguese and Lebanese princes, the Emperor's brother, the Prince of Wurtemburg, the Prince of Monaco and Admiral Gydenlove[23] were among those visiting Portsmouth during these years. Besides the set-piece festivities invariably provided on such occasions, the region derived many spin-off benefits as well. There was work for interpreters, some of whom may have come from Portsmouth's Jewish community. Goods and services were in demand in various ways, while many of the region's inhabitants became more than passingly familiar with a number of strange tongues. And yet the majority of Europeans who came to the Portsmouth region did not do so for pleasure.

England's prolonged involvement in European wars during this period, culminating in the Revolutionary and Napoleonic struggles, left major marks upon the Portsmouth region. Foreign troops were frequently to be found in and near the town. At least once during the War of the Spanish Succession (1702–1713), Swiss and Walloon troops were marched from London to Portsmouth and from thence to the Isle of Wight.[24] Sustained Anglo-Russian naval co-operation after 1750 meant that Russians were no strangers to the region. In December 1769 Russian ships were repaired in Portsmouth yard, their officers and crews being lodged in Hilsea barracks. During the 1770s, regular visits took place by Russian squadrons. On occasion, considerable numbers of ailing officers and crew were admitted to Haslar hospital, causing increased employment opportunities by virtue of their numbers and a welcome bonus for local food producers who contracted to supply that institution. Supplies of locally-brewed beer were ferried out to Spithead and still more money was injected into the local economy. A vivid impression of some of these visitors was left by Benjamin Haydon in 1809:

> As we passed through the Russian fleet the sailors stared at us – so unlike English sailors, their lips covered with dirty red mustachios, some in hairy caps, some in green jackets, and some in none. When they laughed, they looked like animals. Their ships appeared to be strongly built.[25]

The majority of Europeans in the region, however, arrived as prisoners of war. The three conflicts against the Dutch in the 1650s, 1660s and 1670s saw large numbers of captives dumped at Portsmouth and redistributed to communities such as Fareham and Winchester. In 1666, Fareham's inhabitants petitioned Charles II for payment 'for taking care of sick seamen and soldiers placed upon them. . . .' Portchester Castle, England's oldest regular war prison and capable of holding up to 8,000 internees,[26] was frequently used to house prisoners. During the War of Austrian Succession (1739–48), overcrowding resulted in a disease outbreak at Portchester in 1747, with serious repercussions for both Fareham and Southampton. While rankers were herded together, officers, considered gentlemen, gave their word, or 'parole', that they would not escape and were quartered upon private households. Officers ordered to be released and repatriated in 1748 included Messieurs Boullanger and Musalary at Petersfield and Messieurs Bouillon, Dieval and Rodez at Fareham.[27] But honour was not always observed. It was reported in April 1757, during the Seven Years War, that 'Sixty French Officers were brought from Petersfield to Portchester Castle by a guard of Napier's regiment, to be confined there, some having gone from their parole.' One officer who escaped and made his way back to France was promptly ordered back to England by Louis XV to complete his sentence.[28]

There was, needless to say, always the danger and fear of a break-out, a psychological threat that hung over Portchester's inhabitants for much of the period under consideration. When prisoners were put to work as construction gangs, in remodelling Portsmouth's defences in the 1660s and 1670s and in road building in various parts of the region during the eighteenth century, the risks were probably at their greatest. In September 1778, some fifty-seven American prisoners of war escaped from Forton prison, near Gosport, described as 'by no means adequate to the purposes'. In April 1793 an attempted break-out by the 850 French prisoners held there was discovered and thwarted.[29]

The effects upon the region of this European presence were diverse. While money could be made housing, feeding and entertaining prisoners of war, as well as from repatriating them, there were always serious risks, not least being those to local health and morale. In a similar fashion, provision of entertainment and lodging for important European visitors injected more money into the region's economy. Even so, there were still dangers. Queen Anne fretted, in 1704, over possible adverse effects upon the King of Spain's health while he waited in Portsmouth for a ship, the town having 'no very good reputation as to the wholesomeness of the air'. When, in 1708, the Queen of Portugal was entertained at Portsmouth, it was at the home of egregious brewer Thomas Ridge, generally considered to have the only decent house in the entire town.[30]

While the term 'variety' could be applied to the region's European visitors, it was equally applicable to its trading patterns. Trade in the Portsmouth region could be divided into overland, sea-borne and illicit. Overland trade through the region was both diverse and important, and was exemplified by a Meonstoke yeoman having West Country cheeses in his possession in 1686. Traders travelled from neighbouring communities to buy and sell in Portsmouth. Into this category fell William Avenall, who journeyed from Petersfield to sell pears in July 1685, and Jane Deane from Bedhampton, who took apples to Portsmouth market for sale in March 1695. When Anne Wheeler of Warblington set out to do the same thing in January 1735, she had the apples stolen from her before actually reaching her destination. A similar fate befell Hambledon shoemaker William Moody who had goods stolen 'from his Stall or Standing in the Market Place at Portsmouth' in March 1748. There were also itinerant traders travelling the region, sellers of vegetables and china, or men like Benjamin Dennis, a petty chapman, who wandered from Winchester to Portsmouth in November 1671 selling knives, scissors, lace and combs. Some traders came from still further afield. In December 1679 William Peagan made his way from London, via Guildford, Godalming and Chichester to Portsmouth.[31]

The region's communities were well served with fairs, all following a well-arranged, time-honoured 'season' but varying in both number and type. By the late eighteenth century eleven communities in the region held fairs, some, such as Titchfield and Hambledon, having as many as three per year. Emsworth could boast two, one on Easter Monday, the other on 18 July. The two fairs at Rowlands Castle, held on 12 May and 12 November, were for horned cattle and hogs. The solitary fairs at Southwick and Wickham, in April and May respectively, were primarily for horses. Other fairs specialised simply in toys, as happened at Gosport every 4 May and 10 October, and at Fareham on 29 June. Only one fair, that held at Titchfield on 25 September, was described specifically as a hiring fair. The largest of the region's fairs was, without doubt, Portsmouth's Free Mart fair, attracting traders from as far away as London, Lewes and Yorkshire. With its giants and dwarfs, puppet shows, trinket and book stalls, the fair was a 'must' for local residents. It should, of course, be remembered that, while fairs attracted many purchasers from the surrounding countryside, they were also lures for members of the criminal fraternity and made ideal hunting grounds for recruiting sergeants.[32]

Fairs tended to deal in commodities which were purchased infrequently. Items bought regularly from week to week would be acquired at markets and among such wares would undoubtedly have been salt, a commodity in constant demand but produced in relatively few locations. One of these was the Portsmouth region. From the various Portsea Island salt works, supplies were distributed regularly throughout the area. The opening of further workings on Hayling Island in the early 1730s increased supplies and created more employment.[33] Heavy goods were also moved, belying the myth that roads must have been uniformly poor. Southwick-grown timber was regularly hauled by road to Portsmouth yard for ship construction. From Egham in Surrey, timber supplies were carted to the small, but nevertheless thriving, Gosport shipyard in the 1740s for use in the construction of heavily-armed East Indiamen.[34] Iron and butter were two other bulky commodities frequently to be found being moved by road.[35] A regular carrier and waggon network through the region encouraged and facilitated such movement; from Portsmouth numerous waggon, carrier and van services provided links with London and elsewhere. From Gosport in the 1780s waggon services operated to both Salisbury and London, halting at the Royal Oak in Fareham for passengers and parcels. There were strong links between overland and sea-borne trade. Wines and linens were landed at Portsmouth from Cowes in the 1660s and 1670s and then distributed inland to keep the cellars of inns and large private houses well stocked.[36]

The region's sea-borne trade was just as diverse, much of it being concentrated on Portsmouth, though both Fareham and Emsworth served as small feeder ports. Coastal shipping links were established with West Country ports, with Cowes and Chichester, all important for the shipment of cereals, paper and other essentials. The inward coastal shipping details for Portsmouth in 1679 are typical of the entire period. During that year vessels arrived from Southampton, Chichester, Cowes, Plymouth, London and Poole. Commodities shipped in included wines and brandy, cloth, particularly West Country serges, Virginia tobacco, salt, cheese, timber, sugar, fish and soap.[37] From further afield came the slow-moving colliers, bringing much-needed supplies of coal from Newcastle and Sunderland. Despite Protector Oliver Cromwell's conviction that Hampshire possessed coal deposits, supplies throughout the period 1640–1815 had to be shipped in. During 1731, for example, colliers from Newcastle brought 3,060 chaldrons of coal into Portsmouth. The cargoes went to the many coal-merchants and coal meters to be found in Portsmouth and from there to communities such as Gosport and Hambledon.[38] From even further afield came those vessels engaged in foreign trade. Ships arrived from the New World, the Baltic, the Iberian peninsula, the Middle East and distant India. During 1720–60 several leading local merchants had important trading interests in North America. William Rickman and his associates regularly sold to the Portsmouth naval authorities train oil, extracted from whales for use as a lubricant and England's only direct import from Newfoundland in the early eighteenth century.[39] Sweden and Muscovy, major sources for much-needed naval supplies, exported directly to Portsmouth by the early eighteenth century.[40] During the 1750s, at least one Portsmouth ship traded regularly with Portugal. In mid-April 1757 Clatworthy Thackstone, master of the *Sarah*, a local merchant craft, told how that February Richard West had signed on for a voyage to Oporto, on Portugal's west coast, only to desert before leaving harbour.[41] Vessels engaged in the lucrative but dangerous Levant and India trades could be found at Portsmouth, especially as the town was a major departure point for silver supplies, passengers and East India Company employees making the hazardous journey out to the East.[42]

There was also a third type of commerce to be found in the region – the illicit. Excessive import duties and high-handed official actions drove people to smuggle, and the coastline between Titchfield and Emsworth was particularly rife with such activity. In September 1679 Richard Norton, Southwick landowner and JP, complained that 'the trade had increased . . . of late. Some scores, if not hundreds of tuns, have passed at first in the night, but of late in the daytime.'[43] Both complex and dangerous, smuggling involved people whose organisations were far-reaching and ruthless. In July 1735 officers clashed with ten smugglers at Kingston Point on Portsea Island and impounded a consignment of brandy. A second encounter several months later resulted in the capture of supplies of tea. Wines brought ashore illicitly at Hillhead, 'a great smuggling place', were taken inland and lodged at Wickham.[44] All participants, as well as customs officers, ran the risk of extreme violence. The cruelty inflicted upon Galley, a customs officer, and Chater, a shoemaker of Fordingbridge, in 1748 by smugglers with a network operating inland from Rowlands Castle north to Liphook, showed just how far such ruffians were prepared to go.[45] It should, of course, be noted that customs officers were just as capable of meting out harsh treatment, often on only the flimsiest of evidence. Witness, for example, officer John Arnold's rough search of Norton family property at Southwick on the pretext of involvement in 1723.[46]

Many of the travellers, merchants, and smugglers took rest and shelter in the region's numerous inns. Throughout the period 1640–1815, the region's inns were a great deal more than just drinking shops. Convenient meeting places for turnpike and charitable trusts, they were also centres for the exchange of news, gossip and business information and for auctions, as well as offering rudimentary banking facilities and coming into their own at election times. The region was well served with inns as Table 1 indicates.

TABLE 1

INNS AND THE PORTSMOUTH REGION 1686

Community	Guest Beds	Stabling for Horses
Alverstoke	3	–
Bedhampton	3	–
Catherington	1	–
Emsworth	11	13
Fareham	45	48
Gosport	61	48
Havant	31	36
Hillhead	2	–
Hook	2	–
Horndean	4	6
Langstone	4	4
Lovedean	1	1
Portsea	6	–
Portsmouth	164	87

Community	Guest Beds	Stabling for Horses
Rowlands Castle	1	–
Titchfield	58	46
Warblington	1	–
Wickham	20	23
Total	418	312

Source: *P.R.O. W.O.30/48, pp.159–67.*

That the five communities of Fareham, Havant, Portsmouth, Titchfield and Wickham were well served is explained not just by their activities as market towns, but also by their location on important routes. Thus Fareham, Havant and Wickham were the last stopping-places for travellers making for Portsmouth from Southampton, Chichester and Winchester respectively. Beyond these communities, however, the facilities offered were of a limited but adequate nature. In a few instances their names provide further clues to the region's trading patterns. Gosport's inns included the India Arms, the Newcastle upon Tyne, the Sunderland Pink and the Dutch Pilot Boat. Across the harbour in Portsmouth, hostelries included the Coach and Horses, the North Country Pink, the Guernsey, the Pack Horse, the Plymouth Trader, the West India Tavern, and the Southampton Hoy.[47]
One further use to which inns were put occasionally was for bankruptcy hearings, as happened at Horndean's Bell and Ship in December 1711.[48] During the century after 1695, some 114 men went bankrupt in the Portsmouth region. The failures were scattered throughout the region, as Table 2 illustrates.

TABLE 2
BANKRUPTCIES AND THE PORTSMOUTH REGION 1695–1795

Alverstoke	1
Emsworth	2
Fareham	6
Gosport	18
Hambledon	1
Havant	5
Horndean?	1
Portchester	2
Portsea	24
Portsmouth	47
Southwick	2
Titchfield	2
Wickham	3

Sources: *London Gazette, 1665–1715, passim; The Gentlemen's Magazine, 1731–95, passim.*

When considered chronologically, bankruptcy material reveals one very striking correlation. The heaviest concentration of failures by decade were in 1706–15 with nineteen, in 1746–55 and 1766–75 both with fourteen, and in 1776–85 with thirty-five. In other decades the figures were low; for 1696–1705, for instance, the figure was only five. Quite clearly the heaviest failures coincided with the conclusion of hostilities. Local tradesmen, while coping with the artificially prosperous boom caused by the War of Spanish Succession or of that with the American Colonies in the 1770s and 1780s, failed to adjust to changed circumstances once peace returned. Thus there was a heavy preponderance of slop-sellers, vintners, bakers and butchers amongst those going bankrupt. On a broader scale, such a situation must have had serious repercussions for the entire region, with alternating periods of prosperous expansion and depressing contraction. In more than a few ways the region's lifeline was tied to the armed forces and, therefore, to decisions made in London.

Between 1640 and 1815 there were various links between the Portsmouth region and London. Young lads regularly went for training at the Inns of Court or for apprenticeship with one of the city's many livery companies. During the years 1660–1720 there was a heavy imbalance against those going for legal training. The Civil War period had seen a decline in numbers attending Inns of Court, a trend which continued in the case of south-east Hampshire during the years after the Restoration. Only four admissions from the region were made to Lincoln's Inn, for example, between 1660 and 1720. Edward Norton from Southwick went in 1699, Charles Francklyn from Chalton in the following year, Gibson Dalyall from Portsmouth in 1715. The fourth admission, Titchfield's John Barton in 1703, was probably honorific rather than for formal legal training, since he was an adult. Some Inns of Court, of which Grays Inn was one, admitted no young men at all from the region during the six decades after 1660. There are, however, glimpses of local lads attending other Inns. Henry Stanyford, for example, son of a prominent Portsmouth merchant, entered the Middle Temple in January 1720.[49]

Many more youths went for apprenticeship with the livery companies. Between 1660 and 1720, the Barber-Surgeons Company took on twenty-two apprentices from the region. The majority, thirteen, came from Portsmouth. A further three came from Gosport, while Meonstoke, Fareham, Southwick, Titchfield, Wickham and Wymering each sent one. In contrast, only nine went to be apprentices with members of the Stationers Company. Between 1660 and 1680 only three were apprenticed, one each from Hambledon, Havant and Portsmouth. The next two decades saw a slight increase, with two lads from Portsmouth and one each from Fareham, Portchester and Southwick. The years 1701–20, however, saw only one Stationers Company apprentice from the region, when Thomas Glover or Gover, son of a Gosport bookseller, was bound to James Leake, a Fleet Street printer, in 1720. Two years later the lad was turned over to a neighbouring printer, Samuel Richardson, to complete his apprenticeship.[50] The London livery companies had, however, an effect upon the region that extended beyond training facilities. The Grocers Company, for example, was represented by the Portsmouth trading interests of Abraham Jaggard in the mid-1660s. Some companies, however, made only a later appearance. It was not until January 1760, for example, that the Society of Apothecaries opened a medicine and drug warehouse in Portsmouth.[51] The greatest degree of immediate control was exercised by the Goldsmiths Company, empowered to summon erring goldsmiths to London, to reprimand them for illicit practices and fine them accordingly. In this way Stephen Woolriche, a Portsmouth goldsmith, was fined in 1699. In 1718, Derbyshire-born John Leake, Portsmouth goldsmith, alderman and London freeman, was fined for selling sub-standard gold and silver wares.[52]

There were, however, further ways in which the region was linked with London. Considerable amounts of the region's money were invested in the great contemporary trading concerns, deposited in London's banks and sent to the capital in various state payments. Sir John Biggs, Portsmouth's conscientious Recorder, had East India Company investments of between £300 and £500. Twice during the 1680s the company authorised payments in excess of £1,000 to Richard Norton of Southwick for unspecified purposes. Between 1746 and 1788, George Huish jun. was not only Portsmouth's town clerk and coroner, but also acted as the East India Company's agent, filled the same office for its Dutch counterpart and was additionally consul for Holland.[53] John Vining, Portsmouth's powerful mayor, had stock in both the South Sea Company and the Bank of England, while Alderman John White invested a small sum in the Royal African Company. Other local figures took their involvement even further; thus Chamberlain Atkins left Portsea to become the Royal African Company's factor at Cape Coast Castle on the coast of Guinea.[54] Southwick's Richard Norton ran an account with goldsmith-banker Edward Backwell, with a balance of £400 during 1669–70.[55] Quite obviously, only the more prosperous could afford to dabble in such ventures and the region was by no means short of such men. There was the roguish merchant-prince, Thomas Missing of Titchfield (d. 1733), whose monument in the parish church describes him as having died possessing a large fortune, but which erroneously states it was 'acquired by honest abilities'. Brewer William Pike of Portsmouth was described in 1775 as 'Eighty-four Years of Age with between 3 and £400,000'.[56] Many of the region's less wealthy inhabitants remitted money to London as payments to the central government. The so-called 'Free and Voluntary' present to Charles II in 1661, which appears to have been neither free nor voluntary, produced various contributions from the region. From Widley two 10s. donations were sent from Clement Kent and John Hunt. Wymering contributed £1 4s., while Rowner sent 12s., and there were gifts of 3s., 4s. and 5s. from John Feilder, John Bassett and Robert Stares respectively.[57] Others with wealth left money to charitable London ventures, such as the £50 bequest of Portsmouth general dealer and tallow chandler Thomas Appleford to the London Foundling Hospital in January 1753.[58] At the same time, reverse links were to be found, since some London residents had property interests in the region. Thus Thames Street dyer Daniel Peck had 'an Estate in Land in Riplington and Droxford' in 1703. And there were other links inasmuch as some local residents acted as agents for London fire insurance companies. In 1784 the Sun Fire, the Royal Exchange and the New Fire Office retained agents in Portsmouth, William Baker also acting for the Sun Company in Portsea as well. That same company also had an agent across the harbour in Gosport.[59]

Much of the wealth to be found in Portsmouth and her neighbouring communities in the late eighteenth and early nineteenth centuries was occasioned by war. Even so, during the Revolutionary Wars (1793–1802) and the struggle against Napoleon (1803–15), there were dark episodes such as the Spithead Mutiny in 1797 and the nation's loss of Nelson eight years later. However, there were other aspects to life as well. Indeed, what might almost be called a 'carnival' or holiday atmosphere can be detected locally during these years. This was certainly the case in June 1794 when 'Black Dick' Howe returned to Spithead with his victorious fleet and six French prizes. One local family 'took a trot over to Portsmouth', hired a packet and sailed round the victorious wooden walls, the day before George III and his family arrived for an official visit. The Bramstons were rather concerned to:

> see the poor wounded french, brought on shore, they were as quiet as ever I saw poor Creatures, did every thing they were bid, and never murmurd or Complaind on being moved, tho ma[n]y died before they got a mile. . . . [60]

A naval lieutenant could take time off after Christmas 1804 to go shooting at Fratton, only to be killed by his own gun, triggered off by brambles through which he was endeavouring to cut a swathe. During her Portsmouth honeymoon in 1812, at the height of the war, Mrs Montefiore, who had found Horndean a 'pretty little village', could still go with her enlightened husband on a 3-hour dockyard tour.[61] This clearly relaxed atmosphere reached its apogee with the patriotic concerts of the day and with the visit by the Allied Sovereigns in June 1814.

Thus it may be seen that during the crucial period 1640–1815 the Portsmouth region enjoyed both prosperity and gloom, the one usually following hard upon the heels of the other. The armed forces, in so many ways, provided the region's economic lifeline as well as generating more than a few of its many social problems. If there was one characteristic which predominated, it was the cosmopolitan nature of the area. Any visitor to the region after 1650 was likely to rub shoulders with Swedish or Russian sailors or with the crews from Dutch, Spanish or Portuguese merchantmen. Lebanese princes visited Portsmouth, as did traders from Danzig and representatives of the North African regencies. This social richness was further accentuated by the presence of Cherokee chiefs in 1762 and by that of Omai the Tahitian, returned to the Sandwich Islands by Captain Cook in Autumn 1777.[62] In many instances, lavish official entertainment was provided and yet more money was injected into the local economy. The wealth so generated was poured, in many instances, into substantial estates outside Portsmouth, such as those at Southwick, Posbrooke, Soberton and elsewhere. Marked social differences became apparent between Portsmouth's population and the inhabitants of neighbouring communities. With both good reason and perception, James Wolfe wrote of the 'diabolical citizens' of Portsmouth, while another contemporary pointed out that the absence of local gentry as parliamentary candidates explained why 'our Representatives are always sent us from a-loft'.[63] In the hinterland some communities such as Havant and Wickham waxed fat. Others, such as Portchester, dwindled to become, as Southampton-born itinerant cleric Richard Pocock explained, 'a village of houses scatter'd on each side of a street half a mile long'.[64] Even so, such communities had their interesting residents, men such as Melchior Collart, 'an Hungarian by Birth', who married Portchester girl Rebecca Cheesman in May 1746. The region also had contacts with the exotic and the distant. Early in May 1802 curiosities such as Cleopatra's coffin, statues and the hand of a figure 'which is said to be eighty feet high' were landed in Portsmouth, as part of Lord Elgin's Egyptian spoils.[65] Some years before, in May 1787, a fleet of eleven ships, led by Captain Arthur Phillip, had left Portsmouth for a distant destination – New South Wales.[66] In the preparation for this and subsequent expeditions a role was played by Portsmouth dockyard – a fluctuating element in the region's fortunes.

6
THE NINETEENTH CENTURY

R.C. Riley and John Chapman

Seldom can a town of 33,000 inhabitants have been so dominated by a single enterprise as was Portsmouth by its dockyard at the onset of the nineteenth century. Certainly, settlements like Cromford in Derbyshire,[1] specifically designed to house workers employed by one firm, were springing up, but they were hardly the size of Portsmouth. Indeed, both the constraints of capital and of demand obtaining in the eighteenth century combined to inhibit the construction of private-sector industrial plants of any great size, let alone one employing very nearly 4,000 workpeople. It is most likely, therefore, that the naval dockyards, in particular those at Portsmouth and Chatham, represented the largest industrial undertakings in the country at the time of the Napoleonic Wars. Since there were considerable numbers of sailors constantly in the town, together with a permanent garrison whose brief it was to defend both town and dockyard, it is clear that the yard's direct influence was by no means restricted to those employed within its walls. Such was the dockyard's central role that it was the fundamental determinant of both the speed and nature of the region's economic expansion throughout the nineteenth century.

Just as Portsmouth was overshadowed by the dockyard, so in turn the town of Portsmouth dominated south-east Hampshire, as can be seen in the population data. In 1801 the town housed slightly more people than resided in the remainder of the region, and this at a time when agricultural mechanisation had hardly begun to influence rural areas and when increasing output and land use had created more employment opportunities. From such beginnings it is hardly surprising that as the century wore on, Portsmouth first overtook its region and then palpably outdistanced it, becoming, by the 1870s, three times more populous. A major national characteristic of the nineteenth century was the rapid growth of urbanisation, but to the influences at work in the market economy were added, in Portsmouth's case, the contingency plans laid down by the government for the defence of realm and Empire. In consequence, the population greatly increased in both time of war and its perceived threat. The greatest intercensal population increase on Portsea Island was one of almost 36 per cent between 1841 and 1851, growth that may largely be ascribed to the prosecution of colonial wars in India and Burma, and to the decision by the Admiralty to employ steam propulsion and to embark upon the construction of a steam basin, engineering workshops and iron foundries in the dockyard. The impetus of these decisions carried over into the 1850s, giving rise to a 31 per cent increase in the town's inhabitants between 1851 and 1861; events in the Crimea exacerbated the trend. The Napoleonic conflict and the dockyard expansion programme led by Bentham[2] were largely responsible for the 22 per cent population growth in the first intercensal period of the century, and inevitably rearmament and additional productive capacity in the yard engineered increases of 24 per cent and 18 per cent in the 1880s and 1890s respectively. Similarly, the cessation of hostilities with the French in 1815 engendered the collapse of the hitherto buoyant urban economy, giving rise to the modest population increases of 10 per cent and under 4 per cent in 1821–31 and 1831–41 respectively. Since the Navy was able to victual its expanding fleet without a concomitant expansion of the Royal Clarence Yard, not least the result of the innovatory activities of Thomas Grant,[3] Gosport failed to share the development experience of its neighbour. With 11,295 inhabitants in 1801, Gosport was one-third the size of Portsmouth, but, lacking naval shipbuilding facilities, it ended the century only one-sixth as populous.

Outside the two core settlements, apart from Fareham which was used as a residential area by some serving officers, other towns were less influenced by the naval presence and did not share the great surges of population growth enjoyed by Portsmouth. Nevertheless, Fareham, Havant, Warblington (which included Emsworth) and, until the latter part of the century, Titchfield managed to match Gosport's performance in relative terms. Fareham, indeed, exhibited an expansion of 172 per cent between 1801 and 1901 compared with the 156 per cent increase experienced by Gosport. These apparently impressive increases pale into insignificance when contrasted with events in Portsmouth where the population increment between 1891 and 1901 alone was the equivalent of Gosport's total population in the latter year and where the century's growth was some 466 per cent. Fareham's growth was perhaps a function of its position between the two large towns of Portsmouth and Southampton, thereby encouraging interaction in both directions. Moreover, it was a port in its own right. By the same token, the more sluggish expansion of both Havant and Emsworth, whose populations grew by 118 per cent and 98 per cent respectively between 1801 and 1901, might be explained by the absence of a large settlement to the east. Beyond the towns mentioned lay a number of smaller settlements which, by virtue of their agricultural emphasis, would be expected to exhibit a declining population. However, in south-east Hampshire at least, rural depopulation was relative rather than absolute: former market towns such as Hambledon and Droxford, having reached their apogee in the 1840s, exhibited only imperceptible change to the end of the period, despite the allure of the towns, above all for the young women who bore the burden of the Victorian middle-class ethic that equated social standing with the number of servants kept.

Inevitably the rural–urban dichotomy so evident in population data displayed in Table 1 is reflected in the occupational structure. From the rudimentary evidence provided by the early census reports, it is clear that the rural areas were largely agricultural, with between a fifth and a quarter of the population of parishes such as Soberton, Hambledon and Droxford employed in such activity at the beginning of

TABLE 1

POPULATION CHANGE IN S.E. HAMPSHIRE DISTRICTS 1801–1901

	1801	1861	1901
Portsmouth	33,226	94,828	188,123
Gosport	11,295	22,653	28,879
Fareham	3,030	6,197	8,246
Titchfield	2,949	4,043	1,569*
Havant	1,670	2,470	3,837
Warblington†	1,433	2,196	3,639
Hambledon	1,358	1,891	1,922
Droxford	1,199	2,194	2,609
Soberton	672	1,136	1,189

* Figure negatively influenced by boundary changes.
† Includes Emsworth.

Source: *Census Reports, 1801, 1861, 1901.*

the century.[4] Conversely, agriculture was of negligible importance in Portsmouth and Gosport, although it was of rather more significance in some of the region's other towns, accounting for 6 per cent and 8 per cent respectively of the total inhabitants of Fareham and Havant. The drift to the towns, coupled with improved farming techniques, ensured that the proportion of those employed in agriculture would dwindle, a trend influencing both rural districts and smaller towns alike. By 1831 not a single parish in the region had more than a fifth of its working population employed in agriculture and only four – Meonstoke, Soberton, Boarhunt and Hayling – had more than a sixth so employed; agriculture in Fareham and Havant could claim but 5 per cent and 6 per cent respectively of the employed population in that year. Trade and manufacture were the province of the towns and it is to be anticipated that the sophisticated urban economy of Portsmouth would have engendered relatively large numbers in these sectors. That the relative proportions of those engaged in trade and manufacture in Havant, Warblington, Fareham and Gosport should, in 1801, exceed Portsmouth is doubtless indicative of the presence of large numbers of naval and military personnel on Portsea Island, thus reducing the importance of other activities. Hence the subsequent reduction in the armed services caused Portsmouth's occupational structure to become closer to that expected, although in 1831 both Havant and Emsworth still had proportionately slightly larger numbers in retailing and handicraft than Portsmouth. However, the addition of those classified as labourers to the retailing and handicraft category in all districts reasserts the pre-eminence of Portsmouth and Gosport.

Less predictably, the 1801 census reveals that, far from being clustered in the largest towns, those employed in the professions were quite remarkably evenly distributed among all but the smallest parishes. Even Droxford and Hambledon had virtually the same percentage of professional people as the old town of Portsmouth, arguably the cultural and civic centre of the region. It is possible that this class had already begun to exhibit a dislike of the crowded and somewhat unhealthy confines of both Portsmouth and Portsea and to transfer their place of residence to a more bucolic and prestigious setting. The location pattern of the middle class is largely reflected in that of servants. Not only were they numerous, but once again Portsmouth did not command a lead, having proportionately fewer servants than Farlington and Bedhampton, while Wickham and Emsworth were not far behind. By contrast, as befitted an emergent working-class town linked inextricably to the dockyard, Portsea had the smallest proportion of servants (see Table 2).

TABLE 2

OCCUPATIONS IN SOME S.E. HAMPSHIRE DISTRICTS, 1831

| | Agriculture | | Retail/ Handicraft | | Professions | | Servants | | Total Population |
	%		%		%		%		
Portsmouth	2	–	763	9	152	1.8	606	7	8,083
Portsea	327	0.8	4,168	10	586	1.6	431	3	42,306
Gosport	177	1	1,070	8	259	2	561	4	12,637
Fareham	214	5	358	8	65	1.5	281	6	4,402
Warblington*	183	9	218	10	14	0.7	137	6	2,118
Havant	127	6	251	12	29	1.4	114	5.5	2,083
Hambledon	313	15	122	6	33	1.6	105	5	2,026

* Includes Emsworth
Source: *Abstract of Answers and Returns under the Population Act, 11 Geo.IV.c.30.*

The importance of the naval and military presence in Portsmouth, regarded as a key issue in the operation of the local economy in the early nineteenth century, may be put on a quantitative footing from 1841 onwards by virtue of more comprehensive census data concerning occupations. From a position of marginal numerical superiority over servants in 1841, the services became an increasingly large component of the total population, reaching 11 per cent by 1861 and remaining at this level until 1871. Major extensions to the dockyard in the 1840s and early 1850s signalled the advent of the steam navy, larger vessels and bigger crews, while the Crimean crisis which immediately followed made Portsmouth a hive of activity as a major point of shipment for troops and supplies. No sooner had the Russian dispute been resolved, than the national alarm at the perceived threat of invasion by the French in the years 1859–60 gave rise to the frantic construction of a powerful ring of seven land- and four sea-forts to protect Portsmouth Harbour. Begun in 1860, the land-forts were complete by 1868, but the civil engineering difficulties involved delayed the commissioning of the last sea-fort, No Man's Land, until 1880, by which time the whole *raison d'être* for 'Palmerston's Folly' had evaporated.[5] The forts, which made Portsmouth and Gosport the most heavily fortified towns in Europe at the time, had nevertheless to be manned, military increments consequently accruing to the population of Portsmouth and Gosport alike. Spurred on by the arguable technical superiority of the French ironclads, the Admiralty embarked upon what was known locally as the 'Great Extension' of the dockyard between 1867 and 1881.[6] This development was rendered unnecessary by improvements in Anglo-French relationships, which resulted in the declining importance of the services in the 1880s; by 1891 they represented only 5 per cent of the population. However, subsequent fear of German aggression occasioned a quite formidable shipbuilding campaign as part of rearmament, ensuring that the services' earlier numerical strength in the town was restored by 1901. This great resurgence in naval activity, causing some 20,000 sailors, or one in every five employed persons, to be in port in 1911, simultaneously discriminated against the military, who had in 1841 outnumbered the Navy, particularly in Gosport. To the doubtful value of the land-forts could be added the tactical futility of the Portsmouth and Portsea fortifications. These were demolished in the 1870s, when Portsmouth reverted to being a naval port, rather than a garrison town with a naval presence which it had been in the early Victorian period. None the less, there remains a powerful military legacy for, the forts apart, the architectural richness of Cambridge Barracks, built in the High Street in 1856, St George's Barracks in Forton Road, Gosport, erected in 1859, the Royal Marine Barracks of 1862–7 at Eastney and above all the remaining section of Clarence Barracks, completed in 1898, adds both variety and stature to the environment.

Given the paramount importance of the armed services to Portsmouth, that they should have accounted for between one-fifth and more than one-quarter of the working population between 1851 and 1911 is not altogether surprising. Less expected is the remarkable similarity between the numbers of servicemen and those employed in manufacture. In 1901 both sectors could claim 25 per cent of the workforce and ten years later they each accounted for some 27 per cent of the total. It was as though the strength of manufacturing industry was no less related to foreign policy than was service activity in the town. Yet since the dockyard was at the very core of industrial production, fluctuations in its fortunes were therefore more likely to be mirrored in figures for the borough as a whole. Between 1841 and 1911, dockyard workers represented between 32 per cent and 49 per cent of Portsmouth's industrial population,[7] establishing the yard as very much a leading sector in the urban economy. The arrival of steam-powered vessels in the 1850s was matched by an increase in the number of engineering workers, just as the ironclads of the 1860s and later boosted the ranks of the metalworkers and the Dreadnoughts the ranks of the electrical workers in the first decade of the twentieth century. The numbers of sailmakers, sawyers and ropemakers were, by contrast, decimated by these developments.

Decisions made by the Admiralty on grounds of economy and quality control encouraged the dockyard to follow a policy of self-sufficiency as far as was possible, thereby reducing the scope for local manufacturers and substantially contributing to the dominance of the yard. While materials such as timber, hemp and metal were supplied from without, the production of hulls, masts, rope, chains, copper sheeting and anchors was effected from within. Bread, ships' biscuits and beer were produced in the Victualling Yard at Gosport, while potential local economic benefit from the expansion programmes went unrealised following the discovery that clay excavated for the new docks made excellent bricks and that convicts proved to be redoubtable kiln operators. A few contractors like Benjamin Bramble[8] might have benefited, but singularly few links were forged between yard and town. The experience of William Treadgold, a Portsea iron merchant, was typical. His day book for 1866 reveals that, while he enacted no direct business with the dockyard, 17 per cent of his transactions for the year were with government contractors, some of whom were involved in dockyard extension work.[9] Far from engendering the associated growth of small firms, the dockyard merely provided a source of employment for wage labour, leaving scant opportunity for the rise of an incipient middle class so characteristic of many industrial towns elsewhere.

It is entirely justifiable to raise the question of why a private-sector shipbuilding industry failed to develop, given the abundant local timber supplies, the physical advantages bestowed by Portsmouth Harbour and the lengthy shipbuilding tradition of the locality. Nine ships privately built in Portsmouth did participate in the Napoleonic Wars and, although this was fewer than those launched at Buckler's Hard and Cowes,[10] it suggested that the activity had a future. That this proved not to be the case was, in all probability, the result of subtle pressures by the Admiralty who wished to restrict commercial activity in the harbour. Thus proposals tabled in the 1850s and backed by the borough council for commercial docks dug from the Mill Pond between the dockyard and the old town of Portsmouth were ruled to be 'entirely inadmissable' by the Sea Lords.[11] Their refusal to sanction a railway line between the town station and the Camber, where John Read and later H.E. Vosper had yards, worked in the same direction. Additionally, the advent of the iron-hulled ship gave locational advantage to the Clyde and Tyne shipyards, further reducing the scope for local builders. In the absence of commercial docks on the scale of the general cargo ports, it is hardly surprising that the numbers of merchant seamen should be small. In 1851 they represented 3.6 per cent of the working population, but by 1911 they mustered less than 1 per cent of the total. Apart from shipbuilding, the most important Portsmouth industry was clothing manufacture, which accounted for between 38 per cent and 45 per cent of the manufacturing workforce in the period between 1841 and 1911. Even after making allowances for the importance of clothing manufacture in Victorian towns, it is apparent that the activity was well developed in Portsmouth and indeed did not differ unduly from shipbuilding in the numbers employed. The requirement for sailors and officers to purchase their uniforms until free issues were introduced in the latter part of the century explains the proliferation of naval tailors, but local market factors can hardly have been at the root of the expansion of other clothing sectors. There seems no doubt that the explanation lies in the availability for work of large numbers of women, consequent upon the almost entirely male workforce of the dockyard and the presence of so many sailors' and soldiers' wives, most of whom received scant remittances from their absent menfolk. Disasters befalling Portsmouth ships, such as the *Birkenhead* which went down in 1852 with the loss of 436 lives, caused severe financial hardship among dependants and, as Father Dolling showed half a century later, such relief funds as were collected were not always as fairly distributed as would have been wished.[12] Dockyard redundancies following governmental economy decisions placed a further onus upon wives to seek work. Abundant female labour enabled unscrupulous entrepreneurs to exploit the possibilities of low wages and many merely established warehouses from which materials were supplied to women, who were obliged to carry out the work at home after the classic fashion of the putting-out system.

Within clothing manufacture one sector stands out. So distinctive was corset-making that throughout the seventy years after 1841, in relative terms, there were between twelve and fourteen times as many employed in the industry in Portsmouth as there were so occupied in England and Wales, a specialisation at least as great as in carpet manufacture at Kidderminster or Axminster. The labour force was almost entirely female in receipt of low wages and, although this was a contributory influence upon the expansion of the industry, it fails to explain the initial momentum that enabled producers to break into other urban markets, long before the arrival of the railway in 1847 facilitated inter-urban trade. Growth may credibly be ascribed to the dynamism of a few manufacturers in respect of design and marketing methods. Certainly Portsmouth corset firms had a very favourable record of patents taken out between 1860 and 1899, and the manner in which a few men belonging to the Reynolds and Leethem families dominated the industry exemplifies the importance of dynamic leadership and imitative behaviour in explaining economic activity.[13] Corset production, together with brewing, gave rise to the only substantial industrial premises in Portsmouth outside the dockyard, yet, although it generated some work for the local engineering industry and led to the manufacture of cardboard boxes and steel springs, it was notable principally for the employment it created rather than for its regional multiplier effect.

Between them, the shipbuilding and clothing industries accounted for 80 per cent of employment in Portsmouth's manufacturing sector. The remainder was mostly involved in the production of goods and public utilities for the urban population. In other words, this sector was supportive of those whose activities were directly a result of the town's principal function. It may thus be argued that almost all manufacture was either directly or indirectly linked to the needs of the dockyard. The strength of one activity, brewing, was particularly related to the serviceman's requirement for a substantial alcohol intake; indeed many topographers erroneously assumed that the presence of so many sizeable breweries, such as those operated by the Long, Brickwood, Carter and Jewell families, was synonymous with extensive employment. Yet in 1871 the industry employed only 190 persons, representing a mere 1.7 per cent of the working population. Brewing may have incurred the wrath of the temperance movement and the church, but it certainly generated wealth for the brewers and, in the case of the Carters, helped to provide a financial base for political ambition. More permanently, the multiplicity of brewing companies gave rise to great variety in public house designs, most notable of which are A.E. Cogswell's half-timbered 'manor' houses erected for Brickwoods' brewery at the turn of the century, standing out incongruously from their mean artisan environment.[14]

Brewing, like other manufacturing activity in the region, was a major influence on the development of a transport network which was itself both a cause and a result of economic growth, the process intensifying after the arrival of the railway in the 1840s. By virtue of their coastal location, Portsmouth, Gosport, Fareham and Emsworth were able to make good use of maritime transport, which contributed to their size through warehousing, shipbuilding and a variety of tertiary functions. At the same time, road transport played a key role in the economic organisation of rural districts and urban areas alike;[15] certainly Portsmouth-made corsets were being marketed nationally by the 1830s, by carriers who worked the turnpikes for much of the century until competition from the railways became crippling. Notwithstanding the importance of other means of transport, the railways had the greatest impact during the nineteenth century. They provided rural areas with an efficient means of exporting agricultural produce, even though the Meon valley line was not completed until 1903, and they encouraged growth in the larger coastal towns, all of which were included in the network between 1841 and 1848.[16] The dockyard obtained its own branch shortly after the opening of the line into Portsmouth and the significance of the railway to the yard may be judged from the existence of some twenty-five miles of track therein by the end of the century. There can be little doubt as to the role played by the railway in the growth of the tourist industry, above all in Southsea, and to a lesser extent on Hayling Island, at Stokes Bay and Lee-on-the-Solent.[17]

Public utilities developed tardily in the first half of the century, largely because society maintained an ignorant or ostrich-like attitude to the perils of inadequate drinking-water supplies and rudimentary drainage. Some improvement occurred in 1811 with the inauguration of the Farlington and Portsea Island Water Companies, but without the provision of mains drainage it was understandable that the death rate should exceed the national figure, given the community's crowded conditions. In the old town of Portsmouth, for instance, there was an average of 9.68 persons per house in 1861, contrasting starkly with rural areas such as Soberton (4.56) and Hambledon (4.63).[18] Between 1841 and 1847 some 25.37 per 1,000 persons were dying annually, a figure that rose sharply with the cholera epidemic of 1848 which claimed 152 lives in July and August alone.[19] The unfavourable Rawlinson Report of 1850 did much to alert public opinion to the dangers of inactivity.[20] Even so, mains drainage was not introduced until 1867 and it was not until 1873 that the Borough of Portsmouth Waterworks Company provided piped water for all. The gas industry employed many more workers than the other public utilities and, although it lacked the social implications of water and drainage services, the extension of the supply of gas for lighting, and later cooking, by the Portsea Island Gas Light and Coke Company nevertheless made an important contribution to the amelioration of social conditions.

Exceptionally aware of the niceties of social position, the Victorians were not slow to equate the number of servants a man possessed with his status in society. Throughout the century the servant population maintained a close numerical relationship with the number of inhabitants in Portsmouth, remaining close to 4 per cent until 1901 when the sheer weight of servicemen caused the share to dip to 3.4 per cent. The momentum of rearmament accelerated the process and, as a result, by 1911 the figure had fallen to 3.1 per cent. For much of the period, servants represented nearly one in ten of the employed population, a figure by no means excessive for the time owing to the importance in the town of non-commissioned servicemen, very few of whom could afford domestic assistance. The spatial distribution of servants reflected that of social class, so that from the 1840s onwards they were markedly clustered in Portsmouth's middle class suburb of Southsea. Here a number of developers, notably Thomas Ellis Owen, had constructed distinctive terraces and garden-encircled villas. Southsea originated as the residential area for serving and retired officers; indeed, in 1851, half the heads of households in Owen's properties belonged to this category. Such respectability attracted the wealthy in no small measure, with the consequence that property owners, fund-holders and annuitants represented a further quarter of the heads of households.[21] Small wonder, therefore, that servants bulked large in such an environment, accounting for more than one-third of the population in Owen's houses and being the principal cause of a remarkable imbalance between the sexes which saw females outnumbering men by three to one.

Once more the social milieu may be said to have been strongly influenced by the naval and military presence. The subsequent welding of tourist functions on to Southsea, causing the middle class to vacate many of their early homes overlooking the sea as lodging houses and hotels were able to afford such prime sites, may have reduced the influence of the dockyard, but it was nevertheless national pride in the Queen's Navy that drew many tourists to the resort, above all for the fleet reviews at Spithead.[22]

Continuing population growth brought in its train a constant demand for housing, with the consequence that the built-up area of Portsmouth underwent a massive expansion which dwarfed all that had happened before. The outward march of dwelling houses was a reflection of changing housing conditions, for while the squalid, overcrowded courtyard dwellings of Portsea remained to horrify observers throughout the century,[23] rather more spacious artisan dwellings were gradually developed outside Southsea, creating a lower density of urban population. By the beginning of World War I, almost the whole of Portsea Island was devoted to some form of urban land use; and Portsmouth had engulfed the neighbouring agricultural communities, though Milton could still be described as 'a rural village' in 1911.[24]

This extension of Portsmouth's urban area was made possible by a developing communications network, making it a practical possibility for the workforce to live further from their place of employment. The gross overcrowding of the early period of urbanisation was not due simply to an indifference to the living conditions, but also to the necessity for proximity between workers and workplace. Given the long hours of toil, it was natural that a tiring walk before and after work was regarded as impracticable by the majority. Urbanisation of the northern and eastern parts of the island had therefore to await the coming of the tramway in the 1860s, although at the outset, owing to the prices charged, it was the middle class who were convenienced.

The spatial pattern of Portsmouth's growth in the immediate post-1815 period was largely controlled by the existence of the remains of an open field system. Though the system had been disintegrating for some time, most properties in the adjacent agricultural land were still held in long narrow strips,[25] so Portsmouth could not expand in large, carefully planned blocks without a formal enclosure or an extensive programme of land purchase and exchange. Instead, the urban area developed piecemeal wherever landowners could be persuaded to release land for building, producing a street pattern controlled by the old property boundaries,[26] which affected Landport and adjacent areas east to Fratton Road and Kingston Road and north as far as Kingston Crescent.

Beyond these limits larger-scale development was possible. Beeston Field, to the east of Kingston Road, and Pitcroft Field, north of Kingston Crescent, were formally enclosed under an 1817 Act of Parliament. The open fields of Hilsea were abolished under the 1812 Wymering Act, while those of Milton and Copnor had been enclosed centuries before.[27] In each case, the effect was to produce larger compact properties susceptible to a more planned development, with the result that these areas are largely characterised by long straight rows of terraces, which decrease in age but increase in size and amenities.

The growth of Portsmouth cannot be viewed in isolation, for the phenomenon obviously had a major impact on the surrounding area. On the one hand, there was an ever-growing market demand providing a stimulus for agricultural development; on the other, there was the disruptive effect of the urban demand for land, which not only destroyed the agriculture of the immediate urban fringe, but was also increasingly felt in more remote localities as wealthier individuals bought substantial plots and developed large villas beyond the reach of the sprawling town.

The destruction of local agriculture has already been noted. The town had begun to impinge on its adjacent fields centuries earlier, but they had not been eroded seriously before the eighteenth century. Until then, they continued to perform their rôle of feeding the town, though the relaxation of the traditional rotations had allowed farmers to diversify into new products, notably vegetables.[28] By 1815, however, Town Field in Landport had been seriously affected and Cherry Garden Field, north of Lake Road, was under threat. Over the next twenty-five years, the former succumbed to the town's voracious appetite for land and the latter moved far along the way to obliteration.

As the nearby fields were thus absorbed by the town, the more distant ones were presented with an opportunity to fill the vacant niche, an opportunity further increased by the growing size of the market. There was thus an incentive to maximise production and one means of doing so was by enclosure. Until the nineteenth century, the Portsmouth area had been little affected by the growing Parliamentary enclosure movement, relying largely on enclosure by agreement, and only Southsea Common had been subjected to formal Parliamentary procedures.[29] There were thus substantial amounts of both open field and common waste requiring attention. The Napoleonic Wars, however, offered an additional spur to action and in the early years of the century there were seven local Acts, followed by two more shortly afterwards.[30]

The effects of this movement were felt throughout the coastal strip from Fareham to Warblington and into the Chichester area of West Sussex.[31] Both open field, as in the Wymering, Cosham and Hilsea enclosure, and common, as at Fareham, were involved and, although a number of the awards were concerned with less than 200 acres each, the total was substantial. There seems little doubt that the primary motive for these enclosures was to take advantage of the agricultural opportunities now available, though the stated aims must be treated with some caution. Phrases about agricultural improvement had become an accepted convention and only rarely did the bill's promoters admit to a desire for unencumbered building land. It may be suspected that the 1817 Beeston and Pitcroft enclosure was carried out with at least one eye to the area's building potential, though in the short-term agriculture may have been the primary concern. Additionally, although the intention in enclosing the Forest of Bere by the Act of 1810 was undoubtedly for agricultural purposes, it was, nevertheless, appreciated that there were other possibilities. Land sold by the commissioners to raise money for the costs was advertised as being in a 'situation for elegant villas',[32] a clear indication of the distance at which Portsmouth's influence was being felt.

The post-Napoleonic War period was one of economic difficulties for most of Britain's agriculture, and the problems must have been particularly acute in south-east Hampshire with the sudden decline in military and naval activity. Thus, only two new enclosures, those for Beeston Field and for Warblington, were initiated before the late 1830s. Nevertheless, Portsmouth still provided a large and growing market and must have aided local recovery greatly. William Cobbett's description of the cornlands of Portsdown Hill, even allowing for his habitual exaggeration, bear witness to that area's agricultural significance in the 1830s.[33]

The latter half of the nineteenth century saw a further wave of enclosure in the Portsmouth area, stimulated by the massive expansion of the town together with the cheaper, simplifed procedures instituted by the General Enclosure Acts of 1836 and 1845. In all, nineteen enclosures were carried out, together with at least one common regulation, including that of Alverstoke in 1887–88.[34] Some of these involved mere scraps of land, much of which was common waste and of very doubtful agricultural value, as was the case with the Crofton enclosure of 1867 consisting of 38.23 acres of marsh and foreshore. Thus it seems that a distinction must be made between the more distant enclosures in, for example, Hambledon and Meonstoke, where the improvement of substantial tracts for agriculture remained the prime objective, and a zone closer to Portsmouth where non-agricultural purposes were to the fore. In the latter, direct enclosure for building land may have been limited, but the consolidation of estates primarily for amenity purposes seems to have been a motivating force. Much of the area covered by the Havant enclosure of 1864–70 was subsequently developed for woodland, but commercial exploitation of this for timber seems to have been only a secondary objective. The main purpose of the enclosure seems to have been to permit the creation of an attractive wooded setting for the numerous substantial houses built in the area.

However much it may be argued that the Portsmouth region comprised a hierarchy of a large town, a fringe of small settlements and rural areas beyond, such was the town's demographic and economic dominance that the nineteenth-century history of the region is very much the history of Portsmouth. Indeed, the borough's influence grew as the period progressed. This growth was intimately related to the vagaries of foreign policy, while the influence of the dockyard, which had become the very *raison d'être* for the town, permeated not only the employment structure and the social system, but also the urbanisation process itself. In more ways than one, Portsmouth was the premier naval dockyard town of the realm.

7

THE POPULATION OF THE PORTSMOUTH REGION[1]

Barry Stapleton

Although the Portsmouth region has probably been inhabited for nearly a quarter of a million years, for the vast majority of that time it is impossible even to guess at the size or density of the area's population. Only in the last two centuries, with the introduction of decadal censuses, does it become possible to establish with any accuracy how many people lived in the region and where their homes were located.

Even so, archaeological evidence indicates that man has exploited the region's resources for over 200,000 years. In the Palaeolithic (Old Stone Age) and Mesolithic (Middle Stone Age) periods man was a nomadic hunter-gatherer and theoretically signs of his presence could exist anywhere in the region. In practice, for much of the prehistoric era, the known sites of early man's habitation fall mainly into two groups, those along the littoral where man could have exploited the resources of both sea and land, and those on hilltops which provided more easily defensible locations.[2] However, these represent only those dwelling places which have been discovered and there could be many more remaining to be unearthed. Clearly hilltop sites have been explored because they have remained largely undeveloped by modern man whereas coastal areas, subjected to recent development, have also provided archaeological evidence of early habitation. Where urban growth has taken place over the last few hundred years, however, evidence of early man's possible presence has remained hidden.

With the coming of the Iron Age and the development of iron-tipped coulters for ploughing, it is probable that man was able to till not just the lighter soils of the chalk downs, but some of the heavier ones away from the hilltops. As a result, greater population dispersal would have occurred in the region, a process which may have continued throughout Roman and Anglo-Saxon times, although much settlement remained on previously inhabited sites. Certainly new centres of population emerged at Fareham and Havant,[3] but it is not until the early Norman period that it becomes possible to estimate the relative importance of the region's centres of habitation from Domesday Book. Primarily produced as a land survey

83

for purposes of royal taxation, the book provides some substantiation of the archaeological evidence of the established importance of some communities. For example, the downland areas around Chalton[4] appear to have contained a greater population than many other parts of the region, some 104 tenants, each presumably head of a household, being listed in the four downland communities in Finchdean Hundred.[5] Fareham, Alverstoke, Wymering and Droxford were other important centres of population. Hayling Island, with over three times as many tenants, was demonstrably more populated than neighbouring Portsea Island, seemingly confirming the archaeological evidence which indicated that the former was of importance as a religious centre,[6] thus perhaps attracting increasing numbers to provide various services to the clerics. Nevertheless, the region's largest single community may have been Fareham, although the large spatial parish of Titchfield, containing a number of small hamlets, probably included more residents in total.

It must be noted, however, that Domesday Book was intended to show William I what his recently-acquired province was worth in taxable value and not to indicate the size of its population. Even so, it is possible to use the information to provide a guide to the distribution and density of the region's population by assuming that each tenant numbered was head of a household and then apportioning these households to the relevant ecclesiastical parish. In total, just over 900 tenants are recorded as living in the Portsmouth region in the late eleventh century; assuming that each tenant represented a household of 4.5 inhabitants,[7] then the total population would have been over 4,000. Since the total acreage of the region's parishes was 96,860,[8] a density of one household to over 100 acres or 27 persons per square mile is obtained. However, the population was unevenly distributed, large numbers living to the west where the four parishes of Titchfield, Alverstoke, Rowner and Fareham contained 30 per cent (272) of the households. Since they occupied over 27,000 acres, producing a density of one household to every 100 acres or 28.8 persons per square mile, their distribution was very close to the mean for the region. By comparison, the northernmost parishes of the region – Meonstoke, Droxford, Soberton and Hambledon – were the most thinly peopled, only 122 households being recorded in the 24,730 acres they contained, a density of one household to over 200 acres or 14.4 persons per square mile. These figures were influenced strongly by Hambledon in which only 14 households were recorded for the large parish of over 9,600 acres. Both the central part of the region – Wickham, Boarhunt and Southwick – and the north-east – Chalton, Clanfield, Blendworth and Catherington – had below average densities (see Table 1). By contrast, the coastal parishes of Portchester, Wymering, Widley (Cosham), Farlington and Bedhampton had a greater than average density with their 10,000 acres holding 132 households, producing a density of one household per 76 acres or 38.25 people per square mile.

However, it was in the east of the region – Havant and Warblington parishes and Hayling Island – where population was thicker on the ground with the 8,620 acres containing 176 households thus averaging 76 acres each. Surprisingly, it was Hayling Island which had the greatest population density with its 3,670 acres supporting 94 households averaging only 39 acres each or 74.25 people per square mile. This contrasted sharply with Portsea Island where just over 5,000 acres were occupied by less than one-third of the number of households of Hayling Island, only 31 being listed in Domesday Book. With over 164 acres per household or 18

TABLE 1

POPULATION DENSITIES

	1086		1525		1603		1676		1725		1801	
	Persons per sq. mile	Acres per person	Persons per sq. mile	Acres per person	Persons per sq. mile	Acres per person	Persons per sq. mile	Acres per person	Persons per sq. mile	Acres per person	Persons per sq. mile	Acres per person
North	14.4	44.7	27.2	23.6	49.5	13.0	54.9	11.7	50.6	12.7	91.1	7.0
N. East	24.3	26.5	30.7	20.8	49.7	12.9	56.5	11.3	50.1	12.8	67.8	9.4[3]
Central	23.0	24.9	33.1	19.4	72.2	8.9	73.3	8.8	183.3	3.5[1]	117.9	5.4
West	28.7	22.2	43.7	14.7	66.0	9.7	137.0	4.7	197.0	3.7	167.6	3.8[4]
South	38.0	16.8	43.0	14.9	56.8	11.3	68.2	9.4	63.7	10.0[2]	151.7	4.2
East	58.0	11.0	78.4	7.8	115.7	5.5	113.0	5.7	121.7	5.2	272.6	2.3
Portsea Is.	17.4	36.5	78.8	8.0	163.6	3.9	811.2	0.8	1,188.0	0.5	4,153.3	0.15
Alverstoke & Gosport											1,792.9	0.36

North – Droxford, Hambledon, Meonstoke and Soberton
N. East – Blendworth, Catherington, Chalton and Clanfield
Central – Boarhunt, Southwick and Wickham
West – Alverstoke, Fareham, Rowner and Titchfield
South – Bedhampton, Farlington, Portchester, Widley and Wymering
East – Havant, North Hayling, South Hayling and Warblington
Portsea Is. – Portsea St Mary's and Portsmouth St Thomas's excluding the northern part of the island which was included in the parish of Wymering

[1] Wickham only – Boarhunt and Southwick omitted in original return.
[2] Portchester, Farlington and Bedhampton only – Widley and Wymering omitted in original return.
[3] In the 1801 census, Catherington's population was returned as 1199 (829 males and 370 females). In the light of earlier estimates and later censuses (1811 –607; 1821–798) this figure was clearly too high. The 1851 census subsequently referred to the 1801 figure as an erroneous return and estimated the 'real' figure as 559. This total has been incorporated in the table.
[4] Alverstoke with Gosport excluded and tabulated separately.

persons per square mile, Portsea Island's population density was over four times less than Hayling's and, apart from the northern parishes, was the most thinly peopled area of the region. It is not easy to explain this discrepancy, particularly since access from the mainland to Hayling would seem to have been more difficult than to Portsea because of the wider channel. As noted earlier, the greater population density may have been connected with Hayling Island's early development as a religious centre. In addition, William I had granted to the Abbey of Jumièges[9] a religious settlement on the island in 1067 and this would, presumably, have attracted more people. Alternatively, the island's proximity to West Sussex and the large and important medieval city of Chichester may have been an influence on population growth.

Meanwhile, Portsea Island's much smaller number of inhabitants could reflect its inhospitable nature especially on the periphery where, most probably, the land would have been subject to regular flooding. In support of this view, it is noticeable that of the three small communities recorded in Domesday Book – Copnor, Buckland and Froddington (Fratton) – the last two were located along the central spine of the island where the land was slightly higher (8m) than elsewhere and Copnor was around the 6m mark (see Map 1). Whatever the reasons, it is quite clear that in the late eleventh century Portsea Island cannot be regarded as an important demographic or economic centre in the region. In early Norman times, Fareham, Wymering, Hayling Island, Alverstoke, Droxford and Titchfield had much stronger claims to such importance.

Unfortunately, Domesday Book, by the nature of its evidence, allows only a static and blurred 'snapshot' view of population. Even so, no other source of such quality survives for the rest of the medieval period. Thus, no direct evidence of the dynamics of population change exists and it is only indirectly that it becomes possible to indicate medieval demographic fluctuations. It seems unlikely, however, that the Portsmouth region would have escaped the considerable variations which occurred in the nation's medieval population. Generally, the period from 1086 to the early fourteenth century was one of growing numbers of people. England's population between 1086 and 1377 has been variously estimated either to have more than doubled from 1.1 million to 2.23 million[10] or to have risen from 2.6 million to 3.4 million,[11] depending on assumed household size.[12] These national figures have been derived from information in Domesday Book and the Poll Tax of 1377, neither of which was intended to count the numbers of people, and hence no firm estimates of population size can be soundly made. However, between 1086 and 1377 England's population did not experience continual growth since early fourteenth-century famines and disease, especially the Black Death of 1348–49, reduced the numbers from a pre-plague peak estimated variously at either 3.7 million or between 6 and 7 million.[13]

Even though regional variations must have occurred in this pattern of rising then declining population in medieval England, the Portsmouth region appears to have experienced the nation's trend of growth in the twelfth and thirteenth centuries. The most obvious manifestation was the appearance of new settlements, the outstanding example of which was the founding of Portsmouth in about 1180. Further evidence is provided by the establishment in the early twelfth century of Southwick Priory and of Titchfield Abbey a century later. The creation of new markets at Havant (1200), Emsworth (1239), Wickham (1268) and Portchester

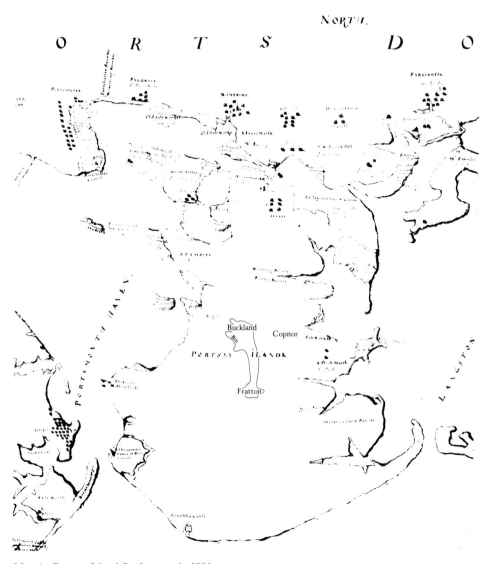

MAP 1   Portsea Island Settlements in 1086
Based on De La Fabvolliére *c*.1665
The central spine of the island, an approximate 8m contour, includes the locations of Buckland and
Fratton, Copnor about 6m above sea-level, nearer the salterns to the east

(1294) similarly testifies not only to growing numbers of consumers but also of
urban centres. However, rural areas also experienced growth in the numbers of
people, a trend demonstrated again in the thirteenth century by increasing land
sales and subdivision of larger peasant landholdings into smaller plots, as happened
on the Titchfield Abbey estates.[14] Increased landlords' incomes, resulting from a

rising number of manorial court cases and the growing frequency of offences such as trespass, when land shortages caused actions to be brought against people and animals, as on the Southwick Priory estates in 1279,[15] are further evidence of population pressure.

In an agrarian nation with a relatively static agricultural technology, feeding rising numbers of people could only be achieved either by an extension of the cultivated area or by a more intensive use of existing farmland. Both solutions were apparently being carried out in the Portsmouth region. New settlements indicate that land use was extended and subdivision of holdings suggests more intensive farming was being practised. Inevitably, however, subdividing landholdings resulted in some plots of land being smaller than the ten acres considered to be the minimum requirement to support a peasant family at subsistence level.[16] By 1259 smallholders with under ten acres accounted for half the tenant population on the Bishop of Winchester's estates, and the manor of Bishop's Waltham, on the western edge of the Portsmouth region, showed an increase in the proportion of smallholders with less than ten acres from 42.6 per cent in 1259 to 51.5 per cent in 1332.[17] It seems unlikely that neighbouring manors to the east, in the Portsmouth region, would not have been similarly affected. Additionally, if those peasants unable to inherit land because of growing population pressure are taken into consideration, the average holding per family on the Bishop of Winchester's estates, which included the manors of Fareham and Hambledon, was a mere two acres.[18] Thus, with the increasing numbers of inadequate landholdings and landless peasants, many must have fallen perilously close to, if not below, the margins of subsistence in late thirteenth-century southern Hampshire, and particularly so since the extension of the cultivated area must have meant that progressively less fertile land remained to be farmed, the best having already been exploited.

The results of these trends can be seen in the late thirteenth and early fourteenth centuries in increasing mortality during bad harvest years such as those of 1272, 1277, 1283, 1294 and especially those years culminating in the great famine of 1315–17.[19] The fact that in the Portsmouth region during this period the impoverished suffered considerably more than their better-off contemporaries is amply demonstrated on the Winchester manors of Meon, situated in Titchfield parish, and Fareham, as well as the neighbouring one of Bishop's Waltham where, from the 1290s, there was a steep rise in the number of poor dying, especially in years of deficient harvests and in particular from 1316 to 1319. Implicit in this evidence is that the region was relatively over-populated and the associated declining living standards left many particularly vulnerable to bad harvests.[20] It also seems reasonable to argue, therefore, that the rise in the region's population came to an end, not in 1348–49 with the Black Death, but with the Great Famine of 1315–17. Such a view is supported by data on the movement of wages, for whereas money wages on the Winchester manors, as elsewhere in thirteenth-century England, were relatively stable, rising prices of most agricultural produce meant that real wages fell by some 25 per cent.[21] The increased labour supply occasioned by population growth had clearly kept wages down, but from the 1320s money wages on the Winchester manors, including Meon, began rising and kept on doing so for over a century.[22] Since it has been estimated that the 1315–17 famine resulted in an increase in mortality of some 10 to 15 per cent of the population,[23] it seems likely that the origin of the rising wage-levels lay in that period of crisis. Such a level of population loss, however, would seem small by comparison with the consequences of the Black Death of 1348–49 which, it is estimated, was responsible for national mortality of between 30 and 45 per cent of the population.[24] The number of deaths varied from region to region, but the national estimate certainly does not seem too high when local evidence is examined. In Droxford deanery, which included the Portsmouth region, up to 47 per cent of the clergy died, Portsmouth and Hayling Island being particularly affected.[25] On the nearby manor of Bishop's Waltham, 65 per cent of the tenants died[26] and at Titchfield a massive 80 per cent perished.[27] The inhabitants of Hayling Island petitioned Edward III in May 1352 for relief from taxation, stating in 'Stoke, Estoke, Northwode, Southwode, Mengham, Weston and Haillyng, in the island of Haillyng, a very great number of . . . men have been destroyed by the said mortal pestilence.'[28] In response, a royal declaration stated 'Moreover since the greater part of the said population died whilst the plague was raging, now, through the dearth of servants and labourers, the inhabitants are oppressed and daily are falling most miserably into greater poverty.'[29] Accordingly, a reduction in taxation was granted.

Despite the evidence of substantial local mortality, the plague visitation of 1348–9 could not alone have been responsible for the continued labour shortage reflected in the rising wage-levels for at least another three-quarters of a century. The population would have recovered its numbers before then had it not been for repeated plague epidemics, first in 1361–62, when Bishop's Waltham manor lost a further 13 per cent of its population,[30] secondly in 1369 and again in 1374–75, when many towns in southern England were said to have been ravaged by the 'Fourth Pestilence'.[31] No figures of the local mortality levels of these epidemics are available, although estimates of 18 and 19 per cent of the national population having died have been made.[32] Whatever the level of loss, there seems little doubt that not only did these plague outbreaks prevent the population from recovering, but also reduced it still further, thus creating increased problems of labour shortage. In the Portsmouth region the effects of the decline in the numbers of agricultural labourers can be seen in the local landowners' reactions to the changing circumstances. Titchfield Abbey attempted to solve its labour problems by converting from direct farming to leasing to tenant farmers. By 1381 all the land in the open fields of Crofton manor had been enclosed into smaller fields manageable by individual peasants, and similarly at Funtley manor all but one acre had been converted. By this process, the abbey needed no direct labour for its manors and was able to maintain its income, since enclosed land fetched higher rents than open fields. At Fareham, labour services were converted progressively into money payments as labour became scarcer. Before the Black Death in 1346 only £1 12s. 9d. was received from tenants in lieu of services, whereas this sum had risen to £9 6s. by 1352 and to £12 12s. 6d. by 1421.[33]

It would thus seem that in Fareham manor the labour supply remained deficient until at least 1420. Given that the plague, either nationally as in 1390–91 and 1405–7 or regionally as in frequent years, remained endemic,[34] keeping numbers low or further reducing the population, it is probable that the bottom of the trough of demographic decline was not reached until about 1440 when the nation's population had shrunk almost to its Domesday level. Perhaps a decline of some 60 per cent in the population of England had taken place from the peak numbers achieved before 1348.[35] Certainly the evidence of wage movements from the

Winchester manors supports such a conclusion, since agricultural wages rose between the 1340s and the 1440s by 50 per cent,[36] a figure which probably understates the real increase, since the highest wage manors of the bishop were leased out as his demesnes ceased to be cultivated. This increase in leasing by landlords of their demesne lands in the late fourteenth and fifteenth centuries presents a problem of diminishing evidence of change on the manors of south-east Hampshire and, thus, even the indirect measures of population size become increasingly less available. In the 1530s many of these less adequate series of manorial accounts cease completely with the dissolution of the majority of monastic houses, including those at Southwick and Titchfield.

Fortunately, from the sixteenth century, other sources become available in the form either of tax returns or ecclesiastical counts of those attending church. Like Domesday Book, they allow only static and unclear views of the possible population, albeit at rather more frequent intervals. Prior to the first census of 1801, there are five examples of such surviving evidence appertaining to the Portsmouth region. First, the lay subsidy (taxation return) of 1525;[37] secondly the Liber Cleri (communicants list) of 1603;[38] thirdly the Compton Census (communicants list) of 1676;[39] and finally the two Visitation Returns of the bishops of Winchester in 1725 and 1788[40] which numbered the inhabitants ('souls') in each parish. These disparate sources provide information which is not easily compatible, especially since the coverage of each one is uneven. Only the lists of 1603 and 1676 include all the parishes of the region, but even in those, as in the others, there are unknown levels of omission as well as problems of estimating what proportion of the population is listed. Some entries by the rounded nature of the numbers, as in 1676 and especially in 1725, give clear evidence of rough estimation rather than counting of inhabitants.

Nevertheless, the numbers the sources provide, when converted into parish population totals, afford a general indication of the long-term trend of population change. Between 1525 and 1603 a growth of some 60 per cent is indicated for the region's population, excluding Portsmouth and Portsea, for which adequate data have not survived. Had those two communities been included, it is likely that population growth would have been greater since, if the hundred or so houses on Tudor maps[41] are any guide, and if each contained a household of an average size of 4.5 people,[42] then some 450 people would have lived in Portsmouth about 1552. As, by 1603, there were perhaps nearly 800 inhabitants in the town, a growth of 74 per cent in Portsmouth's population is indicated in the second half of the sixteenth century. Certainly such a growth seems plausible considering that Leland had noted in about 1540 the vacant spaces within the town's walls.[43] Within the region there were considerable variations in the rate of sixteenth century population increase. The market towns of Hambledon and Wickham showed particularly high levels of growth with 164 per cent and 153 per cent respectively while, in complete contrast, Portchester and Bedhampton appear to have had declining populations. Most probably these latter estimates are indicative of inadequate source materials. Portchester's figures were suspiciously rounded, while Bedhampton's were probably affected by unstated levels of nonconformity, at least until 1725 when almost 40 per cent of its inhabitants were said to be Roman Catholics. A survey of Bedhampton manor made in 1633[44] provides further evidence that the 1603 estimate understates the village's population, since it indicates there were 33

TABLE 2   POPULATION ESTIMATES 1525–1725

	1525	1603	1676	1725
Meonstoke	158(35)	205(123)	467(280)	225
Droxford	346(77)	497(298)	612(367)	c.568
Soberton	243(54)	410(246)	n.g.	460
Hambledon	302(67)	798(479)	1,040(624)	≥700
	1,049(233)	1,910(1,146)		
Catherington	180(40)	382(229)	377(226)	c.322
Clanfield	86(19)	140(84)	227(136)	c.130
Chalton (+ Idsworth)	212(47)	308(185)	368(221)	c.400
Blendworth	117(26)	135(81)	125(75)	c.120
	595(132)	965(579)	1,097(658)	
Wickham	144(32)	365(219)	435(261)	c.550
Boarhunt	90(20)	137(82)	155(93)	n.g.
Southwick	216(48)	480(288)	407(244)	n.g.
	450(100)	982(589)	997(598)	
Titchfield	981(218)	1,372(823)	1,530(918)	1,500
Rowner	41(9)	47(28)	137(82)	90
Fareham	617(137)	808(485)	1,667(1,000)	1,300
	1,639(364)	2,227(1,336)	3,334(2,000)	
Portchester	207(46)	200(120)	533(320)	300
Wymering	212(47)	320(192)	233(140)	n.g.
Widley	72(16)	152(91)	118(71)	n.g.
Farlington	63(14)	122(73)	82(49)	180
Bedhampton	117(26)	92(55)	98(59)	161
	671(149)	886(531)	1,064(639)	
Havant	450(100)	752(451)	615(369)	c.780
Warblington	284(63)	300(180)	393(236)	c.500
North Hayling	{	245(147)	350(210)	{
South Hayling	{ 324(72)	265(159)	168(101)	{ 363
	1,058(235)	1,562(937)	1,526(916)	
Alverstoke	176(39)	}	{	{
Gosport	45(10)	} 583(231)	{2,500(1,500)	{ 4,500
	221(49)			
Portsea	?	527(316)	220(132)	1,500
Portsmouth	?	782(469)	4,270(2,562)	c.8,000

Sources: *1525 – P.R.O. E179/181 and 182 Lay Subsidy return using multiplier of 4.5 to convert taxed heads of households to population total. 1603 – B.L. Harleian 495 ff.237–39 Liber Cleri communicants list using multiplier of 5/3 to convert adults to total population. 1676 – William Salt Library, Stafford, MS. Salt 33 Compton Census communicants list using multiplier of 5/3 to convert adults to total population. 1725 – H.R.O. B/2/A Visitation Return (2 vols), numbers 'souls' per parish. Figures in parentheses are the original numbers returned.*

families in the community, suggesting a population approaching 150. This would imply a growth of over a quarter in the numbers living in Bedhampton in the century after 1525 (see Table 2).

Such corrections to the figures of individual communities, however, are unlikely to change the general direction of the trend revealed by the data. If the evidence is acceptable, then it demonstrates that even in the sixteenth century Portsmouth was still not the dominant community in south-east Hampshire. In terms of numbers, this distinction appears to belong to Titchfield parish, though its large spatial area included a number of smaller communities. Furthermore, as in 1086, so in 1525 the eastern part of the region remained the most densely populated although, had the evidence survived, it is likely that by the mid-sixteenth century Portsea Island would have run it very close. If to the 100 houses in Portsmouth in about 1540 are added the 40 listed in Portsea in the 1525 tax return,[45] then Portsea Island would have become more densely populated than Hayling Island. Generally speaking, however, apart from Portsea Island, the distribution of the region's population in the early sixteenth century remained much as it had been indicated in Domesday Book, although its overall density had increased some six and a half times (see Maps 2 and 3). Nevertheless, even as late as about 1600, Portsmouth may well have been only the fourth or fifth largest parochial community within the region. The

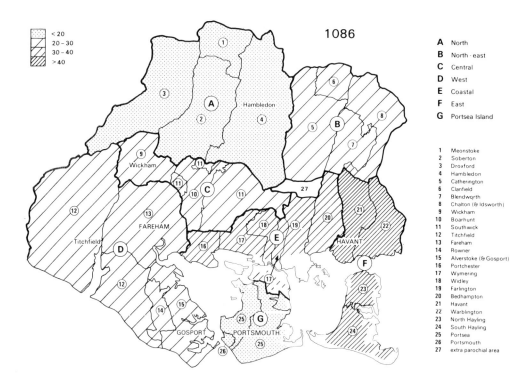

MAP 2   The Portsmouth region: Population density 1086

parishes of Titchfield, Fareham and Hambledon, all holding markets, apparently contained larger numbers than Portsmouth, and Havant was approximately the same size. Titchfield's prominent sixteenth-century position may well have been influenced by the presence in late medieval times of its important religious establishment, as well as its market function and port facilities which would have attracted traders.[46] If total numbers are converted to population densities, however, there can be no doubt of Portsmouth's growth by 1603, since Portsea Island was clearly more densely peopled than any other part of the region, having about 40 per cent more inhabitants per square mile than the eastern part of the region which was still more densely settled than the remainder (see Table 1).

For the bulk of the seventeenth century, between 1603 and 1676, the population of the Portsmouth region appears to have continued to grow from over 10,000 to over 19,000 people, a rise of 83.5 per cent. Increasingly, however, that growth was dominated by the emergence of the two expanding naval communities of Portsmouth on one side of the harbour and Gosport on the other. This growing regional dominance is clearly seen when comparing sixteenth- with seventeenth-century estimates, for whilst population in the Portsmouth region as a whole probably grew by 60 per cent between 1525 and 1603, when Portsea Island and

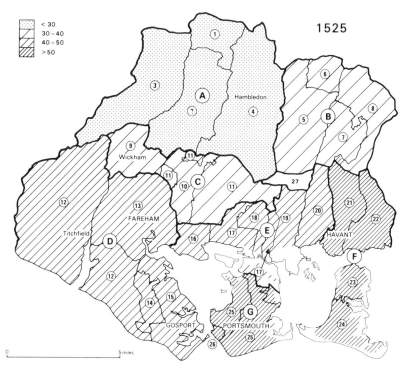

MAP 3   Population density 1525

Alverstoke with Gosport are excluded, growth was still as much as 56 per cent. Between 1603 and 1676, however, of the 83.5 per cent growth the vast majority occurred in the two naval communities, growth in the rest of the region accounting for only 18.8 per cent of the total (see Maps 4 and 5). Thus, while Portsmouth and Gosport were growing rapidly in the seventeenth century, the evidence from the rest of the region suggests that growth was slowing down. Not surprisingly, these changes are reflected in the population densities of the region. By 1676, Portsea Island was almost six times more densely peopled than elsewhere in the region and the eastern part had been overtaken by the west, Gosport's growth having influenced the density of that part of the region, since Alverstoke parish had almost half as many people per square mile as Portsmouth. This growing seventeenth-century demographic dominance of Portsea Island was achieved despite the depredations of the plague in 1665–6. The resident Navy Commissioner in Portsmouth in August 1665 had disclosed his fears of an outbreak of the epidemic, then seriously affecting London 'amongst so crowded and miserably poor a population',[47] as he described the people of Portsmouth. He had ample justi-fication for his misgivings since exceptionally high mortality was to be experienced in 1666 and to a lesser extent in 1665 itself. Nevertheless, Portsmouth's population recovered rapidly from such setbacks with little noticeable effect on the general

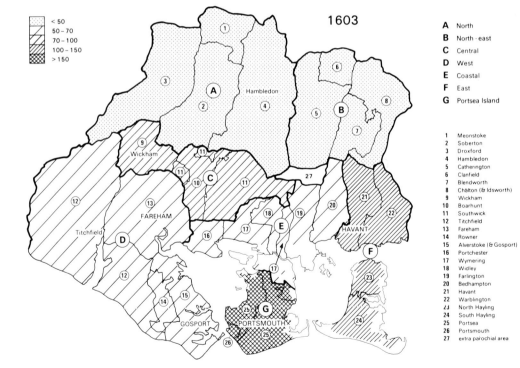

MAP 4   Population density 1603

level of baptisms being caused by the high death rate, suggesting rapid replacement by immigration.

The only other reasonably complete source of information from which the region's population can be calculated before the first census is the Bishop of Winchester's Visitation Return of 1725. This indicates that the rate of population growth for the region as a whole had slowed down in the preceding half century, an estimated increase of only 24 per cent from a total of over 18,200 to over 22,600 people being recorded.[48] However, if Portsea Island and Gosport are excluded from these calculations, the remainder of the region's population appears to have declined by 6 per cent whereas that of the two naval communities rose by 56 per cent, eloquent testimony to the importance of the Portsmouth Harbour settlements to the whole region by the early eighteenth century. By this time the distribution of the region's population had also been altered radically, with Portsmouth and Gosport containing considerably more people than the rest of the region, some 14,500 out of 22,649 (64 per cent), a consolidation of the position the communities had been well on the way to achieving in 1676 when they comprised some 47 per cent of the region's population. No wonder that Defoe could write of Portsmouth at the time of the 1725 Visitation Return as a town 'well-inhabited, thriving, prosperous', with naval docks and yards 'now like a town by themselves'.[49]

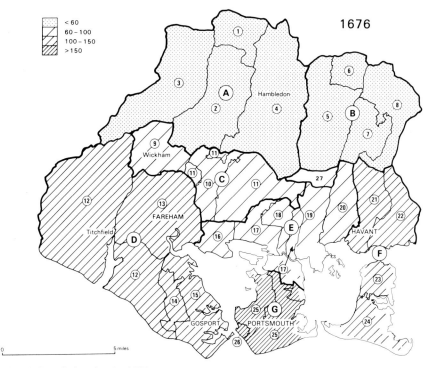

MAP 5   Population density 1676

The returns to the Bishop's Visitation enquiries of 1788 survive for less than half the parishes in the Portsmouth region and thus it is not possible to calculate the total population or its density and distribution. Of the surviving returns, the great majority are in rounded numbers, casting doubt on their accuracy. Titchfield was estimated to have 3,000 souls, twice the number it contained in 1725, and Gosport and Alverstoke's population had risen from an estimated 4,500 in 1725 to an estimated 6,815. These perhaps are indications of the population beginning to show an increasing rate of growth yet again, but the best source with which to compare the estimates from the 1725 Visitation Return is the Census of 1801, which provides the first population figures in English history that can be accepted with greater confidence. In those cases where the parishes are directly comparable it can be calculated that the region's population, excluding Portsmouth and Gosport, increased from about 8,650 people in 1725 to over 16,400 in 1801, a rise of 90 per cent. When the two naval towns are included, the increase becomes one from about 22,650 people to over 60,900, a remarkable growth of 169 per cent. Thus it can be seen that the numerical dominance of the Portsmouth Harbour communities was strengthened throughout the eighteenth century when, after a period of slow growth or even decline in other parts of the region in the late seventeenth or early eighteenth centuries, the region's population began to grow more rapidly once again (see Maps 6 and 7).

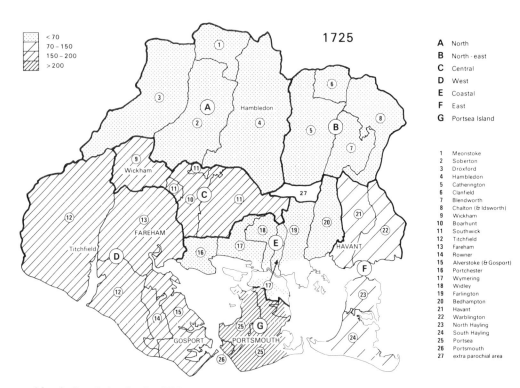

MAP 6   Population density 1725

This apparent pattern of population change in the Portsmouth region from the early sixteenth century to the end of the eighteenth century is, in many ways, a microcosm of the nation's population experience. The number of people in England increased in the sixteenth and early seventeenth centuries; the increase slowed and numbers probably fell in the late seventeenth century, only to rise to new heights in the eighteenth. At the same time, the nation's capital city, London, consistently increased its domination of the national population until by the mid-eighteenth century it contained more than one in ten of the native populace.[50] The Portsmouth region's population experience has more than an echo of this national pattern, with Portsmouth itself accommodating an increasing proportion of the local people, its share rising consistently from 7.5 per cent in 1603, to 22 per cent in 1676, approximately 33 per cent in 1725 and 52.7 per cent in 1801.

Such an analysis, based for the most part on disparate sources, widely spaced chronologically and intended for purposes other than demographic, must raise questions not the least of which concerns the accuracy of the estimates produced. Nevertheless, there are reasons for supposing that the results are not greatly at variance with reality. In the case of most of the local communities, it is possible to

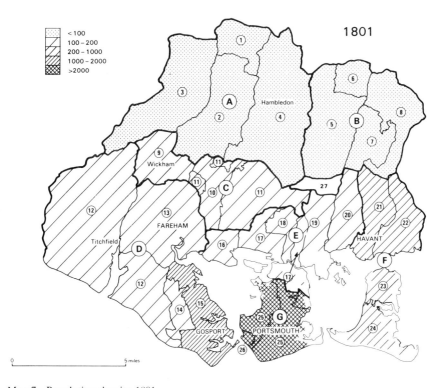

MAP 7 Population density 1801

check the accuracy of their population estimates in the late seventeenth century by comparing the Compton Census of 1676 with an earlier Hearth Tax return compiled at Easter 1665.[51] The total estimated population of the former at 15,747 indicates a 7.5 per cent increase in 11 years on the 14,625 population estimate from the Hearth Tax. These figures would appear to be reasonably compatible and suggest an acceptable degree of accuracy in the two estimates, since it is most unlikely that two sources of information drawn up by different institutions for entirely dissimilar purposes would engender the same margins of error. Thus, although the derived figures cannot be regarded as anything but estimates, they can be reasonably taken as indicators of the general trend in population. However, because the sources are not only limited to static single year views spaced from 49 to 78 years apart, it is difficult to know when changes in population trends occurred. It is quite possible, for instance, that the trend of a declining population noticed in much of the region between 1676 and 1725 began earlier than 1676, but cannot be discerned because it had been masked by considerable growth in the earlier part of the period between 1603 and 1676.

Fortunately, a method of confirming the population trends and the dynamics of change can be ascertained from another source – the Anglican parish registers of baptisms and burials for the twenty-six parishes in the region.[52] Like the other sources, the registers were not maintained for estimating the numbers in local populations, but they have increasingly been exploited for estimating long-term population trends.[53] In theory they should all begin in 1538.[54] In practice few surviving ones do so, and in the Portsmouth region only those of Chalton survive back to that year, although Farlington registers begin in 1539. Many have been lost, only half the region's parishes having registers which commence in the sixteenth century. Those of Bedhampton start as late as the 1680s.[55] The problems of missing parish registers are compounded by gaps in the existing ones, burial registers being worse than baptism ones in this respect. Gaps of only a handful of years are not particularly serious, but ones over ten years are, thus the Boarhunt register with two substantial gaps in both baptisms and burials has its value reduced. It is also the most inadequately maintained of all the region's registers, with infrequent and haphazard entries much of the time. This highlights another problem of parish registers, that of the conscientiousness of an incumbent in recording parish events. However, most registers are adequately kept for most of the time, although in the eighteenth century they are increasingly affected by nonconformity. In the Portsmouth region, nonconformist groups keeping their own registers are known to have grown in Gosport, Havant, Portsea and Portsmouth.[56] The omission of nonconformists from the Anglican registers, although reducing the real number of baptisms and burials, is unlikely to alter the population trend for the region as a whole. In fact, their inclusion would serve to enhance whatever trend was perceived.

However, there are clear problems in interpreting the population trend for a whole region from only a proportion of its parishes, particularly if those parishes for which registers survive are not the most important or sizeable demographically. Not until 1688 do all the registers come into observation (although Gosport was not created until 1697) and those for Portsmouth and Portsea, arguably the most important, only begin in 1654. Thus for the sixteenth and early seventeenth centuries the available evidence comes from a minimum of three and a maximum of thirteen parishes out of a total of twenty-six. What the aggregation of the baptisms and burials of these parishes shows is baptism surpluses in all decades to 1640. Decades such as the 1560s and 1600s have substantial surpluses whilst others have more moderate increases, but the impression given is of a growing population in the second half of the sixteenth century and first decade of the seventeenth, a finding which would not conflict with the analysis of the 1525 and 1603 returns (see Figure 1). From the 1650s, however, the introduction of the Portsmouth and Portsea registers into the data set produces quite the opposite effect. Portsmouth, in particular, had such massive burial surpluses that its experience overshadowed the rest of the region.

Even so, the parish register evidence seems to suggest that when Portsmouth is disaggregated from its region there is little indication of the population growth suggested by the 1603 and 1676 counts, at least after the middle of the seventeenth century, implying that growth had been concentrated in the first half of the century. The slower growth after 1650 may have been affected by increasing mortality since, in the 1670s, half the parishes in observation had burial surpluses. Not only those on Portsea Island, but also all the eastern parishes and three of the four northern ones were affected. The 1680s were almost as bad, eight of the eighteen parishes in

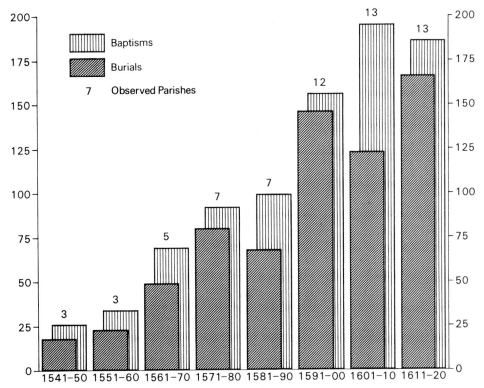

FIGURE 1   Average annual baptisms and burials 1541–1610

observation being affected, though this time the western group of parishes was worst hit. After a decade where few burial surpluses were recorded, the turn of the century saw another increase in deaths with eleven out of twenty-five parishes in observation having burial surpluses, the southern coastal parishes suffering the worst of the mortality on this occasion as they did in the second decade of the century. From then on only the 1740s were to prove a decade of high mortality with the worst affected areas to be found around the whole of Portsmouth Harbour. This pattern of mortality, with four of the five decades from 1670 to 1720 showing between 40 per cent and 50 per cent of the parishes having burial surpluses, would certainly support a view of little or no population growth in the region, outside Portsmouth and Gosport, as the 1676 and 1725 counts indicated.

For the rest of the eighteenth century, burial surpluses in individual parishes are, apart from the 1740s, at lower levels and especially so in the last two decades when only 2 and 3 parishes respectively indicate such a phenomenon. The cause of the rise in burials in the 1740s can at least be partly explained by an outbreak of disease among prisoners of war at Portchester which had serious repercussions in Fareham – and, sure enough, one of only two decades when Fareham had a burial surplus was the 1740s.[57]

It does seem that the population of the south-east Hampshire region from the late seventeenth century onwards was to be increasingly affected by Admiralty affairs for deliberate decisions were taken to expand the naval dockyard. In 1687 this industrial unit employed 294 men. Consistent growth, except for the years 1698–1700, meant that by 1711 it employed over 2,000. It was not the Industrial Revolution – but equally clearly it cannot be classed as proto-industrialisation. Whatever its designation, an almost seven-fold increase in the workforce could hardly not have had its effect on population growth, and such a rapid increase in just over two decades must have created housing shortages and overcrowding leading to disease and high mortality. Not surprisingly burial surpluses were particularly high in the first decade of the eighteenth century.[58]

Dockyard growth was inevitably connected with war which brought increasing numbers of sailors, marines and soldiers into Portsmouth. These, too, caused population to grow and baptisms can be seen to climb when war broke out, and decline again after the cessation of hostilities. But the presence of the armed forces was not without its problems. In 1697 the Mayor of Portsmouth, John Mounsher, wrote to the Secretary of War complaining about the cost of a regiment which, after being billeted on the town, had left without paying. The authorities feared another regiment was coming.[59]

As Portsmouth's population fluctuated with war and peace, so did the dockyard labour force. After 1711 its numbers fell and probably did not reach 2,000 again until 1756, the very year the Seven Years War broke out. After 1762 numbers employed declined again, though from 1771 a consistent level of 2,000 or more workers was maintained and from 1795 over 2,700 were employed, again growth connected with war. From that year annual baptisms rose to over 400 in Portsmouth for the first time and over 700 in Portsea. War was thus a boost to Portsmouth's population and peace similarly caused a reversal of the process.[60]

No doubt local traders and merchants measured the benefits of increased economic activity occasioned by the onset of hostilities and so, no doubt, did undertakers for, in every measurable decade from the 1650s to the 1770s inclusive, burial surpluses are found, making Portsmouth the unhealthiest place in the region. However, that title passed across Portsmouth Harbour in the 1780s when the 'honour' became Gosport's, which had burial surpluses in every decade from the 1720s. Similarly, Farlington, Wymering and Widley, situated on the mainland at the head of Portsea Island, were unhealthy places in which to live. Clearly life around Portsmouth Harbour for many of the migrant workers attracted from far and near was hazardous. At the other end of the mortality spectrum were the four north-east parishes which had fewer decades of burial surpluses than any other group – Blendworth and Chalton having only two and Clanfield and Catherington only one.

Despite the hazards to the health of the population of Portsea Island, growth was maintained and by 1800 over 1,000 baptisms were being registered each year in Portsea, whilst Portsmouth's registrations rose to half that figure. However, in the first decade of the nineteeth century, while Portsea's growth continued so that by 1810 over 1,500 baptisms were being recorded each year, Portsmouth's baptisms declined to an average of not much over 300. Bearing in mind the growth of nonconformity in the late eighteenth and early nineteenth centuries, these figures clearly understate the reality of growth. Portsmouth's baptisms are only marginally affected by surviving nonconformist registrations, but the Baptist and Congregational chapels in Portsea increase that parish's total by approximately an additional 200 baptisms per annum by the beginning of the nineteenth century. From the mid-eighteenth century Portsea, demographically, appears to have achieved self-sustaining growth and there seems little doubt that the major force behind such growth was dockyard expansion, since the development of commercial shipping was not only not encouraged by the naval authorities but positively opposed. As late as 1851 the Board of Ordnance refused permission for Portsmouth Borough Council to establish a commercial port at the Mill Pond located north of the town between it and the dockyard.[61]

For the nineteenth century it is possible, through the availability of census data, to establish with confidence the demographic trends of the Portsmouth region. The century saw the culmination of the increasing dominance of Portsea Island. Whereas in 1801 Portsmouth contained 52.7 per cent of the region's population, by 1851 it accommodated 61.1 per cent and by 1901 some 72.8 per cent. If Gosport with Alverstoke's population was added to Portsmouth's, then the two naval communities would have provided over 70 per cent of the region's population in 1801, over 75 per cent in 1851 and nearly 84 per cent in 1901. Thus, even though the region's population as a whole continued to grow in the nineteenth century, expanding by more than fourfold, from over 63,000 in 1801 to 258,600 in 1901, Portsmouth expanded even more rapidly, experiencing an increase of over five and a half times, from more than 33,000 people in 1801 to over 188,000 at the end of the century. Almost 80 per cent of the region's total nineteenth-century population growth took place on Portsea Island. Inevitably, despite the fact that all parishes in the region grew in population size in the nineteenth century (see Table 3),[62] the rest of the region, excluding Portsea Island, contained a declining proportion of the population. Only two other parishes, Farlington and South Hayling, maintained their proportional share. Having only small populations at the beginning of the nineteenth century, they had space for expansion, and also became desirable residential areas – Farlington just north of the increasingly crowded

TABLE 3 CENSUS POPULATION TABLE 1801–1901

	1801	1811	1821	1831	1841	1851	1861	1871	1881	1891	1901
Titchfield	2949	3227	3528	3712	4030	3956	4043	4369	4571	5412	6734
Fareham	3030	3325	3677	4402	6168	5842	6197	7023	7183	7934	8246
Rowner	105	99	138	140	134	133	147	491	187	271	374
Alverstoke	11295	4424	4788	12637	4648	7062	11384	15220	(21581	(25454	(28884
Gosport		7788	6184		8862*1	9846*1	11269	7424	(	(	(
	17379	18863	18315	20891	23842	26839	33040	34529	33522	39071	44238
Meonstoke	289	300	368	382	459	431	429	550	474	431	431
Droxford	1199	1378	1410	1620	1942	2005	2194	2325	2285	2381	2609
Soberton	672	760	882	931	954	1147	1136	1245	1097	1185	1189
Hambledon	1358	1495	1886	2025	2069	2052	1891	2040	2047	2026	1922
	3518	3933	4546	4958	5424	5635	5650	6160	5903	6023	6151
Catherington	559	607	798	944	1003	1094	1151	1293	1321	1413	1356
Clanfield	153	163	196	210	239	263	265	271	279	247	213
Chalton	127	252	249	235	263	303	286	244	208	241	202
Idsworth	303	321	310	315	396	402	333	394	395	362	420
Blendworth	174	236	249	246	280	236	219	284	298	291	268
Waterlooville							243	283	246	436	609
	1316	1579	1802	1950	2181	2298	2497	2769	2747	2990	3068
Wickham	901	978	1134	1106	1164	1069	1034	1139	1101	1161	1162
Boarhunt	133	165	205	225	232	283	267	271	288	333*2	352
Southwick	569	714	711	723	749	596	609	649	664	643*2	561
	1603	1857	2050	2054	2145	1948	1910	2059	2053	2137	2075
Havant	1670	1824	2099	2083	2101	2416	2470	2634	3032	3474	3837
Warblington	1433	1657	1850	2118	2270	2302	2196	2438	2374	2840	3639
N Hayling	254	247	295	294	277	272	262	281	268	278	279
S Hayling	324	373	443	588	669	824	777	858	1066	1217	1333
	3681	4101	4687	5083	5317	5814	5705	6211	6740	7809	9088
Portchester	917	818	757	739	767	729	771	779	772	839	888
Wymering	566	740	625	578	748	751	1071	1206	985	1123	(2859
Widley	277	422	544	512	607	565	725	874	1069	1350	(
Farlington	302	453	553	778	793	812	931	1218	1223	1352	1388
Bedhampton	305	427	413	537	533	586	576	715	709	700	712
	2367	2860	2892	3144	3448	3443	4074	4792	4758	5364	5847
Sub Total	29864	33193	34292	38080	42357	45977	52876	56520	55723	63394	70467
Portsmouth	7839	7103	7269	8083	7135	8218	10346	11169	7591	7661	(47797)
Portsea	8348	11004	12622	13919	14177	16383	19967	18430	17183	14730	(53022)
Kingston	6909	9107	10442	11499	12105	17626	23089	28541	39127	56581	(43144)
Landport	10130	13353	15315	16888	17139	26742	41426	55455	64121	80306	(44170)
	33226	40567	45648	50389	50556	68969	94828	113595	128022	159278	186133
Military & Convicts		1020	1095		2502	3157					
Portsmouth Parish	7839	7103	7269	8083	9354	10329	10883	11569	7967	(	(
Portsea Parish	25387	34484	39474	42306	43678	61767	83966	102000	120022	(	(
	33226	41587	46743	50389	53032	72096	94779	113569	127989	151590	188133
Regional Total	63090	74780	81035	88469	95415	·118103	147704	170115	183745	222672	258600

*1 Includes Military and Marines in Barracks 1841 – 790, 1851 – 943
Haslar Hospital, Patients and Seamen 1841 – 204, 1851 – 382
Haslar Hospital, Officers and Family 1841 – 198, 1851 – 257
Convicts in Hulks 1841 – 650, 1851 – 850

*2 Boundary changes in 1891

Figures for Portsea Island in 1901 are in parentheses because changes in census registration districts make direct comparison with previous decades impossible

Portsea Island on Portsdown Hill's lower slopes and South Hayling as a seaside development.

As is well known, the nineteenth century was one of national population growth, its most rapid expansion being experienced in the first half of the century when the population of Great Britain doubled from approximately nine to eighteen million. The Portsmouth region matched this rate of growth by rather more than doubling. However, in the second half of the nineteenth century, whilst the national rate of population growth slowed down, an increase of 80 per cent being experienced, that of the Portsmouth region accelerated to twice the national growth rate. That more rapid rate was, by and large, the product of Portsmouth's expansion, since its growth alone represented an astonishing 83 per cent of the region's increase between 1851 and 1901. This dominance of Portsmouth was assisted by the failure to grow, or even the decline, of some of the region's northern and central parishes. Meonstoke, Soberton and Wickham were virtually stable, whilst Chalton, Clanfield, Hambledon and Southwick all demonstrated declining populations. These, mainly agriculturally-based communities, were experiencing the onset of agricultural mechanisation and consequent declining employment opportunities. Doubtless, many of their residents travelled the short distance to expanding Portsmouth and its increasing prospects of employment, so much so that, as the nineteenth century unfolded, the region's history became increasingly the history of Portsmouth.

In this context the census figures show that the rapid population growth, demonstrated by the baptism registrations at the end of the eighteenth century, not only continued in the first half of the nineteenth century, but also accelerated in the second half. The population of Portsea Island, excluding the northern periphery which lay in Wymering parish, more than doubled between 1801 and 1851 and increased over two and a half times from 1851 to 1901. However, the growth was more uneven when analysed decade by decade. There were particularly large population increments in the first ten years, the two middle decades, 1841–60, and in the last twenty years of the century. These increases were entirely consistent with expanding dockyard and military activity either because of war or the need to defend a world-wide Empire or a combination of both. In the early years of the century the Napoleonic Wars enhanced dockyard employment, whilst in the middle years the development of an enlarged dockyard for a steam navy as well as wars in Burma, China, India and the Crimea caused further growth; in the closing years of the century rearmament had a similar effect.

Thus, the first decade saw population grow by more than 25 per cent, an increase entirely within Portsea and its two expanding suburbs of Kingston and Landport, which all had populations growing by 32 per cent. Portsmouth not only did not grow but actually declined (see Table 4). There can be little doubt that the overall growth of over 25 per cent in the decade was related to the expanding dockyard activity during the Napoleonic Wars. The contemporaneous decline in Portsmouth's population is more difficult to explain. Possibly a number of the less well-off inhabitants moved out as rates and rents rose to levels they could not afford. Equally, some may have moved to better properties in the expanding suburbs. Alternatively, if the first two censuses are an accurate reflection of the town, then there were nearly fifty fewer houses occupied in 1811 than in 1801, so perhaps some older properties had become uninhabitable or been demolished and new ones had not yet replaced them (See Map 8).

TABLE 4 PORTSMOUTH BOROUGH – CENSUS TOTALS AND INTERCENSAL CHANGES

PORTSMOUTH BOROUGH	1801	1811	1821	1831	1841	1851	1861	1871	1881	1891
Portsmouth Town	7839	7103 (-9.4%)	7269 (+2.3%)	8083 (+11.2%)	7135 (-11.7%)	8218 (+15.2%)	10346 (+25.9%)	11169 (+8.0%)	7591 (-32.0%)	7661 (+0.9%)
Portsea Town	8348	11004 (+31.8%)	12622 (+14.7%)	13919 (+10.3%)	14177 (+1.8%)	16383 (+15.5%)	19967 (+21.9%)	18430 (-7.7%)	17183 (-6.8%)	14730 (-14.3%)
Landport (including Southsea)	10130	13353 (+31.8%)	15315 (+14.7%)	16888 (+10.3%)	17139 (+1.5%)	26742 (+56.1%)	41426 (+54.9%)	55455 (+33.9%)	64121 (+15.6%)	80306 (+25.2%)
Kingston	6909	9107 (+31.8%)	10442 (+14.7%)	11499 (+10%)	12105 (+5.3%)	17626 (+45.6%)	23089 (+31%)	28541 (+23.6%)	39127 (+37.1%)	56581 (+44.6%)
TOTAL	33226	40567 (+22.1%)	45648 (+12.5%)	50389 (+0.4%)	50556 (+0.3%)	68969 (+36.4%)	94828 (+37.5%)	113595 (+19.8%)	128022 (+12.7%)	159278 (+24.4%)

Percentages in brackets are the intercensal changes in population

In each decade from 1811 to 1841, unlike other major urban centres, Portsmouth's rate of growth progressively declined, although Portsea, Kingston and Landport had almost identical growth rates. From 1811 to 1821 they were in fact unvarying at just under 15 per cent; from 1821 to 1831 they increased by 10 per cent or so, and from 1831 to 1841 Portsea and Landport grew by less than 2 per cent and Kingston by just over 5 per cent. It seems improbable that the decline in dockyard employment, from a peak in 1814 of approaching 4,000 to less than 2,000 by 1832, did not influence this declining growth rate, particularly when it is seen that well over half (58 per cent) of Portsmouth's industrially occupied male labour force were dockyard workers in 1841.[63] By then some 2,227 workers were employed, indications of a slight recovery from the trough of 1832. Similarly, between 1810 and 1813 there were 19,200 naval and marine personnel in Portsmouth, but between 1816 and 1830 these had declined by 80 per cent to 3,800.[64] However, in the 1840s unequivocal growth was once again experienced. The overall intercensal increase on the island was 36 per cent, but there were exceptionally large increments in Landport, including the emergent Southsea, of over 56 per cent and in Kingston of 45.6 per cent. Portsea was still growing, but by only 15 per cent, as also was Portsmouth in this decade. Even so, in this latter case, the increase only a little more than restored the previous decade's losses. It would seem that both the fortified towns were beginning to reach the limits of expansion inside their walls. Portsmouth apparently had done so in the eighteenth century, growing by under 5 per cent between 1801 and 1851, and, despite a later boost resulting from the presence of military personnel, the town ended the century with a smaller population than at the beginning. Portsea, with fortifications completed only in 1809, found them a limiting factor by the mid-nineteenth century. Even so, by then it had almost doubled (96 per cent increase) its population in fifty years and was then twice the size of its parent community (see Map 9). However, it was in the developing surburban sub-districts of Kingston and Landport that the most dramatic population increases were experienced. Between 1801 and 1851 the former had an estimated increase of 155 per cent and the latter one of 164 per cent. In any case, the Landport sub-district was estimated to have been larger than either of the towns as early as 1801 and Kingston became so by 1851, by which time Landport and Southsea had a greater population than both towns combined. Landport's spectacular growth in the 1840s can be ascribed to two major causes. First, the development of larger, steam-powered ships necessitated an extension of the dockyard, a seven-acre Steam Basin being built between 1843 and 1848, and a 600ft. long steam factory being opened the following year.[65] Not surprisingly, the dockyard labour force was increased, reaching nearly 3,000 in 1851, representing some 63 per cent of male industrial workers in Portsmouth. Secondly, came the continuing development of Southsea as a residential suburb and its beginnings as a seaside resort. In the early nineteenth century, while Landport was already developing east of Portsea, Southsea, yet to be named as such, was emerging east of Portsmouth in a small area known as Croxton Town (see Maps 8 and 9) and in which the houses of artisans, most probably dockyard workers in the French Wars, were predominant.

Expansion to the north-east resulted in Landport and Southsea merging in the 1840s. To the south-east, expansion reached the sea front by the 1850s, new villas extending along the northern edge of Southsea Common which had fortunately

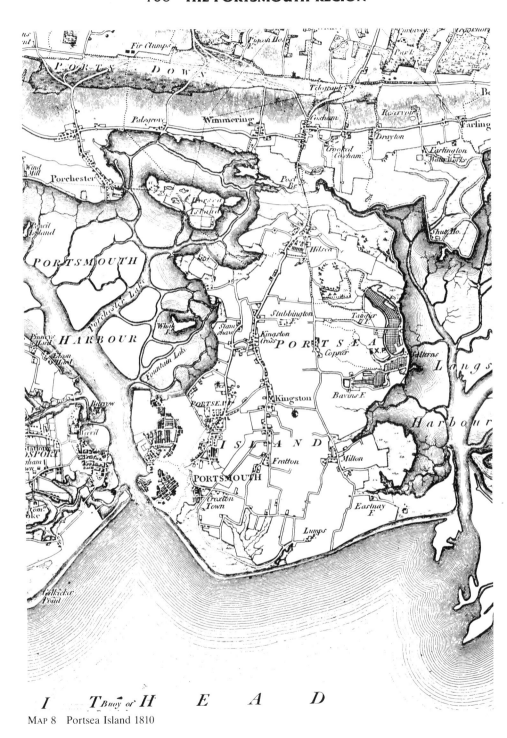

MAP 8   Portsea Island 1810

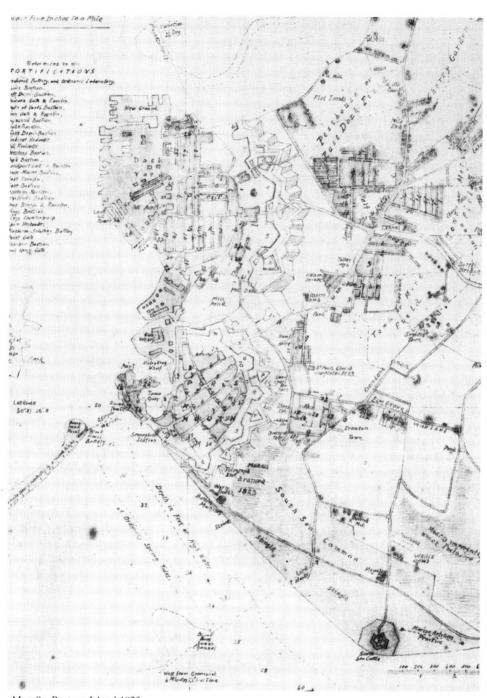

MAP 9   Portsea Island 1823

been drained and levelled between 1823 and 1843. What was significant about this two-directional development was that, unlike the old town of Portsmouth, distinct social stratification emerged. The northern sector possessed many of the characteristics of Landport. It was overwhelmingly artisan in nature, housing many dockyard workers or those employed in the yard's support services. It was, in its density of development and its lack of open space, very much, as Landport was, a working-class residential area. The southern sector contained development of an entirely different nature, spacious houses set in their own grounds being scattered thinly over the district, clearly confirming its middle-class standing (see Maps 10 and 11).[66] However, in the 1840s Southsea began to attract seaside visitors,[67] though it was not until the second half of the nineteenth century that tourism developed along the sea front. Until then, Southsea had expanded as a middle-class residential suburb of Portsmouth, providing spacious housing for military and naval personnel and those profiting from supplying them.

The scale of development can be estimated from the figures of inhabited houses provided in the decadal censuses. Whereas Portsmouth Town had almost exactly the same number of houses in 1851 as in 1811, it had fifty-four (4.5 per cent) less than in 1841. These figures reflect both the fact that Portsmouth had no space to grow within its defences and that the 1840s saw some people leave the town to settle in Southsea. Portsea parish, meanwhile, saw its occupied housing grow from 4,393 in 1801 to 5,768 in 1811, 7,527 in 1821 and 8,215 in 1831, an increase of 87 per cent whilst population grew by two-thirds. From 1841 to 1891 it is possible to separate Portsea Town housing figures from those for the rest of the parish. It is noticeable that, between 1841 and 1851, Portsea's housing stock, unlike its population, had begun to decline. In 1841 Portsea possessed 2,979 houses whereas in 1851 this had shrunk to 2,831, a loss of 5 per cent. Implicit in these figures is that, while Portsea's population had increased by some 2,000 people in the 1840s, thereby considerably exacerbating its overcrowding, some of the better off had migrated to the developing spacious suburb of Southsea as well as to Landport and Kingston, the last named also being considerably expanded by the dockyard's growth.

The 1850s saw the problem of Portsea's overcrowding worsen since, while the housing stock remained much the same, the population increased by over 3,500, nearly 22 per cent. For the next thirty years, however, both the number of houses and the population steadily declined. Total houses fell from 2,831 to 2,611, whilst population shrank from nearly 20,000 to under 15,000. Thus Portsea's houses, which contained an average household of 7.5 persons in 1861, were less crowded with an average of 5.5 persons in 1891.

Similarly, the town of Portsmouth had declining numbers of both houses and people in the second half of the nineteenth century. Between 1851 and 1891 the housing stock declined by 149 (14.4 per cent) and simultaneously the population, after initially rising to over 11,000 in 1871, fell to 7,661 in 1891. These fluctuations were influenced heavily by the presence or absence of service personnel. For example, in 1871, five naval ships were in port containing nearly 2,300 men, but only two ships were enumerated in 1881 with under 500 men listed as being on board. Thus, whereas total personnel in ships and barracks in 1871 numbered nearly 5,000, there were less than 2,000 in 1881. Hence, most, though not all, of the population decline of over 3,500 between 1871 and 1881 can be attributed to movements of service personnel, as could the growth of population between 1851 and 1861.

Map 10   Portsea Island 1853

MAP 11   Portsea Island 1856

That factors other than the movement of service personnel were affecting the population of Portsea and Portsmouth, however, is amply demonstrated in the 1871 census, where it was noted that there had been 'a gradual removal of residents from the business centres of Portsea and Portsmouth to the modern suburbs outside the walls. Landport, one of these suburban parts, possesses the attractions of a large open common and a long stretch of sea-beach. . . . Another cause of the increase of population is the growing reputation of Southsea as a watering-place, and the consequent great demand for houses of a superior description' (see Map 11). Nevertheless, the census officials were not unaware of the consequences of the services, for the entry also stated that the 'naval and military (and consequently to some extent the civilian) population is liable to great fluctuation.' Furthermore, the important effect of the dockyard on the island's population was recognised since the note continued 'Government works now in progress (the principal of which is the extension of the dockyard) employ several thousand men, a large proportion of whom live outside the town.'[68]

Not surprisingly then, it is the housing figures of the 'modern suburbs' which indicate clearly where urban growth on Portsea Island in the 1840s was taking place. Kingston in 1841 had a stock of 2,618 houses, but in 1851 this had expanded to 3,621, excluding 64 in the process of being built. Landport, which included Southsea, had even more phenomenal growth, its houses increasing from 3,880 to 5,957, excluding 107 being built. Respectively, these were increases of 38 per cent and 54 per cent and represented substantial benefits to employers and employees alike in the building industry, which demonstrated a rise of 82 per cent in the numbers employed between 1841 and 1851. The number of enumerated builders rose from thirty-four to fifty-seven and identifiable building workers from 398 to 729.[69]

These increases heralded a half-century of Victorian expansion in the two suburbs. Whereas in the 1840s and 1850s some 3,000 new homes were constructed, the '60s and '70s each saw the figure rise to about 4,000 before the astonishing boom of the '80s when almost 7,500 houses were built. Until 1871 approximately two-thirds of this growth of housing stock took place in Landport, mostly in the Southsea part of the suburb. In the '70s, however, slightly more than half the new houses were constructed in Kingston, which in the 1880s had a doubling in its newly-built housing to nearly 6,000. As would be expected, such growth was reflected in the number of employed building workers which rose to over 1,600 in 1881.[70] By then the number of carpenters and joiners had risen to over 1,400 and since the navy was rapidly becoming an ironclad one, it would seem likely that most of these men must have been employed in the building sector.

The other sector of employment to benefit from Southsea's growth was domestic service. In 1841 some 2,750 were employed as domestic servants, rising to over 4,000 in 1851, most of whom were females. One factor which helped to make this increase in female employment possible was the curiously imbalanced sex ratio of the population on Portsea Island. Between 1801 and 1841 there were never less than 3,500 more females than males in the population and a peak of over 6,500 surplus females was reached in 1831, representing 13 per cent of the total population.[71]

The next three censuses show that this unbalanced ratio was reduced, until, in 1861, males and females were present on Portsea Island in almost equal numbers.

However, that even distribution did not remain. By 1891 the number of surplus females had risen once more to over 6,000. The requirement for increasing numbers of domestic servants in expanding Southsea is clearly not a complete explanation for such fluctuations and when marital status and age structure are added to the overall totals of males and females some interesting differences are observed. Despite the general surplus of females, the censuses show that among single people aged twenty and over there were always considerably more males than females, fluctuating between a low of almost 2,000 in 1891 to a peak of over 6,300 in 1871 (see Table 5). Thus, it was among the married and the widowed that females predominated. In fact, the number of surplus married females rose steadily from over 1,700 in 1851 to more than 4,600 in 1901, whilst there were never less than nearly 2,000 surplus widows and as many as over 4,700 in 1891. However, when the distribution of males and females in the most fertile age groups between fifteen and thirty-four is examined, it was always in Portsmouth and Portsea that the surpluses of young men were to be found and in Landport (including Southsea) and Kingston, the expanding suburbs, where the surpluses of females were resident. The two former districts were those containing most of the army barracks and naval ships and hence provide an explanation for the fluctuating numbers of surplus young men.

It is to be expected that most ports having commercial shipping and fishing as important sectors of employment would enumerate surpluses of females in their census returns. Additionally, since many soldiers and naval seamen married locally, Portsmouth had a problem of one-parent families when husbands either put to sea or were posted away. Inevitably, absent husbands meant that the incomes received by their wives could be spasmodic or non-existent. Some husbands never returned, being killed or lost abroad. It would seem that the majority of absent soldiers and seamen were resident in Kingston and Landport and hence the suburbs' surpluses of married women were directly related to the military and naval presence. Clearly a potentially most volatile situation pregnant with possible social problems was created by the imbalanced marital structure of the island's population. The loss of a Portsmouth-based ship could only create even more difficult circumstances since inevitably an increase in the number of widows would follow, with serious consequences ensuing as no provision was made by the Admiralty for them. In any case, sailors and soldiers were among the low paid of the nineteenth century, their incomes being frequently inadequate to maintain families. Dockyard workers were also among the ranks of the lower income earners, their wages not matching those of men employed in early nineteenth century commercial shipyards.[72]

Consequently, many wives and widows living in Portsea, Kingston and Landport were forced to find some form of employment. Those with children to support often needed to work from home and in nineteenth-century Portsmouth employment which was specifically geared to their needs was developed in the clothing industries. Since free uniforms were still not issued to naval and military personnel in the mid-nineteenth century, the tailoring trade continued to flourish. Dockyard self-sufficiency had not developed to the exclusion of all Portsmouth manufacturing, even if it had almost entirely done so in metalworking and engineering. However, the majority of tailors were male – 80 per cent of those over nineteen years old in 1841 and 90 per cent in 1851. It was dressmakers, seamstresses and

TABLE 5 SEX RATIO 1801–1901

PORTSMOUTH BOROUGH		1801	%	1811	%	1821	%	1831	%	1841	%	1851	%	1861	%	1871	%	1881	%	1891	%	1901
Portsmouth	M	3148	(40.2)	2887	(40.6)	2881	(39.6)	3347	(41.4)	4800	(54.0)	5784	(58.4)	6405	(61.9)	7425	(66.5)	4580	(60.3)	5184	(67.7)	
Town	F	4691	(59.8)	4216	(59.4)	4388	(60.4)	4736	(58.6)	4093	(46.0)	4113	(41.6)	3941	(38.1)	3744	(33.5)	3011	(39.7)	2477	(32.3)	
Portsea	M	3798	(45.5)	6041	(50.2)	6793	(49.5)	6026	(43.3)	6725	(45.5)	9574	(54.0)	12000	(60.1)	11226	(60.9)	10306	(60.0)	8699	(59.1)	
Town	F	4550	(54.5)	5983	(49.8)	6924	(50.5)	7893	(56.7)	8043	(54.5)	8161	(46.0)	7967	(39.9)	7204	(39.1)	6877	(39.1)	6031	(40.9)	
Landport (including Southsea)	M	4618	(45.6)	6104	(45.7)	6927	(45.2)	7326	(43.4)	7520	(43.6)	11904	(44.4)	19005	(45.9)	25357	(45.7)	28798	(44.9)	35493	(44.2)	
	F	5512	(54.4)	7249	(54.3)	8388	(54.8)	9562	(56.6)	9707	(56.4)	14894	(55.6)	22421	(54.1)	30098	(54.3)	35329	(55.1)	44813	(55.8)	
Kingston	M	3280	(47.5)	4334	(47.6)	4919	(47.1)	5203	(45.2)	5546	(45.6)	8223	(46.5)	10915	(47.3)	13573	(47.6)	18739	(47.9)	27178	(48.0)	
	F	3629	(52.5)	4773	(52.4)	5523	(52.9)	6296	(54.8)	6624	(54.4)	9473	(53.5)	12174	(52.7)	14968	(52.4)	20388	(52.1)	29403	(52.0)	
TOTAL	M	14844	(44.7)	18346	(45.2)	20425	(44.7)	21902	(43.5)	24582	(46.4)	35473	(49.2)	48325	(49.9)	57581	(50.7)	62417	(48.8)	76554	(48.1)	91069
	F	18382	(55.3)	22221	(54.8)	25223	(55.3)	28487	(56.5)	28450	(53.6)	36623	(50.8)	46503	(50.1)	56014	(49.3)	65605	(51.2)	82724	(51.9)	97064

Discrepancies in the figures for 1841 and 1851 are caused by the inclusion of convicts and military personnel in the sex ratio statistics but not in the population figures in Table 4.

Portsea is similarly affected in 1811 and 1821.

It must, however, be remembered that the figures for the four districts on Portsea Island between 1801 and 1841 are estimates produced in the 1851 census, Vol I p.49

Alterations in the census enumeration districts in 1901 prevent statistical analysis of the four separate communities.

staymakers who collectively filled over 1,100 jobs for women in 1841 and over 2,800 in 1851. Even allowing for some possible under-enumeration in 1841, an increase of over 150 per cent is impressive growth. Dressmaking was an activity to be expected in all large towns in nineteenth-century England and was only slightly over-represented in Portsmouth. Seamstresses, however, were more than five times more numerous in Portsmouth than in the rest of England and the staymakers over fifteen times. Clearly some form of industrial concentration had taken place. Most of the seamstresses appear to have been involved in shirtmaking, advertisements being placed in local newspapers by Landport agents for women to work at home. One advertisement in 1846 was for '600 white shirtmakers',[73] to work at home and, if demands for labour of this size were being met, then not only was the domestic (putting-out) system expanding in mid-nineteenth-century Portsmouth, but also an explanation of the rapid growth of the clothing industries in the 1840s is provided. However, a greater proportional expansion occurred in staymaking, with a rise of 168 per cent in its labour force in the 1840s making Portsmouth England's most important centre for the corset industry in the nineteenth century.[74] When the industry developed in Portsmouth is not clear. There were two staymakers noted in the town in the late 1790s and six in the eighteenth century as a whole.[75] In 1831, nineteen male staymakers aged over nineteen were listed in Portsmouth and its suburbs, including Gosport and Alverstoke. By 1841 there were fifty-three males, representing 26 per cent of total staymakers. If the number of males employed remained proportionally similar in 1831, then some sixty or so women were likely to have been employed at that time. All would have been domestic workers and probably their products were supplied to the local officers' wives and the rising middle class. By 1841, however, with 233 employed and the industry expanding, the market must have been wider than local, especially when ware-houses were established by those organising the putting-out of work.[76] That would certainly have been essential in the 1840s, since by 1851 over 500 workers were employed.

Clearly, Portsmouth expanded 'domestic activities', both in service and industry, to take advantage of the surplus cheap female labour available. One other classification of women enumerated in the census helped to solve the employment problem for surplus females. In 1841 over 1,800 women were stated to be of independent means, compared to only 421 men. In 1851 the numbers were respectively under 600 and under 100. Obviously some reclassifying had taken place. Even though more women were widowed than men, some 1,800 women of independent means in 1841 calls for an explanation, particularly since their numbers were greater than those in both the clothing industries and domestic service. The only satisfactory interpretation would seem to be that many of these women belonged to a 'profession' for which Portsmouth had long been known. In 1795 one visitor, less than captivated by the charms of the town, felt it necessary to state that

> . . . hordes of profligate females are seen reeling in drunkenness, or plying upon the streets in open day with a broad immodesty. . . .
>
> To form to yourself an idea of these tender, languishing nymphs, these lovely, *fighting ornaments* of the fair sex, imagine a something of more than Amazonian stature having a crimson countenance, emblazoned with all the effrontery of Cyprian confidence and

broad Bacchanalian folly; give to her bold countenance the warlike features of two wounded cheeks, a tumid nose, scarred and battered brows, and a pair of blackened eyes, with balls of red; then add to her sides a pair of brawny arms, fit to encounter a Colossus, and set her upon two ankles like the fixed supporters of a gate. Afterwards, by way of apparel, put upon her a loose flying cape, a man's black hat, a torn neckerchief, stone rings on her fingers, and a dirty white, or tawdry flowered gown, with short apron, and a pink petticoat; and thus will you have something very like the figure of a 'Portsmouth Poll'.[77]

This colourful, if not lurid, description of Portsmouth's prostitutes suggests that, at least in wartime, they existed in large numbers and it seems more than likely that many of the 1,800 women described as 'of independent means' in the 1841 census would have been members of the 'oldest profession'. Even in peacetime, in the nineteenth century, it was stated that large numbers of prostitutes frequented Portsmouth, some 1,355 being registered in 1865.[78]

The existence of such large numbers of prostitutes is explained not only by the need of many women without husbands to seek financial support, but also by the presence of large numbers of single young men with no counterbalancing proportion of single young women. It seems likely that these prostitutes acted as a damper on the potentially explosive mix of the sexes on Portsea Island since, despite the imbalanced sex ratio and marital status, illegitimacy ratios did not rise. Illegitimate births actually fell from just over 4 per cent of registered births in 1861 to just over 3 per cent from 1871 to 1901, lower than was the case for the rest of Hampshire.[79] ·

Despite the decline in the proportion of illegitimate births in Victorian Portsmouth, it could be expected that, with the island's population growing more rapidly than the nation's, births generally would be at a high level and that consequently the proportion of children – those under fifteen – would be greater than in England as a whole. Especially should this be the case since the island's population growth was fuelled by in-migration, the proportion of residents born outside the county rising from 42 per cent in 1851 to 50 per cent in 1871. Since most migration was over short distances, if migrants from the rest of Hampshire were to be included, then the real levels of migration into Portsmouth must have been considerably higher. As the majority of migration was undertaken by young people in the child-bearing age groups,[80] high birth rates should have been recorded in the second half of the nineteenth century. Yet, while under-fifteens in England formed over 36 per cent of the nation's population between 1851 and 1871,[81] unexpectedly in Portsea Island from 1841 to 1881 children formed a smaller proportion of the population, representing from 32 to less than 35 per cent of the total. The explanation for such a relatively small child population lies in the numerous military and naval personnel distorting the age structure. Since most of the servicemen were based in the town of Portsmouth or in Portsea, when the island's population is separated into its four districts, it is in these two districts that numbers of children are at their lowest. In Portsmouth Town, where proportionately more service personnel were present between 1851 and 1881, children constituted only 22–25 per cent of the population; in Portsea they formed 24.5–27 per cent of the total. The suburbs of Kingston and Landport, conversely, demonstrate the high child population which would be expected in rapidly growing communities. Over the same period Landport's under-fifteen population formed between 35.4 and 37.3 per cent of the population whilst Kingston's rose from 37 to 39.4 per cent, thus almost matching the nation's largest ever cohort of under-fifteen-year-olds in 1826.[82] By contrast, of course, Portsmouth Town and Portsea had considerably larger proportions of their populations in the working age groups of 15 to 60, rising to as much as three-quarters of the total in the town in 1881, and more than that in Portsea in the same year. Kingston and Landport, with much larger dependent sectors of children, had only between 53 and 57 per cent of their populations in the working age groups. The elderly, those over sixty years of age, were some 4–8 per cent of the total population of the various districts, the lowest proportion of the elderly being in Portsmouth Town and the highest in Kingston, giving that suburb the largest combined dependent sector of all four districts.

With Portsea Island by 1901 containing nearly three-quarters of the region's population, its importance cannot be doubted and it is noticeable that, if Gosport and Alverstoke are added to the island's total, then nearly 84 per cent of the total regional population was provided by the two harbour communities. Growth elsewhere, as in Fareham, the third largest community in the region with over 8,000 people, as well as Wymering and Farlington, was equally likely to have resulted from Portsmouth's increasing influence.

In the two and a half centuries from 1650 to 1900, Portsmouth had grown by more than forty-fold. No community could have expanded at such a pace without the attendant problems of overcrowding, sanitation, water supply, drainage, vice and poverty. Portsmouth was no exception, as was demonstrated in the description of crowded Messum's Court in Old Portsmouth:

> Below sea-level, and therefore very damp . . . reached through a tunnel only two feet wide. Here 116 people lived, some of them in cellars, with one privy between them and one standpipe which supplied water for perhaps ten minutes a day. Through the court ran a large open drain as well as an open midden and when this was emptied the contents would remain for three days on the surface opposite the exit, suffocating the whole area with its stench.[83]

Overcrowding in life was paralleled in Portsmouth by overcrowding in death. Local doctor, Henry Slight, commented in 1850 on the burial grounds in both Portsmouth and Portsea. Of St Mary's churchyard, Portsea, he stated it was 'full even to repletion' and of St Thomas's, Portsmouth, he noted 'if the walls were to give way, the bodies would fall into the street. . . . The gasses of putrefaction . . . readily escape, poisoning the atmosphere and dealing death and disease in all directions.'[84]

Slight was commenting in the wake of Portsmouth's only major epidemic of the first half of the nineteenth century – the cholera outbreak of 1848. However, the average annual death rate in Portsmouth in the 1840s prior to the cholera outbreak was over twenty-five per thousand and, since the recently formed national Board of Health was empowered, on request, to investigate any area where mortality exceeded twenty-three per thousand, an inquiry began in December 1848. Robert Rawlinson, Superintendent Inspector of the General Board of Health, heard the evidence and reported in 1850. His major findings concerned the 'ill-paved and unclean streets, imperfect privy accommodation, crowded courts and houses with large exposed middens and cesspools.' Disease was 'traced to the undrained and crowded districts, to deficient ventilation, to the absence of a full water supply, and of sewers and drains generally.'[85] Rawlinson also commented on the lack of adequate powers of local government and the detrimental effect of the fortifications of Portsmouth and Portsea in interfering with natural drainage. These were both factors which were clearly not unconnected with the restrictive naval and military presence in Portsmouth.

Finally, what may well have been the best solution for Portsmouth's economic and social problems would have been the ability to develop its economy on a broader base and be less dependent on the dockyard. There is little doubt that the borough authorities were conscious of this need, attempting to expand commercial trade in the harbour. The Admiralty, however, was opposed to such developments, so much so that the authorities explored the possibilities of locating commercial docks on the eastern side of Portsea Island in Langstone Harbour away from the town and the dockyard.[86] The cost of this proposal, which included a ship canal from east of Southsea Castle to Langstone Harbour, was to be £2 million, an astonishing sum for the town in the 1840s. There were clear disadvantages to this scheme, not only Langstone Harbour's inadequate entrance necessitating the canal, but also the limited deep water anchorage. Hence, the council yet again in 1851 approached the Board of Ordnance to see if the defence authorities would allow the development of the Mill Pond as a commercial dock. Once again permission was refused.

That Portsmouth consequently grew on a narrow economic base was noted in White's *Directory* (1878), the entry stating that the 'borough derives considerable support from its extensive dockyard and naval and military establishments, but these have prevented it from rising to that commercial importance to which it would have risen if the government would have allowed the construction of large Commercial Docks.'[87] Had the government done so, it can hardly be doubted that the region's population in general and Portsea Island's in particular would have seen even more phenomenal growth in the nineteenth century. But the truth was that it was in distant London that decisions were made which determined not only Portsmouth's port development but also its population growth.

PART THREE

THE NATURAL
ENVIRONMENT

8

GEOLOGY AND PHYSICAL LANDSCAPE

Brian Daley and David Carter

A relatively simple relationship exists between the major rock types and landforms of the Portsmouth region. The Portsdown ridge, the area's most prominent landform, is developed on the Chalk, an erosionally resistant rock in comparison with the softer sands and clays to the north and south which support areas of low relief. A variety of geological and geomorphological features provide insights into environmental change extending over many millions of years, the last two of which have witnessed exceptionally frequent and marked fluctuations in climatic and sea-level conditions. These changes have been significant influences on local variations in the character of the physical landscape of the region.

Until the second half of the nineteenth century, few publications on the geology of the Portsmouth region had appeared.[1] Soon after 1850, the earliest geological maps of the region were published by the Geological Survey. Following a resurvey of the area on a six-inch scale, one-inch geological sheets were published for Portsmouth in 1893, Fareham in 1900 and Southampton in 1899.[2] The Portsmouth and Fareham sheets in slightly amended form are still in use today, whilst, following a recent resurvey, a new Southampton sheet is currently in preparation. From the 1860s, a number of papers on the local geology appeared, including Meyer's account of the London Clay,[3] facilitated by excavations for the extension of Portsmouth Dockyard, and a description of the Stubbington section by Fisher in a classic paper on the Bracklesham Beds.[4] The first two decades of the twentieth century were marked by more comprehensive publications, including the 'Sheet Memoirs' of the Geological Survey, an account of the water supply of Hampshire and descriptions of the local Chalk.[5]

More recently, there has been renewed academic and commercial interest in the geology of the region. British Petroleum's search for oil resulted in the production of a report on the first deep borings undertaken in southern England.[6] The publication of the 'Wight' 1:250,000 geological map, which includes the distribution of offshore outcrops and both Bouguer gravity anomaly and aeromagnetic maps, in part reflects an increasing emphasis on economic investigations.[7] Recent academic work has led to a number of publications, particularly on the Tertiary strata.[8] Chatwin's *The Hampshire Basin and Adjoining Areas*, recently revised by Melville and Freshney, places the Portsmouth region in a broader geological context, whilst West's review of the Solent area provides a concise compilation of contemporary and earlier research.[9]

Britain is richly endowed with a variety of rocks, some thousands of millions of years old. Those which crop out in central southern and south-eastern England are comparatively young, less than 135 million years old, and comprise relatively gently folded sedimentary strata of Cretaceous and Tertiary age. The Tertiary strata are preserved in two downwarped tectonic basins – the London Basin and the Hampshire Basin – the Portsmouth region being situated on the northern margin of the latter. The rocks of the Portsmouth region comprise the Chalk, which outcrops both on Portsdown Hill and further north on the dip slope of the South Downs, the relatively soft Tertiary sediments to the north and south of Portsdown, and the variety of Quaternary deposits forming a veneer over the 'solid' strata. The outcrop pattern of the Chalk and the Tertiary rocks emphasises the region's superficially simple structure (Figure 1), although it is now known to have had a more complex tectonic history. Portsdown Hill is located on the approximately east–west asymmetrical Portsdown Anticline, a fold with dips of two or three degrees on its southern flank (limb) and none above twelve degrees on its northern limb. The Portsdown axis actually runs south of Portsdown Hill, extending along a line from Bosham through Farlington, passing near the Nelson Monument and north-westwards to Knowle Farm near Whitely.

To the south of the Portsdown axis, the Tertiary strata dip southwards at a few degrees on the northern limb of the Solent Syncline, the axis of which crosses the northern part of the Isle of Wight. Between Portsdown and the northern margin of the Portsmouth region, Tertiary strata are preserved in the Forest of Bere (or Chichester) Syncline. The asymmetry of this fold is clearly indicated by the variation in width of the London Clay along the strike. The axis runs just north of west, passing north of Havant and Bedhampton and almost through Southwick, close to the steeper southern limb of the fold where small outliers of Bracklesham Beds are preserved. The syncline deepens to the west of the River Meon where the Bracklesham Beds outcrop is more extensive (see Figure 1).

There is little indication of geological faulting of any magnitude in the rocks exposed in the Portsmouth region, but evidence of some movement may be seen in the presence of crushed flints in such localities as Downend Quarry, Portsdown, and the displacement of outcrops to either side of the Meon Valley perhaps indicates the existence of a hitherto unrecorded fault running approximately north–south (see Figure 1). It is, however, now widely recognised that the major folds of this and other adjacent areas were produced not by compression, but in response to the movement of large deep-seated faults.

The oldest strata exposed in the Portsmouth region are of Upper Cretaceous age (93 to 65 million years ago). Whilst some understanding of the subsurface rocks and structure has been derived from geophysical studies, more detailed evidence of the stratigraphical sequence is limited to data derived from the Portsdown Borehole (Figure 2) and what may be extrapolated from the few other deep boreholes within the Hampshire Basin but outside the Portsmouth region.[10]

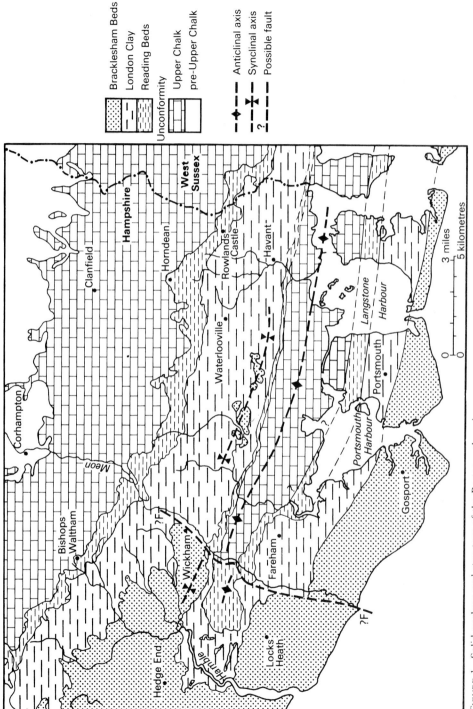

Bracklesham Beds
London Clay
Reading Beds
Unconformity
Upper Chalk
pre-Upper Chalk

Anticlinal axis
Synclinal axis
Possible fault

FIGURE 1   Solid geology and structure of the Portsmouth region

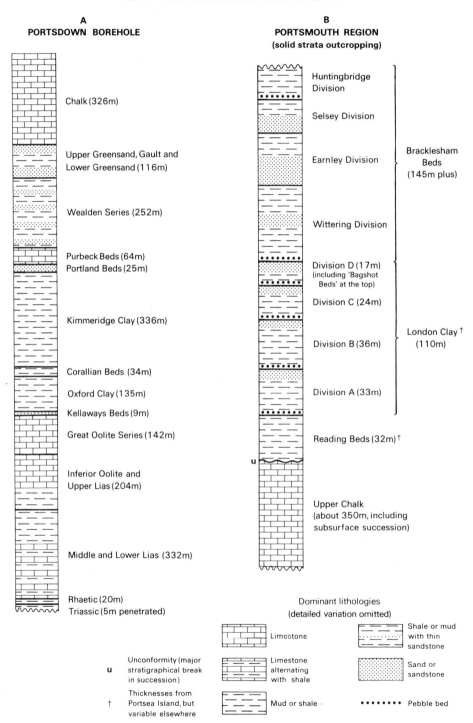

FIGURE 2   The geological succession in the Portsmouth region. (A(Portsdown Borehole) after Taitt and Kent, 1958)

The Portsdown Borehole penetrated 1,998m of sedimentary strata and ceased 4.9m below the top of the Triassic (see Figure 2). It seems clear that for much of the Jurassic and Cretaceous (from about 190 to 65 million years ago), the Portsmouth region was part of a subsiding sedimentary basin. Much of the sequence represents marine deposits. Shallow water marine conditions are indicated by such strata as the Great Oolite Limestones whilst deeper waters are represented, for example, by the thick Kimmeridge Clay, a formation which is thought to have been the source rock for some of the petroleum currently being extracted to the west in Dorset. The former presence of hypersaline surface waters is represented by thick calcium sulphate deposits in the basal Purbeck Beds, whilst the Wealden strata are essentially fluvial (river) deposits developed during an extensive period of marine regression (retreat). The variations in the environments represented, from deep and shallow marine to fluvial, may reflect vertical movements of the sedimentary basin, whilst actual breaks in the rock succession suggest early tectonic movement perhaps associated with faulting along what is now the Portsdown Axis. Evidence from the recent Marchwood Geothermal Borehole near Southampton indicates that the Jurassic rocks of the succession thin rapidly westwards (757.4m compared with 1,280m at Portsdown).

The greater local knowledge of the Chalk and the younger rocks of the Portsmouth region reflects their presence in surface outcrop. Even so, exposures are very limited; the coast is flat-lying and only in a few places are there low cliff sections (e.g. Lee-on-the-Solent) or foreshore sections not covered by recent material. The Chalk may be examined in quarries, such as those at Paulsgrove and Downend,[11] whilst local brickpits, when operative, provided useful sources of information. Data from numerous wells and shallow excavations have been of considerable value. Useful information was obtained from dockyard excavations in the nineteenth century; in more recent years, the M27, A3(M) and other road-works have provided opportunities for further research.

The oldest exposed rocks, the Chalk, brought the long period of marine Upper Cretaceous sedimentation to an end. The Chalk, over 326m deep in the Portsdown Borehole, represents about 12 million years of geological time and formed in a sea which covered much of Europe for this period. A white limestone, the Chalk is mainly composed of minute planktonic plants called coccoliths. Macro-fossil remains of sea urchins, bivalves and other invertebrates also occur and it is now considered that the Chalk accumulated in marine waters 100–600m deep.[12] The Upper Chalk is about 98 per cent pure calcium carbonate, apart from the characteristic flint which formed secondarily after deposition, following the redistribution of silica probably derived from the dissolution of fossil sponge remains.

The Chalk is overlain unconformably by sediments of Palaeogene (Lower Tertiary) age (65 to 26 million years ago), although the Palaeogene rocks of the Portsmouth region accumulated in a few million years from about 50 million years ago. No angular discordance is locally apparent between the Palaeogene and Cretaceous strata, although the unconformity represents a break of some 15 million years following a period of late Cretaceous warping.

In Palaeogene times, the Portsmouth region was in a different geographical situation. It was some 12° of latitude south of its present position [13] and the climate, as inferred particularly from the fossil record, was neotropical.[14] Furthermore, it was located in an essentially shallow westward extension of a sea which spread over much of northern Europe. The local Palaeogene sediments reflect the fluctuating environments of this marginal marine location and the varying position of the Palaeogene shoreline.

Geological Survey maps show four Palaeogene units present in the Portsmouth region (the oldest at the bottom):

> Bracklesham Beds
> Bagshot Sands
> London Clay
> Reading Beds

Current usage is such that the Bagshot Sands is best considered as a sandy unit within the London Clay. Hence, a three-fold major subdivision of the Palaeogene strata may be recognised (see Figure 2).

Formerly called the 'Red Clay' or 'Plastic Clay', the Reading Beds locally comprise mainly colour-mottled clays and thin sandstones. The formation outcrops to the north and south of Portsdown and on the northern side of the Forest of Bere Syncline, though exposures are exceptionally poor. White mentioned that the Reading Beds were visible in low cliffs near Stoke on Hayling Island and that, in foreshore exposures, the typical red colour facilitated the recognition of the formation.[15] In the nineteenth century, the formation was worked in a number of brickpits and the 'Stamshaw Clay', as it was called locally, was found to be ideal for rendering the dockyard 'dams' watertight. The Reading Beds vary in thickness from about 30 to 38m, with 32.3m recorded from a well in the dockyard, and 30m at St James' Hospital.[16] The contact with the Chalk is rarely seen, although it was exposed during improvements to the A3 near the Admiralty Research Establishment when large solution hollows in the Chalk, filled with Reading Beds sediments, were visible. The Reading Beds are locally unfossiliferous, perhaps not surprisingly, since their characteristic red mottling is thought to indicate some degree of weathering during early Palaeogene times.[17] In all probability, the Reading Beds represent fluvial deposits, the margin of the sea having retreated eastwards at this time. The London Clay mainly comprises silty clays, together with sands and thin pebble beds, representing a transgressive marine phase over much of northern Europe. In the Portsmouth region, the London Clay occurs to the north of Portsdown Hill in the Forest of Bere Syncline, and also to the south where it forms an outcrop from 1 to 3km wide. Exposures are very rare. Extensions to the dockyard from 1867 onwards, when excavations extended down to some 13m below low water, provided a major opportunity for study,[18] whilst wells, site investigation boreholes and excavations for drainage tunnels have provided further information.[19] Amongst former exposures to the western end of the region were those at Fareham[20] and the now disused brickpit at Lower Swanwick,[21] whilst an extant but small section occurs north of Elson in Fareham Creek.[22]

The London Clay succession at Portsmouth has been described by King (Figure 3) who recognises four divisions or sedimentary cycles, A, B, C and D in ascending order.[23] Each comprises a basal pebble bed, followed by silty clays passing stratigraphically upwards into sandy clays and sands. The upper, sandier part of Division D includes what was formerly mapped as the Bagshot Sands. Marine fossils characterise the succession, although Division D is unfossiliferous. Large

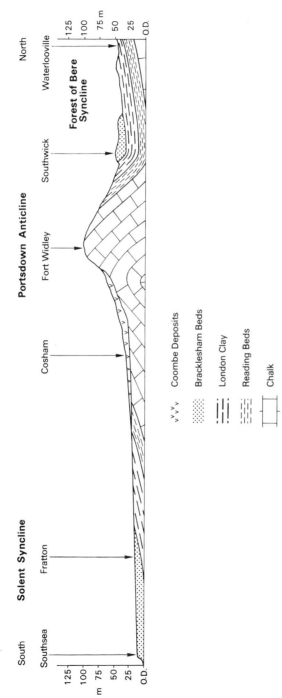

FIGURE 3   North–south geological and topographical section across the Portsmouth region

concretions near the top of Division A contain abundant molluscs, whilst some eighty species are recorded from the top part of Division B. Palaeoenvironmentally, each division began with a marine transgression, the pebbles perhaps representing the remains of nearshore shingle bars. Above, the silty clays resulted from slow deposition in a low energy marine environment. The build-up of sediment led ultimately to shallowing and the progradation seawards of coarse silts and sands from the margins of the marine basin, such sediments probably representing nearshore sand bars or tidal channels. There is no indication that non-marine conditions were ever established in the Portsmouth region at this time. However, the succession thins westwards to about 80m at Lower Swanwick, whilst in east Dorset contemporary deposits in part represent fluvial deposition.[24]

Nowhere within the Portsmouth region is the full sequence of the Bracklesham Beds present. To the north of Portsmouth, small outliers mark the axis of the Forest of Bere Syncline, although the outcrop widens to the west of the River Meon. The formation outcrops in the south of Portsea Island on the shallow dipping northern limb of the Solent Syncline, from Gosport to the Hamble, mainly under a cover of Quaternary material, and is developed thickly below the Spithead Forts.[25] The Bracklesham Beds comprise sandy clays, often greenish in colour due to the presence of the mineral glauconite, as well as lighter-coloured sands and laminated carbonaceous deposits; pebble beds also occur at various levels. The northern outliers are poorly fossiliferous, whilst the coastal outcrops are rich in fossils. Like the London Clay, the Bracklesham Beds are cyclic, reflecting alternations of advancing (transgressive) and retreating (regressive) marine phases. Unlike the London Clay of the Hampshire Basin, there is clear evidence that, whilst marine conditions predominated in the east, to the west an area of non-marine, fluvial sedimentation existed.

Exposures are relatively poor, although the formation may be studied near Lee-on-the-Solent where it appears in low cliff sections below Quaternary gravels and on the foreshore at low water, particularly during spring tides. The section was first described by Fisher who recognised over 32m of fossiliferous sandy clays and sands.[26] These beds have recently been redescribed and assigned to the two uppermost sedimentary cycles of the Bracklesham Beds, known as the Selsey and Huntingbridge Divisions respectively.[27] The section has been known for its fossils since the early nineteenth century; besides molluscs and other invertebrates, shark, ray and other fish teeth and even occasionaly bird, reptile and mammalian bones occur.[28] Further details of the formation to the west of the region have also been obtained from temporary sections, whilst earlier descriptions appear in White.[29]

No younger Palaeogene strata occur in the Portsmouth region, although the more complete succession in the Isle of Wight clearly indicates that sedimentation continued in what is now southern Hampshire at least until early Oligocene times (about 36 million years ago). Subsequently, the succession was affected by mid-Tertiary earth movements which led to the development of the essentially east–west trending folds of southern England. When the climax of these earth movements occurred is uncertain, but it was probably in late Oligocene or Miocene times (around 30 to 20 million years ago). Mention has already been made that such folds reflect movement along deep-seated faults, structures which had first developed some 200 million years previously. Occasional earth tremors suggest that some minor earth movement still occurs within the region.[30]

Though debate exists as to the duration of the so-called mid-Tertiary earth movements,[31] the contribution of combined uplift and folding to the physical landscape of the Portsmouth region has been decisive. It has created the Portsdown Anticline and complementary synclines of the Forest of Bere and the Solent. Although substantially modified by subsequent denudation, these fold structures provide the essential framework for the development of the region's geomorphological character. In this respect, the region has much in common with the landscape character of large areas of south-central and south-eastern England.

Rock outcrop trends are approximately east to west, following the orientation of the principal fold axes (see Figure 1). In part, landforms reflect contrasts in the erosional resistance of these rocks; thus, the principal geomorphological sub-regions also have a general east–west alignment. The Chalk ridge of Portsdown is the dominant feature, flanked to the south and south-west by a narrow coastal plain just above sea-level, and to the north by an area of limited relief where mechanically weak Palaeogene sands and clays have been readily eroded. Geomorphologically, Portsdown was once a considerably larger feature, for much of the southern limb of the fold has been truncated by erosion and subsequently concealed beneath a veneer of geologically very recent deposits. The former extension of Portsdown can be determined from shallow boreholes and by the outcrop of Chalk in some of the low bluffs around the margins of Langstone and Chichester harbours (see Figure 1). Thus, although the Chalk is demonstrably more resistant than the Palaeogene formations, due partly to its permeability and high porosity which removes running water from the surface, it has not been immune to long-term denudation.

In places, more subtle contrasts in rock lithology and their contribution to landform development may be identified. An example is the discontinuous low, north-facing escarpment within the Forest of Bere area, particularly near West Walk and North Boarhunt, where a pebbly horizon within the 'Bagshot Sands' provides a more resistant and protective cap rock to the underlying weak sands and clays. The feature is not continuous because stream erosion has removed a considerable proportion of this once more extensive outcrop. Elsewhere, in the area between Fareham and Titchfield, geologically recent gravels have offered protection to the underlying solid rocks, resulting in the very level and slightly elevated plateaux of this district.

The north–south geological section (see Figure 3) illustrates the influence of structural and lithological factors on the primary form of the local landscape, as a view from the summit of Portsdown convincingly shows. To the south, beyond the steep eroded slope of Portsdown, is the flat coastal plain, partly flooded by the 'bottleneck'-shaped estuaries of Portsmouth and Langstone harbours. Further south, the synclinal basin occupied by the Solent, Spithead and the northern, relatively low-lying Palaeogene sediments of the Isle of Wight, is ultimately bounded by the central Chalk ridge of the island. The view to the north is somewhat analogous, since, beyond the lower elevation and limited relief of the Forest of Bere Syncline, the Chalk may be seen to re-emerge from beneath the Palaeogene strata to form the backslope of the South Downs. The gradient of this feature is gentle, but rises steadily to culminate in the prominent summits of Old Winchester Hill, Butser Hill and West Harting Down, each located at the boundary between the backslope and the steep scarp slope of the Chalk upland.

The influence of rock and dependent soil types on the contrasting character of the rural landscape is very apparent, for whilst the Chalk supports an 'open' landscape of large arable fields and a general absence of woodland, the Palaeogene country is a more detailed mosaic of woodland, heathland and small fields mostly devoted to permanent pasture. Historical factors partly explain this striking contrast,[32] but geological, geomorphological and pedological factors remain the prime determinants. The sympathy between geological structure and rock types and geomorphological character is by no means consistent. Such is the case with the drainage patterns, for whilst the upper and middle sections of the River Wallington conform to the influence of regional slope and geological strike, there are other drainage elements which appear to be independent of these usually strong influences. The River Meon flows almost due north–south and the lower Wallington also has this alignment, both rivers cutting across east–west fold structures. This discordance presents challenging interpretational problems. Explanations from the local landscape alone are difficult to find and need to be related to the overall pattern of drainage discordance that characterises much of central-southern and south-eastern England.

Jones has argued that north–south orientated 'master' streams evolved prior to the development of the full amplitude of the folds across which they flow.[33] Such rivers would have had to entrench valleys at a rate at least equivalent to the rate of uplift associated with the folding. Drainage elements that conform to the east–west geological trend may be considered as later additions which developed as tributaries along outcrops of relatively weak rocks. This hypothesis suggests that the north–south rivers are very ancient landscape elements and this view has received the support of other researchers,[34] despite the difficulty in proving it from field evidence. In the case of the lower Meon, the coincidence of the river valley with the

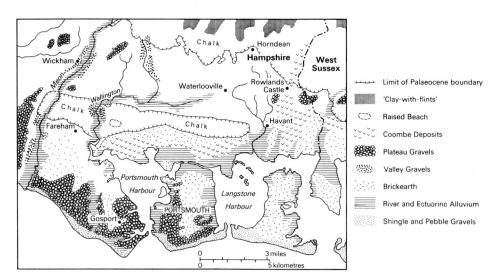

FIGURE 4 Drift deposits of the Portsmouth region

fault postulated earlier implies that this part of the river cannot be older than the mid-Tertiary period of deformation.

This drainage hypothesis conflicts with what was, until recently, the definitive explanatory model of landscape evolution in south-eastern England proposed by Wooldridge and Linton.[35] They placed emphasis on the rôle of the Calabrian (now Waltonian) marine transgression of early Quaternary times, arguing that the ensuing rise of sea-level (up to about 220m above Ordnance Datum (OD)), transformed all southern and south-eastern England below this level to a marine sediment-covered surface. As the sea withdrew, rivers developed down the southward-declining regional slope and without reference to the underlying geology. They became progressively more entrenched as the sea-level continued to fall and as their erosional energy increased, thereby reviving differences of relief that reflect the underlying contrasting lithologies. The River Meon and other local landscape features have been cited in support of this hypothesis, but field evidence is at best scanty and ambiguous, and at worst non-existent. The evidence which most strongly influenced their denudation chronology hypothesis is found in the North Downs, but even this has been subject to reinterpretation.[36] Thus, although the reality of the Calabrian transgression is not denied, its long-term significance is seriously questioned. The assumptions on which this 'superimposed' drainage hypothesis is based are now seen to be insecure.[37]

Although the region's drainage pattern is probably much older than the two to two and a half million years implied by Wooldridge and Linton, the landforms of valleys, hill-slopes and summits are much younger, as they continue to be affected by surface denudation. Large amounts of erosion were accomplished in the Neogene (from 26 to approximately 2 million years ago), but there are some interesting legacies from earlier times. One example is the 'sub-Palaeogene' surface of marine erosion below the Reading Beds. Where the latter has been removed, this ancient surface, over 50 million years old, has been exhumed. It is best seen to the north of the Reading Beds outcrop within the Forest of Bere Syncline, where the 'Clay-with-Flints' deposits may be interpreted as degraded Reading Beds.[38]

The geomorphological evolution of the Portsmouth region during the Quaternary period is indicated by both sedimentological (Figure 4) and morphological evidence.[39] Constructing an agreed chronology of events is difficult, partly because the field evidence is incomplete and partly because the relevant deposits are impossible to date accurately.[40] Important evidence is provided by erosional platforms and terraces within the major valleys, notably that of the Meon, and grouped according to height-range in an attempt to reconstruct former stationary sea-levels.[41] Some are purely morphological forms, whilst others support gravel deposits. Those sloping towards present-day rivers, for example near Wickham at 97m, 70m, 45m and 21m OD, are interpreted as being of fluvial origin. Together they indicate a progressive but spasmodic fall of sea-level throughout the Quaternary period, with sea-levels much lower than that of today implied by buried terraces, channels and gravel deposits beneath the Solent.[42] During these phases of low sea-level, which may be correlated with periods of world-wide expansion of ice-sheets and glaciers, the 'Solent River' had a clear identity. This river, with its roughly west–east alignment, is an ancestral element of the regional drainage pattern and was the 'master' stream to which all other rivers, the Meon, Hamble and those now flooded by Portsmouth and Langstone harbours, were tributaries.

The 'Solent River' appears to have been an eastward extension of the River Frome, now draining into Poole Harbour to the west, which lost its identity following the most recent sea-level rise severing the Isle of Wight from the Hampshire mainland.

The overall fall of sea-level throughout the Quaternary is complicated by the superimposition of climatically-controlled oscillations. The 'lows' approximately correlate with glacial maxima, the 'highs' with warmer, intervening, interglacial phases. The modern period of rising sea-level, resulting in the flooding of the Solent, Southampton Water and the lower portions of their tributary valleys, may represent no more than another interglacial. This post-glacial period is designated the Flandrian Stage and has been operative for about 11,500 years. The evidence for periods of higher sea-levels includes erosional surfaces that maintain a very restricted height-range over a wide area. These 'horizontal segments' occur at two general levels in the Portsmouth region and are specifically represented by the 'Raised Beach' deposits at Down End, near Fareham, at 39m OD and the 'Lower Beach' deposit at Cam's Hall at 2.9m OD. The sediments preserved at these sites appear to indicate storm beaches associated with ancient cliff-lines at these heights.[43] The evidence for these two former shorelines is much more extensive and more fully interpreted in the West Sussex coastal plain and adjacent backslope of the South Downs.[44] The higher shoreline may date from the penultimate interglacial of the Quaternary, the Hoxnian, whilst the lower records the most recent complete interglacial interlude, the Ipswichian. An alternative interpretation,[45] involving a pro-glacial Lake Solent and glacio-fluvial deposition of the higher level sediments at the time of extensive glacier ice presence in the central English Channel, has not received serious support. The Ipswichian age is determined by the fossils from peat horizons incorporated within coeval deposits, at Selsey, Stone and also near Lepe and Calshot.[46]

Although glacial conditions need not be implicated in the deposition of these evidently marine sediments, they are strongly suggested by numerous erratic blocks that occur along the foreshores and at some inland locations within the coastal plain of the Portsmouth area. Immediately to the east, they are common in Bracklesham Bay within pits on the surface of the Palaeogene rocks exposed over the shore platform.[47] Many of the blocks, some of considerable size, are locally derived, but others originated as far west as Cornwall and in the Channel Islands. Several of the larger blocks have been incorporated into older buildings such as St Peter's Church, North Hayling, since they represented a locally rare resource of good building stone. Nineteenth-century geologists noted their frequent presence on Portsea Island[48] and good examples of sarsen erratics can still be seen on the Lee-on-the-Solent foreshore and between Hill Head and Warsash. Their presence throughout this area defies easy interpretation, but they were perhaps transported by floating ice or icebergs that were 'grounded' on the shoreline, implying a sea-level close to that of the present time but coinciding with the later part of a glacial period.

The terraces of both fluvial and marine origin, forming a partially destroyed morphological 'staircase' throughout the Portsmouth region, support spreads of poorly-sorted, angular to sub-angular flints collectively termed Plateau Gravel (see Figure 4). There is no obvious textural differentiation between the gravels at various altitudes, but those nearest to modern sea-level are the most extensive and are regarded as younger than those at greater elevations. They occupy the area west of Portsmouth, especially between Hill Head and Warsash, much of the

Gosport peninsula and southern Portsea Island, and are best exposed in the low cliffs between Hill Head and the Hamble estuary. The higher gravels have doubtless been re-eroded to contribute to the larger gravel spreads near the Solent coastline. Fabric and textural analysis of the extensive Plateau Gravels in the southern New Forest has indicated that they were deposited by rivers with discharges and sediment loads much greater than those of their modern successors.[49] The equivalent deposits of the Portsmouth region are thought to have had a similar origin. The anomalously large size of the valley accommodating the present-day rivers implies that the latter were once more powerful, whilst the lack of sorting of the gravels suggests the former presence of braided streams or periods of flood deposition.

The environment at the time of gravel deposition may have been periglacial, that is, comparable with tundra conditions in high latitudes today. Flint implements have been identified in the Plateau Gravels, although they do not indicate an unambiguous age since they could have been reworked from older deposits. None the less, detailed research on the micromorphology of shaped implements may give additional information on their post-depositional history.[50] The impact of periglacial climatic phases is further evidenced by deposits of Coombe Rock, a usually poorly-sorted but occasionally stratified accumulation of chalk and flint fragments in a matrix of comminuted chalk, with clay and sand particles.[51] Such deposits occur only within or adjacent to the chalklands, especially in the bottoms of dry valleys and as low-angle fans leading away from chalk outcrops. Extensive spreads of Coombe Rock, whilst present in the West Sussex coastal plain contiguous with the backslope of the South Downs, are largely absent from the equivalent location in the Portsmouth region. Coombe Rock does, however, form the low-gradient surface south of Portsdown between Cosham and Fareham and occurs below the more recent deposits of northern Portsmouth Harbour. It is the product of freeze–thaw weathering of the Chalk and subsequent slow downslope movement of this debris when saturated by water during short summer periods and when the climate improved. Periglacial phases have contributed substantially to the weathering and erosion of the landscape. Notable legacies of such phases were dry valleys on the chalklands, which were eroded when subsurface ice rendered the Chalk temporarily impermeable. An alternative view is that these valleys predate periglacial conditions and have only been modified by them. Detailed study of the sediments and non-marine molluscan fossils of Coombe Rock infilling dry valleys has given valuable information concerning late Pleistocene and post-glacial climatic changes in this area.[52]

A fine-grained silty loam deposit, known as the Brickearth, forms a discontinuous veneer over Quaternary drifts. It may have accumulated at the end of the last periglacial period, settling out in standing water after transportation to this area by strong winds associated with permanent anticyclonic air masses.

The last 12,500 years accommodate the post-glacial Holocene period during which the climate has improved and environmental changes crucial to the geomorphological evolution of the Portsmouth region took place. The most important of these changes was the rise of sea-level following worldwide melting of once extensive ice-sheets, which drowned the Solent River valley and the lower reaches of some of its tributaries. Thus, Portsmouth, Langstone and Chichester harbours developed by inundation, as did tidal channels such as Alver Creek, Fareham Creek, the Hamble estuary and Titchfield Haven, prior to its reclamation.

During the Holocene, the present-day character of the coastline evolved. The rise of sea-level was initially rapid, but slowed over the last 5,500 years. Whilst thick silty clays have accumulated in both the Solent and the harbours during this time, interbedded peats provide evidence for short-lived regressions. Peat deposits have been identified from boreholes in Portsmouth and Langstone harbours, and also from Wimbledon Park, Southsea[53] at depths of −18.2m, −11.9m, −10.75m, −4.1m and −0.6m OD. The two shallowest of these horizons indicate the existence of forest cover and probably correlate with the submerged forest occasionally seen between Lee-on-the-Solent and Hill Head at low-water spring tides. Above the more recent buried peats, adjacent to the present-day coastline, are layers of flint shingle representing beach material built up by wave action as the sea-level subsequently rose. Thus, the shingle beaches of the open coastline of Portsea Island, Hayling Island and Gosport are the presently active components of barrier features which have been developing for at least 3,000 to 4,000 years. Much of the flint originated from the marine erosion of Plateau Gravel cliffs and by the reworking of now submerged Solent River terrace deposits. Landward migration of these barriers is associated with the infilling of former embayments, exemplified by the gravel plain of Browndown, Gosport. Lagoons existed behind some of the shingle barriers, and their former sites, subsequently infilled by sediment, include Salterns at Hill Head[54] and the Great Morass and Little Morass of Southsea and south-western Portsmouth respectively. The Canoe Lake near South Parade Pier, Southsea, is the only remnant of the former open water environment of the Great Morass recorded on earlier maps, but finally reclaimed in the late nineteenth century.[55] Sediment profiles from the Great Morass area indicate that there were episodes when the confining shingle barrier was breached and marine deposits accumulated.

Within the almost land-locked harbours, low energy sediment accretion persists under the domination of intertidal processes within salt marsh, tidal flats and channels. On the exposed shores, shingle continues to be reworked by relatively high wave energy; sandy shores are not developed except at the south-western corner of Hayling Island, where there is a small development of dunes which are the product of onshore winds. Patterns of flow and sedimentation at the harbour entrances with their opposed spits are more complex. Research has attempted to clarify the complicated patterns of sediment movement locally, concluding that there are discrete 'cells' of onshore, alongshore and offshore sediment transportation. This, together with research on waves in the Solent, is currently enhancing understanding of the marine processes which have shaped and are still shaping the region's coastal margins.[56]

No account of the geology of the Portsmouth region would be complete without some consideration of its economic significance. In an area lacking good building stone, but rich in clays, brickmaking became an early-established industry traceable back to Roman times. In nineteenth-century Hampshire, between 100 and 150 works produced bricks, tiles and pipes. Both the Tertiary clays and the appropriately named Quaternary 'Brickearth' were utilised. The Reading Beds were worked at Rowlands Castle, Fareham, Gosport, Bedhampton and Emsworth and exploited on Portsea Island as 'Stamshaw Clay'. The London Clay was also worked, the major pit within the Portsmouth region being at Lower Swanwick which closed in 1975. The Bracklesham Beds were little used in the region, but the

Brickearth was widely worked locally and utilised in the construction of many houses in the Milton and Copnor areas.[57]

For many years sand, such as the 'Bagshot Sands' at West Walk near Wickham, has been extracted on a very modest scale for building purposes. The increasing use of concrete to support the rapid post-1945 urbanisation of the coastal region has led to a considerable need for aggregate. Quaternary Plateau Gravels for this purpose are worked at Peel Common, Lee-on-the-Solent and in the Warsash area, whilst flint gravel from Coombe Rock deposits is extracted north of Emsworth. Offshore gravels are also of local importance and there are a number of concession areas to the west of the Solent and south-east of Spithead from which gravels, formerly laid down as terrace deposits by the Solent River at stages of lower sea-level, are dredged. Offshore gravels are unloaded and graded at installations such as that on the western shore of Langstone Harbour. Because of the problems of land-use conflict and amenity preservation presented by the expansion of inland gravel extraction, as well as the additional marginal cost of site restoration, an expansion of offshore gravel production can be anticipated. Any such expansion will need to be based on a careful consideration of the coastal sediment balance in order to ensure the maintenance of an appropriate dynamic equilibrium between supply and removal.

Of the major chalk quarries at Paulsgrove and at Down End, near Fareham, the first is a distinctive landmark on the south-facing slope of Portsdown and dates from the early nineteenth century; both quarries have been extended in recent years to supply foundation materials for the M27 and A3(M) motorways and other major local road-works. The polder reclaimed for IBM in the north-east part of Portsmouth Harbour, which partly accommodates the M27 and the M275 spur, also consumed considerable quantities of chalk.

The water supply of the area is essentially dependent on the Chalk, but other aquifers have been exploited on a local scale in the past as a source of either spring or well water.[58] The 'Bagshot Sands' were formerly important around Gosport, whilst reasonable water yields were also obtained from the Bracklesham Beds in locations such as Horse Sand and No Man's Land Forts in Spithead, which obtained their supplies from shallow wells. Quaternary drift deposits, such as the Plateau Gravels and, to a small extent, the Brickearth, have also provided sources of water for domestic and agricultural use. All these minor aquifers presented problems, including variable yield, contamination by sea water and, in the more populous areas, serious pollution prior to the provision of adequate sewerage.[59]

As both population growth and industrial development in the nineteenth century necessitated a more abundant and reliable source of water, attention turned to the Chalk, from which most of the region's present-day supply is obtained by the Portsmouth Water Company.[60] The company has traditionally concentrated on the exploitation of over twenty prolific artesian springs in the Bedhampton and Havant areas. The catchment area supplying these springs comprises a wide area of the backslope of the South Downs (Figure 5)[61] from which the flow of ground water appears to be concentrated into a number of flowlines using major joints or fissures widened by solution. The rapid movement of water from the zone of infiltration to the springs has been demonstrated by a recent tracer experiment. This indicated a direct link between sink-holes at Hazleton Wood, Horndean, and the springs and demonstrated a rapid subsurface flow of 2.21km per day.[62] The ease whereby such

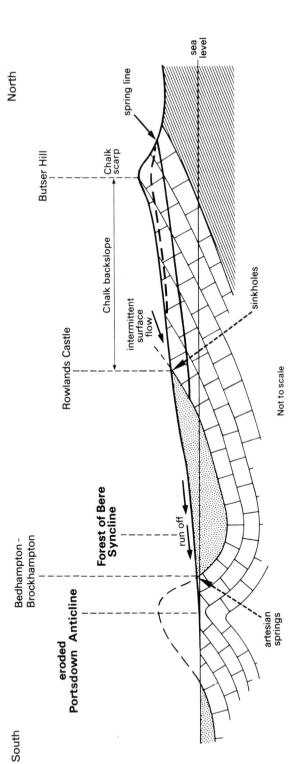

South

Bedhampton -
Brockhampton

eroded
Portsdown Anticline

**Forest of Bere
Syncline**

Rowlands Castle

Butser Hill

North

Chalk scarp

spring line

Chalk backslope

intermittent
surface flow

run off

artesian
springs

sinkholes

Not to scale

sea
level

Generalised saturation levels
in the Chalk

– – – End of winter

——— End of summer

Palaeogene

Chalk

Upper Greensand,
Gault Clay

FIGURE 5 Generalised vertical section from Bedhampton to Butser Hill to illustrate regional
hydrological relationships

sources can be contaminated and the need for the careful control of the surface drainage of such roads as the A3(M) was also demonstrated in this study.

Various authors have recorded fluctuations in the level of the ground-water table in the Chalk.[63] Most fluctuations are seasonal, with higher levels in the late winter and early spring. Longer-term fluctuations reflect climatic events such as the drought of 1975–76, but the yield of the Bedhampton Springs complex has been maintained at a remarkable mean of 101 megalitres per day since its initial exploitation as a major source of public water supply over a century ago.

Some 40 per cent of the region's water supply is obtained from this source and nearly 35 per cent from wells. The remainder is derived from surface drainage, from such rivers as the Meon and Upper Ems whose discharges are maintained by ground water from the Chalk. The annual flow of such rivers shows only limited response to rainfall and other seasonal variations, for whilst the Chalk surface immediately accepts all inputs of precipitation because of its high permeability, any fluctuations in supply are 'smoothed out' by the time and distances taken for such water to reach outflow points.[64] By contrast, rivers draining the Palaeogene strata, particularly where there are large outcrops of impermeable Reading Beds and London Clay, have a much more variable flow regime reflecting a fairly rapid response of discharge to rainfall. The Wallington is a good example of such a river, its hydrograph contrasting with that of the Meon (Figure 6).[65] Clearly, the smaller and more variable discharge from rivers draining the Tertiary outcrop makes them less attractive as sources of public water supply than the Chalk rivers.

Within recent years, there has been a revival of interest in the possible existence of oil and natural gas reserves at considerable depths below the surface of southern England and offshore beneath the English Channel. The Portsdown exploratory borehole of 1936, and another at Arreton in the Isle of Wight in 1945, reported no commercially exploitable hydrocarbons, but the more recent discovery and successful development of the Wytch Farm oilfield in east Dorset has stimulated some reappraisal. Borehole information has indicated that both potential petroleum source and reservoir rocks occur at depth in the Portsmouth region and adjacent areas, while geophysical and borehole information has shown that the deep burial of the sedimentary sequence provides circumstances which elsewhere have led to the generation of large quantities of oil.[66] It may also be that structures associated with the Dorset oil extend eastwards into this region.

There is little doubt about the interest of oil and gas exploration companies in this part of southern England and the adjacent offshore area. Over the last eight years or so, the Department of Energy has issued a number of exploration and production licences. At one stage, the apparent abandonment of the Sandhills Borehole near Porchfield on the Isle of Wight in 1982, and the lack of positive indications from other borehole investigations, suggested that earlier optimism needed to be qualified.[67]

In February 1982, however, Carless Exploration struck oil at Pyle Farm, Horndean, and subsequently mounted a programme of exploratory drilling to evaluate the field's extent. The oil occurs in fault traps, similar to those of the Wytch Farm Field and are associated with fault blocks that developed in mid-Cretaceous times. The migration of the oil into such traps took place long before major Tertiary folding developed, explaining why no oil was found as a result of earlier drilling into the potentially promising anticlinal traps. Much of the recent

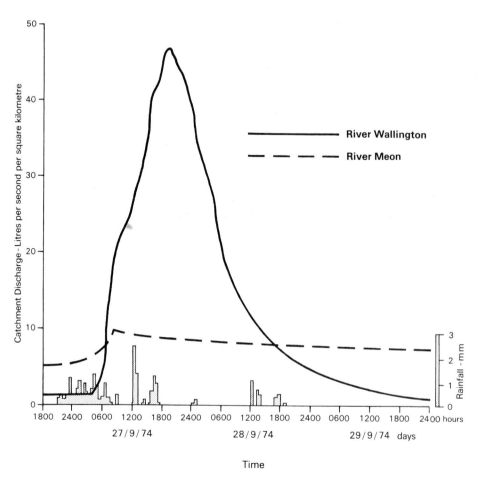

FIGURE 6 Sample hydrographs for stations on the Rivers Meon and Wallington

success reflects the increasing sophistication of geophysical (seismological) exploration technology, which has improved the chances of finding suitable geological structures from about 1 in 20 to about 1 in 3. Seismological investigations can apparently predict the depth at which strata may ultimately be penetrated by drilling to ±1 metre at depths of about 1,000m. Indeed, in the Horndean Well, for example, the accuracy of such methods was clearly demonstrated where, for one geological horizon, the seismologically predicted depth turned out to be only one-third of a metre out. At present, whilst petroleum is being produced from the Humbly Grove Oilfield in the northern part of Hampshire, there is currently no extraction of oil in the Portsmouth region. Whether local oil has commercial potential remains to be seen. Certainly, while world petroleum prices remain depressed, production from small fields is clearly both uncompetitive and unprofitable.

Geological and hydrological resources have provided a basis for the development of the human environment of the Portsmouth region and contributed substantially to urban growth. Much of the region's infrastructure reflects the past and present availability and influence of these resources. Geomorphological conditions, both inland and coastal, have been decisive in determining the critical location of early settlement, the subsequent growth of the built environment and the patterns of commercial and other social development. Indeed, the very existence of Portsmouth as a port has depended fundamentally on its geological and geomorphological endowment of a fine natural harbour. Throughout the entire region, factors such as lithology, water supply, drainage conditions, soils, coastal erosion and sedimentation continue to exert both direct and subtle influences on the economy and human activity. Perhaps the presence of oil beneath the Portsmouth region will have similar effects in the future. How significant this will be as an influence on the area's future economic development must, however, remain a matter of conjecture.

9

CLIMATE, SOILS AND THE TERRESTRIAL FLORA AND FAUNA

Fred Haynes and Fay Stranack

More than 5,000 years of human settlement and land manipulation is undoubtedly the key factor which has determined the present distribution of flora and fauna in the Portsmouth region as elsewhere. The species which were available to colonise the habitats created by man have been selected by chance and local circumstances from a variety of organisms suited to a region of temperate climate. This region, while including a maritime element, lacks both high altitude and hard rocks. Thus animals and plants characteristic of mountains and cliffs are absent, and most of the buildings and walls are too greatly affected by sulphur dioxide pollution to carry more than a very depauperate representation of saxicolous mosses and lichens. Only untended gravestones and farm buildings provide an indication of what might have grown under different topographical conditions.

The presence of chalk within the region supports a distinctive collection of organisms linked to the particular nutritional limitations imposed on the plants by the alkaline soils. Furthermore, the geographical location of south-east Hampshire, midway along the south coast of Britain, determines that the region lies just to the west of the main area of species associated with a continental climate and just to the east of that for species associated with damper Atlantic conditions. The swings of climatic variation through the decades may have added and subtracted species of these two biogeographical elements from the region.

The Portsmouth region enjoys a mild and equable climate (see Table 1), characterised by no great fluctuations about the diurnal or annual means. Precipitation is only moderate and sunshine figures are high. Winters are mild, snowfall infrequent and months with frost are few. Winds are mainly from the west, but strong winds are fewer than in more westerly south coast locations. Mild winters

TABLE 1

CLIMATOLOGICAL AVERAGES FOR SOUTHSEA COMMON

Month	1931–60 Mean Max Air Temperature °C	1931–60 Min Air Temperature °C	1931–60 Mean Air Temperature °C	1931–60 Daily Mean Sunshine Hours	1916–50 Average Rainfall mm
JANUARY	7.4	2.6	5.0	2.08	78.2
FEBRUARY	7.6	2.4	5.0	2.86	54.1
MARCH	10.2	3.8	7.0	4.34	46.7
APRIL	13.3	6.0	9.6	6.18	47.5
MAY	16.6	8.9	12.7	7.21	44.5
JUNE	19.6	12.2	15.9	7.85	36.3
JULY	21.0	14.1	17.5	7.02	50.8
AUGUST	21.1	14.2	17.7	6.79	55.4
SEPTEMBER	18.9	12.4	15.6	5.25	55.6
OCTOBER	15.0	9.1	12.1	3.85	76.7
NOVEMBER	11.0	5.8	8.4	2.31	82.8
DECEMBER	8.5	3.9	6.2	1.78	77.0
YEAR	14.2	7.9	11.1	4.80	58.8

Source: *Meteorological Office*

Source: *S.J. Harrison, 'Local Climate of the Portsmouth Area' in Portsmouth Geographical Essays, II, ed. D.J. Mottershead and R.C. Riley (Portsmouth 1976), pp. 51–65.*

favour plant growth, but this is sometimes checked by a shortage of rain from March to June.

Local climatic variations within the region are small, but there is increased rainfall over the higher ground of the South Downs (Map 1), and at Southsea Common a consistently 2°C to 3°C higher temperature than at Butser Hill.

Along the coastal fringe, particularly between May and September, onshore breezes may locally modify the wind direction and bring greater humidity accompanied by a fall in temperature. Portsdown Hill is recognised by many local commuters as the landward boundary of the sea's climatic influence, but the land climate sometimes retreats to a frontier along the mass of the chalk upland of the South Downs. The same chalk mass may also initiate land breezes, which can occur on any clear night, the air drifting down the slope.

Ground frosts are absent from late May to early September and, near the coast, the crucial horticultural months of May and October are also often free of frosts.

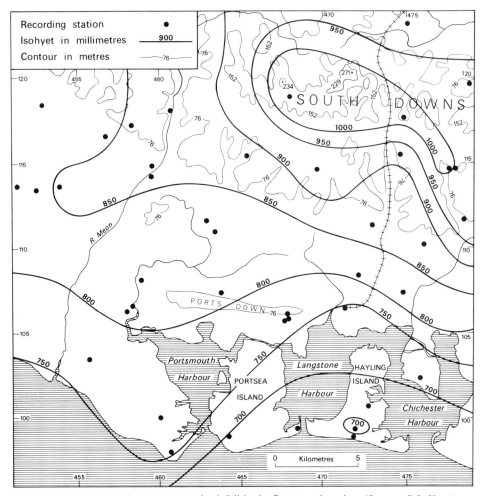

FIGURE 1 Distribution of average annual rainfall in the Portsmouth region. (Source: *S.J. Harrison , 'Local Climate of the Portsmouth Area' in Portsmouth Geographical Essays, II ed. D.J. Mottershead and R.C. Riley (Portsmouth 1976), pp. 51–65.*)

Inland, however, the mildly varied topography contributes to the occurrence of frost hollows. One such site at Fareham, now occupied by housing, is called Frost Hole Crescent (SU 563/074).

Aspect does not seem markedly to influence the present distribution of plant communities, though mosses and liverworts (bryophytes) appear more luxuriant on north-facing grassland.[1]

Soils are classified by the appearance of a vertical section through the soil, known as the profile. The characteristics of a profile are determined by:

1)   the nature of the mineral fraction which has been derived from the parent material;
2)   the climatic, hydrological and biotic factors pertaining during soil formation;
3)   the age of the soil;
4)   the degree of disturbance.

A mature soil contains a mixture of mineral grains and organic matter. Under natural conditions, and when the situation is suitable for earthworm activity (neither too acid nor too wet), the litter is transformed into a *mull* humus which becomes incorporated into the mineral fraction, the combination forming a dark-coloured zone in the upper layer. If the soil is too acid, too wet or too dry, a distinct organic layer (*mor*) accumulates at the surface with an upper zone of undecomposed litter overlying a zone of decomposed, compacted humus. A half-way stage between mull and mor, known as *moder*, is particularly characteristic of acid woodland and is found under some of the very old oak trees of the district. In moder, mixing is not as thorough as in mull and the humus plus mineral zone forms an abrupt boundary with the purely mineral lower zone, instead of merging imperceptibly into it as is found below a mull. Under cultivation these distinctions disappear. The combination of manure, fertiliser and plough leads to a mull-like humus, which is more rapidly oxidised and so destroyed when the soil is bare than when it is protected by turf and trees. Accumulation of organic matter under totally waterlogged conditions produces peat, but this is very rare in the region.

The water regime of a soil is controlled both by the permeability of the substrate and by its location relative to a river or the sea. Underlying many of the superficial deposits there are beds of clay which are often near to the surface; also some of the parent materials themselves are not very permeable to water and as a consequence waterlogging of the lower portion of the soil profile is not uncommon. Seasonal variations in water-level provide alternating oxidising and reducing conditions, changing the chemical constitution of the soil to provide ochrous and greyish-blue colours respectively. Soils having profiles which show this pattern are called *gleys*.

Even over the past 7,000 years there have been periods of relatively rapid rise in sea-level. Peat overlies much of the chalk bed in the north of Langstone Harbour below the alluvium, and samples from near Farlington seem to be of Atlantic age and include plants characteristic of species-rich, wet woodland. With sea-level changes, extensive drainage and reclamation, the hydrological conditions have obviously varied but, where waterlogging is a consequence of impermeable substrate, such changes have probably had only local effects on the extent of the gleyed areas.

During the winter months there is an excess of rainfall over water lost by evaporation and transpiration. The weakly acid rain percolating down through the soil removes the soluble components (*leaching*). The material leached out from the upper layers either drains away or is redeposited at a lower level. Plants whose roots absorb the nutrients can return these soluble chemicals to the surface via leaf fall. In the ideal natural system such cycling of materials maintains the fertility of a soil and, in Britain, leads to the formation of a mull-type humus. The presence of moder under old oak trees suggests a failure in the long term efficiency of this natural cycle, but, by the nature of woodland changes, some trees such as birch are soil improvers and the natural successor to the oak might enhance the soil. In the agricultural system the leaching is offset by applying fertiliser and lime. Many local soils have been treated with lime, including some that have now reverted to semi-natural vegetation. This use of lime to preserve fertility keeps the soil slightly acid (pH 6). An excess of calcium carbonate can render the soil alkaline (pH greater than 7). Such conditions occur over the Chalk and deposits derived from the Chalk (Brickearth and Coombe deposits). If the soil is undisturbed and deep, leaching can have washed all the free calcium carbonate out of the superficial layers and it is only near the chalk outcrop that the surface horizons contain free carbonate. This is rarely sufficient to raise the pH to levels which provide the plant with problems of nutrient availability. Only in the shallow soils of the Chalk does this occur. These soils, *rendzinas*, are dark-coloured with mull humus and lie directly over the Chalk which may be only a few centimetres below the surface. Slightly deeper soils have been extensively ploughed, for the Chalk holds water for plant growth and is readily comminuted by the combined action of frost and plough. Cereals do particularly well in such soils.

Without man's intervention, how deep would these chalk soils have been? It has often been suggested that downland soils were shallow before the advent of cultivation. Would they have been sufficiently deep for their upper layers to have been leached of the excess calcium carbonate? At the bottom of dry valleys on the Chalk, soils of up to 1m overlie the 'head' of glacial times and investigations suggest that much of this material has been washed down the slopes following the removal of woodland cover initiated in neolithic times.[2] Such evidence, combined with a knowledge of the changes which have occurred since the decline of the rabbit, make it not unlikely that much of the downland could have been covered by wood little different from that of the clay lowlands, and that only the oversteep slope and the area of natural catastrophe would carry the shallow rendzina soil. It must not be thought that soil erosion in England was only a product of ages when its consequences were unknown. During the 1980s the rate of erosion in England was twice the natural rate of replenishment, according to the National Soil Survey. Now, as in the past, present gain has predominated over future good, a policy to which downland soils bear mute testimony.

The woodlands of the lowlands would mostly have been on the major group of soils known as *brown earths*, i.e. well- to moderately-drained soils, with mull humus more or less uniformly incorporated. These soils are usually brown with variation according to the parent material. Whereas the true brown earths are now mostly under cultivation, many of the semi-natural woodlands are on *acidic brown earths*.

On drift material derived from the Chalk (for example, Coombe Deposits) the soils resemble brown earths, but the higher chalk content distinguishes them as *calcareous brown soils*. They provide good arable conditions with a distinctly reddish colour to their lower horizons.

Brown earths with mottling in the lower horizons due to waterlogging are classified as *brown earths with gleying*. They grade into less structured soils, lacking the features of the brown earth. The waterlogging is a consequence of impeded drainage so such gleys are termed *surface water gleys*. Gleys are particularly associated with the Eocene clays. The semi-natural vegetation of these areas is generally woodland, but cultivation has usually concentrated on pasture with the liberal addition of lime to offset the acidity.

In the river valleys where waterlogging is a consequence of a high water table, *ground water gleys* are encountered. Initially carrying alder or willow marsh and fen, they are now rich grazing land with soils showing the enforced influence of the water-borne material including the lime from the streams' Chalk origin.

Extreme leaching produces a mor-type humus overlying a distinctly stratified soil with a layer of whitish sand from which all the clay, humus and iron compounds have been removed. The iron is redeposited at a lower level. Such a profile typifies a *podsol*. Only prolonged mismanagement could produce such a condition over the local parent materials. A few isolated examples occur, usually associated with frequently burnt scrub. Outside the region in the New Forest podsols are frequent.

It is clear that the development of the different types of soil is a consequence of interactions which have a large biological component and that this development takes time. The abundant evidence of Ice Age activity (raised beaches, solifluction and loessic deposits) indicates that the oldest soils cannot be more than about 10,000 years old, but the degree of disturbance by man has been such that most of the soils found in semi-natural situations will have their age numbered in hundreds rather than thousands of years. Gravel, sand, shingle and bare chalk also support plant growth, but a mature soil is absent. Such *skeletal* soils are a feature of many areas of waste and dereliction, but the intertidal silts and sands can be grouped in this category being almost permanently waterlogged with saline water. Reclamation of silts, however, has provided grazings with a fresh water table that fluctuates with the periodicity of the tides.

In very broad terms the soils of the region can be related to the parent geology. Sands and gravels of recent marine deposits together with some Eocene deposits (Reading, Bagshot and Bracklesham Beds) have free draining earths with a tendency towards the formation of acid brown earths and even podsols. The silts and loams of the Coombe deposits and Brickearth range from brown calcareous soils through brown earths to surface water gleys, while flinty inclusions become increasingly common as the chalk outcrop is approached. The steep chalk slopes carry rendzinas. The London Clays typically produce brown earths with gleying. River valleys have relatively narrow strips of ground water gleys on the alluvial silts, but the alluvium of marine origin provides a comparable gley of much lower fertility. There is no detailed account of the soils of the region, but a full description of the similar soils of the West Sussex plain is to be found in the Soil Survey account written by Hodgson.[3]

The landscape around Portsmouth is remarkably well wooded (OS Sheet 196, The Solent, 1:50,000) considering that it is an important farming and market gardening area, although at present too much woodland is being lost too quickly. Woods of varying sizes may be found, from small copses, spinneys and shelter belts such as those on the Southwick Estate, to quite large tracts of woodland, for example, West Walk near Wickham. The woods are composed of a wide range of tree and shrub species, and support a diverse ground flora. Many species of animals are likely to live in the woods, especially insects,[4] but these remain to be studied thoroughly. Roe deer abound, a few badgers still remain and foxes are common. The smaller mammals are probably present in large numbers, but have not been systematically studied.[5] The birds, which are more easily observed than mammals, are better known and include all the common woodland species with reports of the occasional nightingale.

The present pattern of flora and fauna has developed over centuries, since man started clearing the primaeval woodland to graze his domestic stock and grow crops. About 8000 BC, Hampshire, like the rest of lowland England, was largely covered with deciduous forest dominated by oak, elm and lime, with hazel, birch, alder, willow and other species in smaller quantities. Evidence from pollen analysis suggests that elm and lime were the first species to diminish in numbers. Early stock farmers probably cut elm foliage for cattle food when grass was scarce and selectively removed limes as they demand a richer soil than other tree species, since such soils were preferred for agriculture. Subsequently, with more sophisticated knowledge, machinery and technology, farmers were able to cultivate the more difficult soils and further woodland clearance took place. The expansion of sheep rearing helped to clear any residual woodland from the chalk downs and also prevented its regeneration. Clearance of alder and willows from the flood plain of rivers with calcium carbonate rich waters, such as the River Meon, was a necessary prelude to the development of water meadows. This grazing regime is now obsolete, but the remains of carriers and drains may still be seen, for example, at Corhampton.

Much of the woodland of south-east Hampshire was originally part of the Royal Forest of Bere and owes its survival to the legal protection afforded to such royal hunting preserves. The ancient Forest of Bere stretched eastward from the River Test to the Sussex border and from the north slope of Portsdown Hill to the foot of the South Downs. As with the New Forest, use of the Forest of Bere and all its products was reserved for the Crown, except for certain common rights such as those of pasture and mast for feeding stock, and collecting fuel.

The primary purpose of the royal forests was to provide facilities for hunting deer. Timber derived from the oaks of the royal forests was used for the construction and maintenance of royal buildings, was granted to loyal and deserving subjects and religious foundations, and sold to the Royal Navy for shipbuilding. The proximity of the Forest of Bere to several shipyards, on the River Hamble and around Portsmouth Harbour, ensured a steady drain on woodland reserves, though hedgerow and park oaks provided the timber of particular shapes for the specialised frames of ships. During the years 1808–14, the Crown relinquished the Forest of Bere. Parts of it were sold to private landowners, enclosed and subsequently cleared for agriculture or replanting with conifers. Eventually, part of the woodland area passed into the hands of the Forestry Commission which was established in 1919.[6]

A small estate in the Forest of Bere was given by the Crown to Southwick Priory when it moved from Portchester to Southwick in 1153. The estate gradually grew in size by gift and purchase. On the Dissolution of the monasteries in 1538, the estate passed into secular ownership and has remained as a unit ever since, with the result that much of the woodland has been conservatively managed and has survived to the present day.[7]

Ever since Anglo-Saxon times, and probably earlier, woodland management followed the coppice-with-standards pattern in which oaks were selectively encouraged to grow to maturity, providing structural timber, whereas the smaller trees, hazel, field maple and willow, were cut at regular intervals, from seven to twelve years, to provide a continual supply of wood for tools, thatching spars, the basis of wattle and daub panels, hurdles and firewood. The majority of woodland in south-east Hampshire shows signs of this practice, with hazel as the main coppice species and oak as the standard tree, though the alien sweet chestnut, introduced by the Romans, may be found filling both roles. Elm and lime are extremely rare in the area, hornbeam occurs occasionally, beech is quite frequent and, of other tree species, holly, hawthorn, field maple and bird cherry are found in good quantity.

Many of the woods have been clear felled and replanted either with conifers – larch, spruce, fir and pine, all of which are introduced species – or with a mixture of hardwoods, predominantly oak, but also some beech, interplanted among a protective crop of conifers. A few areas have been newly planted and added to the total woodland coverage, notably Walton Heath and Lodge Moor on either side of the B2177 west of Southwick. Neither of these sites was shown as woodland on the 1810 Ordnance Survey map or the 1840 Tithe map, but both appear as woodland on the 1897 Ordnance Survey map. The long-continued growth of trees on the same pieces of land for centuries has resulted in a very diverse ground flora containing a good proportion of ancient woodland indicator species.[8]

Recently, the Nature Conservancy Council and, of late, Hampshire County Council, provoked by the widespread clearance of ancient woodland throughout the country, have gathered together into several publications the scattered information on plant communities characteristic of different types of woodland in Hampshire. From these studies it has become apparent that some herbaceous plants are only to be found in woods with a long continuous history, such as those on the Southwick Estate. The nutrient status of the soil also plays a part in the diversity of plants to be found, chalk soils supporting a greater richness of plant life than poorer clay- and sand-based soils. Plants such as woodruff, greater butterfly orchid, herb Paris and the rarer woodland grasses will only be found on chalk deposits, though species such as primrose, wood anemone, early purple orchid, yellow archangel and many more are especially common in woods on soils derived from the Tertiary strata. One plant of particular interest, Solomon's seal, is a speciality of Hampshire woodlands and occurs in abundance in ancient woods.[9]

Some insect and snail species are also known to be confined to ancient woods though these have been studied less thoroughly in the region. A few insect groups, notably Lepidoptera (butterflies and moths), Coleoptera (beetles) and Hymenoptera (bees, wasps and ants) have been investigated[10] and a number of rare and local species identified, especially in Botley Wood, but the species restricted to ancient woodland need to be more precisely selected and more work undertaken on the woodland fauna before any conclusions can be drawn.

Coppicing, the practice of felling small trees with subsequent regrowth of multiple stems on a seven to twelve year rotation, has the major benefit of letting light through to the woodland floor in one area after another. This allows the richly diverse spring flora to develop in each patch in turn, though suppressed as the coppice stools regrow and cut out the light. Consequently, neglected woods, where the coppicing cycle has not been maintained, tend to lack the colourful flowering plants and animal communities of consistently managed woodlands.

The dominant plants of local woods give an indication of soil type, the acid brown earths supporting bramble and honeysuckle, with bracken on drier soils, while the poorly-drained, but more basic, clay soils carry dog's mercury, sanicle, pignut, bluebell, bugle, lesser celandine and sedges. The bryophytes are remarkably lacking in diversity, particularly in the woods on acid brown earths where *Hypnum cupressiforme* and *Mnium hornum* dominate the list, but a move to the richer damper soils would add *Bracythecium rutabulum*, *Eurynchium praelongum* and *Catharinia undulatum* to the list with thalloid and leafy liverworts by the streams. On the sandy soils *Dicranum* species come to prominence. The range is undoubtedly less than in the New Forest and, though diligent search in the valley bottoms can increase the total number of species growing on trees, moss and liverwort species remain few in number. Fungi are well represented though dry years may restrict their fructifications. The colourful genera *Amanita*, *Boletus* and *Russula* are common, while an autumn foray usually provides a satisfying collection of the expected and occasionally a species not previously found in the locality.

The scattered woods and hedges which remain are fragments of the prehistoric deciduous forest which formerly covered most of the land surface. The vast majority of native plant and animal species in Britain are adapted to the woodland ecosystem and depend upon it. Consequently, removal of woodland has reduced the extent of their preferred habitat, restricting their numbers as living space decreased. Some species, such as starlings, are sufficiently adaptable to take advantage of changed conditions and others, jays for example, have more stringent requirements. Inevitably, the latter have suffered more than the former from loss of habitat.

The coastal region of south-east Hampshire, with its productive Brickearth soil, has long been known for its excellent wheat-growing potential, commented on by William Cobbett as a result of his ride along the length of Portsdown Hill.[11] Much of this land is now covered by urban development. The market gardens further west may possibly share the same fate as the Portsmouth conurbation spreads inexorably, but, currently, vegetables and soft fruits, especially strawberries, are cultivated on the light dry soils around Titchfield and Wickham.

North of Portsdown Hill mixed farming has developed on the relatively mediocre soils of the Hampshire Basin.[12] Much of the land is poorly drained, but grows grass well and is used for cattle rearing, predominantly of Friesian dairy herds. On the drier slopes of the Chalk Downs, barley and wheat are grown. An increasing number of sheep are to be seen both on the traditional sheep-rearing areas of the Downs and on the lower land. Rarely do they graze on the short, springy, flower-strewn turf characteristic of the old sheep runs, but are to be found on grass leys composed of a monotonous rye grass sward specially selected for nutritive value and encouraged by applications of artificial fertilisers, the broad-leaved 'weed' competitors being eliminated by selective herbicides.

Modern agricultural techniques of deep ploughing and application of chemicals have resulted in the displacement of the wildlife, except for the common species able to adjust to rapidly changing conditions, such as starling, dandelion and dock. While the land subjected to continual cultivation cannot support a permanent wildlife community, none the less some animals are seen feeding in or passing over the fields, for example, fox, roe deer and wood pigeon throughout the year, fieldfare and redwing in winter, the lark soaring in spring, many seed-eating birds at harvest time and invertebrate feeders following the plough.

The more common butterflies, red admiral, small tortoise-shell, meadow and hedge browns, marbled white and common blue, may also be seen over cultivated land. All feed in their larval stages on common plants, nettle for the first two, grasses for the next three and bird's foot trefoil for the last one. Clover, grown as a fodder crop, inadvertently provides food for bees and other nectar-feeding insects.

Not surprisingly, the more mobile animals, birds and butterflies, are more common on farmland as they can avoid the hazards of machinery and sprays, but they only visit the fields to feed, retreating to safer locations to breed.

The efficiency of modern farming is nowhere more evident than in the scarcity of cornfield weeds. Cornflower and corn-cockle are extinct, ox-eye daisy, corn marigold and poppy are rarely seen, since the cereal seed sown is so clean and selective herbicides are most efficient. The disturbed soil around the margins of arable fields and on tracks supports communities of annual plants such as scarlet pimpernel and mayweed:

Rising gradually from the Eocene clays and sands in the south of the region, the predominantly arable fields of the Chalkland Coombe Rock stretch northward to the watershed of the South Downs. Most of the woods, as in the lowlands, are coppice with standard oaks, but there is, however, a perceptible increase in the frequency of such shrubs as maple, wayfaring-tree and bloody dogwood, while the ash becomes a common tree of spontaneous regeneration and clematis begins to festoon the wood margins on the brown calcareous soils. The ground flora changes from the ubiquitous bramble, honeysuckle and wood soft grass of the more acidic lowlands to a cover of dog's mercury and wood melick in which bluebells flourish, producing in spring an almost hallucinatory blue mist.

On the steeper slopes of the dry valleys, for instance around Hambledon, similar woods occur but extending downwards towards the damper lower slopes where lesser celandine, cuckoo pint and enchanter's nightshade become prominent. The soil on these slopes mostly remains deep with beech replacing oak as the dominant tree. Only rarely do these chalk valley slopes carry the shallow rendzina soil characteristic of beech or yew 'hangers', where the dominant trees exclude most ground-cover plants.

The classic short turf of Chalk Downland is now a thing of the past except where it is recreated by precise and careful management in open-air museums such as the nature reserve at Old Winchester Hill. Rarely in history can man have inflicted such severe stress on an area and have been rewarded by such floristic diversity. This colourful and fragrant variety of plants is reflected in the works of English lyric poets and fortunately it survived sufficiently long to be recorded by the more precise methods of early ecologists. For centuries the Downs were subjected to heavy sheep grazing, a pressure intensified by a superabundance of rabbits, causing loss of both vegetation and soil.[13] A decline in sheep flocks during the 1930s and 1940s, followed by the near extinction of the rabbit, produced a dramatic change during the 1950s. Grasses, such as false oat and upright brome, previously kept at bay by intensive grazing, swept to dominance and tor grass, previously confined to small patches, spread laterally, turning hillside slopes from green to pale yellow, restricting the diversity by eliminating the range of herb and grass species. Simultaneously, shrub seedlings free from destruction by herbivore and shepherd grew to small bushes. At some locations bloody dogwood, wayfaring-tree and maple predominated, a combination that in autumn with its colourful admixture of foliage turned the hillside into a riot of yellow and red. Elsewhere, hawthorn and sloe provided the main seed stock and in spring their white blossoms shimmered on the hill slopes.

Around these bushes the original vegetation, protected from grazing, grew taller and the soil became damper with each patch becoming a centre for nutrient enrichment in a nutrient poor terrain. Crosswort, marjoram and wild parsnip flowered here in profusion and for a while the orchids survived, even flourished, but as the bushes became trees the grasslands dwindled and the mellifluous lark and pippet were dispossessed.

Most of the original trees of the coombes were yew, growing along the upper margins of valleys, as chance or the market forces controlling grazing density permitted. Initially the yew seedlings had been protected by juniper, a shrub now rare in the south. Many of the young yews in pictures from the 1930s have since grown to form mature woodland, their sombre greens intensified by the flaming white of occasional whitebeams. The post-myxomatosis scrub is now a continuous and impenetrable cover in which yew often regenerates, unless the area is ploughed or is part of a grassland reserve. The planning and work required to maintain the downland sward is well evinced at Old Winchester Hill where livestock grazing and mowing are all carefully regimented. Now only sheep can create and maintain a close sward, for the rabbit population remains too depleted to do more than assist. Their abandoned warrens are marked by clusters of old elderberry trees under which a tangle of brambles and herbs has sprung up. Cattle are too heavy to be allowed to graze on the steep slopes all the year round and their feeding method of tug and pull is less selective and generally more destructive than the shearing action of the sheep. Mowing twice a year preserves some of the herbs which are food plants for butterflies and moths, but only sheep seem able to recreate the short springy turf of cherished memory with its aromatic thyme, sedges, vetches, scabious, eyebright, daisies, salad burnet and a wealth of grass species all competing with mats of moss.

The taller herbage, including bellflower round the scrub and wood margins, requires constant regulation so that there is always some short grassland to restart the succession naturally. The scrub forms a habitat for many full-throated passerines such as warblers, yellow hammers, dunnocks and finches, while adders and lizards find cover in its margins. The orchids, most wayward of species in their success, require further research and understanding or the restricted areas in which they now grow may prove too small and isolated for their continuity. Nests of yellow ants with their characteristic and individual plant growth of speedwells, thyme, lady's bedstraw and squinancywort also require herbage control. They increased with the reduction in grazing earlier this century and decrease in the tall grass. Over the chalk grasslands, yellow with hawkbit, cowslip and vetches, flit the butterflies, particularly blue ones. Most are the common blue, but the chalkhill blue and the rare Adonis blue may also be seen where their food plants, kidney vetch and horseshoe vetch are present, as well as small heaths, meadow browns and fritillaries.

As subsidies and fertilisers encouraged the spread of arable farming over the ancient downland, so the remains accessible to the public declined. Moreover public mobility increased. Heavy trampling by visitors in these restricted areas compacts the soil and has resulted in further vegetational changes, plantains and daisies having increased, for example, at the expense of less robust species.

The Portsmouth region does not extend far enough to include plateau woods on acidic clay-with-flints, but an odd patch of gorse may mark where this geological material has slid over the rim of a coombe as at Butser, whilst very restricted patches of chalk heath occur over similar substrates.

Portsdown Hill used to carry many of the vegetation types of Chalk Downland, but excavation and farming have destroyed them leaving only some of the characteristic species in disturbed areas.

If you visit a reserve tread softly for you are treading on a realised dream of Old England and this creation is fragile. Economically worthless, and the product of over-exploitation and nutrient depletion, it is aesthetically and biologically beyond price.

The most convenient heading under which to group a range of habitats which have yet to be restored after disturbance by extractive industries, waste disposal or building, together with those inconvenient and uneconomic corners of plots and fields is wastelands. To the older generation they were places where brass-knobbed bedsteads grew. Now they seem to produce old tyres, colourful plastic bags and portions of cars. Near habitations, they are often enriched with the garden refuse eschewed by the official disposers of waste. There are gradations from the general rubbish tip to derelict paddock, newly-created road cuttings or grassed tip.

What all these habitats have in common is their comparatively recent initiation from a substrate lacking vegetation and sometimes even lacking soil. This situation creates relatively extreme environmental conditions, but little competition and restricts the range of species which can colonise such sites. Those that succeed are often intolerant of competition and, as the succession develops, such plants are soon crowded out. Weeds from abroad, inadvertently introduced in bird seed or with imported materials, often succeed for a generation but either do not set seed or do not become established as native species. However, there is a group of British plants which are successful despite the rigours of the habitat. These have been present in Britain since the Late Glacial period when they colonised the wastes of boulder clay and moraine left by the retreating ice. Because of this ability to invade and establish themselves on open ground they tend to be thought of as weeds. Some members of the daisy family, in particular, occur with high frequency. They include the mugworts and wormwoods, a group confined almost entirely to wastelands. Equally characteristic are orache, fat hen and good king Henry, members of the *Chenopodiaceae*, all moderately tall plants of mealy appearance which produce copious seed and thus supplement the diet of certain birds. Such plants are common around allotments and in areas where organic rubbish accumulates. Nettles, too, flourish wherever there is nutrient enrichment and these plants are very attractive as food for the larval stages of butterflies such as the small tortoise-shell, peacock, comma and red admiral. An increasingly common plant of local wastes is Japanese knot-grass, a tall woody herb which rapidly forms dense thickets by the invasive growth of its stems. It is apparently ideal for making pea-shooters, but it causes fierce blistering when in contact with the skin. Also notable in the grassy waste areas, especially during the spring, is the hoary pepperwort which forms a locally dominant cover.

If succession has had to start in an area of purely silicious minerals, the early colonisers are remarkably constant suggesting highly effective powers of dispersal. Road-side chippings frequently become decorated with silverweed, dry sandy wastes with wall barley and soft brome and gravelly surfaces with plantain, mouse-eared hawkweed and daisy. As such silica-rich sites develop towards grassland, weeds once associated with cereal crops appear, such as poppy, ox-eye daisy and pineapple weed, as well as ragwort which is poisonous to stock but essential food for the orange and black caterpillars of the cinnabar moth.

Chalk is widely used as infill in the region, as at North Harbour and beneath the A3(M) motorway, with the result that these wastelands distant from the bed-rock chalk resemble recolonised marl or chalk pits. Steep slopes of the cuttings and infill material carry some chalk grassland plants, with clematis from the hedgerows an unexpectedly successful coloniser of the bare limestone. Standard rubbish-tip weeds are less successful in such locations and the early stages of colonisation can be of considerable interest. Buddleia, a noted butterfly lure, exhibits a liking not only for abandoned chalk pits but also for building rubble.

Time brings uniformity to the untended dry wasteland: brambles, wild roses and goose-grass combine to create an impenetrable tangle in which shrubs, usually hawthorn or elder, establish themselves. Roadside margins tend to resemble old-fashioned hay meadows with a high proportion of flowering plants including knapweed, bush vetch and cow parsley, more picturesquely known as Queen Anne's lace. Motorway verges, increasingly being seeded with native plants, are becoming sites of biological importance, giving a twist to the meaning of a 'central reservation'. Some artificial depressions and pits are damp enough for the establishment of plants associated with gleyed soils, for example the highly fragrant meadow sweet lines many a roadside ditch. Common rush grows above blocked field drains and marsh plants appear in old marl pits. Later stages of succession may produce thickets of alder and willow. Clearings in woods often include a patch of wood ash on which the moss *Funaria hygrometrica* flourishes and is rapidly succeeded by the tall dark-green plants of the rose bay willowherb or fireweed and marsh thistles, whilst around the periphery of the clearing docks and foxgloves precede brambles, which pave the way for shrubs and trees.

Proximity to the sea leads to the occasional appearance of Alexanders, a striking yellow umbellifer, as well as the aromatic fennel species which, while not confined to the shore, seem to flourish best on wasteland in reach of sea breezes. By the sea itself, plants of the upper salt marsh and shingle find a congenial home on rubble and waste tips. The strand line, too, with its piles of drifted seaweed, crates and planks, has much in common with the rubbish tip, but has the additional feature of high salt content, which excludes many plants.

There is an air of dereliction about many of these wasteland sites which, it should be stressed, are amongst the few wild places in the region. Their origin lies in neglect and abandonment, while most habitats are a product of continued management. The range of plants found on such sites encourages a diversity of insects, often of importance as pollinators. Spiders' webs glisten with morning dew and amongst the vegetable detritus false scorpions may be found, though they are often overlooked. Mice, voles and fiercely voracious shrews seek food in these locations and find cover from the predatory owl, kestrel and fox. These sites, ranging from open waste to tangled damp thicket, can yield a remarkable variety of birds including larks ecstatic above grassed tips, goldfinches on the thistles, bullfinches far from the buds of ornamental trees, tits, warblers and buntings. The wastelands bring wilderness to the countryside and a hint of country to the town.

In spite of being one of the most densely populated cities in Britain, Portsmouth has a number of open and undeveloped spaces ranging from well-managed formal parks, such as Southsea Common, private gardens and cemeteries, to fortuitously preserved semi-natural habitats, such as Hilsea Lines. Parks and gardens tend to contain alien species and garden varieties of plants: tombstones are often encrusted with lichens, though atmospheric pollution diminishes the variety of these interesting plant associations, while the semi-natural areas may still retain numerous native plants and animals.[14]

Although the shoreline of Portsea Island is largely built-up, the intertidal zone along the south, east and north shores shows a range of substrate types of different particle size from shingle to mud, each with its characteristic living community. Man-made 'rocks', usually stone or concrete blocks left over from sea defence works, together with piles, provide the solid surface necessary for the attachment of seaweeds, barnacles, sponges and the many other species normally to be found on rocky shores. Very little animal and plant life can exist among shingle, especially if it is constantly shifting under wave action, but the muds are rich in burrowing and surface-dwelling animals, the sands rather less so. Here the large populations of lug- and rag-worms are exploited by bait diggers; many other worm species are also present, together with burrowing molluscs and surface-living crabs and other crustaceans.

Plants typical of shingle above high tide, such as yellow horned poppy, sea kale, sea bindweed, sea campion and the less common Nottingham catchfly, grow at Eastney. In Portsmouth Harbour, Horsea Island, having been stabilised and enlarged by chalk dumping, now supports typical grassland plants as well as marsh orchids, but in recent years has become largely covered by scrub.

Hilsea Lines, built in the 1860s, is a system of ramparts and a moat which rapidly became obsolete and fell into neglect. The woodland and rough grassland which developed on the chalk embankment now support a number of common species of birds, including wood pigeon, blackbird, robin, willow warbler, chiff-chaff, tits, chaffinch and owl. Butterflies present are large and small white, orange tip, common blue, wall brown, small tortoise-shell and peacock. The trees consist mainly of sycamore and poplar, with a few ash, much hawthorn, some willow and field maple, and elm regenerating from suckers left after the formerly dominant trees had succumbed to Dutch elm disease. Some large old walnut trees at the western end were probably planted soon after the ramparts were finished. The ground flora is poor, dominated by ivy, with wild arum, goose-grass, nettle, cow parsley and the willowherb species which provide food for the caterpillars of the elephant hawk moth. Japanese knotweed is invading the more open areas. Foxes, rabbits, woodmice and field voles have been seen in the open grassland which is rich in buttercups and daisies.

The moat is fed from springs, but the salinity of the water is variable due to seepage through the sluice from Port Creek. There are several reed beds and other emergent vegetation among which damselflies and dragonflies may be seen. Swans and mallard nest along the moat and there is a resident population of kingfishers, coots and moorhen. Pond skaters, water measurers and water boatmen can be seen on the surface and molluscs, crustaceans and midge larvae in the water. Alexanders grows along the north bank of the moat's western section, which is managed as a coarse fishery for carp, roach, tench and perch.

The other major area of biological importance on Portsea Island lies beside the Eastern Road at Milton and consists of ponds excavated to take drainage water from the adjacent former tip, now landscaped and grassed over. Since pollution from the tip ceased, Milton Lakes have developed to support several species of water birds: swans, mallard, coots, moorhen and great crested and little grebes can be found all the year round. Wildfowl visit in winter and in the reed beds in summer sedge warblers and reed bunting breed. A few willows grow near the ponds which are surrounded by open grassland where common lizards are sometimes seen, together with crickets, grasshoppers and a variety of butterflies – green-veined whites, large and small whites, small tortoise-shells and peacocks. The herbs include hoarycress in quantity, also tansy, yarrow, mugwort, common mallow, fennel and nettle.

Other urban areas of south-east Hampshire show a similar range of habitats to those of Portsea Island. Portchester, Fareham and Gosport all have muddy shores supporting marine invertebrates which in turn provide food for fish and birds. Gosport has defensive structures at Forts Brockhurst, Rowner and Monckton, while Portchester boasts the unique habitat of its castle walls with their specialised flora, including wallflower, thick leaved stonecrop and wall rue. The shingle at Browndown has a flora similar to that of Eastney beach, but is more diverse and of greater extent, supporting almost prostrate wind-pruned oaks loaded with oak apple and marble galls, evergreen oak, large patches of burnet rose, heaths, and Nottingham catchfly. In Gosport, the Wild Grounds, bordering on the Alver valley, is a natural oak wood with trees of a wide age and a shrub layer of rhododendron, left over from game conservation and ornamental planting. The built-up areas have some open spaces such as cemeteries and recreation grounds, all with trees, where birds are usually conspicuous. The rough areas of local golf courses sometimes retain interesting plants, including orchids at Crookhorn and sand dune plants at Hayling Island.

Steadily increasing public awareness of, and interest in, wildlife has resulted in an increase in the number of some species, since many people feed birds and cultivate buddleia and other nectar-secreting plants in their gardens to attract butterflies. The highly adaptable starlings and house sparrows are commonly to be seen in urban surroundings readily accepting scraps at the bird table. Most civic centres have their quota of feral pigeons and the monotonous cooing of the collared dove is a familiar sound to urban residents. Orange patches of lichen may be seen on roofs and walls, while mosses develop readily in rain water gutters and assorted small 'weeds', mainly pearlwort, thrive between paving stones. Some wild visitors to human habitation are less welcome, for example, house flies, clothes moths and carpet beetles. But perhaps the most spectacular wild inhabitant of towns is the kestrel which accepts ledges on buildings as a substitute for cliff-nesting sites. The small mammals living in rough grass constitute prey as they probably also do for the foxes, which scavenge from suburban dustbins as well.

The south of the region is now predominantly urban and industrial. The range of habitats for wildlife has been curtailed drastically and the spread of the town has been very rapid. Towns are inimical to wildlife for they are specifically designed and created for the material benefit of one species – man. Changes in the rural environment have been almost as far-reaching. Successful agriculture and forestry demand high yields and these are obtained by making the maximum use of land for planted crops. The semi-natural grasslands are replaced by seeded leys. The mosaic characterising the coppice-with-standards woodland has been replaced either by even-age plantations or abandonment, which has resulted in a uniform tree cover. Many hedges have been eradicated and in those that remain herbicides and pesticides control the range of species tolerated.

Many indigenous species are now confined to nature reserves and wasteland. The economics of progress have continually caused the depletion of wildlife and the changes are now more rapid than ever before as the south coast is an attractive area for human activity. To retain some of the flora and fauna enjoyed by previous generations will require effort, ingenuity and money. To lose it would impoverish human experience culturally, aesthetically and scientifically.

10

AQUATIC FLORA
AND FAUNA

Fred Haynes and Fay Stranack

Natural boundaries can be extremely difficult to determine with precision, and a question arises as to the point at which the aquatic habitat ceases and the terrestrial one begins. Traditionally marsh and fen are included under the heading of wetlands as part of the aquatic habitat, but in such areas a distinction is made between submerged and emergent species. Moreover, in aquatic habitats, the fundamental chemical distinction between fresh and saline water results in an almost total disjunction between freshwater and marine species; furthermore the blown sea spray produces such a characteristic maritime component amongst the species of dune and shingle that it becomes convenient to separate plants of the sea coast and littoral from other aquatic or terrestrial habitats. The problems relating to salinity are exemplified by the estuary of the Hamble. The salt marshes at its mouth support typical halophytes, such as sea purslane and sea plantain, but at the estuary's head the channel is fringed by the common reed (*Phragmites communis*) which can flourish in brackish conditions. However, the reed grass (*Phalaris arundinacea*), only found in fresh water, is absent. Both types of reed, moreover, are characteristic of inland lakes. Another example which illustrates overlap of aquatic and terrestrial habitats can be seen at Hook Common where the shingle along the foreshore supports sea kale with its handsome blue-green foliage and the floriferous sea campion, whereas the short turf of the embankment embraces primarily inland species into which sea campion and sea plantain extend. The common itself carries a mixture of grassland and wetland plants, including species tolerant of brackish conditions. Bordering the adjacent Hook Lake, blackthorn, a very common scrub plant of sea coasts, contends with willow. Blackthorn is normally regarded as a precursor of oak wood, such as may be found a hundred metres inland, while willow at such a location is indicative of the gradation from reed swamp to fen carr.

The brackish water conditions normally associated with estuaries are relatively unimportant in the region's three harbours because the freshwater input is too

156

slight to influence significantly the salinity. It is better to think of them as lagoons. The combination of fully saline sea-water and sheltered conditions is rather rare outside the Solent area and contributes much to the uniqueness of the maritime zone. Among other factors affecting the habitat, consideration must be given to the region's rapidly rising population since World War II, which has led to greatly increased sewage discharge into the upper reaches of Portsmouth and Langstone harbours. By comparison, the Fareham discharge has now been diverted from Portsmouth Harbour to Peel Common, from where it goes directly into the Solent. This situation has increased the nutrient content of the harbour waters for plants, a process supplemented in Langstone Harbour by the acquisition of some of the returning Portsmouth effluent. The planned extension of the Portsmouth discharge pipe should reduce the total effluent load in the harbour. Nutrient levels have risen to a point at which detrimental effects might be expected from the excessive growth and subsequent decay of plants. Eutrophication of this type is usually marked by 'blooms' of microscopic plants of the phytoplankton, a feature seen, for instance, in the upper reaches of Southampton Water as a red colouration in early summer. However, in the local harbours excessive growth is evinced by species of the larger green algae (*Ulva* and *Enteromorpha*) which in summer make up a thick cover over the muds known locally as 'slob'. Its decay contributes a characteristic sulphurous odour and significantly influences mud invertebrates and the behaviour of mudland birds.[1]

The waters of both Langstone and Portsmouth harbours are slow to disperse into the general waters of the Solent, for the twice-daily tidal influx brings back water that has just been carried out. Nevertheless, slow mixing does occur and, together with the input from rivers and outfalls, contributes to the fertility of the inshore waters which contrast so markedly with the nutrient deficiency of the open ocean.[2]

In the Solent anglers have recorded more than fifty species of fish caught. A similar number have been found within Langstone Harbour.[3] The fish taken most commonly in the Solent are bass, pouting and flounder with seasonal plaice, mullet, pilchard and black bream. Sole, mackerel, sea trout and turbot are also found occasionally. In common with the whole of the western portion of the English Channel, the herring has declined and been replaced by the pilchard since the 1940s. The salmon is extremely rare despite its presence in the more favoured angling rivers such as the Test and Itchen to the west, but, with no major rivers entering the harbour confines, this is not surprising. By comparison, molluscs are filter feeders and can thus accumulate bacteria released from the sewage outfalls. Cockles, for example, are locally abundant and oysters have staged a resurgence following previous overfishing, the late 1970s bringing the Solent to a position of importance among naturally occurring British oyster beds. During this period huge quantities were gathered and exported before the slow process of legislation brought some control over their exploitation. Meanwhile, an effort to re-establish the old oyster fisheries on the Hayling shore has failed after some massive earth-moving exercises. Although the tradition of oyster rearing has continued uninterrupted at Emsworth, an opportunity to harvest the sea without detriment to its natural history seems to have been lost, for in spring 1986 a new oyster disease entered the area, though its impact has yet to be thoroughly assessed. It would appear that future success will lie with those who can control their stocks. Contamination by heavy metals is fortunately not a feature of the local marine environment and radioactivity never rises above acceptable background levels, despite the presence of a reactor to the west at Winfrith, Dorset.

The food sustaining the larger animals such as fish, birds and man is derived from, firstly, the photosynthetic activity of microscopic plants of the phytoplankton, of which there are at least forty species in Langstone Harbour; secondly, the diatoms of the mud surface which, when very abundant, often colour it a greeny-brown; thirdly, the decomposed remains of the higher plants of the saltings, together with the fungi and bacteria which induced this action; and finally, the larval forms of the sea-floor invertebrates providing nutrition for plankton, the microscopic animals which float in the upper layers of the sea.

Portsmouth's intertidal zone lacks one of the most interesting marine coastal habitats – the rocky shore. With the removal of many of the rocks and boulders off Southsea Castle, the best which can be seen are a few species representative of intertidal rocks present on sea walls at Southsea, Titchfield Haven and on the Mulberry harbour remains in Langstone Harbour, or where large pebbles are mixed with the mud, as occurs not only by Hayling Bridge, but also off the tip of Farlington Marshes, in Tipnor Lake and along the shores at Hill Head.[4]

Sand near the mouths of each of the harbours and mud in their upper reaches have been extensively investigated and documented, Langstone Harbour particularly so.[5] Of especial interest to marine biologists is the discovery of several discrete populations of the rare worm-like sipunculids *Golfingia vulgaris* and *Golfingia elongata* in Langstone Harbour and the hemichordate *Saccoglossus* which provides a touch of the unusual to the standard species of bristle worms, molluscs and crustaceans.

In view of the absence of rocky shores, the list of seaweeds is surprisingly long, there being over a hundred species in Langstone Harbour.[6] The mudflats of tidal creeks carry a *Fucus* of uncertain nomenclature and several introduced species from the Pacific, including *Grateloupia* species and *Sargassum muticum*, whose floating thallus forms a perfect propeller trap for small boats and has rendered some of the channels unnavigable. Consolation may be provided to the nature lover by the thought that, contrary to previous opinion, *Sargassum muticum* is associated with a large range of invertebrates and has not so far ousted any of the indigenous algae.

The littoral has been attractive to man throughout the ages. Mesolithic shell-fishing, Celtic trade and Roman defence have all left tangible remains and similar economic and military activities continue to be important in the region today. Medieval and early-modern workings, and eighteenth-century reclamation, illustrate the widening economic interests that continued to justify the transformation, even obliteration, of the natural habitat. During this century, waste disposal and industrial development have caused the loss of many acres of aquatic environment and the recent spectacular rise in demand for water sports facilities has spawned a litter of moorings, boat compounds and marina proposals.

Recent encroachment has been primarily at the expense of intertidal muds. Concurrently, but for unrelated reasons, the flowering plants of the remaining mudland areas have changed markedly since the beginning of the twentieth century. The attractive mixed saltmarsh community, of which only small scattered remnants survive, formerly provided an extensive sward with the colourful flowers of sea lavender and sea spurrey among a diverse mixture of species. This sward

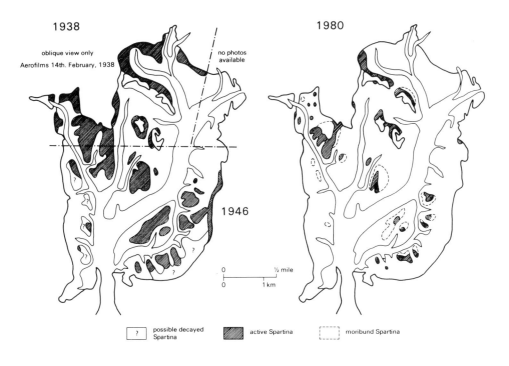

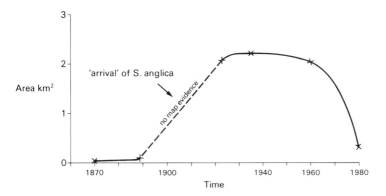

FIGURE 1   Change in extent of Spartina cover at Langstone Harbour 1938–1980. (Source: *F.N. Haynes and M.G. Coulson 'The decline of Spartina in Langstone Harbour, Hampshire' Proc. H.F.C., 38 (1981)*)

has now been reclaimed or taken over by rice grass (*Spartina*). The extensive mats of eel grass (*Zostera*), which supported a wealth of animals, declined in the 1920s, but during the 1970s staged a dramatic spread.[7] Equally striking was the spread of a hybrid variety of rice grass (*Spartina anglica*) during the early years of the twentieth century, colonising, stabilising and trapping mud to form extensive saltings.[8] This was followed, inexplicably, by decline in its vigour and by death, leading to widespread erosion of these same saltings so that the harbours have a more extensive cover of *Zostera* and green seaweed than of the once dominant *Spartina*.[9]

The genus *Spartina* is native to Britain, but the particularly vigorous strain specified as *Spartina anglica* is the consequence of a succession of natural crosses involving the native species and introduced American species, both of which are present in the harbours. Hybrids were first found in the western Solent at the end of the nineteenth century and, aided by planting, spread throughout the Solent harbours and estuaries. Showing a remarkable ability to accrete mud, they colonised mud surfaces from mean tide level upwards, rapidly raising them by as much as 2m, forming monospecific swards over them and invading and eventually dominating many of the older mixed marshes. Elsewhere, particularly in the north and west of Britain, *Spartina* continues to advance and its advent is followed by a marked decline in the numbers of birds utilising the intertidal area. *Spartina*'s ability to accumulate mud has been successfully utilised in reclamation schemes in many countries of the world, for example, China and New Zealand, but despite much study the reasons for the local decline and failure of this landscape, initiated indirectly by man, remain elusive. For a while, the roots of the decayed *Spartina* stabilise the mud and scenes of desolate devastation are created. After a decade or so, however, the hummocks erode and new, more smoothly undulating plains of soft mud are formed, possessing a resistance to erosion greater than might be suspected from their particle size because the mucilage produced by minute algae and bacteria on their surface helps to bind the fine particles together.

Nowhere in the intertidal area of the region, however, are there any clear signs of the succession described for south coast marshes,[10] though all the plants specified as participating in it are to be found. An area by the Eastern Road bridge at Farlington seemed, perhaps, to be initiating new growth,[11] but by 1986, ten years after the first observations, no change had occurred beyond the contribution of some marker canes to the landscape.

Other parts of the non-urban littoral have sand-dunes, shingle or reclaimed marshland. Dunes are one of the most fragile of habitats and, of the quondam sand-dunes, those at Hayling Island provide the greatest interest. They are floristically abundant and contain a surprising number of unusual and often handsome species, such as sea lyme grass and species of evening primrose. The golf-links retain patches not only of 'grey dune', where lichens and moss predominate, but also enclaves of carefully protected uncommon plants reminiscent of species-rich dune 'slacks'.

Much of the shingle above high-tide level is far too disturbed to bear much resemblance to the characteristic shingle 'community'. It is seldom in any situation very rewarding in terms of the number of species of either animal or plant, but it might be claimed that examples in this region have had their diversity increased by human interference. At Eastney, for instance, vegetation from the tip which filled the 'Glory Hole' invaded the shingle area before the hole was re-excavated to form a marina. Nevertheless, this location, together with Sandy Point on Hayling Island and Browndown, musters typical shingle plants such as the yellow horned poppy, sea campion and sea holly. As a consequence of habitat destruction elsewhere on the Hampshire coast, as in England generally, these sites must now be unique in the region for their range of maritime plants.

Of the reclaimed salt-marsh areas the most extensive to have survived the spread of industrial and residential use are those at Farlington. Fortunately for the wildlife of the area, these have been leased by Portsmouth City Council to the Hampshire and Isle of Wight Naturalists' Trust. Throughout the Solent region such reclaimed lands have been most economically maintained as pasture, though with the addition of fertilisers reasonable haycrops can be obtained. Farlington Marshes are best known for their bird life, but they also carry an interesting flora.[12] The strengthening of the sea-wall during the 1970s placed a number of plants in jeopardy. The old wall had provided an approximation to a cliff habitat with cracks and ledges for colonisation. The path along the top of the wall had maintained a constant cycle of temporary habitats, the plants of which provided a seed source for perpetuating the species as new temporary sites appeared. Wholesale reconstruction using heavy earth-moving machinery broke this cycle, but constant vigilance by the Trust ensured survival of the threatened species. Present-day control of the traditional grazing regime at Farlington marshes aims to provide a variety of grassland sites for ground-nesting birds and for those which use the site as a high-water roost and feeding area. The presence of a lagoon and the recent excavation of pond and 'scrapes' greatly increase the feeding resources, whilst the scatter of shrubs in this protected area provides a habitat for a wide range of birds. It is unusual for a season to pass without some exotic species being sighted, a situation typical also of the comparable reserve at Titchfield Haven. Over two hundred bird species have been seen on Farlington Marshes. An unusually complete record of bird-counts has been kept for Langstone Harbour, facilitating a study of the trends in numbers with a view to elucidating possible reasons for variation.[13]

The intertidal zone and shallow seas provide a feeding ground for waders, ducks, brent geese, grebes and cormorants, and also for terns and gulls. The number of birds of certain species present in the three harbours of Chichester, Langstone and Portsmouth form a significant percentage of their total European population, wherein lies the international importance of the harbours.[14] Langstone and Chichester harbours rank among the twenty most important British intertidal systems for their wader populations.

The dark-bellied brent goose, a winter visitor from northern Siberia, is the bird for which the harbours are most noted. It has reputedly declined in numbers following the widespread disappearance in the 1930s of the eelgrass (*Zostera*), then thought to be its staple diet. Certainly, when the first reliable counts started in 1951, the brent geese numbers were below 300. The birds were shy, easily disturbed and they fed at some distance from the shore. It is now known that they not only feed extensively on the green seaweeds covering the mud surface, but also on grasslands. Since the 1950s their numbers have risen dramatically, so that the maximum winter counts have exceeded 10,000 since the mid-1970s and both

TABLE 1
AVERAGE MIDWINTER COUNT OF SOME BIRD SPECIES IN THE THREE HARBOURS
1971–2 TO 1974–5

	Average Count	% of British Population	% of European/ North African Population
Dunlin	61,721	9.5	4.4
Dark-bellied Brent Goose	9,844	38.0	16.6
Shelduck	4,644	6.6	1.9
Curlew	2,134	2.8	1.4
Oystercatcher	2,045	1.0	0.4
Redshank	2,007	2.0	0.8
Grey Plover	1,518	18.9	3.5
Bar-Tailed Godwit	1,460	2.4	0.5
Black-tailed Godwit	1,189	8.5	1.7
Ringed Plover	339	3.2	0.8

Source: *C.R. Tubbs, 'Wildfowl and Waders in Langstone Harbour', British Birds, 20, 1977, pp.77–99.*

Chichester and Portsmouth harbours have joined Langstone as major areas for their overwintering. During this period of population increase, the geese have become much less shy and can now easily be observed by casual strollers round the margins of the harbours. During the thirty-five years since 1951, a number of factors may have influenced the increasing numbers of brent geese: *Zostera* has resumed its importance as an intertidal species, the green algae have spread over large areas of mud in response to nutrient enrichment, wildfowling is a controlled and responsible practice, and many suitable wetlands for brent in other areas have been destroyed. It is not clear which, if any, of these factors, may have led to the brent's increase in numbers in this region.

The population of the large, colourful shelduck also rose in Langstone Harbour from mere hundreds in 1953 to several thousand birds in each one of the next seventeen years. Then, for unknown reasons, it declined to just below one thousand where it has remained ever since. For most avian visitors, other than for curlew and redshank, the Solent harbours seem to be an increasingly popular winter resort.

While the salt-water harbours are notable features of the region, the west and east boundaries are formed by two important freshwater rivers, the Hamble and Ems respectively. Two other rivers, the Wallington and the Meon, run through the region. Apart from these, and their tributary streams, south-east Hampshire is remarkably devoid of biologically interesting freshwater habitats. There used to be a number of mill and village ponds, for instance at Rudley Mill between

Hambledon and Wickham and in Denmead, but these have disappeared almost entirely either by development or neglect, resulting in siltation and vegetation growth. Such stretches of water used to harbour newts and frogs which now find the majority of their breeding sites in suburban garden ponds. It is a matter for regret that so many ponds have been eliminated as no longer useful, thus depriving youngsters of the delight of pond dipping.

One of the better remaining ponds is at Funtley Brickworks which, though threatened by development, is still full of aquatic life, especially the emergent vegetation so necessary for dragonflies when they metamorphose from the larval aquatic stage into aerial adult life. Indeed, at least eight species of dragonfly have been identified at this pond. Rushmere Pond and Langstone Mill Pond have recently been restored. Repeated removal of silt from the latter will be a necessity if the pond is not to dry out altogether. One other pond worth mentioning is Soake Pond, Waterlooville, which is largely artificial, oblong in shape, managed by an angling club, crossed by a pylon line and threatened by infilling and pollution from an adjacent tip. Though it contains nothing of particular interest, it does support a range of common aquatic plants and animals, including the not so common frog.

Undoubtedly the finest freshwater habitat in the locality is the River Meon which rises in the chalk hills north of the region and flows across the Hampshire Basin to the sea at Titchfield Haven. Stretches of the river are managed as a trout fishery and, because its waters are calcium-rich and pollution-free (though major slurry pollution killed the fish in a four-mile stretch during summer 1986), it contains a wide variety of emergent and submerged plants. These include water crowfoot in shallow reaches, aquatic larval stages of insects, crayfish and other crustaceans, species of molluscs and flatworms, and the water vole. Herons, kingfishers and grey wagtails nest beside the river which is overhung in places by willow and alder. Fringed with marsh and fen plants, the Meon flows through pastoral countryside studded with attractive villages. Where it approaches the sea, the river threads its way through two adjacent nature reserves occupying the former estuary on which Titchfield was a small port. The sea was excluded by an embankment constructed in 1611, at the behest of the second Earl of Southampton, and the river now empties through sluice-gates into the Solent. Some marine influence is still apparent in the salt-marsh flora of Lower Titchfield Haven. Both the Upper and Lower Haven of Titchfield Haven Nature Reserves are well populated with wildfowl and waders in winter and harbour-breeding small birds in the extensive reed beds in summer. The Lower Haven is owned by Hampshire County Council, the Upper by the Hampshire and Isle of Wight Naturalists' Trust. Public access to both reserves is restricted in order to avoid undue disturbance to wildlife.

The estuary of the River Hamble is largely devoted to sailing and includes many moorings and two marinas. From 1939 several breaches developed on the east bank of the river resulting in the former meadows being converted to salt marsh. Restoration of the embankment at Bunny Meadows has recently been carried out by Hampshire County Council so as to retain the salt marsh, the tide being admitted through a series of sluices. This wet area is used by wildfowl in winter for roosting and feeding and is to be conserved by declaring it a local nature reserve. Additional reserves are proposed for the adjacent coastline and in the tributary valley near the river mouth. Much of the River Hamble is inaccessible to the public from the land, which is privately owned, but in the National Trust reserve, further upstream at Curbridge, saline, fully freshwater and totally terrestrial habitats may be seen along the river bank, each with its characteristic vegetation.

The Wallington river further east has suffered episodes of pollution both by oil and other chemicals, agricultural and industrial. It now contains very little of interest to the naturalist. Southwick Lake, through which the river flows, is steep-sided and overhung all round with trees, so that little light reaches the water and this, together with pollution, has resulted in minimal biological diversity. However, some wet meadows, bordering the tributaries of the Wallington, support common freshwater plants with a few rare species among them.

Even small insignificant wet areas may be attractive and of interest to naturalists: the colourful pink and white flowers of codlins-and-cream, deep-pink ragged robin, creamy meadowsweet, brilliant marsh marigold and white hemlock, and water dropwort grow in roadside ditches. In one ditch, near Titchfield, the rare great bitter cress occurs; its more familiar relative, lady's smock, sprinkles unimproved meadows with its lilac blossoms.

Small freshwater sites, by their very nature, are temporary and liable to dry up; they may be polluted accidentally or deliberately, are often enriched with fertiliser, natural or artificial, and seem to be regarded as suitable sites for rubbish dumping. Consequently, the flora and fauna of any one site is subject to extreme fluctuation in quantity and composition.

Aquatic habitats generally are very vulnerable to changes of any sort – innate successional change, climatic variation or human activities. Consequently, description of the flora and fauna of such systems is likely to prove inapplicable after a lapse of time. Wetlands are disappearing fast as sophisticated drainage techniques are applied widely for agriculture or development. It is notable that the only valuable freshwater habitats are those which have been conserved for fishing, such as the River Meon, or are designated nature reserves, as at Titchfield Haven. Nature reserves have also been established in the maritime environment at Farlington Marshes and in part of Langstone Harbour. However, the maritime habitat of the littoral has been almost obliterated and the intertidal lands have been progressively encroached upon by reclamation, despite their biological productivity and the bird life they sustain. Commercial fish stocks, subject to controls on over-fishing, are also in part dependent on food exported from salt marshes and mudlands. Langstone Harbour constitutes a breeding area for some fish species and a 'nursery' for the young. Without enforced legal protection the aquatic animals and plants of the region are likely to be severely depleted both in numbers and diversity. If the retention of the specialised wetland communities is desirable, then constant vigilance, protection and habitat maintenance must be long-term objectives to ensure their survival.

PART FOUR
TWENTIETH-CENTURY PORTSMOUTH

11

THE TWENTIETH-CENTURY ECONOMY

Hugh Mason

During the first half of the twentieth century Portsmouth could be described as a community built upon shifting sands. Throughout the period its economy and that of large parts of the surrounding area was substantially based directly or indirectly upon the employment provided by the Navy and by the dockyard.[1] It was thus tied closely to the role which the United Kingdom played as a world power. This nexus lay at the root of many of Portsmouth's problems during the period as the nation passed by way of two world wars from the noon to the twilight of world wide imperial power. Not merely did the position of Britain in the world change, however, but the world itself was changing as new technologies were developed, as the economy successively grew and faltered, and as peoples' aspirations for their own lives changed. All of these, and many other changes, affected both the economic life and the physical appearance of the Portsmouth area.

At the beginning of the century Portsmouth might have been described as a 'northern city' in a southern setting since it was dominated by one industry. The naval dockyard itself was, in 1900, employing 7,976 men and had a wages bill of almost £575,000. In both size and technology the dockyard was in a period of change. Employment had risen by 1,700 men (27 per cent) between 1890 and 1900, and the census of 1901 revealed that the old trades associated with the sailing era had all but disappeared, whilst new trades had grown during the previous decade. In particular, since the introduction of the new water tube boilers in the mid-1890s, the number of boilermakers employed had risen rapidly and the 1901 census recorded 650 men employed in that trade living in Portsmouth, the majority of whom would have been employed in the dockyard.

This establishment, however, was not the only way in which the Navy underpinned the area's economy. The 1901 census recorded that 17,567 servicemen were living in Portsmouth, Gosport and Alverstoke. Their importance in the area can be gauged from the fact that the 13,559 naval personnel in that total accounted for 39 per cent of the whole Navy complement recorded in barracks or in home waters.

The service personnel were supported by a large, and perhaps larger, group of civilians, both those employed directly in shore establishments and those working in a wide variety of trades and professions, including such occupations as brewing and tailoring, which relied upon the armed forces for a substantial proportion of their custom.

During the decade which followed, the importance attached to the Navy grew and its shore establishments were both enlarged and modernised.[2] In the years 1903 and 1904 the Steam Factory, a large workshop extending over 4 acres and employing 650 men, was built. From 1906 onwards the majority of the dockyard equipment was overhauled and new technology, including electric power, was introduced. The 1911 census showed great changes in employment. The number of boilermakers in the town had risen to 962 and for the first time a large number of electricians were recorded, the majority of whom were probably employed in the dockyard. The changes in the dockyard's needs were also reflected in new courses being provided for the apprentices in the dockyard schools.

With the increased capability larger ships were constructed with increasing frequency. In 1904 the *New Zealand* and the *Brittania*, the last pre-Dreadnought battleships, each of 16,350 tons, were launched. These were followed in 1906 by the *Dreadnought* itself, a battleship of 17,900 tons, incorporating the latest in naval design and equipment. From then until 1914 one battleship a year was launched at Portsmouth. The Dreadnoughts were followed from 1911 by the Super Dread-noughts, a class which culminated in the *Royal Sovereign*, a massive battleship of 27,500 tons, launched in 1915 and completed the following year. So great were the demands for ship construction that, to supplement dockyard activity, minor shipbuilding works were carried out at the Haslar gunboat yard.

By the outbreak of war in 1914, the dockyard had been extensively modernised and was working at full pressure. It was, by then, employing some 15,000 men, of whom 11,500 were employed in the industrial departments. The increased amount and pace of war-work led to the numbers employed rising to approximately 23,000 at the height of activities in 1917.[3] In addition to the construction of capital ships, submarines were built and there was a heavy programme of maintaining and servicing major naval vessels. Completion of the Dreadnought programme in 1917 marked the end of an era of expansion and of frenetic activity. With the cessation of hostilities, the need for work decreased still further and men were laid off, employment falling to 9,000 by 1921. This caused considerable distress, both in the town and the surrounding area, especially amongst those who had moved to the region to obtain work in the dockyard.

The post-war years were certainly ones of anticlimax, such work as there was for the dockyard being mainly concerned with the rehabilitation of warships. By the mid-1920s the number employed had shrunk to 8,000 men and it was expected that with added government economy measures this number would be further reduced.[4] However, after the lean years of the early 1920s, when only one warship was launched from Portsmouth, the second half of the decade saw some increase in activity with the building of three County Class destroyers. None the less, government retrenchment and increasing economic difficulties in those years kept the dockyard at a low ebb and by 1931 the number of men employed was only two-thirds, and the number of shipwrights only a half, of the totals of 1914.[5]

The lean years gradually came to an end in the 1930s when government policy again began to pay more attention to defence. It was realised that the fleet had been reduced to very low levels and after 1933 the modernisation of capital ships provided a succession of jobs for the dockyard. Work further expanded after 1936 with the conversion of ships to new functions such as the transformation of light cruisers for anti-aircraft warfare purposes. When hostilities broke out in 1939, dockyard employment had been restored to approximately the level of 1914, with a little over 14,000 men being employed. In addition, reflecting the changes which were taking place in the structure of employment, 132 women were at work.

Although the increase in personnel, reaching 16,820 at the height of operations, to meet the packed programme of emergency and refit work during the war, appears slight when compared to that of the First World War, there was a considerable change in the structure of employment. Many skilled workers were transferred from the dockyard to emergency repair bases and consequently increasing numbers of semi-skilled and temporary workers were employed and trained. This number included many women workers and unskilled men. Rapid changes in the skills of the dockyard were also brought about by the speedy technological changes of the war period. Radar was introduced and wholly new types of work such as that on the Mulberry Harbour were undertaken by the dockyard and by other establishments. Despite the very heavy bombing of the dockyard, and the other shore establishments in Portsmouth, work continued unabated throughout the war.[6]

Just as the wartime expansion in employment had not been as marked as that in the First World War, so the subsequent decline in activity was not so serious. The numbers employed in the dockyard itself fell from 16,820 in May 1945 to 14,799 in May 1948. Similar declines were recorded in other shore establishments. The short-term future was secured in 1948, however, when the Admiralty set in motion the first stage of its plan for modernising the fleet. The modern specialisations which had been developed in wartime were of considerable value in the refitting and major overhaul work which provided the dockyard with a continuing role.

At mid-century the naval base and the dockyard still provided the *raison d'être* for the whole conurbation. The dockyard remained by far the largest employer and the 1951 census recorded 16,582 men in the armed forces resident in Portsmouth and a further 9,872 in the remainder of the conurbation which included Gosport, Fareham, Havant and Waterlooville. Voices were already being heard at this time questioning the yard's long-term future and even that of many of the nearby shore establishments. As a result, greater attention was beginning to be paid by the City Council to the development of other industries.

Gradually through the century the industry of the Portsmouth area became more diversified, although the dockyard remained dominant. Even as late as 1968 the internal industrial labour force in the dockyard was about 8,500, although thereafter a sharp decline set in. It is, however, somewhat surprising that an area endowed with a wide range of industrial skills should have been so tardy in developing a variety of alternative successful industries. Although it was widely believed that the Navy was not happy with the prospect of any other industry developing and competing with it for labour in any dockyard town, the effect of the naval dockyard seems to have been a negative force retarding development rather than a positive force preventing it. The dockyard and the shore establishments provided comparatively secure, if not well-paid, work for their labour forces. The skills of those workers developed often through yard apprenticeships were, in many cases, very specialised and not easily transferable to small commercial ventures. Moreover, by the very comprehensive way in which the dockyard was organised, ancillary commercial operations which might have facilitated the growth of more widely ranging industry were discouraged. Even so, the naval establishments and the Navy itself provided the stimulus for the development of much of the commercial industry. The initial stimulus and continuing demand which kept the industry alive in many cases may be seen as a response or reaction to the defence 'industry'. In some cases, therefore, supplying defence needs provided the stimulus for the establishment or growth of enterprises. In other cases the collapse of defence work forced individuals and companies to seek new outlets and products. Sometimes the same company experienced both effects at different times.

Two further features characterise many of the industries of the Portsmouth area during the first half of the century – a lack of capital and a pattern of merger or takeover. The stresses and changes thus caused appear most frequently at times of trading difficulty and here, once again, the dominance which the dockyard and the Navy exercised over the whole economy of the area is clearly demonstrated.

One industry which illustrated many of these features was brewing, dominated by the growth of two major firms, Brickwoods, at the beginning of the century by far the largest brewers in Portsmouth, and the Portsmouth United Brewery which challenged their supremacy. The latter well illustrates growth by merger. It had been founded by Thomas Dupree in the 1890s upon the combination of the Cosham Brewery, the Beehive Brewery and John Miles Elm Brewery. During the early years of the century the firm expanded by either outright purchase of, or the acquisition of controlling interests in, other small breweries. Thus, by 1913, despite having had some capital problems, it was supplying 200 licenced houses. The much increased demand during the First World War, from civilian workers, servicemen and contracts to supply the forces, led to a very rapid increase in trade. Between 1913 and 1918 public trade sales rose by 96 per cent from £107,000 to £210,000, and contract sales rose by 294 per cent from £50,000 to £197,000. The down-turn in trade, which predictably followed the war, as did persistent unemployment, produced a decline in both aspects of sales. The contract trade fell to £39,000 in 1924 – less that 20 per cent of its high point six years earlier – and Portsmouth United Brewery faced considerable problems. Its future was eventually secured, however, by a further merger in 1928 with the Rock Brewery of Brighton. It remained thereafter the major rival to Brickwoods until it was itself taken over by Brickwoods in 1953.

The First World War brought a number of enterprises into being, some of which were short-lived, whilst others were able to diversify sufficiently to continue trading. The Gosport Aircraft Company, established jointly in 1916 by Charles Nicholson, of the Camper and Nicholson Yacht building family, and Sir Charles Allen, was an example of a short-lived venture.[7] The firm was concerned mainly with the building of flying boats and its first order, which served to establish the company, was for fifty such aircraft for the Royal Naval Air Service at Lee-on-the-Solent. Other contracts followed, but the company was perhaps too specialised to be able to make the transition to peace-time requirements and, after a brief attempt at some desperate measures including furniture manufacture, the company closed in 1920. The Mayfield Clothing Company of Gosport, in contrast, whilst initially making clothing for the Navy, was able to diversify sufficiently to remain in business. Similarly, the Portsmouth Steel Company, established in 1915 initially to make the corset steels previously imported from Germany, diversified into a variety of sprung steels and by the early 1920s had further extended its activities into bedding manufacture.[8]

The period following the end of the war produced both a decline in trade in Portsmouth and much increased unemployment. In February 1922, when unemployment had reached 6,225 in the town, the *Evening News* reflected a campaign to encourage the buying of locally-made goods in a series of articles about Portsmouth-produced manufactures. The variety of products was impressive, ranging from the pianos of Papps Piano Factory to the cigarettes of the St Petersburg Cigarette Company. Despite all attempts, the area faced difficulties throughout the decade and the latter years of the 1920s saw registered unemployment in the Portsmouth Employment Exchange area hovering around the 5,000 mark.

Innovation there certainly was in the inter-war years, but it was always interwoven with difficulties. The Osborn Engineering Company, which produced the technically advanced OEC motor cycle, was founded in 1919 and acquired the Lees Lane, Gosport premises of United Aircraft, a casualty of the ending of hostilities. It would probably have been a very short-lived enterprise had it not, quite early in its existence, acquired the contract to assemble Blackburn engines which certainly helped to keep the company solvent. However, the firm continued to experience financial problems, although later in its history it benefited from a financial linking with Glanfield and Lawrence, the motor-cycle agents of Portsmouth. The firm exemplified the view that between the wars British engineering was more interested in craftsmanship and technical perfection than in mass production.[9]

The quest for perfection did not always produce continuous crisis as was shown by yacht-building, one of the most successful industries of the inter-war period. Although the Gosport firm of Camper and Nicholson was founded in the eighteenth century, it came to prominence after control of the firm passed in 1906 to Charles Nicholson. Under his direction, the firm specialised in the building of ocean-racing yachts. The almost fanatical interest of the wealthy in ocean-racing in the inter-war period brought a steady stream of work to Camper and Nicholsons at a time when other industries were in the doldrums. Not merely did the building of the highly successful and very expensive J Class and 23m yachts provide employment in a town described as having a dingy and depressed appearance, but the success brought benefits to other firms linked with the yachting world.[10] Ratsey and Lapthorn, sailmakers, producing special sails for racing yachts, small manufacturers of yachting equipment, ships chandlers and even tailors and photographers benefited from the money being spent on the enthusiasm of ocean-yachting.

Far removed from the glamour of yachting, firms manufacturing low-cost necessities were also able to weather the difficulties of the inter-war period. Although there were few such firms in the Portsmouth area, one example was John Palmer & Co., brush manufacturers established in 1869. The firm had slowly expanded its operations following the opening of new premises in Somers Road, Portsmouth, in 1902, enlarging its factory in 1911 and again in 1914 to meet War Office demand. Like many other firms, it suffered major difficulties coping with the rapid and severe contraction of demand at the end of the war, but the firm remained successful enough even during the depression and was able to open a new and modern factory in Nancy Road in 1933 and new showrooms four years later.[11] Similarly, in the corset industry, the pattern of a stable demand and the flexibility produced by subcontracting part of the work to home-based workers, enabled firms such as Leethems to maintain their position during these difficult years.

These well-established local firms were joined in the 1930s by branches of a number of companies based or founded elsewhere which, for reasons of growth or relocation, sought new premises. Despite the difficulties faced by the unemployed, many consumer industries, and most especially those catering for new or changed tastes, found the period to be one of expansion. One such was the Sanderson Wallpaper Company, based at Perivale, Middlesex, which, in order to cater for an increasing demand for higher quality wall coverings, opened a branch factory at Lees Lane, Gosport, in 1932.

These developments, even when supported by the many short-lived enterprises which provided some employment, were insufficient to prevent the inter-war years being ones of continuous high unemployment in the Portsmouth area. The restricted opportunities in the reduced dockyard, and the resultant effects on the whole area's economy, produced a high level of unemployment especially amongst young adults. Although the mid and late 1930s brought significant improvements, unemployment was not overcome until the outbreak of the Second World War which brought a rapid change with the frenetic activity of a wartime economy. Even more, perhaps, than during the First World War, all sectors of the economy were caught up in the business of providing for the war effort. At the centre of this activity were the manufacturing industries. The aircraft manufacturers Airspeed, for example, had been one of the city's less successful enterprises. Established at York in 1931, it had moved to Portsmouth where, had it not been for the efforts and, perhaps more importantly, the funds of Lord Grimethorpe, its principal backer, it would probably have foundered given the fitful demand for aeroplanes.[12] The war brought defence contracts and security to this and other such firms. Once again all manner of businesses were drawn into the war effort. Palmer's Brushes, for example, instituted double shifts in 1940 in order to cope with the vast number of government orders and, even after much of their plant was destroyed in an air raid early in 1941, production continued in temporary factories at Stakes in Purbrook and Southbourne. Such was the demand for production, whatever the difficulties, that the firm used Mr Palmer's home at Purbrook as a temporary warehouse.

The cessation of hostilities in 1945 brought the inevitable reduction in employment affecting all branches of manufacturing industry and, although the decline was neither so sharp nor so severe as that following the First World War, unemployment rose to levels which were comparatively high for the south of England. By January 1948 in the Portsmouth Employment Exchange area, the number out of work had risen to 2,250 and by 1950 had reached 4,136, or 5.1 per cent of the employed population. Although the government was advised against scheduling Portsmouth as a Development Area, there was both considerable local agitation for government assistance and, on the part of the local councils, considerable effort to attract new industry. The City of Portsmouth scheduled 510 acres for industrial expansion and in the late 1940s firms new to Portsmouth, such as GEC and Frigidaire, were attracted to the region. By 1950, therefore, the local economy was clearly changing. Although the dockyard remained by far the largest employer, whilst other manufacturing industry was both very much in second place and often heavily dependent itself upon the defence market, new industries were being attracted and the groundwork had been laid for the great diversification of the area's economy which occurred from the 1950s.

One characteristic of this diversification was that few of the industries were either Portsmouth-based or had links with the traditional industries. Onto the new industrial estates at Paulsgrove, Wymering and Farlington the city attracted, in the early 1950s, branch plants of manufacturing firms such as Canda, Smiths Crisps and Johnson and Johnson. Similarly the estates at Havant, Gosport and Fareham saw both relocations of industries and branch plants. As a result the area's economy became less distinctive and industrially self-contained. Indeed, with the attraction of IBM to Havant and later the office developments of IBM and Zurich Insurance in Portsmouth, the area began to develop an international dimension.[13]

Although the dominant features of the Portsmouth economy have long been industry and commerce, by far the greatest proportion of the land area was, at the turn of the century, being farmed. Even in the Borough of Portsmouth, 445 men were recorded in the 1901 census as being in agricultural occupations and, although this number included 283 gardeners and nurserymen, there were also 20 farmers, 130 agricultural labourers and a single shepherd among others. In the Fareham Urban District, 14 per cent of the occupied men were still engaged in agriculture. Despite its importance, however, the agriculture of the area was in relative decline; the amount of arable land in Hampshire had been falling for thirty years and, with the exception of the period 1916–1918, when the requirements of meeting wartime shortages led to land being ploughed, it was to continue to decline until the outbreak of the Second World War. Overall, arable land in Hampshire and the Isle of Wight fell from 422,209 acres in 1901 to a mere 248,617 acres in 1938. In some places, especially on the chalk soils, land reverted to pasture and even to rough grazing.[14] There, as elsewhere, the laying down of arable land to permanent grass was accompanied by the overstocking of pastures with sheep and a consequent deterioration in land quality. Much land was lost to agriculture altogether as suburban growth around the towns spread rapidly, developers benefiting from the depressed price of agricultural land.

Two sectors showed development, however, amidst the overall decline. A gradually increasing demand for dairy produce helped to maintain the dairy cattle sector whilst small-scale market gardening, particularly for strawberries, prospered fitfully in the area to the west of Fareham and especially around Titchfield. In neither case were fortunes readily made although enterprises such as the Co-op (PIMCO) and Tom Parker of Fareham came to operate quite extensive farms. The strawberry cultivation was always on a small scale. From its beginnings about 1880, it had grown by 1914 to a total extent of about 4,000 acres, mostly cultivated by growers with less than 4 acres. In the immediate aftermath of the 1914–18 war there was a short-lived expansion in acreage when, with only limited prospects in either industry or commerce, many people moved into smallholding, despite the price of strawberry land being between £100 and £150 per acre. The inter-war activity settled down after this little boom to a size of about 3,000 acres. A yield of about 200lb. per acre was necessary to cover costs and few smallholders made a good living, although in a period of general economic difficulty in agriculture the number of chip baskets of strawberries, each containing 2lb. in weight, dispatched by rail (the usual way of sending fruit to market), hovered around the two million mark during the inter-war period.[15]

The period around 1930 was the nadir for agriculture in the Portsmouth area. The exempting of agricultural land from rate charges in 1928 and the setting up of marketing boards under the Agricultural Marketing Act of 1931 gave some relief to an industry hard pressed by falling prices. However, by the end of the 1930s, much of the countryside still had an air of neglect and housing rather than food provided the most profitable return for good agricultural land. Green, writing of Portsdown Hill at the end of the decade, noted that 'much first rate arable land with a south aspect is now being swallowed up in what are, compared with Portsmouth itself, admittedly attractive sites for building development.'[16]

The picture of neglect was, however, changed by the outbreak of the Second World War. Land which had been laid to grass for decades was ploughed and, although much good land had been lost forever to housing, south Hampshire agriculture regained its vitality. Whilst the pressing demand for home-produced food receded in the post-1945 era, Government policy of providing support for agriculture prevented a return to the depressed condition of the inter-war years. The pressure of the housing market for land remained strong and, although some landowners, such as those holding the Southwick Estate, resisted the attractions of housing development, it was clear by the 1950s that land was, and would continue to be, lost to housing and other building especially in the zones between the existing built-up areas.

Even though the basic support for the town and its surrounding area was provided by the Navy, and to a lesser extent by manufacture and agriculture, these economic sectors created opportunities for the development of a wide range of other employment. The distributive trades were especially extensive. The 1938 'Return of Insured Persons' showed that some 18 per cent of the insured population was engaged in these activities. Even at the time, this was recognised as being high and the city was often referred to as 'overshopped'. While some of the firms in the retail business were successful, the vast majority suffered from a lack of capital and a consequent lack of stock. Their owners were often making a poor living in a competitive market.

New trends became apparent during the early years of the century and became increasingly important in the inter-war period – these were the development of multiple and department stores. The multiple stores included Portsmouth-based enterprises such as Timothy White, the chemist and general hardware merchant, and Pinks the grocers, who had a number of retail stores in the area, as well as national chains such as Woolworths. The department stores, such as the Landport Drapery Bazaar in Commercial Road and Handley's in Palmerston Road, Southsea, were established on the solid foundation of drapery.

The Co-op, or more properly the Portsea Island Mutual Co-operative Society, operated both as a multiple and a department store. It expanded its service as the town grew, opening branches on new housing estates.[17] Before the First World War it had opened branches in Havant, Fareham and Chichester and it further expanded by absorbing the co-operative societies at Bognor in 1913 and Petersfield in 1919. Its central premises were, however, at Fratton and these were developed into a substantial department store in 1907. These premises, destroyed by a spectacular fire in 1934, were rapidly rebuilt in a modern and spacious manner.

The Second World War brought extensive destruction to large parts of major shopping areas such as Commercial Road, Kings Road and Palmerston Road, leading to a brief boom in peripheral shopping areas such as Albert Road, Southsea. The destruction also caused the demise of some substantial local businesses and when Commercial Road and Palmerston Road were rebuilt after the war they became largely the preserve of the national multiple stores. The trend was also set by the Co-op which in 1947 opened the first self-service grocery store in the country at Albert Road, Southsea, a trend which would lead eventually to the Co-op Hypermarket at Havant.

Substantial changes also took place in the sector of personal services. In 1901, the census recorded 6,878 female domestic servants in Portsmouth itself, a number which constituted about 8 per cent of all women over the age of 10 living in the town and over 25 per cent of all employed women. The large number, even in the context of the period, is not surprising in view of the many Army and Navy officers who lived in Portsmouth and who would have employed servants. The number of domestic servants, having increased to 7,159 in 1911, fell substantially after the First World War. Even so, as late as 1951, there were still some 2,997 domestic servants in employment.

Other service industries grew and flourished during this period. Education expanded at all levels, but especially in the older age-groups. The Day Training College for teachers which had opened in 1907 and the Municipal College, established a year later, provided the basis for a slow but steady growth in tertiary education. By the time of the National Union of Teachers' Conference in Portsmouth in 1937 some 77 students each year obtained a teaching certificate from the Day Training College and, in addition to a large number of people obtaining technical qualifications, an average of 27 people each year were obtaining London University external degrees from the Municipal College.[18]

In the primary and secondary education sectors, schools were built to meet the needs of the expanding towns. Gosport Council, which became responsible for its primary schooling under the 1902 Education Act, erected three new public elementary schools before the outbreak of the First World War. However, the same Act removed to Hampshire County Council control of the Gosport and Alverstoke Technical Institute which had been proudly opened in January 1902 with 32 pupils. The County promptly changed the Institute into a grammar school, much to the annoyance of many local residents.[19]

In the inter-war period the local authorities opened primary and secondary schools to meet new needs. As in many other services, the public provision was mirrored by that in the private sector and private schools flourished in consequence. These ranged from the prestigious Portsmouth Grammar School, which obtained new large premises by acquiring the former Cambridge Barracks in 1928, to a number of small preparatory schools offering little or nothing educationally which could not have been obtained freely in the local authority schools. By mid-century these minor schools were in decline as, following the 1944 Education Act, their ability to compete, both in terms of education and social cachet, had declined.

One characteristic of Portsmouth, shared by the other towns of the area to only a limited extent, was its wide range of civic enterprises. In this, Portsmouth was in many ways similar to a number of cities of the north of England, a factor partly responsible for the comment that the community was a northern city in a southern setting. An important aspect of Portsmouth's civic enterprise was transport. In 1901 the tramways were taken over by the municipality and the system subsequently extended. It was later supplemented by motor buses and then replaced by trolleybuses, thus providing a service throughout the community.[20] The town also operated for some years a municipal telephone service, opened in 1901 and which, by 1911, had some 2,600 subscribers. In addition to the municipal docks, at the Camber and Flathouse Quay, the further development of which was constrained by the naval presence along much of the island's western shoreline, the municipality in 1930 purchased land on the north-east of Portsea Island for an airport, which was opened two years later. Not content with this, Portsmouth fitfully promoted the case during the late 1930s and 1940s for the establishment of an 'Empire Air Base' for long distance sea planes on Langstone Harbour.

The Second World War of necessity extended the city's range of activities. On the practical front, new services such as municipal restaurants, including the largest on the south coast, were opened. The city set about replanning with a will. The Replanning Committee, established by the Council in 1941, produced a far-reaching set of interim proposals two years later. In the post-war period the scope of planning was enlarged with the production of a design for the development of Portsmouth by Max Lock,[21] and the planning process bore fruit with the Council promoting industrial estates in the north and east of the city.

A further area where municipal enterprise was important was the holiday industry. Southsea was never a resort to rival the great names of the south coast, but it was a substantial second order seaside town. In the early years of the century it had received minor setbacks when the Queen's Hotel was destroyed by fire in 1901 and South Parade Pier in 1904, but the rapidity of rebuilding testified to the resort's success. The Council did much to develop Southsea in the inter-war period, purchasing the common in 1923 and laying out the 'Ladies' Mile' in 1924. A few years later, Victoria Pier was purchased and a new one constructed together with pavilions, shops and kiosks. In the early 1930s, Portsmouth's publicity office was active in promoting the resort and distributed over 30,000 copies of the holiday brochure each year. The Second World War produced a hiatus, but the recovery was rapid and tourist guides of the late 1940s reveal Southsea as a small, fairly conventional, but flourishing resort. Gradually, from the 1950s onwards, a decline in the holiday trade, as the continent became financially more accessible, led to a greater emphasis on the day tourist and to a consequent period of difficulty for the hotel trade.

Whilst Southsea was the more formal resort, the 1920s and 1930s saw a substantial holiday trade develop both in Lee-on-the-Solent and on Hayling Island. In both cases the guest house trade was supplemented by organised camping and other forms of self-catering accommodation. Efforts were made to develop Lee in the 1930s, despite the closure of the railway branch line to passenger traffic. In 1935 a tourist complex, including an observation tower, was designed for the landward end of Lee's pier and, although it was never a great financial success, it added to the attraction of this small resort.[22]

It was not only the resorts which changed in appearance, for the whole region would have been hardly recognisable had the visitor of 1900 returned half a century later. The most obvious change was in the physical scale of the built-up area, for the individual towns and villages of 1900 had, by mid-century, merged into a conurbation stretching across most of the South Hampshire Plain. At the beginning of the twentieth century, Portsmouth was concentrated into the southern and western parts of Portsea Island but was growing rapidly. By 1904 new housing at Milton had led to the opening of a Co-operative store to serve that locality and the Society opened another in Tangier Road, Copnor, in 1912 to meet the town's further eastward expansion. Similarly in Gosport the population had grown and extensive infilling had occurred between the town and Alverstoke during the years before the First World War.

The first decade of the century also saw deliberate attempts to improve housing in Portsmouth. In 1912 the Corporation replaced some of the worst slum dwellings to the south of Queen Street by the spacious and well-planned homes of Curzon Howe Road.[23] After the First World War, using the more extensive provisions of 1919 legislation, the Corporation began to build estates of council houses. What was described in 1923 as a 'charming site of some 500 acres on the south side of Portsdown Hill'[24] was developed as the site for 200 houses at Paulsgrove and the hope was expressed that private developers would create a garden suburb in that locality. Later in the decade, Bransbury Park estate was developed by the Council, each of the houses having a substantial front and back garden.

In Portsmouth, as elsewhere, the 1930s witnessed an explosion of private house building as the depressed price of land and comparatively low cost of building brought the possibility of home ownership to a much wider section of the population. A number of developments took place on the periphery of the city including the Highbury Estate, planned for some 3,500 houses, at Cosham. Extensive estates of houses and bungalows were built on the outskirts of Gosport and on a smaller scale around Fareham, Havant and Petersfield. Many were well, if conventionally, planned, although unplanned developments in places such as Hayling Island produced buildings and developments unrivalled in their unloveliness.

However, the most extensive housing development was brought about by the Second World War, when the Replanning Committee was faced with wholesale destruction. By late 1944, some 6,625 homes had been destroyed and only slightly fewer had suffered serious damage. The Council was actively seeking to purchase land beyond the city's boundaries. Approaches were made unsuccessfully to the Southwick Estate. However, in 1944 the Council purchased 497 acres of the Leigh Park Estate and 1,174 acres of adjoining land to the north of Havant. Plans were drawn up rapidly and, during the late 1940s and 1950s, the area was developed extensively.

With the rebirth of private housing in the 1950s, available land in the proximity of the main roads was developed rapidly and by the end of the decade it was less easy to view Portsmouth, Gosport, Fareham and Havant as visually separate and distinct towns. To the north of the coastal conurbation, although the London Road as far as Horndean was sandwiched in a ribbon of building by the mid-1930s, the 1950s and 1960s saw the development of a substantial dormitory suburb, the areas of Cowplain and Waterlooville being affected. To the west, Stubbington and the western part of Fareham experienced considerable growth, increasing car-ownership encouraging the suburbanisation process as it had to the north. By the time the South-East Study was published in 1964, it was no longer fanciful to consider the development of a South Hampshire Corridor of urban growth from Southampton to Havant.[25] The pattern, however, was not uniform. Ministry of Defence lands broke up the continuous development of Fareham, Lee, and Gosport. What was by some viewed almost as a *cordon sanitaire* separated Waterlooville from Leigh Park and the Southwick Estate strongly resisted attempts to purchase, thus producing asymmetrical development along the A3 between Portsdown and Waterlooville, land to the east being largely built-up and to the west containing much open country.

The unprecedented rate of change during the twentieth century in economy, technology and society has affected almost every aspect of British life, and to a great extent the changes which occurred in the Portsmouth area were no different from those taking place elsewhere. As a result, Portsmouth has undoubtedly become a less distinctive place; the extensive suburbs, the multiple retailers, the patchwork of office, light industrial and service employment can be replicated in almost every sizeable town in the land. Nevertheless, the city retained a degree of distinctiveness, largely stemming from its links with the sea. Although the dockyard ceased to be a builder of huge warships, Portsmouth retained a national prominence, with naval heritage opening a new and visibly stimulating chapter in the tourist trade. The development of the commercial port, and the combined presence of yacht-builders and associated service industries, underlined the region's links with the sea. The changes were many, even if their implications were not always noted at the time. The general standard of life improved in most respects during the century which had witnessed two world wars, imperial decline and the ebb and flow of economic prosperity. Few, however, would deny that for the city, its region and its inhabitants there had been more growth than decay, success than failure and more improvement than decline.

12
LEISURE AND CULTURE

Nicholas Fox

The story of leisure and culture in twentieth-century Southsea and Portsmouth is one of a peculiar civic relationship, not only in the dichotomy of an elegant seaside resort and a hard-headed entrepreneurial municipality, but also in the pervasive influence of a large naval and military presence, from the heyday of empire to its decline and beyond.

The resort trade, which had developed with the nineteenth-century growth of Southsea, was twice steered onto a new course by a combination of these municipal and military forces, firstly after the Great War, in order to bring into the town sorely-needed finance from the holiday trade following the rundown of naval and military activity, and later after the Second World War, when the defence interests were once more in retrenchment and there was a change of emphasis towards 'Heritage Portsmouth' – the defence of the realm and its historic setting. The municipal authorities took every possible opportunity to acquire useful vacant land and historic sites in the borough, responding to the demands of the 1920s and '30s for more recreational and leisure facilities, and seeking to exploit the general increase in the amount of free time available to the working man and the gradual introduction of paid holidays. Later, when the advent and spread of television dealt a damaging blow to much of the traditional indoor activity of theatres and cinemas, the Corporation was in a position to respond to changing tastes with enhanced outdoor and indoor sporting amenities and restored heritage sites. Throughout the century, Portsmouth was strong in amateur musical and dramatic art and this tradition facilitated the launch in the 1970s of major cultural and artistic programmes in which the excitement and flair of the Edwardian period was revived, reinterpreting the one-time cosmopolitan naval scene for an essentially civilian, but equally international, population.

A picture of Portsmouth's cultural and leisure activities at the beginning of the century can be obtained from a substantial guidebook produced for delegates to the 1899 British Medical Association conference.[1] The guide indicated that there were vocal and military concerts 'confined to sacred music on Sundays' on Clarence Pier, from whence steamer excursions departed to various Solent and other resorts. In addition, there was the rather disconcerting note that the pier and adjacent hotel

179

PLATE 1   Ladies Mile

were 'liable to be cleared away at a day's notice in the event of war'! The esplanade was liberally supplied with seats and shelters, and there was an asphalted walk across the common known as the Ladies' Mile, 'where beauty and fashion display themselves after church on Sunday morning'. Two other piers existed – the South Parade and Victoria, the latter 'much frequented by invalids and amateur photographers'. There was also a museum, the new Town Hall with Saturday organ recitals, military bands playing in Victoria Park, two theatres – the Princes and the Royal, a music hall – the Empire Palace (later Coliseum) – and regular concerts at other venues including the Portland and Victoria Halls. The venturesome could take a ride into the countryside to Milton – 'quite the most umbrageous nook on Portsea Island' – or visit the picturesque ruins of Portchester Castle by train. Accommodation was to be had in eleven general, three commercial and two temperance hotels.

In addition to these fairly limited amenities, the town did possess one attribute very desirable to the Victorian middle and upper classes – a healthy climate – and the Corporation had for a quarter of a century been assiduously promoting this natural asset in persuasive and extravagant terms. 'Come to Sunny Southsea, where the death rate is only nine per 1,000 and the other rates 6/4*d*. in the pound', ran the opening of the official guide for 1908, stressing all the available healthful outdoor pursuits,[2] such as skating on South Parade Pier, golf at Hayling Island, Rowlands Castle and Lee-on-the-Solent, cricket, tennis, croquet, bowling, cycling and yachting. The Portsmouth Swimming Club, founded 1875, had no equal and claimed to be the world's largest with 1,500 members. Many of the borough's

PLATE 2   Old Town Hall (Museum)

PLATE 3   Town Hall

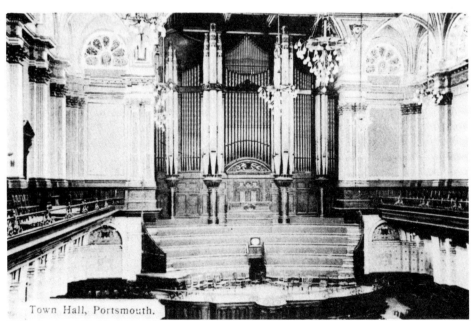

Town Hall, Portsmouth.

PLATE 4   Town Hall interior

PLATE 5   Swimming Club

popular assets were relatively new, for example the Town Hall of 1890 and the Empire Palace of 1891, as well as the famous Theatre Royal where Charles Kean, Henry Irving and Ellen Terry played, which was rebuilt by Frank Matcham in 1900.[3] Nor were more academic pursuits lacking. Although Portsmouth had been reluctant to adopt the Public Libraries Act of 1850, a Libraries and Museums Committee had been formed by 1882 and by 1900 three public libraries had opened as well as a museum in the old Town Hall in the High Street. A Literary and Scientific Society, of which Conan Doyle and Dr Watson were members, had existed in various guises since 1818.

In Edwardian Portsmouth, the naval and military presence, as might be expected, provided the most ostentatious opportunities for social activities. Thus the population and the borough authorities were presented, not only with ready-made spectacle, but more especially with occasions for demonstrating lavish hospitality and celebrating *entente* in style. In 1907 for example, a not untypical year, there were visits from a Russian squadron in March, the colonial premiers in May, the King and Queen of Denmark in June, two Japanese cruisers in July, a Swedish squadron and Edward VII for a review in August and the Kaiser with a German squadron in November. On each occasion rounds of entertainment were given. When the French fleet visited in 1905, the crews were carried to a fête at North End Recreation Ground in gaily decorated tramcars, a banquet was held for the officers in the Town Hall, a garden party in Victoria Park and there were stirring scenes in the streets as the populace fraternised joyously. For the Coronation Review in 1911, some 50,000 people greeted George V and Queen

PLATE 6   French Fleet visit 1905

Mary at the harbour station, 45,000 schoolchildren were entertained at an open-air party and the days were filled with civic receptions, garden parties and banquets.[4] On the occasion of the 1914 fleet review, the largest ever *feu de joie* was given in three volleys by a three-mile line of soldiers drawn up along the sea front from Southsea to the Round Tower and from Fort Blockhouse to Fort Gilkicker on the Gosport side. The assembled fleet totalled 648 ships in eleven lines and stretched for forty miles.[5] Likewise during this period, garrison regiments provided the immensely popular church parades at Governor's Green in Old Portsmouth, which were a colourful spectacle and *de rigueur* for the fashionable population as well as entertaining for the lower classes.

It was not, however, simply in armed forces' affairs that the borough enjoyed a reputation for hospitality. Numerous national bodies held their conferences in the town, enjoying both the reception and the facilities provided. To give encouragement and impetus to this lucrative trade, a Southsea and Portsmouth Entertainments Committee was formed in 1905 independent of the Corporation, although most of its members were councillors. This body undertook to supply all the necessary equipment and facilities to add to the attractiveness of Southsea and eventually in 1920 it became the Beach and Publicity Committee of the Corporation,[6] concerning itself with both indoor and outdoor activities.

Indoor pastimes, in this early period, were mainly dramatic and musical. When the first South Parade Pier burnt down in 1904, the Corporation purchased the site and opened a new pier, including a large theatre and skating rink, four years later. A new music hall, the Hippodrome, opened in 1907, as did the King's, another

SOUTHSEA

AND

PORTSMOUTH

Coronation

Souvenir Guide.

The World's Greatest Naval Port.

A Charming Summer & Winter Resort.

PLATE 7   Official Guide 1911

THE HIPPODROME,

COMMERCIAL ROAD, PORTSMOUTH.

Proprietors - - *The Portsmouth Hippodrome, Ltd.*

MANAGER DIRECTOR—MR. WALTER DE FRECE.

The
Hippodrome
is a
Favourite
place of
Amusement.

THIS MAGNIFICENT BUILDING,

THE HANDSOMEST & MOST LUXURIOUS HOUSE OF ENTERTAINMENT ON THE SOUTH COAST,

⚓ IS NOW OPEN. *⚓*

The Entertainment is modelled on the system of

Two Performances Nightly,

Commencing at **6-50** and **9-0**. All Artistes appear at each performance, and both performances are alike. The Artistes will be booked in conjunction with the other establishments controlled by the De Frece Circuit, which include—

Palace Theatre, Manchester.	Empire Palace, Wolverhampton.
Tivoli Palace, Liverpool.	The Hippodrome, Southampton.
Palace Theatre, Belfast.	The Hippodrome, Colchester.
Royal Hippodrome, Dublin.	The Hippodrome, Boscombe.
Royal Hippodrome, Edinburgh.	The Hippodrome, Margate.
The Palace Theatre, Leeds.	The Hippodrome, Wolverhampton.

Stoke Newington Palace of Varieties.

It is the desire of the Management to make the Hippodrome a FAMILY RESORT, and they guarantee that the performance will be at all times refined and of the highest class.

A feature of the Entertainment is the Magnificent Orchestra of 20 Selected Musicians.

Prices of Admission—3d., 6d., 1/-, 1/6, 2/6, 10/6, 15/-.

PLATE 8 Hippodrome

Matcham theatre, complementing the Royal, Princes, and Empire Palace showing straight plays, melodrama and variety respectively.[7] Six cinemas opened in 1910, a further five in 1911, and by 1914 there were some eighteen in operation.[8] Musical entertainment was provided by the Temperance Choral Union, founded 1880, giving sacred concerts and an annual *Messiah*. Additionally, military and marine bands performed in several bandstands, whilst Saturday morning organ recitals, given by prominent local musicians, took place in the Town Hall.[9] For entertainment of a different kind, the town was still notorious for the enormous number of licensed houses which played their traditional rôle in the pleasures of the working class and armed forces. In 1905 there were 995 of these houses for a population of only 190,000. By 1930 there were still 782.

The Portsmouth area naturally offered a wide variety of outdoor leisure opportunities. Excursions could be taken to Leigh Park, opened to the public by Sir Frederick Fitzwygram; to Horndean and to the tea gardens and fairs on Portsdown Hill via the light railway opened in 1903.[10] Portchester could be reached by train, as could Farlington with its racecourse opened in 1891 complete with royal box.[11] However, with much of Portsea Island undeveloped, it was unnecessary to go far for simple pleasures such as blackberrying around the Canoe Lake or ball games on the common.[12] The sea provided more free entertainment, with mixed bathing allowed as early as 1910. Also on the sea front, soap-box oratory at Speakers' Corner could be enjoyed, or concert parties and troupers performing nearby on makeshift box or trolley stages.[13] Elsewhere in the town itself the crowded Charlotte Street market was a source of fascinating variety, especially for children, who at other times played out in the streets and alleys of Landport and Portsea.[14] Whilst all these activities were free, at Fratton Park the public could pay to watch Portsmouth Football Club, founded in 1899. Playing in the Southern League, they became champions in 1902.[15]

A Parks and Open Spaces Committee had been established in 1891 and a number of astute moves by the Corporation prior to the Great War added to their ownership some large private estates which were often turned, at least partly, to recreational use. Thus Alexandra Park was opened in 1907, land was acquired at Milton in 1911 on the death of Mr James Goldsmith, from which developed Milton and Bransbury Parks, whilst Baffins was landscaped the following year. In 1914, a small golf-course was opened at Southsea and some bowling greens by the Canoe Lake, and there were moves to acquire the Great Salterns estate on the east side of the island.

The Corporation also took the opportunity in 1904 to purchase the Landport house where Dickens was born and to convert it into a museum. They were also persuaded to accept a library for Fratton from the celebrated philanthropist Andrew Carnegie, which the noted Southsea architect A.E. Cogswell designed free of charge in 1906.

The outbreak of the Great War had an immediate effect on the cultural life of Portsmouth and Southsea, ending the church parades, forcing suspension of societies for lack of members, closing some cinemas and halls, and seeing the takeover of parks and open spaces for allotments or military purposes, as at Southsea Common and Farlington racecourse. Southsea front was almost completely closed off by barbed wire and the town filled up with large numbers of military and naval personnel, eventually totalling some 30,000 in the various barracks.[16] Women began to take over men's jobs in the dockyard and public

PLATE 9   Dickens Birthplace Museum

services from 1916 and a committee was formed for entertaining the wounded, using the Town Hall, South Parade Pier and Victoria Park as venues. Performers gave their services gratuitously and free public transport was provided on the trams for the servicemen.

As the town emerged unscathed from Zeppelin attack,[17] so the cultural and leisure aspects of life, dormant during the war, were revived without much difficulty in 1919 and the peace treaty was celebrated enthusiastically with a pageant, banquets, garden parties and tattoos. At the same time, the Corporation was considering how best to combat the inevitable decline of dockyard and service activity and the ensuing economic slump. Accordingly, the authorities decided to adopt a vigorous policy for the development of the tourist and resort industry, whilst embarking on major job-creation projects such as the building of the Eastern Road and the extension of the sea front promenade, which would both help unemployment in the area and generate business.[18]

After the war, the policy of acquiring vacant land where possible was retained and in 1920 the Corporation resolved to purchase the Great Salterns estate for development, to include a 126-acre golf course opened in 1926. In 1921 the sea front esplanade was extended to Eastney using government grants to help employment and then in 1922 the momentous decision was taken to purchase Southsea Common from the War Office – paid for from War Loan profits – which ensured that the future development of the major part of the resort's sea front was firmly in the hands of the elected members. Anxious to press on with its landscaping, the Parks Committee approved development of ornamental and rock

PORTSMOUTH SPORTS STADIUM

Target Rd. Tipnor. In the heart of the Town. Take N°.3 bus to Alexandra Park

Perfectly Presented

GREYHOUND RACING

Under the Rules of the National
Greyhound Racing Club

Electric Totalisator in Operation

Thrilling

SPEEDWAY RACING

Under the Rules of the Auto Cycle Union

Provincial League Matches

See Tonight's **PORTSMOUTH EVENING NEWS** for *particulars of this week's arrangements*

PLATE 10   Greyhound stadium

gardens, an aviary, fountain and children's paddling pool near the Ladies' Mile. New bowling greens at Alexandra Park and a swimming pool at Stamshaw were opened in 1924. The Corporation thus tried, by the development of extra facilities and the consequent employment generated, to alleviate for the town the hardship of the inter-war depression. Further purchases of land were made by the Parks Committee in 1928 at Portsdown, Hilsea and Southsea whilst, despite unanimous disapproval from the Council on moral grounds, greyhound-racing and speedway tracks were opened at Stamshaw.[19]

The Corporation's vigorous publicity campaign for the encouragement of tourism involved the distribution of vast quantities of free town guides, railway station advertising, inspection and listing of hotels and boarding houses, and the provision of new sea-front kiosks, pavilions and chairs. Applications for guide-books trebled between 1927 and 1928, and in the summer months there was an almost continuous succession of attractions – civic week, children's week, Navy week, carnivals, galas, competitions, garden parties and pageants. Stress was laid also on the attraction of a long season and this encouraged large numbers of day-trippers and holidaymakers to take the numerous through trains from the Midlands and the North, to the extent that even the fashionable Southsea stores began to take an interest in catering for the holiday industry.

Theatrical and musical activity had resumed after the war, with major London stars and productions appearing regularly at the King's Theatre and at the Theatre Royal, the latter advertising itself as 'the premier theatre of the south coast'. Variety and revues took place at the Hippodrome and Coliseum. The King's became notable

PLATE 11   Southsea Beach

PLATE 12   South Parade Pier

PLATE 13 Pavilion interior, South Parade Pier

for the flying matinée system, whereby West End shows were rushed down to Southsea for the afternoon and back to London in time for an evening perform-ance.[20] A Young Citizens' Music Festival in the Town Hall in 1921 attracted 1,200 competitors and developed into the still flourishing Musical Competition Festival. Four years later the Town Hall organ was restored and an official organist appointed. In March 1929, the first Portsmouth Music Festival since the nineteenth century took place. The Portsmouth Players, formed in 1926 to produce light opera and musical comedy with local talent, performed at the South Parade Pier theatre, and by the 1930s musical and dramatic activity flourished widely, with numerous new amateur groups being formed. Among these were the Portsmouth Glee Club (1930), the Southsea Symphony Orchestra (1937), the Tangmere Choral Society at North End (1938) and the Southsea Light Orchestra (1938).[21] Many were to face extinction in the next few years, but a hardy few survived.

For film-goers, a further seven cinemas had been opened by 1928, including Cogswell's exotic Palace near the Theatre Royal in Commercial Road, apparently inspired by a visit which the eminent architect had made to the Khyber Pass. By 1939 there were over thirty cinemas in the town, whilst the theatres continued to attract full houses. All these were mainly private business ventures, but the authorities were persuaded to concern themselves with the provision of extra non-profitmaking facilities. The presentation to the borough of John Pounds' house occurred in 1923, further public libraries were opened at Cosham and Milton in the next two years and the decision was taken in 1925 to develop a library for the Dickens Museum. Three years later the city acquired Cumberland House by the Canoe Lake and converted it into an art gallery and natural history museum.

Less cultivated activities were also promoted, such as the first Southsea Carnival of 1922. Conferences and visits by foreign fleets resumed. The French squadron arriving in 1927 enjoyed concerts, dances, charabanc picnics and suppers, Town Hall banquets, a carnival procession and car pageant, free access to places of amusement and tramcars, a fireworks display, balls, and even columns in French in the *Evening News*. The annual Navy Weeks were immensely popular, attracting enormous crowds of visitors and receiving an important boost in 1922 when HMS *Victory* was towed into dry dock and opened to the public in Trafalgar condition six years later. In 1923 the foundation stone of a Royal Naval Museum in the dockyard was laid by the painter W.L. Wyllie.

Portsmouth's sporting activities and facilities also increased during the inter-war period. There was cycle-racing at Alexandra Park, which was also to be the venue for regular meetings of the Portsmouth Athletic Club from its formation in 1932. Horse-racing took place at Wymering, the Farlington course never having recovered from the Great War. Boating, yachting, bowls, with an Open Tournament from 1928, cricket, hockey and a motor speed rally along the sea front were additional attractions, whilst the dancing and dramatic troupes resumed at Southsea and a large fun-fair grew up next to the Clarence Pier.[22]

The Schneider Trophy races,[23] held over the Solent in 1923, 1929 and 1931, brought the city still more publicity. For the 1929 contest, stands for 10,000 people were erected along the sea front and the beach was packed from end to end. Competitors were naturally entertained at all the usual places such as the Town Hall, Victoria Park and Southsea, where on the Canoe Lake a romantic Venetian evening was enjoyed upon illuminated gondolas.

Portsmouth's national prominence was furthered by the success of the football club. 'Pompey' won the Southern League again in 1920 and became a founder member of the new Third Division, gaining promotion to Division Two in 1924 and to Division One by 1927, the first ex-Third Division club to achieve this feat. Their meteoric rise was crowned two years later by an appearance at the FA Cup Final though, on this first attempt, they lost to Bolton. Their second Wembley appearance in 1934 was again unsuccessful, but finally, in April 1939, their loyal supporters were able to celebrate the capture of the coveted trophy. The city went wild with excitement and by a singular fate Pompey were destined to possess the Cup for a longer period than any other club owing to the intervention of the war. The enthusiasm engendered in local amateur soccer by the club's achievements was such that as early as 1923 the Portsmouth Area Football Association had 350 clubs with over 5,000 players.[24]

In the national depression of the 1930s, with the city's population reaching a peak of 250,000, the Council made strenuous efforts to further the promotion of the resort potential. Summer 1930 was marked with a civic week and shopping festival, the city being gaily decorated and illuminated by 10,000 coloured lights. Lamps were also festooned along the sea front. National associations were encouraged to hold yet more conferences and annual meetings in the town. Some 32,000 guidebooks were issued and each inquirer received a free, forty inches wide, coloured panorama of Portsmouth by Wyllie. The Council acquired part of Hilsea ramparts for public recreation, laid out a small park at Cosham and decided to purchase Pembroke Gardens and the Victoria Pier area. To cater for inclement weather, an eventuality regarded as unthinkable in the official guides, shelters and

PLATE 14   'Pompey' 1939

a large tea house were erected on the sea front in 1931. The airport at Hilsea opened the following year in response to the growing interest in flying and gliding.[25]

The 1930s witnessed a general relaxation in social attitudes towards Sunday observance and in pursuance of this trend the city's parks and golf-courses were opened, additionally, on Sundays from 1933. Other weekend activities included dancing to military bands at various bandstands, roller-skating, picnicking, rambling, cycling, Portsdown Hill fairs and regular sea-front firework displays.[26] The Bastion Roadhouse at Hilsea catered for the motoring fraternity and numerous private operators provided charabanc and coach trips to a wide variety of destinations. In Commercial Road, Portsmouth, and Palmerston Road, Southsea, many of the large stores had tea dances or palm court orchestras.

This transformation of a relatively select Edwardian image to one of abandoned gaiety culminated in 1934 in the famous 'Exit Mrs Grundy' poster and the official proclamation of Southsea as 'the resort with no restrictions'! This development shocked the more conservative elements and local churchmen. In the expansion of cultural activities, the High Street museum was converted that same year into the city's art gallery and the first of a series of municipal concerts was promoted. The area around Baffins Pond was also preserved as a beauty spot by its sale, at a loss, to the Corporation by generous owners.

Silver Jubilee Year (1935) and Coronation Year (1937) were suitably marked by street parties, free cinema admission for children, fireworks, an illuminated tram

PLATE 15   Airport opening

Facsimile of " Mrs. Grundy " Placard

PLATE 16   Exit Mrs Grundy

PLATE 17   Fleet Review 1935

and fleet reviews. On the sea-front, in the mid-1930s, the ramparts from Clarence Pier to Grand Parade were gradually restored and opened to the public, and plans were laid for the landscaping of Lumps Fort near the Canoe Lake, another former defensive work which the city had acquired in 1931 to forestall unwelcome private exploitation. In the north of the island the moats and ramparts of the old Hilsea Lines, purchased in 1930, were also transformed and an important civic amenity provided in the large, modern, outdoor lido which the Corporation opened in 1935 and promoted strongly. Not only was it the first major leisure asset for the new estates springing up on the mainland, but also its position adjacent to the only road into Portsmouth ensured abundant advertising. The attractiveness of the open-air pools served only to underline the aged appearance of the nineteenth-century indoor baths at Victoria Park and the foundation stone of the new baths there was laid in 1939, only for work to be interrupted by war and a final opening delayed until 1962.

Transport developments were to the city's advantage as a resort. The Southern Railway electrified its lines from Waterloo and Victoria to Portsmouth in 1937, bringing more frequent and better quality services, whilst the other companies accelerated their timetables for the through restaurant-car services which brought thousands of holiday-makers from the North and Midlands industrial areas. In 1938 the attraction of flying was demonstrated when the airport was used as the starting point for a race to Johannesburg and through the 1930s various air-ferry services were operated to the Isle of Wight, the Channel Islands, London and other south coast towns. The adjacent Eastern Road had been extended northwards as far as

PLATE 18   Hilsea Lido

the airport by 1938 and its wide modern carriageways proved perfect for sports-car speed trials which attracted entrants from all parts of the country.

Although Portsmouth had ceased to be an agricultural area, nevertheless the public open spaces of the common had been recognised since the nineteenth century as an ideal venue for the Royal Counties Agricultural Show.[27] The Society's first ever meeting was held in 1871 at Portsmouth on the future site of Victoria Park, but thereafter, with one exception, all nine shows held in the town made use of the common. The event was both popular and of great variety. In the four-day shows, from 1914 onwards, attendances averaged 80,000, by far the best anywhere. At the 1931 event, visited by the Duke of York, there were over 200 exhibitors and £6,000 was presented in prize money.

Contemporary photographs from the local newspapers give an indication of the extraordinary popularity of Southsea at this time. The beaches were packed as far as the eye could see with a solid mass of humanity. Rows of coaches parked along the sea front offered day trips into the countryside while the roads were packed with buses and private cars.

With the declaration of war in 1939, all the theatres and cinemas were closed abruptly. Although these restrictions were later lifted, opening hours continued to be curtailed. As in the First World War, Southsea front and both piers were closed to the public along with the kiosks, tea-houses and other sea-front amenities. Within ten months of the outbreak of hostilities the city found itself in the front line

PLATE 19   Bomb damage, Princes Theatre

PORTSMOUTH MUNICIPAL CONCERTS
Under the auspices of the Council for the Encouragement of Music and the Arts (C.E.M.A.)

Kings Theatre   Sunday, 11th July, 1943

ISOBEL BAILLIE	HARRIET COHEN	HENRY WENDON
(Soprano)	(Pianoforte)	(Tenor)
	GERALD MOORE (Accompanist)	

PROGRAMME

1—" Sigh no more, Ladies " ... ...   *G. Aitken*
  " Love's Philosophy " ... ...   *Delius*
  " The Eve of Crecy " ... ...   *Julius Harrison*
  " Roadside Fire " ... ...   *Vaughan Williams*
  HENRY WENDON

2—Prelude and Fugue in A minor ... ...   *Bach-Liszt*
  HARRIET COHEN

3—" O, Ravishing Delight " ... ...   *Arne*
  " With thee the unsheltered moor I'd tread " (Solomon) ... ·   *Handel*
  " O, had I Jubal's Lyre " (Joshua) ... ...   *Handel*
  " O yes, just so " (Phœbus and Pan) ... ...   *Bach*
  ISOBEL BAILLIE

Interval of Eight Minutes

4—" Shepherd's Song " ... ...   *Edward Elgar*
  " Bard of Armagh " ... ...   *Arr. Herbert Hughes*
  " Onaway, awake Beloved " (Hiawatha) ... ...   *Coleridge-Taylor*
  HENRY WENDON

5—" Twilight Fancies " ... ...   *Delius*
  " Færy Song (The Immortal Hour) ... ...   *Rutland Boughton*
  " If my Songs were only winged " ... ...   *Reynaldo Hahn*
  " Spring " ... ... ·   *Ivor Gurney*
  ISOBEL BAILLIE

6—(a) Nocturne in F major
      Etude in F minor   } ... ...   *Chopin*
      Etude in C minor (Revolution)
  (b) Andaluza—The Miller's Dance (from the Ballet "The Three Cornered Hat" *De Falla*
  HARRIET COHEN

7—" Lovely Maid in the Moonlight " (La Boheme) ... ...   *Puccini*
  ISOBEL BAILLIE AND HENRY WENDON

PRICE 3d.   **For next Concert see over**   **PRICE 3d.**

PLATE 20   Municipal concert

C.E.M.A. CONCERTS

The Council for the Encouragement of Music and the Arts
in conjunction with Portsmouth Libraries and Museums
Committee announce a Series of

LUNCH-TIME CONCERTS

NORMAN NOTLEY and DAVID BRYNLEY
Famous Duettists
MARIE KORCHINSKA
Celebrated Harpist
at Angerstein Hall, Angerstein Road,
North End,
THURSDAY, 27th MARCH, 1941.

ROBERT EASTON
Famous Bass
HAROLD FAIRHURST   THOMAS BEST
Popular Violinist   *Well-known Pianist*
at Duchess of Albany Hall, Edinburgh Road,
(Unicorn Road Entrance)
WEDNESDAY, 2nd APRIL, 1941.

THE BLECH STRING QUARTET
at Angerstein Hall, Angerstein Road,
North End,
THURSDAY, 10th APRIL, 1941.

NORA GRUHN
Popular Soprano
JAMES PHILLIPS   HOWARD FERGUSON
Well-known Cellist   *Popular Pianist*
at Duchess of Albany Hall, Edinburgh Road,
(Unicorn Road Entrance)
WEDNESDAY, 16th APRIL, 1941.

TWO CONCERTS EACH DAY
12.10 - 12.50 p.m. and 1.10 - 1.50 p.m.

Admission at doors 3d. each Concert.
Snack lunches may be taken and eaten during concerts.

Enquiries at Central Library (Tel. 4847) or Branch Libraries

PLATE 21   C.E.M.A. concerts

of the Nazi offensive and the first air raids came in July 1940, when three cinemas were hit. The greatest devastation, however, came in a huge raid on 10 January 1941, which demolished the Palmerston Road, Kings Road and Commercial Road shopping centres, together with Clarence Pier, the Hippodrome, four cinemas and the interior of the Guildhall.[28]

Amidst this terrible devastation, the Corporation, intent on maintaining morale, organised in January 1941 the first of a hugely popular series of municipal concerts in the King's Theatre.[29] At the same time a Special Development Committee was appointed to plan post-war recreational facilities.

With the Government's active promotion of 'Holidays at Home', the Council organised service tattoos at Fratton Park, gymkhanas at Wymering racecourse, water sports at Hilsea, lunch-time concerts, boxing and youth tournaments in local halls, and military band concerts at Hilsea, Milton and Southsea at the rate of fourteen a week. Despite the difficulties, two new musical societies, Portsmouth Music Club and the Portsmouth Philharmonic Society, were formed in 1942 and 1944 respectively. The Special Development Committee produced in 1943 a preliminary report[30] recommending acquisition of the remaining historic sea-front fortifications. In acting on this principle after the war, the Corporation set the city on a new course in cultural development.

With the cessation of hostilities in 1945, some facilities, including the three theatres, naval museum, Alexandra Park, where the pavilion had been used as a mortuary, and Hilsea Lido, which had been used for Admiralty experiments, resumed their pre-war activities. Foreign fleet visits recommenced in 1947, but with the Guildhall gutted by incendiary bombs the civic functions were held on South Parade Pier or in suitable hotels and large halls. The city's first music adviser was appointed in 1947. The next year saw the hundredth municipal concert celebrated and in 1949 the resumption of the Musical Competition Festivals occurred. Two new choral societies were formed, the Milton Glee Club in 1947 and the Drayton Choral Society in 1952, whilst new ground was broken in 1954 by the formation of a short-lived Grand Opera Society. Dramatic activities were similarly revived. The Portsmouth Players, the Little Theatre (later Arts Theatre), founded in 1945, and the Southsea Shakespeare Actors, established two years later, performed at the South Parade Pier and later at the King's Theatre.[31]

Outdoor facilities were extended in 1947 when the Council approved the building of a substantial new Rock Gardens Pavilion and in 1948 agreed the provision of a large recreation ground at Cosham with a grant from the King George V Foundation. 'Pompey', which had held the FA Cup from 1939 to 1946 in the absence of wartime fixtures, celebrated its golden jubilee year, 1948–49, by reaching the Cup semifinal and winning the League Championship, setting another record as the first ex-Third Division side to do so, a record they proceeded to repeat the following year.

The early 1950s continued to be a period of celebration in Portsmouth despite post-war austerity. The Festival of Britain in 1951 brought a revival of the old spirit with a searchlight tattoo, carnival, sports and galas, children's week and fairs. In 1953 the Coronation was marked by traditional scenes of fleet review, street parties, Victoria Park garden party, tattoos, fireworks and an illuminated trolleybus.

Meanwhile, the work of reconstructing and developing the city had begun. The Council resolved to rebuild the Guildhall within the shell of the old building, approved the reconstruction of Clarence Pier and planned the shape of the restored shopping centres. In the dockyard the Royal Naval Museum was redesigned and enlarged. New public libraries opened at Southsea in 1953 and at Paulsgrove in 1954 – a temporary building which in fact lasted over thirty years. Portsmouth Museums Society was founded in 1952 with the aim of encouraging the Council to extend and improve the provision of cultural facilities, pressure which assisted in the creation of a part-time post of City Archivist in 1956 and led to the negotiations for the purchase of the Round Tower in 1957.[32] Rebuilding of a different and enlightened sort had occurred in 1949 with the forging of a link with the German city of Duisburg, leading in subsequent years to fruitful exchanges of cultural and sporting activities especially amongst young people.[33] Further links of this nature were later established with Toulon and Caen in France, and Haifa in Israel.

With the task of reconstruction proving costly and perhaps in reaction to military and naval affairs, voices were raised against any resumption of pre-war levels of civic entertainment, especially of foreign naval personnel and matters came to a head in 1956.[34] From this time Portsmouth's traditional naval hospitality declined. Nevertheless, other forms of entertainment resumed. The sea front and rock gardens were illuminated again, the municipal concerts reached their two-hundredth performance in 1957, there were fireworks on the South Parade Pier every Wednesday in the season and the outdoor facilities now included a roller-skating rink in the old Southsea bandstand which was said to be the largest in England. The town still possessed nineteen cinemas, seven musical societies and three drama groups in the mid-1950s. However, the national decline in theatre and cinema attendance, brought about by the spread of television, began to have its effect on the local environment, particularly in those areas of the town which were in economic or physical decline as a result of war damage, changing population and shopping patterns, and the greater mobility of the age. From 1959 cinemas in such vulnerable areas as Stamshaw, Fratton and Eastney began to close, until by 1966 there were only eleven remaining. By 1982 there were five and by 1987 only three, all converted to multiple-screen facilities and none of which was in Southsea. The Theatre Royal just managed to celebrate its centenary in 1956 before the first of many crises caused temporary closure, the final curtain falling in 1960 and ushering in over twenty years of decay until the restoration proposals of the 1980s. The Empire Palace was sold and demolished in 1958. Nevertheless, the gloom of such closures was dispelled somewhat by the opening of a new 2,000-seat concert hall in the rebuilt Guildhall.

By a significant agreement in 1958 the City Council acquired almost all the remaining fortifications in Old Portsmouth including Long Curtain Battery, King's Bastion and the Round Tower. Then, two years later, the Square Tower and Southsea Castle were released by the Ministry of Defence and the city thus found itself owner and user of nearly all the surviving historic military defences on Portsea Island. The tourist and heritage potential of these sites was clear. Similarly, the Palmerston's Folly forts on Portsdown and in the Solent offered the city further opportunities of heritage development. At the same time, in 1959, Farlington Marshes were scheduled as a nature reserve and bird sanctuary.

Since the beginning of reconstruction work on the post-war city, scant attention had been paid to Southsea as a resort and meagre resources channelled in that direction. In consequence a sense of lost direction pervaded the traditional holiday trade, weakening any resistance there might have been to the changing course of the town's cultural and leisure activity. Once-favoured Southsea began to take second place; the *Southsea Guide* became significantly, in 1950, the *Portsmouth and Southsea Guide* and photographs of the sea front were gradually replaced by ones of HMS *Victory* and of the restored fortifications. This policy received the blessing of the British Travel Association in 1964,[35] which encouraged the city to raise its aesthestic standards still further by promoting the military museums and emphasising the city's historical connections, a trend which encouraged the production of several official handbooks on the historic development of Portsmouth and its defences.[36] In 1963 the Parks and Piers Committees of the Council were amalgamated in a further move to broaden the base of general leisure services.

In 1966 the first Records Office was established in the city with a full-time Archivist and the post of City Museums Officer was separated from that of Librarian with an independent department. Southsea Castle Museum opened in 1967, with the restoration of the Dickens Museum as a period house being completed two years later. In 1972 Eastney Pumping Station Museum was opened, as was a large central City Museum and Art Gallery in part of the old Clarence Barracks. Cumberland House remained to be completely restored and refurbished in 1981 as the Natural History Museum, and under an ambitious publicity and exhibitions policy the city museums service has been projected in recent years with great success. Perhaps the crowning achievement – the D-Day Museum housing the Overlord Tapestry – has attracted huge numbers of visitors from all over the world and provided a fitting memorial for the fortieth-anniversary commemorations of D-Day.

During this development of the archives and museums services, the city libraries had remained the Cinderella. However, the construction of a large purpose-built central library in 1976 as part of the civic centre redevelopment, containing a coffee bar, theatre and meeting rooms, rectified this imbalance. Its amenities have proved popular and successful both with local societies and for civic functions, including the Portsmouth Festivals and International String Quartet competitions. A local studies centre for Portsmouth and south-east Hampshire was established at the library in 1977.

Paralleling this development of the city's land-based cultural and historic heritage, exciting naval discoveries and restorations in the 1970s and 1980s have brought 'Defence of the Realm' to the fore in Portsmouth's present-day promotional assets. The spectacular raising of the Tudor warship *Mary Rose* in 1982 and the arrival in 1987 of the restored ironclad HMS *Warrior* to a permanent mooring at The Hard, together with the historic dockyard buildings, museum and *Victory*, have persuaded the Ministry of Defence to set aside part of the naval base area for heritage purposes. Along with the restoration of some of the Palmerston's Follies by the Ministry and local authorities and the opening of a Solent fort to visitors by an enterprising individual, the greater Portsmouth area offers a splendid collection of military and naval defensive works from Roman Portchester to the historic warships in the harbour – all of which can be viewed by resident and tourist alike.

The emphasis on history has not, however, prevented moves towards cultural artistic events on a large scale. An ambitious series of Portsmouth Festivals, mentioned above, began in 1971 bringing distinguished orchestras and artists to the Guildhall, King's Theatre, the two cathedrals, the central library and other venues. With the appointment of a full-time city arts administrator in 1976, a coherent

PLATE 22   Portsmouth Festival 1980

pattern of advanced artistic activity began to emerge. In 1979 a triennial international String Quartet Competition was launched, the first of its kind in the world, under the artistic direction of Yehudi Menuhin, by which the city hoped to rise to the international distinction of Leeds and Harrogate in similar functions. Less elevated, but no less enjoyable, were the establishment of a Craft Fair in 1978 and the revival of the Free Mart Fair in 1974, even though the latter has not yet attained the notoriety of its nineteenth-century predecessor. In traditional musical and dramatic activity the city still proves strong, the Choral Union (no longer Temperance) celebrating its centenary in 1980 and the number of new choral and dramatic groups remaining buoyant.[37] A fire on the South Parade Pier in 1974 destroyed the theatre there, but plays have been performed in the new central library, in the new Hornpipe Theatre, in drama centres and in church halls, in addition to the continuing professional productions at the King's. Moves are also advanced for the reopening of the restored Theatre Royal.

Recent developments in the outdoor and indoor sporting facilities of the town have also been spectacular, with a fine modern complex – the Mountbatten Centre – opened at Alexandra Park in 1983, where events of international quality have taken place. Debate on whether or not to move Pompey's ground to the north of the city did not prevent the club from climbing back to the First Division in 1987, but sadly only for one season. Basketball and boardsailing have come to the fore as popular local sports and the Portsmouth of the late 1980s sees the promotion of modern facilities for shopping, leisure and sport alongside well-presented and documented historical attractions. Interestingly, high-quality hotel and restaurant developments have been encouraged in various parts of the area not previously favoured, including Paulsgrove and Farlington, and indeed Portsea.

The 1980s thus see the city wedded to heritage, history and the arts on the one hand, and to modern tourism and leisure needs on the other. The traditional seaside resort trade lingers in some respects, although electronically updated amusement arcades, spectacular fun-fair attractions, fast food and bingo have taken the place of dancing and bands, whilst a 1986 Sea Life Centre has transformed the old children's paddling pool site, leaving the 1930s miniature railway in uneasy occupation of a reduced area. On the common the annual Southsea Show continues to draw substantial crowds in the summer.

In the city itself, the contraction of the brewing industry has led to a drastic reduction in the number of public houses and the conversion of many into bistros, wine bars, clubs and casinos – reflecting a national trend towards a more elegant style once again. An indoor bowling alley, constructed in Arundel Street during the 1960s redevelopment, has been followed by the conversion of several former cinemas into bingo and snooker halls.

Long-term holiday-makers increasingly sweep into the city on the new motorway (opened 1976), only to take passage at the Continental ferry port for more exotic destinations abroad. In return, the day-trippers are swelled by continental arrivals, for whom the odd traffic sign in French can be noted. With the occasional foreign warship in port to balance the Continental ferry services and with an increasingly Continental style in shops and eating places, Portsmouth once again has the distinctly cosmopolitan air appropriate to the greatest of English naval cities.

13
POST-WAR DEVELOPMENTS

Ron Windle

Under the Local Government Act of 1888, Portsmouth became one of sixty-one county boroughs. It then had a population of 159,000, but its boundaries extended only to the southern and central parts of Portsea Island. Since 1888, the administrative boundaries have been extended three times to include, in 1904, the whole of Portsea Island, in 1920, the mainland districts of Cosham and Paulsgrove and, finally, in 1932, parts of the parishes of Portchester and Farlington. Thus, since then, the City of Portsmouth has had administrative boundaries which encompass an area of approximately 9,300 acres of land and inland waterways (see Map 1). In 1926 the County Borough of Portsmouth was accorded the dignity of a city.

Despite successive boundary extensions in the twentieth century, social, economic and demographic pressures built up to such an extent by 1945 that it was considered these boundaries no longer accorded with the social, economic and demographic dimensions and, from time to time, the city sought unsuccessfully to extend its administrative boundaries. To escape from the confines of the boundaries in the post-war period, the City Council utilised land to the north and north-east of the city as overspill development areas. Land was obtained at Leigh Park in the Borough of Havant in 1944 and, in the 1960s, further land was acquired at Wecock Farm and at Crookhorn. At Leigh Park, housing and industrial development plans were put into effect and housing developments took place in the other two locations. By 1980, more than 40,000 people lived in these overspill areas.

The failure to extend the administrative boundaries had demographic implications for the city, since overspill housing developments induced a population drift from Portsmouth. Between 1931 and 1971, there was a steady decline in the total number of inhabitants (see Table 1).

The population that migrated to the overspill housing developments outside the city's boundaries tended to consist of relatively young families. Between 1931 and 1971 the number of people under 60 years of age residing in the city diminished by

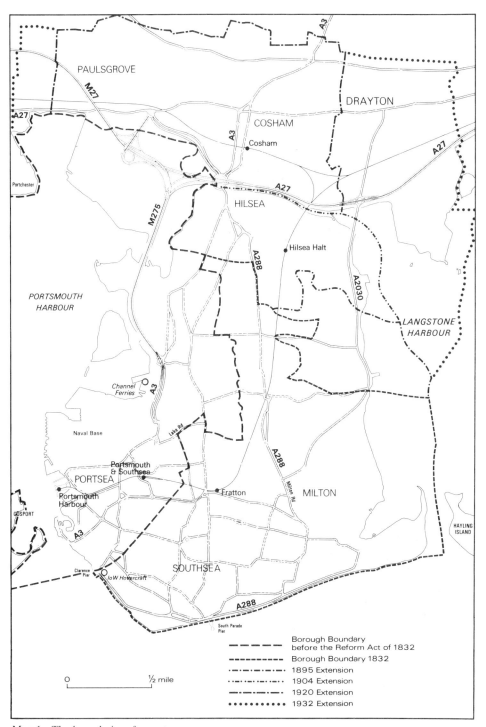

MAP 1   The boundaries of a century

TABLE 1
POPULATION OF PORTSMOUTH, SOUTHAMPTON AND THE UNITED KINGDOM
1931–1971

	1931	1951	1961	1971
Portsmouth	249,283	232,505	215,097	196,950
Southampton	176,007	178,343	204,822	214,820
UK	46,000,000	50,225,000	52,700,000	55,700,000

Source: *Censuses of Great Britain and Northern Ireland.*

over 67,000 and the number of people over the age of sixty increased by nearly 15,000, so that by 1971 there were more than 43,000 people over the age of sixty and approaching 12,000 over the age of seventy-five (see Table 2). Respectively, these groups formed 22 per cent and 6 per cent of the population, compared with 16.5 per cent and 3.7 per cent in 1951, and 11.4 per cent and 2.2 per cent in 1931. Whereas between 1966 and 1971, there was a slight diminution in the number of people aged sixty years or more, 'ageing of the population' between 1945 and 1971 was greater in Portsmouth than in Great Britain as a whole.[1] This was due to two factors. First, there was an increase in the life span of people in Britain: more survived to reach their 'three score years and ten'. Secondly, and more significantly, whilst in Great Britain the number of children in the nation increased after 1945, in Portsmouth there was a decline in the younger age groups, largely as a result of the post-war overspill housing policy, which encouraged the migration of families to new housing estates outside the city boundaries. People over the age of sixty did not migrate to the same extent and remained in Portsmouth to form a larger proportion of the city's population. There is evidence which suggests the crude birth rate in Portsmouth was less than that for Great Britain by the later 1960s, but this would be partly an effect of the ageing of Portsmouth's population.

During the 1960s and 1970s, there was a tendency for economically active males to move out of the city. Whilst the number of armed forces personnel entering Portsmouth was more or less equal to the number leaving in other socio-economic groups, the loss was greater than the gain. The net loss tended to be greater among 'white collar' than 'blue collar' workers. A large amount of the migration out of Portsmouth was merely to adjacent areas in Hampshire where new private housing developments were to be found,[2] a movement which put pressure on the road system at peak times. Consequently, before the construction of the M27–A27, M275 and the A3(M), 'rush hour' travel was a time-consuming and frustrating experience.

Although the population of Portsmouth diminished continually between 1945 and 1971, the density of population, at approximately 21.4 persons per acre, remained higher than elsewhere in Hampshire, being 17.8 in Southampton and 1.1 in the remainder of Hampshire.[3] Despite the city's density of population, the

TABLE 2 CHANGES IN THE COMPOSITION OF THE POPULATION OF PORTSMOUTH 1931–1971

	1931	1951	CHANGE 1931–'51	1961	CHANGE 1951–'61	1966	CHANGE 1961–'66	1971	CHANGE 1966–'71	CHANGE 1931–'71
TOTAL	249,283	233,545	−15,738	215,077	−18,468	201,400	−13,677	196,950	−4,450	−52,333
Ages										
0–4	19,459	19,555	+ 96	15,443	− 4,112	15,720	+ 277	14,510	−1,210	− 4,949
5–9	21,366	17,503	− 3,863	13,482	− 4,021	13,240	− 242	14,050	+ 810	− 7,316
10–14	20,721	14,614	− 6,107	16,678	+ 2,064	12,160	− 4,518	13,015	+ 855	− 7,706
15–19	19,814	16,716	− 3,098	17,134	+ 418	17,010	− 124	14,800	−2,210	− 5,014
0–19	81,360	68,388	−12,972	62,737	− 5,651	58,130	− 4,607	56,370	−1,760	−24,990
20–24	21,380	18,960	− 2,420	16,149	− 2,811	15,810	− 339	18,360	+2,550	− 3,020
25–29	20,991	17,861	− 3,130	12,659	− 5,202	11,630	− 1,029	12,215	+ 585	− 8,776
30–34	18,844	16,779	− 2,065	11,740	− 5,039	9,660	− 2,080	9,940	+ 280	− 8,904
35–39	17,550	15,898	− 1,652	13,359	− 2,539	11,000	− 2,356	9,570	−1,440	− 7,980
40–44	17,023	15,970	− 1,553	13,904	− 2,066	11,750	− 2,154	10,375	−1,375	− 6,648
45–49	16,456	15,083	− 1,373	14,130	− 953	12,560	− 1,570	12,065	− 495	− 4,391
50–54	14,730	13,690	− 1,040	14,549	+ 859	13,150	− 1,399	12,285	− 865	− 2,445
55–59	12,449	12,419	− 30	13,613	− 1,194	13,670	+ 57	12,450	−1,220	+ 1
20–59	139,423	125,620	−13,803	110,103	−15,517	99,230	−10,783	97,265	−1,965	−42,158
60–64	9,818	11,872	+ 2,054	11,940	+ 78	13,220	+ 1,280	12,345	− 875	+ 2,527
65–69	7,713	10,296	+ 2,583	10,240	− 56	10,620	+ 380	10,650	+ 30	+ 2,937
70–74	5,468	7,742	+ 2,274	8,651	+ 909	8,720	+ 169	8,335	− 385	+ 2,867
75+	5,501	8,587	+ 3,086	11,426	+ 2,839	11,480	+ 54	11,980	+ 495	+ 6,479
60+	28,500	38,497	+ 9,997	42,257	+ 3,770	44,040	+ 1,883	43,310	− 735	+14,810

proportion living in overcrowded conditions was less than elsewhere in the country, apart from Bournemouth, and severe overcrowding was markedly lower than in Southampton or the whole of Hampshire, and considerably below that in Britain as a whole.[4]

This apparent contradiction between population density figures and severe city overcrowding is accounted for by the high density of dwellings per acre. The number of occupied dwellings per acre in 1966 was 6.9, compared with 5.6 in Southampton and 0.5 in non-county borough parts of Hampshire, providing one reason why there was so much emphasis after 1945 on 'overspill' housing development.

During the Second World War bomb damage exacerbated housing problems and, when hostilities ended in May 1945, the City Council faced a severe shortage of accommodation. Some 7,000 dwellings had been destroyed by enemy action; a large number of houses were either old and needed replacement or were slums, and there was a rising tide of demand for dwellings from young married couples. The War Office, later Ministry of Defence, a major landowner in Portsmouth, was unable or unwilling to relinquish sites and thus it is hardly surprising that a decision was reached between 1943 and 1945 to pursue an overspill housing development policy. Consequently, during that period, the opportunity was taken to obtain the Leigh Park Estate at Havant (see Map 2).

Local authority housing development, however, was influenced by the policies of central government. In 1919, the Addison Housing Act placed responsibility on local authorities for dealing with housing needs and made subsidies available for house construction for the working classes, thus marking the beginning of local authority housing. After 1944, there was a tremendous increase in the construction of dwellings by local authorities and Portsmouth was no exception. Between 1945 and 1974 some 22,000 dwellings were constructed, of which nearly 10,000 were built at Leigh Park. In the 1940s and 1950s, housing development was concentrated at Paulsgrove, in the north-west of the city, as well as at Leigh Park. In the 1960s and 1970s, the main centres of development were Leigh Park, Crookhorn in Purbrook and Wecock Farm in Cowplain. In addition to these events, clearance and redevelopment programmes were pursued within the city and attention was paid to modernising housing stock in improvement and conservation areas. Clearance programmes were slow because most of the sub-standard houses belonged to owner-occupiers, or to very small-scale landlords, necessitating the use of a large number of compulsory purchase orders, since owners were reluctant to sell at site rather than market value.

Unfortunately, in the 1950s, national ideas about urban renewal inclined towards the allegedly efficient use of land by means of constructing high-rise blocks of dwellings. In 1958 the Housing Subsidies Act linked subsidies with the number of storeys in residential blocks and consequently high-rise blocks of flats mushroomed in almost all urban areas in Britain, including Portsmouth, where land was provided by clearance programmes. In 1956, a development plan was drawn up for the reconstruction of war-damaged areas in Portsmouth and it included slum clearance. Some 7,000 houses were considered to be in need of renewal and between 1956 and 1965 more than 3,000 properties were demolished or closed. In the years 1964 and 1965 there was a major review of the development plan as a result of which, between 1966 and 1976, almost 4,000 more dwellings were cleared. The review of the development plan envisaged the construction of high-rise blocks, so that a population density of 130 persons per acre could be achieved. The construction programme that followed was affected adversely by the Ronan Point disaster when a gas explosion in a tower block in Wandsworth caused the progressive collapse of a number of flats. The block had been built by the apparently well-proven method of

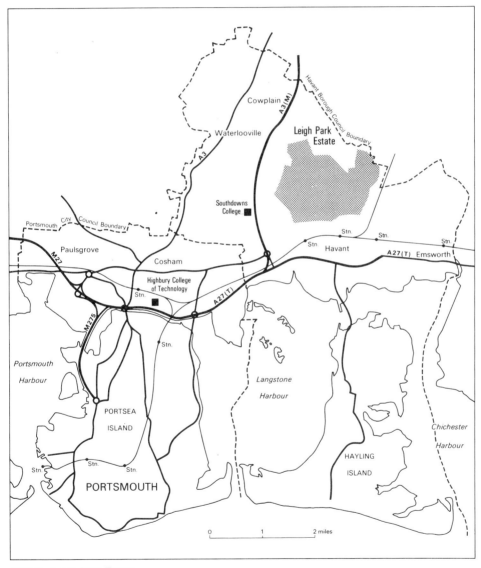

MAP 2   Leigh Park Estate

a panel system of construction with load-bearing walls. In 1968, the Ministry of Housing and Local Government issued a circular, laying down new structural requirements for such high-rise blocks. In Portsmouth there were eight blocks of this nature, containing 995 dwellings, and the City Council had to make very expensive arrangements to conform with the new requirements. Additionally, by 1968 evidence was accumulating nationally to show that such high-rise blocks caused social problems and provided unsatisfactory living conditions.[5] A few years later, the City Council had further problems. On this occasion the Portsdown Hill development of Portsdown Park, designed to accommodate 523 dwellings on an elevated site overlooking Portsmouth Harbour and Portsea Island, suffered severe water penetration of the blocks of flats. A planned, award-winning, prestige development turned out to be just as much of a problem as the eight high-rise blocks previously referred to, although for different reasons. Significantly, the development has now been completely demolished.

Both the South Hampshire Study of 1966 and the South Hampshire Structure Plan of 1973 acknowledged the severity of Portsmouth's housing problems and the need for overspill development. After local government reorganisation in 1974, arrangements had to be made with Havant Borough Council to facilitate administration of the overspill development areas. A Hampshire Standing Housing Conference was established in 1972 and, in 1974, a Joint Advisory Committee, including five members from Portsmouth City Council and five from Havant Borough Council, was formed.

Although the bulk of accommodation provided between 1945 and 1980 was the result of building by the City Council, not all effort was concentrated on local authority housing. In the 1960s, efforts were made to set aside land for privately-owned housing development on sites located near St James' Hospital, at Moorings Way, Pembroke Park, Hilsea Barracks, Leigh Park and other locations.[6] Hence, between 1966 and 1976, out of a total of 10,688 dwellings completed, some 3,366 were in the private sector. The City Council provided mortgages for the purchase of older dwellings and, by 1981, owner-occupation in the city amounted to about 56 per cent, a small contribution to that figure being made by the sale of council houses.[7]

Housing and general improvement policies were pursued energetically from 1964 when the Housing Act of that year authorised local authorities to designate improvement areas. Three years later, in 1967, the City Council obtained the Portsmouth Corporation Act providing additional powers to deal with environmental improvement areas, powers which were subsequently applied to parts of Portsea and Landport. This Act proved to be a forerunner of the Housing Act of 1969 which introduced general improvement areas and was followed by a further Act in 1974 designed to ameliorate the urban environment. The number of grants for improvement in Portsmouth exceeded 5,000 between 1964 and 1980 and helped consolidate efforts to rehabilitate areas of substandard housing in the city and thereby prevent community dispersal which had ensued under the clearance and redevelopment schemes. Improvement schemes had two beneficial effects: they provided work for the small-scale building firms and dealt with houses that were more easily within the economic reach of first-time buyers. The result was a fairly dramatic facelift, internally and externally, for many older houses within the city. An important feature of the improvement of areas of housing that should not escape notice, was the decision to construct community centres, such as those at

Buckland and Tipner, to fill a major gap in social provision. Further housing development was facilitated by the construction of a somewhat unpublicised new sewerage system and the provision of a more powerful pumping station which relieved flooding problems in parts of the city.[8]

A fundamental part of post-war development in Portsmouth was economic diversification which began in earnest in 1948 when, under the Town and Country Planning Act of 1944, the City Council established its first industrial estate at Fratton, to be followed by further developments on land adjoining the former airport site, in areas along the mainland coastal sections within the city boundary and at Leigh Park.

Emphasis was placed on light industry and office development and, by 1966, these economic diversification policies had created some 21,000 new jobs, of which 15,000 were in the city and the remainder at Leigh Park. It was then estimated that a further 21,000 jobs would be needed by the early 1980s,[9] and subsequent major developments included the attraction to the city of firms such as IBM, the Zurich Insurance Company, Schroder Life Assurance, John Brown Constructors Ltd. and a number of Government offices, as well as the expansion of further and higher education.

Economic diversification policies were given new impetus in the 1960s because employment opportunities at Portsmouth Dockyard began to diminish. There were even fears that the yard might be closed and work transferred to Chatham and Devonport. Additionally, by the mid-1960s, it was becoming obvious that the enjoyment of full employment in Britain was not to be permanent; from time to time unemployment became quite serious and by the 1980s had exceeded 3 million. In the 1960s, Portsmouth had more acute unemployment problems than elsewhere in southern England, and job-creation schemes by the City Council became essential.

Whilst land was a very scarce resource that limited the City Council in formulating policies for economic diversification, some of the constraints were diminished in the 1960s and 1970s as the Ministry of Defence began to release land for other uses. By 1969, almost 500 acres had been purchased from the Ministry making possible the expansion of Portsmouth Polytechnic, housing developments at Pembroke Park, Southsea, as well as the Crest Hotel, housing developments at Gatcombe Park, Hilsea, and at Portsdown Park, together with the construction of the Portsmouth Golf Course at Crookhorn and public open-space development on Portsdown Hill. In 1971, Farlington Marshes were purchased to increase public open space in the city. The purchase of 408 acres of tidal mudland and subsequent reclamation north of Horsea Island facilitated construction of IBM's office complex, making Portsmouth a major focal point of this American multinational organisation.[10] In 1973, the decision to close Portsmouth Airport provided the city with a sizeable area of land for development, but it was not until the 1980s that the site's potential began to be realised with a mixture of both housing, at Anchorage Park, and industry.

The process of diversification meant that by the 1970s mechanical engineering, electrical engineering and electronics provided work for more than 15 per cent of the labour force and dominated manufacturing employment.[11] Diversification, however, included more than the manufacturing sector and financial services. It also embraced tourism and leisure, professional and health services, education, employment in the Civil Service, local government and the defence sector, although the latter contracted quite markedly between 1945 and 1980. The City

Council, as a prime mover in the diversification of the economy, negotiated with firms to attract them to sites in the city or to overspill areas, offering housing priority to key workers, making some finance available for the purchase of sites and plants, and supporting applications for requisite industrial development certificates and office development permits. Until 1960, Portsmouth received favourable treatment compared with other parts of southern England in respect of industrial development, but thereafter applications for appropriate certificates had to be on the same terms as elsewhere.

Diversification was further enhanced by the expansion of economic activity in the port. Although quite small compared with docks in major commercial ports, the city docks became a focal point for increasing development in the 1960s and 1970s. Because of access problems, expansion of the Camber docks was difficult and, in 1968, the Albert Johnson Quay was opened near Flathouse Quay at Mile End. A steady expansion of activity ensued which, by 1980, included passenger and vehicular ferry services linking Portsmouth with both the Channel Islands and with mainland Europe.

Progress in diversifying the economy to minimise dependence on the dockyard and a contracting Royal Navy did not necessarily run smoothly. Occasional set-backs resulted from the closure or partial run down of employment by some firms; among those closing in the later 1960s and in the 1970s were Hawker Siddeley, Bailey & Whites, Matburn Surgical Equipment, Leethems (Twilfit) and Sumlock Anita Electronics, while Smiths Foods and Vosper Thorneycroft implemented redundancy policies.

Although never a major facility, closure of the airport in 1973, was, nevertheless, no assistance to economic diversification: in the 1960s it handled only 25,000 to 30,000 passengers a year and could not be used in winter because its small grass runways became unserviceable. In August 1967 two Channel Airways aircraft skidded and overshot the runways. The consequent Board of Trade inquiry resulted in the airport being closed to Hawker Siddeley 847 aircraft because of new landing requirements.

The diversification of the city's economy, the development of overspill areas for housing and industry, and the development of private housing estates, in such places as Bedhampton, Havant, Waterlooville, Horndean and Fareham, made Portsmouth a focus for a complex pattern of journeys to work. The 1971 census revealed that, within the city, there were employed 109,000 people, of whom 34,000 daily came from outside, whilst there was a concomitant outflow of 10,000 people. Initially, there were two access roads to Portsea Island – the A3 and the Eastern Road – and the result, at peak periods, was traffic congestion. Tidal traffic flows were experimented with as a short-term solution, but, in the long-term, road construction became inevitable. By 1980, the M275 provided a new access road and the A27–M27 trunk route had been developed with a link to Petersfield via the A3(M). Connected with these developments were improvements to roads in the city, the provision of car-parking facilities, including charges for sea-front parking, and traffic-free precincts to make shopping areas at Commercial Road and Palmerston Road more attractive.

Portsmouth Corporation Transport Services suffered a marked decline between 1950 and 1980. In 1948 some 88 million passengers were carried: in 1963 the total had declined to 51 million and in 1977 to 33 reflecting trends in Britain as a whole

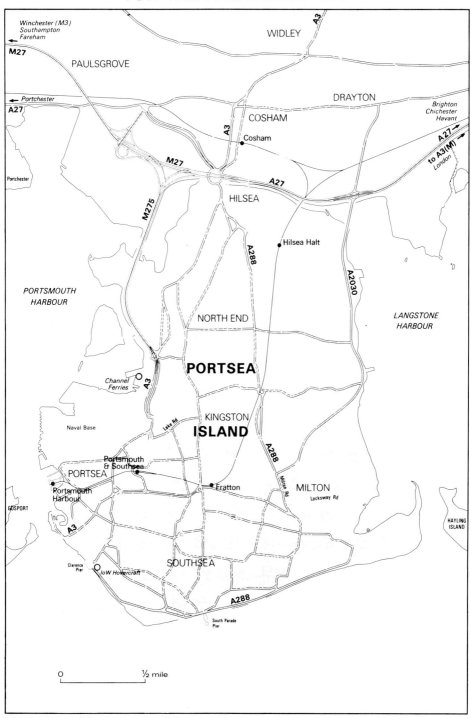

MAP 3   Portsea Island, motorway links

and resulting in a reorganisation of the passenger transport service. In 1963, trolleybuses were finally withdrawn and by 1975 virtually all the city's buses were one-man operated. There was a rationalisation and reduction of route mileage in an endeavour to cut costs, and measures to assist bus movements and quicken journeys were implemented. Limited-stop bus services and bus priority lanes were introduced, but slow adoption meant they were not widely used until the 1970s.

However, the city's economy benefited from the expansion of education, especially in the 1960s. The growth of the Portsmouth College of Technology and, from 1969, its successor Portsmouth Polytechnic, Highbury College of Technology, the College of Art and the College of Education helped to boost demand in the city for goods, services and accommodation. The demand for student lettings in autumn, winter and spring was of especial significance to the boarding house and hotel sectors. In particular, the Polytechnic induced a significant flow of funds into Portsmouth and neighbouring areas and, by the mid-1970s, employed well over 1,000 academic and non-academic staff and had a student enrolment of 5,000 increasing to 6,000 by 1980.[12] The Polytechnic had grown from the Municipal College of 1945 to the Regional College of Technology in 1956 and thence to the Polytechnic in 1969, and established an international reputation as a major institution of higher education, although since 1982 it has suffered staffing cuts as a result of central government finance policies. The College of Education also expanded to cater for a student population of 900 by 1970, but changes in central policy led first to a merger with the Polytechnic and, secondly, to a threat of closure in 1977, only averted by strong representation to central government by Hampshire County Council, the Isle of Wight County Council, Portsmouth City Council and the Polytechnic. Finally, initial teacher-training in Portsmouth, which had experienced great expansion in the 1960s, was subjected to retrenchment in the 1970s and continuing threats of cessation in the early 1980s, culminating in central government's decision to close in 1986. It suffered from the effects of the falling rolls in school populations which tended to veer towards the lowest projection (see Table 3).

When a decision was made that Portsmouth College of Technology should concentrate on advanced courses of further education, Highbury Technical College

TABLE 3

TOTAL SCHOOL POPULATION (THOUSANDS) 1974 PROJECTION

Actual	Hypothetical Highest Projection		Central Projection		Hypothetical Lowest Projection	
1974	1981	1986	1981	1986	1981	1986
8,900,000	9,100,000	9,100,000	8,700,000	8,000,000	8,300,000	6,700,000

Source: DES Report 1974, No. 2, Table 1.

was established in 1963 and expanded very rapidly. By 1980 it was providing courses for more than 10,000 students and had more than 300 members of staff. The college developed a close liaison with commerce and industry in Portsmouth and with the Royal Navy, and was essentially a college with local links, whilst the Polytechnic was a major national institution. On a much smaller scale, the College of Art was also a local institution which lost its advanced work to the Polytechnic in 1969.

After the Act of 1944, education was an important issue in national debate about social policy, especially in the 1950s and 1960s, with considerable controversy centred on the method of organising secondary education. The period 1950 to 1975 was one of increases in public expenditure, in real terms, on education, both nationally and in the city. It was a period of fundamental change, culminating in 1964 in decisions to develop a system of non-selective secondary education and to end single-sex primary schooling in favour of coeducational schooling in Portsmouth. The plan that eventually emerged was for a three-tier school system with first schools catering for 5–8 year-old children, middle schools for the 8–12 year-olds and secondary comprehensive schools for 12–18 year-olds. Furthermore, Portsmouth Grammar School, Portsmouth High School and St John's College lost their Direct Grant status in 1975 and thus left the state sector to become independent secondary schools.

By 1980, schools were feeling the effects of the decline in the birth rate. In England and Wales, the number of births diminished from a peak in 1964 of 876,000 to 725,000 in 1972. In Hampshire, the trends were 24,560 in 1964 and 22,000 in 1972: in the Portsmouth Division the respective numbers were 8,760 and 7,180 and in Portsmouth City – 3,809 and 2,618.[13] By 1982, school reorganisation was again a subject of debate because of the consequence falling school rolls. Some sixth forms in the secondary schools were too small to be viable and a decision was made to create a sixth-form college in 1984, at what had been Great Salterns Secondary School. In the next two years, six middle schools and two first schools in the city were amalgamated to produce three middle schools and one first school, using some existing buildings. Thus, Portsmouth schools, like the College of Education, experienced buoyant times in the 1950s, the 1960s and the early 1970s, but some came under threat of closure as the diminished child population began to have effect by 1982.

While the fortunes of education suffered considerable fluctuations, there was a steadily growing interest in conservation. In Britain as a whole after 1945, and especially in the 1960s, there was an increased awareness, amidst all the changes, that urban conservation should not be ignored. In Portsmouth, bodies such as the Nature Conservancy Group, the Isle of Wight Naturalists Trust and the Langstone Harbour Board acted as conservancy groups and, in 1973, the Portsmouth Society was formed to encourage urban conservation. The City Council and Langstone Harbour Board worked closely with the conservancy groups to safeguard the environment and, after consultation with the Nature Conservancy Council, Langstone Harbour was designated a site of special scientific interest to protect it from over-hasty developments. Emphasis was also placed on tree preservation, a nursery for their cultivation being established at Leigh Park. The 350 acres on Portsdown Hill released by the Ministry of Defence were kept as open space, while improvements to the sea front at Southsea and Portsmouth Harbour shore beyond Stamshaw Bay were made. After much debate, historic buildings, such as the

Theatre Royal, were preserved and attention paid to the landscaping of new roads as well as some existing ones.

Partly associated with attempts to improve the environment, which helped increase the attraction of the city as a tourist centre, was an emphasis on the provision and expansion of leisure facilities. In the South Hampshire Plan, Portsmouth was regarded as a major centre for the development of leisure facilities, especially marine activities. Thus, there was a marked increase in facilities for most sports and, in 1972, the Solent Sailing Conference was inaugurated to review marine leisure provision.[14] The City Council's Parks Department played an important role in the spheres of leisure and environmental improvement. There was an increase in demand for both plants and trees and Leigh Park Gardens were chosen as a centre for horticultural development, leading to a clash with local residents because of a decision to impose entrance charges. Two Havant councillors became well known nationally when they led a revolt against the imposition of a nominal entry charge, one aim of which was to minimise vandalism.[15]

In the field of leisure and culture, an innovation was the staging, in 1970, of the Portsmouth Festival of Arts, which became an annual event, being followed by the creation of the Portsmouth Festival Society two years later and the appointment of a city arts organiser. In 1967, a Museums Department emerged as a separate entity from the library service and, by 1974, was responsible for promoting interest in the Cumberland House Museum, the Beam Engine House Museum, Eastney, the Charles Dickens Museum and the City Museum.[16] Links were forged with the Naval Museum, the Royal Marines Museum and the *Mary Rose* project; in 1967, the '*Mary Rose* Committee' was formed to facilitate exploration of the wreck and, in 1971, a fund of £10,000 was established to help with exploration work.[17] By 1982, plans were well advanced to raise and conserve the remains of the ship.

This active development of Portsmouth's heritage enhanced the city's tourist potential. Coincidentally, in 1969, the Development of Tourism Act resulted in Portsmouth being involved with Southampton in establishing what became the Southern Tourist Board and in that year the City Council formed a Working Party for the Development of Portsmouth and Southsea as a Holiday Resort and a Centre of Recreation.[18] It reported in 1973, producing a somewhat disturbing picture of the city's undue reliance on an ageing clientele. However, between 1945 and 1980 there was a continual improvement in the resort's facilities for the arts and other leisure pursuits, so that the increase in demand was more or less met. Great efforts were made to increase the attractiveness of Southsea as a holiday resort, with improved open spaces, either as parks or for recreation, increased library and museum facilities and the expansion of naval and defence heritage.

After the Second World War, considerable power was wielded by the City Council. The supply of leisure facilities was only one of a considerable array of services provided. However, the City Council of 1982 had quite attenuated powers compared with its predecessor of 1945 for, in three particular years, there was an erosion of the council's powers. In 1948, legislation affecting the Poor Law, the supply of electricity and the provision of hospital facilities under the National Health Service removed some of the services provided by the local authority. In 1967, control of police services was transferred to a new Hampshire Police Authority, which included the former police forces of Hampshire, Portsmouth, Southampton and the Isle of Wight. Finally, in 1974, Portsmouth lost its autonomous status when it became a district of the reorganised Hampshire County Authority, the new City Council emerging as a District Council. Thus, on 1 April 1974, a substantial proportion of the functions of the old City Council were transferred to the new Hampshire County Council, the new Hampshire Health Authority and the Southern Water Authority.[19]

Apart from a brief period between 1963 and 1965, there was a domination of the City Council by the local Conservative Party. Until 1974, the Council consisted of forty-eight councillors representing sixteen wards or electoral districts and fifteen aldermen nominated and elected by existing councillors. One-third of the councillors retired or sought re-election each year and aldermen were elected for six years with one-half of the group retiring every third year. From 1 April 1974, the office of alderman ceased to exist and the draft report of the Local Government Boundary Commission for Hampshire provided for Portsmouth to be separated into fourteen divisions to elect fifteen members to the County Council. The St Mary and Guildhall, Portsea and Nelson wards constituted one division and returned two members, while the remaining thirteen wards elected one member each. The new City Council, like its predecessor, consisted of forty-eight councillors, three being returned from each of sixteen wards. In 1979, a review resulted in the city being redivided into thirteen wards, each to elect, from May 1983, three members to form a City Council of thirty-nine members. From May 1981 onwards, the same thirteen wards elected thirteen members to serve on Hampshire County Council.

It is obvious, then, that the years since 1945 constitute a time of continual change in Portsmouth, change that affected education, housing, health care, personal social services, transport, commerce, industry, the rôles of the dockyard and the Royal Navy in the city and, especially, the structure of local government. Whereas in 1945 Portsmouth had substantial control over its own destiny as a County Borough, in the 1980s it is a mere district of the County of Hampshire. Efforts to extend the city's boundaries to include 'Greater Portsmouth' failed: the economic reality of a 'Greater Portsmouth' was neither recognised in earlier years, nor when local government was reorganised in 1974. As a result, there was a population drift from the city, induced by such factors as the diversification of industry, housing development and the promotion of leisure facilities, which reached beyond the confines of the city's boundaries. A striking feature of the period was the determined attempts to diminish the economic dependence of the city on the dockyard and this, too, involved the city in reaching beyond its administrative boundaries to persuade firms such as IBM and Zurich to utilise Portsmouth as a centre for their operations.

14

PORTSMOUTH – RETROSPECT AND PROSPECT

Barry Stapleton

From its earliest known development in Anglo-Saxon times, when it was among the most thinly populated areas of south-east Hampshire, Portsea Island, over the next 900 years, came to dominate the region. That process of change was not a necessary or inevitable one. Although signs of human presence on the island exist from as far back as about 1500 BC with the discovery of Bronze Age axe heads and necklaces at Fratton and Milton,[1] it is not known whether these archaeological finds represent permanent residence, itinerant craftsmen or maritime trade between England and the Continent. Meanwhile, clear evidence of man's continuous occupation of other sites within the region over a much longer time span suggests that some downland areas have a considerably longer history of habitation.[2]

The earliest verifiable permanent communities on the island, indicated in Domesday Book, were Buckland, Copnor and Fratton.[3] Portsmouth itself simply did not exist until the late twelfth century and, as recently as four centuries ago, the parishes of Titchfield, Fareham and Hambledon seemingly contained larger numbers of inhabitants than Portsmouth.[4]

However, for much of the last 350 years regional development in south-east Hampshire has been closely related to the increasing dominance of Portsmouth. In turn, expansion of the communities on Portsea Island was intimately connected with the growth and physical enlargement of the naval dockyard, as well as being dependent upon the rise of Britain as a world power. This latter achievement necessitated both naval and military forces of considerable size which could be easily transported to actual or potential trouble spots. Thus, alongside the dockyard's augmentation, came the development of fortifications and the erection of barracks for their defenders.

220

The provision of defence works continued well into the nineteenth century with the construction of the ring of forts known as Palmerston's Follies on Portsdown, around Gosport and in the Solent.[5] Unfortunately, the strong ties established between Portsmouth and the defence of the realm were instrumental in causing economic instability with booms of both the economy and births during wartime or the preparations for hostilities and slumps during ensuing periods of peace, a cycle of events which continued into the twentieth century.

From the mid-nineteenth century, however, Southsea's emergence as a centre for seaside holidays, though helping to reduce the most severe effects of boom and slump, did create an alternative cycle of increasing and decreasing economic activity – the seasonal boom of summer visitors which was to last for more than a century, until the growth of affluence and charter air travel took increasing numbers of the British to the more certain climatic shores of the Mediterranean.

Nevertheless, the decision taken in the Government Defence Review of 1981 to reduce the dockyard from a major naval establishment to the lesser role of a ship repair facility ensured that the cycle of boom and slump linked to the yard's activity would, in future, have a substantially reduced effect on the city's economy, except in the immediate planned reduction of 3,500 jobs. Consequently, the city authorities had to look for alternative forms of economic activity and employment, particularly since it was clear, with the growth of cheaper package holidays abroad from the 1960s, that the attractions of Southsea, with its more unpredictable climate than the Mediterranean, were diminishing for holiday-makers. Thus, traditional seaside visitors were declining at a time when increasing numbers of people had more leisure time. Fortunately, a widening availability of leisure facilities was being provided in Portsmouth ensuring alternative, more diverse and less spatially-concentrated employment opportunities than the dockyard had offered. Similarly, the increasing diversity of economic activity which was being attracted to the region did likewise.

Fortuitously, Portsea Island is rich in natural advantages. Set between Portsmouth and Langstone Harbours, with the backdrop of Portsdown Hill to the north and the Solent, with the Isle of Wight beyond, providing both sea and landscape to the south, the island is arguably one of the finer, if not the finest, environmental sites in England. These natural surroundings have increasingly been used, in recent decades, for leisure purposes. The two harbours have both been designated sites of special scientific interest, Langstone Harbour in 1958 and Portsmouth in 1974. Described as of national significance as biological systems, the harbours are also internationally important for their bird populations.[6] Farlington Marshes at the head of Langstone Harbour is a natural sanctuary enjoyed by both increasing numbers of birds, especially overwintering ducks and geese, and bird-lovers alike.

The rising popularity of windsurfing, water-skiing and sailing have multiplied the pressures on both the harbours and the Solent, as have power boats which, along with water-skiing, are less compatible with any other recreational use of water. Even so, the leisure use of boats will almost certainly expand, creating increased need both for more moorings for smaller boats within the harbours and for larger craft based in marinas close to open water. Thus, greater conflicting pressures on the harbours will accrue. In Portsmouth Harbour, reclamation in recent years has led to the construction of large sections of the motorway system, the North

Harbour IBM complex, commercial docks and the cross-channel ferry port. Much needed diversity has thus been brought to the city's port development, although the Navy remains the single major user of land and water in the harbour.

However, it is most likely that any future change in harbour use would see the continued decline of naval influence as commerce and maritime heritage expand. Already, parts of the former dockyard complex have been fenced off for heritage and visitor use, allowing uninterrupted access to the *Mary Rose*, *Victory* and *Warrior*. Since, architecturally, some of Portsmouth's finest buildings lie within the rest of the yard behind the fence, it would seem sensible that future decisions should include the opportunity for visitors and local people alike to see this other, less well known, but equally fascinating aspect of Portsmouth's maritime heritage, particularly since it is situated in such close proximity to the historic ships and would add considerably to their attraction.

A further, and almost inevitable, increasing trend will be the growing importance of both commercial and recreational shipping in the harbour, accompanied by a declining naval presence. In such circumstances, it will be essential to review the tradition that naval ships are accorded priority. Leisure boating is clearly going to expand in both Portsmouth and Langstone harbours. The £100 million Port Solent marina complex is being constructed at North Harbour and will provide 1,000 berths and many permanent jobs, both at the complex and elsewhere through associated spending. In Langstone Harbour, it is intended to develop a marina in the 'Glory Hole' area of Eastney Lake, but the scale and nature of the plan is not being generally supported by local opinion. Eastney is also the area of the island on which the city's untreated sewage storm drain outfalls are concentrated and a further necessity, as environmental standards rise, will be the construction of a modern sewage treatment plant to reduce the amount of water pollution. Clearly, some careful planning of coastal and harbour management will be imperative in the years ahead in order to cater for the conflicting interests of differing users and residents.

Such planning is essential in all aspects of development, especially in a period of adjustment from a city heavily dependent on a major single naval establishment to a more diverse range of activity and employment. Already some considerable diversification has been encouraged. During the last quarter of a century, an increasing contribution to the local economy has been made by firms engaged in the fields of research and development, much of it large-scale and in the electronics industry. Such market-leader firms as IBM, employing over 3,500 are larger employers than the traditional dockyard which now employs only around 2,000. The additional concentration of firms such as Plessey, Marconi and Ferranti in this sector of the economy, plus the arrival of insurance companies such as Zurich and Schroder in the financial services sector, has done much to shelter the region from the worst effects of the economic recession of the late 1970s and early 1980s. Local redundancies have been approximately half those of the nation as a whole.[7] Even so, Portsmouth has not entirely escaped, as demonstrated by the dockyard decline and the closure of some traditional manufacturing firms such as that of Metal Box. Despite the reduction in the dockyard labour force, defence sector employment remains high, not only because of the shore bases and naval establishments as well as the Admiralty Research Establishment, which all employ civilian personnel, but also because Marconi and Plessey are high-technology electronics companies in receipt of large defence contracts. It is the electronics sector on which the manufacturing base of the Portsmouth economy is clearly reliant, not only for existing levels of employment, but also for the creation of new employment opportunities, particularly since it is estimated that, for every two jobs created in this sector, another is generated in the rest of the local economy as a spin-off benefit.[8] However, it has to be noted that large manufacturing firms are geared to national or, more often, international markets and thus their success is likely to be determined by world economic conditions rather than local ones. Unfortunately, little control can be exercised by large firms in these circumstances and the problems of an economic recession can be compounded both by excess capacity in world markets creating increasingly intense international competition and by the volatility and variability of exchange rates.

Smaller local manufacturing concerns will not be so vulnerable to such shifts in the world's economy, except in the case of some new firms established to supply international companies and who clearly would be affected by their client's success or otherwise. New manufacturing firms have been considered as the answer to unemployment problems in the 1980s, but in South Hampshire between 1979 and 1985 some 37,000 manufacturing jobs were lost, while new firms commencing operations between those years employed only 1,525 people.[9] Thus, new manufacturing companies are likely to do very little to reduce unemployment, especially among the unskilled for whom they create little demand. Where these do compete is in the market for skilled workers who are in relatively short supply.

Consequently, it seems Portsmouth will need to look outside its manufacturing sector for major opportunities of job creation into the 1990s and the twenty-first century. It is in fact in the service industries where the real potential lies both for jobs and for the Portsmouth economy's future growth. Whereas the manufacturing sector is likely to expand output in the years up to 1990, it will, at the same time, as its productivity levels rise, be more likely to shed yet more labour than to increase employment. By comparison, the service sector, particularly banking and finance, distribution and miscellaneous services, is not only expected to substantially increase output, but also to create more employment.[10] This trend towards an expanding services sector while manufacturing contracts reflects a maturing post-industrial economy. Once complete, Portsea Island will have changed from its pre-eighteenth-century role as a primary producer in which the majority of people were employed in producing agricultural goods, through the stage of being mostly a secondary producer of manufactures (normally beginning in England with the Industrial Revolution of the late eighteenth century, but commencing in Portsmouth around a century earlier with dockyard expansion), to a mainly tertiary producer with most people employed in the provision of services, both public and private.

The major areas in which the expansion of services have been most visible in recent years are the commercial port and the development of tourist-related activities. In the commercial port, the most important spatial area of expansion has been north of the dockyard. Originally the development of commercial shipping and trade was restricted to the Camber which, with the nineteenth-century growth of both Portsmouth and cargo ship size, was to become increasingly problematic, especially since the Admiralty was not in favour of the expansion of commercial activity. In the post-Second World War period, however, attitudes have been changing and in 1969, with the increasing need to diversify the local economy, the City Council took the decision to transfer the major commercial port activities to the north of the dockyard. Camber Docks, rather than being left deserted, was to remain the home of an enlarged and resited Isle of Wight car-ferry terminal, complete with much larger parking and marshalling area; it was additionally to expand, during the last decade, as a fishing centre with a small but successful fleet, largely based on the growth of Johnson's Sea Enterprises, which also markets the catches of other sea fishermen. The value of fish landed exceeded £1 million in 1986. It is possible that the Camber may be further developed towards pleasure boating, but at the moment it remains an active area for which future expansion must be constrained by its limited size and the consequent inadequacies of mooring provision.

Nevertheless, it is to the north of the dockyard where the majority of commercial port developments have taken place in Portsmouth Harbour. Most of the port's trade has been concentrated at Flathouse and Albert Johnson quays. The former covers a working area of 6 acres and has 300 metres of berth, while the latter was opened in 1968 from 5 acres of reclaimed harbour mudland and with over 150 metres of berth. In 1975 a further 30 metres were added when another 2 acres were reclaimed and, although the quay was originally intended mainly for the Channel Islands trade, it now deals increasingly with Continental and Mediterranean cargoes. Even so, the most important and ambitious development by the City Council was undoubtedly the £20 million Continental ferry terminal opened in 1976. Since then it has been twice expanded, first in 1978 and again in 1983–84 and currently covers some 20 acres. The success of the ferry port meant that over two million passengers, half a million vehicles and approaching 150,000 units of freight were expected to pass through it in 1987. Such achievement – Portsmouth is now second only to Dover in the volume of Continental traffic it handles – creates its own problems. These are concerned mainly with the growing inadequacy of the reclaimed area. Already a temporary overspill exists at Farlington, but the rapid growth rates, especially since 1983, and expected increases of 18 per cent in freight and 13 per cent in passengers in 1987, mean that more marshalling land and freight trailer parking space will be required adjacent to the existing facilities. Similarly, more berths will be required to solve the increasing scheduling problems. Two solutions to the problems have been suggested. One is to expand on the relatively under-utilised Tipner peninsula. However, this is used by the Navy and is separated from the current ferry port by Whale Island. The second solution is to reclaim another 7 acres of mudland immediately to the north of the existing location.

This would probably be the better choice, at least for the near future, particularly since a much improved direct road link with the M275 is now operative. With all these port developments, Portsmouth has become a medium size commercial port of importance. In total, more than one million tonnes of cargo are handled each year; 32 per cent of this is coastal trade, 29 per cent with the Channel Islands and nearly two-fifths (39 per cent) is foreign trade. Exports consist of mainly containerised general cargo from most parts of the United Kingdom and imports are principally of Baltic timber, fruit and vegetables from the Continent, the Mediterranean and North Africa, and South American bananas. Such rapid and substantial developments have altered perceptions of the city as being traditionally dependent on the dockyard certainly for the two million annual passengers and the freight lorry drivers.

However, perhaps the one initiative which most clearly demonstrates the distancing of Portsmouth from its historic naval character is the development of the city's maritime heritage. Curiously enough, much of this is based on the history of Portsmouth's naval dockyard connection and is itself part of the city's attempt to revitalise the local economy and create new employment opportunities following the planned loss of jobs in the dockyard announced in 1981.

Fortunately, Southsea's late nineteenth-century development as a seaside resort meant a range of accommodation was already available for heritage visitors and this is now supplemented by out of town hotels like the Holiday Inn and the Hilton National at Farlington. Additionally, sea-front gardens and promenades were laid out. In the same Southsea area, the history and heritage theme is present in the shape of Southsea Castle and in the D-Day Museum. However, the major heritage attractions lying in the naval base, the sixteenth-century *Mary Rose*, eighteenth-century *Victory* and nineteenth-century *Warrior*, along with the Royal Naval Museum, create a concentrated theme park of maritime history and heritage of national and international importance and, for Portsmouth, a sound base for a successful tourism industry. Such success will be dependent on the provision of adequate facilities such as shopping centres and transport links. The latter have been and continue to be improved, the former have benefited from pedestrian precincts and should shortly be further enhanced by the Moores Square development in Portsmouth. Additionally, attention to general environmental improvement will be essential and one advantage of the heritage development is the boost it gives to conservation and restoration of older buildings as well as their reuse for new purposes. Together with the investment money which is attracted, these factors clearly bring attendant benefits to local residents as does the recirculation of tourist expenditure. Such expenditure is expected to rise substantially in the near future as an additional 30 per cent of visitors are expected between 1985 and 1988 rising to 1.2 million by the latter year. The visitors should generate almost £65 million of direct expenditure and a total spending of over £135 million, and in the process create over 3,000 additional jobs, mainly in the hotels and entertainment, distribution and services sectors, thus replacing most of the planned job losses in the dockyard.

There is little doubt, therefore, that the heritage theme confers substantial economic and environmental advantages on Portsmouth. It will be necessary to continue to develop its potential. The proposal from the Polytechnic to establish a Centre for Local History at Milldam House, close to the maritime heritage area, has not so far received official support, yet it would seem sensible to have an exhibition centre for Portsmouth's history to complement that of the historic ships, and one to which local residents in particular, as well as visitors, could relate. In any case, the more attractions of this nature there are in close proximity, the more visitors will consider they have had 'value for money' and thus act as 'ambassadors' proclaiming the benefits of Portsmouth. Thus the heritage area developments would have an even more major effect on the local economy and especially in the service sector where employment prospects would be considerably enhanced. However, such substantial developments as those already undertaken in the heritage field and in large-scale conference provision, plus others which an imaginative city could develop, should produce substantial spin-off benefits for the rest of the economy and at relatively low cost. If existing developments, as well as possible future ones, realise their full potential, Portsmouth could well become the major visitor centre of twenty-first century England.

GLOSSARY

Aeromagnetic	Referring to magnetism determined by aerial survey.
Amphora	A two-handled vessel for holding oil, wine, etc., usually ancient Greek or Roman.
Anticline	An arch-like fold of rock from which strata dip in opposite directions.
Aquifer	A rock stratum containing commercially extractable water.
Aurochs	An extinct species of wild ox.
Biotic	Of animal life; vital.
Bivalve	A mollusc having a shell of two halves joined by an elastic ligament at the hinge.
Bouguer gravity anomaly	Condition in which the gravitational attraction of a mountain range is less than would be expected if it were just a mass of rock on the surface of the earth's crust. First found in 1735 by Bouguer in the Andes and explained by suggesting that mountains have deep rocks extending into the earth's denser crust.
Bryophyte	Member of the plant group including both mosses and liverworts.
Burin	A prehistoric flint tool with a chisel point used for engraving and grooving.
Carr	An area of bog or fen in which scrub, especially willow and alder, have become established.
Coccolith	Minute calcareous disc-like bodies originating in planktonic alga and common in chalk.
Comminute	To reduce to minute particles; pulverize.
Depauperate	To render poor; impoverish; reduce in quality or vigour.
Diatom	Microscopic minicellular alga having a cell wall in two halves and impregnated with silica, occurring either singly or in colonies in marine or freshwater conditions.
Discordance	An arrangement of rock strata in which older underlying ones dip at a different angle from the younger overlying ones; unconformity.
Downwarped	Depressed.
Einkorn	One of the earliest cultivated species of wheat, still grown in hilly areas of south-west Asia.
Emmer	An early form of cultivated wheat, still grown in mountain areas of Europe.
Eutrophication	Process by which lakes and similar habitats become supplied with an excess of organic and mineral nutrients, so that plants grow to excess and then decay, thereby depleting the oxygen supply.
Fucus	A genus of brown seaweed with flat leathery fronds.
Gleyed	Term applied to a colour-mottled soil showing the slate-grey colour of reduced iron because waterlogging has provided conditions lacking oxygen. Fluctuating water tables provide mottling of grey reduced iron and red oxidised iron.

Graver	A flint tool used for grooving and engraving.
Grey dune	Old, stabilised dunes from which the nutrients have been washed out and where an abundant growth of lichens provide a predominantly grey colour.
Groover	A flint tool for making grooves.
Halophyte	A plant which grows in soil impregnated with salt, i.e. salt marsh.
Hemichordate	Having a partly or imperfectly developed cartilaginous band forming the primitive basis of the spinal column.
Hydrological	Relating to the properties of water and its surface distribution.
Hypersaline	Having greater than normal marine salinity.
Limb	One side of a geological fold.
Lithology	The physical characteristics of rock or the study of the nature and composition of stones and rocks.
Macro-fossil	Fossil large enough to be studied without the use of a microscope.
Microburin	Waste blade fragment from the manufacture of a microlith.
Microlith	A very small geometrically-shaped flint blade for mounting in a wooden handle.
Mucilage	Complex glutinous carbohydrate secreted by some organisms.
Neotropical	Belonging to or characteristic of Tropical and South America as a zoogeographical region.
Palaeoenvironment	Environmental conditions in a past period.
Passerine	Of or about the types of birds which are perchers, e.g. sparrows.
Patent slip	A slipway on which a carriage runs into the sea allowing launching and recovery of vessels.
Pedological	Of, or pertaining to, the scientific study of the genesis and structure of soils.
Periglacial	Geographically adjacent to glacial area or ice sheets.
Phytoplankton	Collective name for all the floating plant life in the sea or in lakes.
Planktonic	Characteristic of drifting organic life found in the sea and in lakes.
Pointillé	A decoration of dots impressed into pottery, etc. with a pointed tool.
Progradation	Outward growth, advance, with reference to a coast or delta, etc.
Quondam	Formerly.
Ring-work	Circular entrenchment.
Samian	Fine kind of pottery found extensively on Roman sites.
Sarsen	Large boulder or block of sandstone comprising an eroded remnant of a formerly overlying rock stratum, found on chalk downs, especially in Wiltshire.
Saxicolous	Growing on rocks.
Siliceous	Containing or consisting of silica.
Sipunculid	A gephyrean worm of the family Sipunculus.
Slack	A small wet hollow, which may be marshy, between dunes.
Solifluxion	A gradual movement or slide of particles down slopes of the earth's surface, especially when soil saturated with salt water slides over a permanently frozen subsoil.
Spandrel	The thickest parts of the arch of a bridge adjacent to the abutments.
Stater	Originally a Greek coin, later copied and developed by Celtic tribes.
Stratigraphy	The order and relative position of the strata of the earth's crust.
Substrate	The matter on which a fungus or other plant grows.
Succession	Progressive changes in species and environment which occur after initial colonisation of an area by plants and animals.
Syncline	A basin-like fold in which strata on opposite sides dip towards each other.
Tectonic	Belonging to the actual structure of the earth's crust.
Thallus	A plant structure in which there is no differentiation into stem and leaves.
Transgressive	Referring to an advance of the sea over the land.

Transpiration	Exhalation of watery vapour from the surface of leaves and other parts of plants.
Tundra	Level treeless region between ice-cap and timber-line having permanently frozen subsoil.
Umbellifer	Member of family of flowering plants having hollow stems, divided leaves and flowers in flat-topped heads like those of parsley and fennel.
Unconformity	Marked break or discontinuity in a geological succession often associated with a period of erosion.
Voussoir	The wedge-shaped stones forming an arch or vault.

NOTES

THE ARCHAEOLOGICAL BACKGROUND

CHAPTER 1 – PREHISTORIC

1. The space available in the text precludes a comprehensive list of sites and find spots, but an extensive sites and monuments record is held by the Archaeology Department of Portsmouth Museums which may be consulted on request. It is this and the prehistoric artefacts held by Portsmouth City Museums that have provided the basic source of information. For a slightly more comprehensive coverage see D.J. Rudkin, *Early Man in Portsmouth and South-East Hampshire*, P.P., no. 31, Portsmouth, 1980.

2. The dates referred to in the text are mainly expressed in calendar years before Christ, abbreviated BC, as opposed to radiocarbon years before Christ, abbreviated bc. However, because of the divergence of earlier radiocarbon dates from calendar dates the former have been corrected, wherever possible, using the Clark calibration curve. For this see R.M. Clark, 'A Calibration curve for radiocarbon dates', *Antiquity*, XLIX, no. 196, 1975, pp. 251–66.

3. J.C. Draper, 'Stone Industries from Rainbow Bar, Hants.', *Archaeological News Letter*, III, no. 9, 1951, pp. 147–9. Letters and numbers in parentheses refer to locations on Map 1.

4. J.J. Wymer, *Lower Palaeolithic Archaeology in Britain*, 1968.

5. M.L. Shackley, 'On the Palaeolithic Archaeology of Hampshire', in (eds.) S.J. Shennan and R.T. Schadla-Hall, *The Archaeology of Hampshire*, Hampshire Field Club and Archaeological Society Monograph no. 1, 1981, p. 6.

6. M.L. Shackley, 'Preliminary Note on Handaxes Found in Gravel Deposits at Warsash, Hampshire', *Proc. H.F.C.*, XXVII, 1970, pp. 5–7.

7. A.M. ApSimon and C.S. Gamble, *The Lower Palaeolithic site of Red Barns, Portchester* (forthcoming).

8. J.C. Draper, 'Upper Palaeolithic type Flints from Long Island, Langstone Harbour, Portsmouth', *Proc. H.F.C.*, XXII, 1961–3, pp. 105–6.

9. J.J. Wymer, *Gazetteer of Mesolithic sites in England and Wales*, C.B.A. Research Report, XX, 1977.

10. R.M. Jacobi, 'The Last Hunters in Hampshire', in *The Archaeology of Hampshire*, pp. 10–25.

11. J.C. Draper, 'Mesolithic Distribution in South-East Hampshire', *Proc. H.F.C.*, 23, 1964–8, pp. 110–119.

12. J.C. Draper, 'Further Mesolithic sites in South Hampshire', *A.N.L.*, IV, no. 12, 1953, p. 193.

13. Draper, *Proc. H.F.C.*, 23, p. 117.

14. Jacobi in *The Archaeology of Hampshire*, p. 18, fig. 7.

15. R. Bradley and E. Lewis, 'A Mesolithic Site at Wakefords Copse, Havant', *Rescue Archaeology in Hampshire*, II, 1974, pp. 5–18.

16. M.F. Hughes and A.M. ApSimon, 'A Mesolithic flint working site on the South Coast Motorway (M27) near Fort Wallington, Fareham, Hampshire 1972', *Proc. H.F.C.*, 34, 1977, pp. 23–35.

17. P.L. Drewett, 'Neolithic Sussex', in (ed.) P.L. Drewett, *Archaeology in Sussex to AD 1500*, C.B.A. Research Report, XXIX, 1978, pp. 23–39.

18. W. Campbell Smith, 'Jade axes from sites in the British Isles', *Proceedings of the Prehistoric Society*, XXIX, 1963, pp. 160–1.

19. I.A. Kinnes, 'Monumental function in British Neolithic Burial Practice', *World Archaeology*, VII, 1975, pp. 16–29.

20. D.J. Rudkin, 'Excavation of the Neolithic long barrow and Anglo-Saxon cemetery at Bevis' Grave, Bedhampton' (in preparation).

21. J.H. Cooke, *Tales of Ancient Wessex: Links with the Past*, Portsmouth, no date, pp. 6–12.

22. A. Fleming, 'Territorial patterns in the Wessex Bronze Age', *Proc. P.S.*, XXXVII, 1971, pp. 138–66.

23. A. Corney, P. Ashbee, V.I. Evison and D. Brothwell, 'A Prehistoric and Anglo-Saxon Burial Ground, Ports Down, Portsmouth', *Proc. H.F.C.*, 24, 1967, pp. 20–41.

24. D.J. Rudkin, 'Excavations at Southwick Hill Crossroads, Portsdown, Portsmouth' (in preparation).

25. L.V. Grinsell, 'Hampshire Barrows', *Proc. H.F.C.*, XIV, 1938–9, p. 361.

26. A. Parkes, 'Recent Discoveries at Warsash', *Proc. H.F.C.*, XVI, 1944–6, p. 191. Deverel-Rimbury Culture is named after the Deverel Barrow, Milbourne St Andrews, and the Rimbury Cemetery, Chalbury, Dorset, which produced a characteristic form of urn when excavated in the nineteenth century.

27. J. Nichols, 'M27 Motorway, Downend Road, Fareham', *South Hampshire Archaeological Rescue Group Newsletter*, IV, 1976, p. 4.

28. E. Lewis, 'Bronze Age, Hampshire, Portsmouth', *Archaeological Review for 1971*, VI, 1971, p. 19.

29. E. Lewis, 'Bronze Age, Hampshire, Portchester', ibid.

30. E. Lewis, 'Bronze Age, Hampshire, Gosport', ibid.

31. B.W. Cunliffe, 'A Bronze Age Settlement at Chalton, Hants (Site 78)', *The Antiquaries Journal*, L, 1970, pp. 1–13.

32. M.J. Rowlands, 'The Organisation of Middle Bronze Age Metal Working', *British Archaeological Reports*, 31, Oxford, 1976.

33. B. Hooper, 'Bronze Age, Hampshire, Portsmouth', *Archaeological Review for 1968*, III, 1968, p. 9.

34. B.W. Cunliffe, 'The Origins of Urbanisation in Britain', in (ed.) B.W. Cunliffe and T.R. Rowley, *Oppida: the beginnings of Urbanisation in barbarian Europe*, 1976, pp. 135–61.

35. R. Bradley and M.G. Fulford, 'Excavations at Tournerbury, Hayling Island, 1959 and 1971', *Proc. H.F.C.*, 32, 1975, pp. 63–9.

36. R. Downey, A. King and G. Soffe, 'The Hayling Island Temple', *Third Interim report on the Excavation of the Iron Age and Roman Temple 1976–78*, 1979. Armorica is present-day Brittany, and Central and Belgic Gaul included much of Northern France and Southern Belgium.

37. D.J. Rudkin, 'Excavations of an Iron Age Site at Clanfield Reservoir, Hants' (in preparation).

38. B.W. Cunliffe, 'Two pre-Roman Iron Age Sites at Chalton, Hants', in *Iron Age Sites in Central Southern England*, C.B.A. Research Report, XIV, 1976, p. 30.

39. M.J. Hughes, 'M27 South Coast Motorway Rescue Excavations of an Iron Age site at Wallington Military Road, Fareham, 1972', *R.A.H.*, II, 1974, pp. 31–96.

40. R. Bradley and E. Lewis, 'Excavations at the George Inn, Portsdown', *Proc. H.F.C.*, 25, 1968, pp. 27–50.

41. Rudkin, 'Excavations at Southwick Hill Crossroads, Portsdown, Portsmouth' (in preparation).

42. B. Hooper, Appendix to R. Bradley, 'Excavations on Portsdown Hill 1963–5', *Proc. H.F.C.*, 24, 1967, p. 58.

43. Cunliffe, *Iron Age Sites in Central Southern England*, pp. 33–5.

44. B.W. Cunliffe, 'Report on a Belgic and Roman site at the Causeway, Horndean (1959),' *Proc. H.F.C.*, Vol XXII, 1961–3, pp. 25–9.

45. R. Bradley, 'Excavations on Portsdown Hill 1963–5', *Proc. H.F.C.*, 24, 1967, pp. 42–58.

46. M. Hughes, 'Excavations at Brownwich Farm, Titchfield, 1971', *R.A.H.*, I, 1973, pp. 5–28.

47. R. Bradley and B. Hooper, 'Recent Discoveries from Portsmouth and Langstone Harbours: Mesolithic to Iron Age', *Proc. H.F.C.*, 30, 1973, pp. 24–7.

48. E. Lewis, 'Pre Roman Iron Age, Hampshire, Havant', *Archaeological Review for 1971*, VI, 1971, p. 22.

49. C.F. Fox, 'Salt Works at Hook, Warsash, Hants', *Proc. H.F.C.*, XIII, 1935–7, pp. 105–9.

50. Cheriton is 6 miles east of Winchester.

CHAPTER 2 – ROMAN TO SAXON

1. Links with Roman Gaul immediately before the Conquest are assumed rather than proved archaeologically, as also is the influence of the more pro-Roman neighbours in the Chichester region.

2. I.D. Margary, *Roman Roads in Britain*, 3rd edition, 1973, pp. 92–4.

3. G. Soffe and D.E. Johnston, 'Route 421 and other Roman roads in South Hampshire', *Rescue Archaeology in Hampshire*, II, 1974, pp. 99–118.

4. M.F. Hughes, *The Small Towns of Hampshire*, 1976, pp. 58–65, 70–7. For Fareham, see also A.G. Holmes, 'Evidence of Romano-British settlement in Fareham', *Rescue Archaeology in Hampshire*, III, 1975, pp. 43–58.

5. M.F. Hughes, (forthcoming).

6. B.W. Cunliffe, 'A Romano-British Village at Chalton, Hants.', *Proc. H.F.C.*, 33, 1976, pp. 45–67.

7. Personal communication from R. Bradley.

8. S. Applebaum, in (ed.) H.P.R. Finberg *The Agrarian History of England and Wales AD 43–1042*,, I, II, 1972, p. 90.

9. *V.C.H. Hants.* 1, p. 310.

10. F. Warren, *Proc. H.F.C.*, X, 1926–30, pp. 286–7.

11. R. Bradley, 'Salt and settlement in the Hampshire-Sussex borderland', in (eds.) K.W. de Brisay and K.A. Evans, *Salt: the Study of an Ancient Industry*, 1975, pp. 20–5.

12. G. Soffe and A. Holmes, (forthcoming).

13. S. Applebaum, *Agrarian History*, p. 229.

14. R. Bradley and M.G. Fulford, 'Excavations at Tournerbury, Hayling Island, 1959 and 1971', *Proc. H.F.C.*, 32, 1975, pp. 63–9.

15. T. Ely, *Roman Hayling*, 1908.

16. R. Downey, A. King and G. Soffe, *The Hayling Island Temple*, Interim Reports 1–3, 1977–9. See also *Current Archaeology* 62, 1978, pp. 83–7.

17. B.W. Cunliffe, *Excavations at Portchester Castle*, 1–3, 1974.

18. B.W. Cunliffe, *The Regni*, 1973, p. 132.

19. Translated D. Whitelock in *English Historical Documents*, I, p. 144.

20. Bede, *Historia ecclesiastica gentis Anglorum*, trans. D. Whitelock, I, p. 15.

21. For the Meonwara see especially M.J. Hare in *Proc. H.F.C.*, 32, 1975, pp. 5–6.

22. S. Coffin, 'Linear earthworks in the Froxfield, East Tisted and Hayling Wood district', *Proc. H.F.C.*, 32, 1975, pp. 77–81.

23. D.C. Devenish and T.C. Champion, 'A sixth century Anglo-Saxon grave at Meonstoke, Hants', *Proc. H.F.C.*, 34, 1977, pp. 37–42.

24. F.G. Aldsworth, 'The Droxford Anglo-Saxon cemetery, Soberton, Hampshire', *Proc. H.F.C.*, 35, 1978, pp. 93–182.

25. G.R.J. Jones, 'Settlement patterns in Anglo-Saxon England', *Antiquity*, 35, 1961, pp. 221–62. In Meonstoke Hundred Domesday Book records a Liss Abbas, so named because it was held by the abbess of Nunnaminster in Winchester.

26. M.F. Hughes, 'The excavations of a Roman and Saxon settlement at Shavards Farm, Meonstoke, 1984/1985', *Archaeology and Historic Buildings in Hampshire Annual Report for 1984–5*, pp. 2–8.

27. M.F. Hughes, *The Small Towns of Hampshire*, p. 143.

28. D.A. Hinton, 'Hampshire's Anglo-Saxon origins', in (eds.) S.J. Shennan and R.T. Schadla-Hall, *The Archaeology of Hampshire*, 1981, p. 61.

29. P.V. Addyman and D. Leigh, 'The Anglo-Saxon village at Chalton, Hampshire', *Medieval Archaeology*, 17, 1973, pp. 1–25; T.C. Champion, 'Chalton', Current Archaeology, 59, 1977, pp. 354–71.

30. Cunliffe, *Portchester*, p. 302.

31. Bede, III, p. 7.

32. M.J. Hare, in *Proc. H.F.C.*, 32, 1975, p. 6.

33. D.A. Hinton, *Origins*, p. 62.

34. All are described in N. Pevsner and D. Lloyd, *The Buildings of England: Hampshire and the Isle of Wight*, 1967. For more recent work see notes 35 and 36 below.

35. M.J. Hare, 'A note on the Anglo-Saxon church at Boarhunt', *Proc. H.F.C.*, 34, 1977, pp. 81–3.

36. M.J. Hare, 'The Anglo-Saxon church of St. Peter, Titchfield', *Proc. H.F.C.*, 32, 1975, 5–48.

37. Ibid.

38. S.E. Rigold, 'Litus Saxonicum – the Shore Forts as mission stations', in (ed.) D.E. Johnston, *The Saxon Shore*, 1977, pp. 70–81.

39. D.A. Hinton, *Origins*, p. 61.

40. M.J. Hare, 'The Watergate at Portchester and the Anglo-Saxon porch at Titchfield: a reconsideration of the evidence', *Proc. H.F.C.*, 40, 1984, pp. 71–80.

41. Between 1961 and 1972.

CHAPTER 3 – INDUSTRIAL ARCHAEOLOGY

1. National Maritime Museum, ADM/B; ADM/B/P., Navy Board Quarterly Returns to the Admiralty.

2. Anonymous, 'Plans of His Majesty's Dock Yard at Portsmouth in the Years 1688, 1698 and 1774', in (ed.) D. Hodson, *Maps of Portsmouth Before 1801*, Portsmouth Record Series, vol 4, Portsmouth, 1978.

3. J.P. Desmaretz, 'A Plan of Portsmouth and the Harbour, 1743', in Hodson, *op.cit.*

4. P.C.L. map no. 1218. John Murray, *Map of Her Majesty's Dockyard at Portsmouth, March 1858.*

5. For specific details of dockyard buildings see Nikolaus Pevsner and David Lloyd, *The Buildings of England: Hampshire and the Isle of Wight*, Harmondsworth, 1967, pp. 407–18; Alan Balfour, *Portsmouth*, 1970; (ed.) Monica Ellis, *Hampshire Industrial Archaeology, A Guide*, Southampton, 1975, pp. 39–41; Jonathan Coad, 'Historic Architecture of HM Naval Base, Portsmouth 1700–1850', *The Mariner's Mirror*, 67, 1981, pp. 3–59; Jonathan Coad, *Historic Architecture of the Royal Navy*, 1983; Pamela Moore, *A Guide to the Industrial Archaeology of Hampshire and the Isle of Wight*, Southampton University Industrial Archaeology Group, 1984, pp. 30–2; R.C. Riley, *The Evolution of the Docks and Industrial Buildings in Portsmouth Royal Dockyard 1698–1914*, P.P. no. 44, Portsmouth, 1985; R.C. Riley, 'Portsmouth Dockyard: An Industrial Archaeological Overview', *Industrial Archaeology Review*, VIII, 1986, pp. 177–93.

6. I am indebted to Cdr. J. Merritt for the dating of the Gosport Victualling (later Royal Clarence) Yard buildings. See also his 'Naval Victualling and the Development of the Royal Clarence Victualling Yard, Gosport', unpublished dissertation for Diploma in English Local History, Portsmouth Polytechnic, 1977. Six-figure map references are provided for all sites outside Portsmouth Dockyard and Royal Clarence Yard, Gosport.

7. (ed.) Monica Ellis, *Water and Wind Mills in Hampshire and the Isle of Wight*, Southampton, 1978, p. 22; R.C. Riley, 'Chesapeake Mill, Wickham', *J.P.C.T.I.A.S.*, I, 1968, p. 39.

8. F.H. Brownridge, 'Lumley Mill, Lumley, Emsworth', *J.P.C.T.I.A.S.*, II, 1969, pp. 50–2; F. Brook, 'The Old Industries of Emsworth', ibid, II, 1969, pp. 18–21.

9. Riley, 'Chesapeake Mill', I, p. 40; J.B. Tappenden, 'The Mill at Wickham, Hampshire', unpublished dissertation for Diploma in English Local History, Portsmouth Polytechnic, 1986.

10. M.D. Freeman, 'Funtley Iron Mill, Fareham, Hants.', *Industrial Archaeology*, VIII, 1971, pp. 63–8; R.C. Riley, 'Henry Cort at Funtley, Hampshire', ibid, pp. 69–76; R.C. Riley, 'Henry Cort's Mill at Funtley: A Remarkable Seat of Innovation', *J.P.C.T.I.A.S.*, III, 1970, pp. 26–31.

11. D.J. Viner, 'The Industrial Archaeology of Hampshire Roads', *Proc. H.F.C.*, 26, 1969, p. 158, pp. 160–1.

12. R.C. Riley, *The Industries of Portsmouth in the Nineteenth Century*, P.P. no. 25, Portsmouth, 1976, p. 6.

13. The Great Stone Dock was 69.4m long by 6m deep at high water springs; No. 1 dock was 77.4m long by 5.9m deep; No. 2 dock was 77.2m long by 7.1m deep; No. 3 dock was 80.5m long by 7.4m deep.

14. K.R. Gilbert, *The Portsmouth Block-making Machinery*, 1965.

15. Dawn Jones, 'Marc Brunel in Portsmouth', *J.P.C.T.I.A.S.*, I, 1968, p. 34.

16. Pevsner and Lloyd, *Hampshire and the Isle of Wight*, p. 414.

17. HMS *Rattler*'s twin-bladed propellor is on show in No. 10 storehouse, near HMS *Victory*. See also E.A.M. Laing, *Steam Wooden Warship Building in Portsmouth Dockyard 1832–52*, P.P. no. 42, Portsmouth, 1985.

18. Ballast castings were iron blocks designed to act as ballast in newly-launched vessels prior to fitting out.

19. The Gosport Victualling Yard became the Royal Clarence Yard on the abolition of the Victualling Board in 1832.

20. Pevsner and Lloyd, *Hampshire and the Isle of Wight*, p. 245 give the date of the bakery and granary as 1853, but there is a wealth of documentary evidence to indicate that they were under construction in 1828–30. Thomas Telford had employed the principle of an open ground floor to maximise quayside area at St Katherine's Dock, London, in 1828, but the Gosport granary pre-dates Jessie Hartley's Albert Dock, Liverpool, by sixteen years.

21. Merritt, dissertation. Thomas Tessell Grant was storekeeper at the Royal Clarence Yard, 1831–51.

22. J. Cramer, 'William Treadgold, Iron Merchants, Bishop Street, Portsea', unpublished dissertation for Diploma in English Local History, Portsmouth Polytechnic, 1982.

23. The ground floor columns are 20.3cm in diameter at their widest and the upper floor ones are 14.6cm.

24. Gordon Biddle, *Victorian Stations*, Newton Abbot, 1973, p. 63; G.A. Allcock, *Gosport's Railway Era*, Gosport, 1975, p. 18.

25. Ellis, *Water and Wind Mills*, p. 11.

26. The track to Portsmouth and Southsea High Level station was lifted in 1982.

27. That the original measurements were metric represents an early augury of changing engineering practice.

28. Lesley Burton, 'Haslar's Historic Ship Tank', *Gosport Records*, III, 1972, pp. 18–24. Froude's father, William, was the originator of the world's first model test tank which he built in Torquay in 1872. He also patented the graph paper ruling machine in 1875 and designed a propeller dynamometer.

29. R.C. Riley, 'The Portsmouth Corset Industry in the Nineteenth Century', in (eds.) John Webb, Nigel Yates and Sarah Peacock, *Hampshire Studies*, Portsmouth, 1981, pp. 242–64.

30. R.C. Riley, 'Rate Returns and Industrial Geography: Nineteenth Century Brewing in Portsmouth', in (eds.) D.N. Mottershead and R.C. Riley, *Portsmouth Geographical Essays*, Portsmouth, 1976, pp. 66–75.

31. For further details of breweries see M.F. Tighe, 'A Gazetteer of Hampshire Breweries', *Proc. H.F.C.*, XXVII, 1970, pp. 87–1.

32. Dawn Jones and P.D. King, 'Rowlands Castle Brickworks', *J.P.C.T.I.A.S.*, II, 1969, pp. 94–8.

33. R.C. Riley, 'The Retort Houses of Hilsea Gasworks, Portsmouth', *J.P.C.T.I.A.S.*, II, 1969, pp. 3–11.

34. E.A. Course, *Eastney Pumping Station*, Portsmouth, 1975.

35. D. Halton Thomson, *A History of the Portsmouth and Gosport Water Supply*, Portsmouth, 1957.

36. T.N. Butters, 'The East Southsea Railway', *J.P.C.T.I.A.S.*, I, 1968, pp. 25–30.

37. M.J. White, 'The Portsdown and Horndean Light Railway', ibid, II, 1969, pp. 87–93.

THE HISTORICAL BACKGROUND

CHAPTER 4 – FROM THE NORMAN CONQUEST TO CIVIL WAR

1. See Table 1, compiled from information given in (ed.) W. Page, *V.C.H. Hampshire*, Vol. I, 1900, pp. 450–503.

2. P. Hase, 'The Development of the Parish in Hampshire', unpublished PhD thesis, Cambridge University, 1975, pp. 96–123.

3. Ibid, p. 107.

4. Margaret Hoad, 'The Origins of Portsmouth', in (eds.) J. Webb, N. Yates and S. Peacock, *Hampshire Studies*, Portsmouth, 1981, p. 16.

5. See Table 1.

6. Other manors in Meonstoke Hundred were Liss held by the nunnery of St Mary, Winchester, Lomer in Warnford, held by the Abbey of St Swithun, Winchester, West Meon and Exton held by the Bishop of Winchester, and Warnford and Westbury in West Meon, held by Hugh de Port.

7. Other manors in Finchdean Hundred were Mapledurham and Sunworth, both being partly in Buriton and Petersfield.

8. These manors were Nytimber (later Wade) in Warblington, and Warblington itself.

9. See Table 1.

10. Churches were recorded in the manors of Crofton, Fareham, Droxford, Corhampton, Meonstoke, *Ceptune*, Warblington, Bedhampton and Boarhunt.

11. These were Crofton, Portchester, Hayling and Nytimber in Warblington. The precise nature of these fisheries is not known. They may not have been fishponds such as those later at Titchfield Abbey, but could have been oyster beds.

12. F.G.S. Thomas, *The King Holds Hayling*, Havant, 1961, pp. 41–45. The exact site of this priory today is not known. It has been variously suggested that it was near South Hayling Manor House, Tournerbury or Mengham House. F.G.S. Thomas thinks that the last named is the most likely.

13. *V.C.H. Hampshire*, Vol. II, pp. 217–19.

14. H.R.O. S.P.R., 1M54/1, f.1, no. 3.

15. Ibid, f.1, no. 1.

16. Emma Mason, 'The King, the Chamberlain and Southwick Priory', *B.I.H.R.*, Vol. LIII, no. 127, 1980, pp. 3–4.

17. Hoad, *Hampshire Studies*, pp. 11–12.

18. The priory held among other estates the manors of Southwick, Belney and Wanstead, both in Southwick, Boarhunt, Stubbington in Portsea Island, Preston Candover, Dean and Colemore, and Fishbourne in Sussex.

19. *V.C.H. Hampshire*, Vol. II, pp. 164–5.

20. D.M. Knowles and R.N. Hadcock, *The Medieval Religious Houses of England*, 1971, p. 174.

21. *V.C.H. Hampshire*, Vol. III, p. 161.

22. Knowles and Hadcock, *Medieval Religious Houses*, pp. 181–92.

23. These estates were the manors of Titchfield, Swanwick, Portchester, Wallsworth and Cosham, and Corhampton.

24. B.L. Loan 29/56.

25. Other manors acquired were Newland, Mirabell, Stubbington, Crofton, Fontley, Warde and Markes, all in the parish of Titchfield, Cadland, and Inkpen in Berkshire.

26. D.G. Watts, 'Peasant Discontent in the Manors of Titchfield Abbey 1245–1405', *Proc. H.F.C.*, Vol. 39, 1983, pp. 121–134.

27. H.P. Wright, *The Story of the 'Domus Dei' commonly called the Royal Garrison Church*, Portsmouth, 1873, p. 2.

28. W.G. Gates, *Illustrated History of Portsmouth*, Portsmouth, 1900, p. 79.

29. Wright, *Domus Dei*, pp. 118–25.

30. The main references for Titchfield Abbey are B.L. Loan 29/55, 58, 59 and H.R.O. Daly MSS, 5M50/1281–1308, 1349–65, and for Southwick Priory are H.R.O. Southwick Priory MSS, 1M54, and Daly MSS, 5M50/1670–1709, 1715–35, and Winchester College Muniments, Nos. 15236–50, 15376–98.

31. D.G. Watts, 'The Estates of Titchfield Abbey 1245–1381', unpublished B.Litt. thesis, Oxford University, 1958, *passim*; Watts, 'The Villages on the Manors of Titchfield Abbey', *Proc. H.F.C.*, XXI (1), 1958, pp. 31–37; Watts, 'A Model for the Early Fourteenth Century', *Ec. H.R.*, 2nd Series, XX, no. 3, 1967, pp. 543–47. For further details of the Black Death and the region see P. Ziegler, *The Black Death*, 1971, pp. 148–52, and J.D.F. Shrewsbury, *A History of Bubonic Plague in the British Isles*, Cambridge, 1971, pp. 90–1.

32. M. Hughes, *The Small Towns of Hampshire*, Southampton, 1976, p. 3.

33. Hoad, *Hampshire Studies*, p. 8. Northern pirates were Danes.

34. Market rights were obtained for Havant in 1200, Emsworth in 1239, Wickham in 1268 and Portchester in 1294: C.J. Longcroft, *A Topographical Account of the Hundred of Bosmere*, 1856, pp. 9, 87; *V.C.H. Hampshire*, Vol. III, pp. 234, 159.

35. *V.C.H. Hampshire*, Vol. III, p. 205.

36. Market rights were granted for Hambledon in 1256 and Boarhunt in 1358: A.W. Goodman, *Chartulary of Winchester Cathedral*, Winchester, 1927, p. 194; *V.C.H. Hampshire*, Vol. III, p. 146.

37. Market rights were granted to Chalton in 1224 and Southwick in 1235: *V.C.H. Hampshire*, Vol. III, pp. 103–104, H.R.O. S.P.R., 1M54/2, f.6, no. 9. At the date of these grants the nearest market to Chalton was possibly Petersfield and to Southwick were those at Portsmouth and Havant. See Notes 34 and 36 above.

38. This area is now known as Old Portsmouth. Until recent research dated John de Gisors' Portsmouth deeds, it had been thought that Richard I founded the town. Suspicions that Henry I may even have granted Portsmouth a charter have also been disproved: Hoad, *Hampshire Studies*, pp. 1–27.

39. R. East, *Extracts from Records of the Borough of Portsmouth*, Portsmouth, 1891, p. 558. This dockyard was allowed to decay within a few years and not fully revived until around 1495.

40. Ibid, pp. 573–76. The original boundaries of the borough included not only the modern Old Portsmouth, but also the rest of the manor of Buckland which had been forfeited by John de Gisors. These boundaries were tacitly confirmed in 1229, while the grant of a Gild Merchant was made in 1256.

41. *V.C.H. Hampshire*, Vol. II, p. 179.

42. H.R.O. S.P.R., 1M54/1,3.

43. Gates, *History of Portsmouth*, pp. 104–107.

44. J.E. Neale, *The Elizabethan House of Commons*, 1961, pp. 321–2.

45. P.C.R.O., GMN 6, p. 323 – 'Item there is to be paid. for expenses of the Burgesses in Parliament when it shall happen for land (within the liberty of Portsmouth) aforesaid – 10*d.*, sometimes more sometimes less.' (*c.* 1381, translated from Latin). Gates, *History of Portsmouth*, p. 86, erroneously gives the sum as £10.

46. Winchester College Muniments no. 15391, 'By gift to the burgesses of Portsmouth, in aid of the same being at Parliament – 22*d.*' (1415); no. 15392, 'To expenses in the said year of Henry Uvedale and Robert Weskham, burgesses at the Parliament of the Lord King, as is accustomed to be allocated – 3*s.* 4*d.*' (1454)*; no. 15393, 'To expenses of the burgesses being at Parliament this year – 5*s.*' (1462)*; no. 15395, 'To expenses of the burgesses being at the Parliament in London in the immediate past year by their sworn account – 11*s.*' (1465)*. Extracts from Stubbington Grange account rolls translated from Latin.* East, *Records of Portsmouth*, p. 626, gives names other than those given for the 1454 Parliament, but makes no reference at all to the 1462 and 1465 Parliaments.

47. Mason, *B.I.H.R.*, LIII, no. 127, p. 2.

48. *V.C.H. Hampshire*, Vol. III, p. 187.

49. Ibid, p. 190.

50. H.M. Colvin, *The History of the King's Works*, 1963, Vol. II, pp. 792–3; D.W. Lloyd, *Buildings of Portsmouth and its Environs*, Portsmouth, 1974, pp. 54–7.

51. The description of Leland's tour of the Portsmouth area is from *The Itinerary of John Leland*, (ed.) Lucy Toulmin Smith, 5 vols., 1964, I, pp. 279–85. See also Margaret J. Hoad, *Portsmouth – As Others Have Seen It; Part I, 1540–1790*, P.P. 15, Portsmouth, 1972, pp. 4–5.

52. M. Oppenheim, *A History of the Administration of the Royal Navy*, 1961 edition, pp. 39–40, 45–8, 68–9.

53. Watts, *Proc. H.F.C.*, XXI, 1958, p. 32.

54. L. Stone, *Family and Fortune: Studies in Aristocratic Finance in the Sixteenth and Seventeenth Centuries*, Oxford, 1973, pp. 209–11.

55. L.F.W. White, *The Story of Gosport*, Southsea, no date, pp. 54–7.

56. P.C.R.O. Madden-Ubsdell Correspondence, 15 Sept. 1847.

57. Wright, *Domus Dei*, 1873, pp. 13–14, 139–53.

58. Leland mentions three brewhouses, but in fact there were at least five: the Lion, the Rose, the Dragon, and the White Hart stood on Four House Green, off St Nicholas Street, and the Anchor, which was also a bakery, in St Thomas's Street. Another bakery, the Swan, was situated near Point Gate: Oppenheim, *Administration of the Royal Navy*, pp. 39–40, 68–9; *Early Portsmouth Maps*, P.R.S. portfolio i, 1978, no. 1.

59. See *Maps of Portsmouth before 1801*, compiled D. Hodson, P.R.S., 1978.

60. For example, the only chamberlains' accounts to survive from the Tudor period, those for 1567–8, suggest a very limited budget (P.C.R.O. CF 1/1). According to the bishops' returns of 1603 (B.L. Harl. MSS 595, ff. 237–40), Portsmouth parish had 469 communicants and the parish of Portsea 305. The most populous place in the area under examination seems to have been Titchfield with 650 communicants. Compare Newport in the Isle of Wight with 1100.

61. W. Camden, *Britannia*, 1806 edition, p. 170.

62. *V.C.H. Hampshire*, II, p. 168.

63. For a brief discussion of the evidence see G.E. Fussell, 'Four Centuries of Farming Systems in Hampshire, 1500–1900', *Proc. H.F.C.*, XVII, 1949, pp. 264–5.

64. Anonymous, *A True Report of the Occurrences at Portsmouth*, 1642, pp. 3–4.

65. H.J. Sparks, *The Story of Portsmouth*, Portsmouth, 1921, pp. 120–33.

66. Camden, *Britannia*, p. 170.

67. Hoad, *Hampshire Studies*, pp. 2–6.

68. *V.C.H. Hampshire*, II, p. 442. In a survey of 1608, the Forest of Bere contained 5,363 timber trees fit for use in the royal dockyards.

69. Oppenheim, *Administration of the Royal Navy*, pp. 68–9.

70. (ed.) R. East, *Extracts from the Portsmouth Records*, Portsmouth, 1891, pp. 609–17, 673–6; A.T. Patterson, *Portsmouth: A History*, Bradford-on-Avon, 1976, pp. 33–5.

71. K.R. Andrews, *Elizabethan Privateering*, Cambridge, 1964, pp. 44–5, 93–4.

72. K.R. Andrews, *Drake's Voyages*, 1967, pp. 107–108.

73. *V.C.H. Hampshire*, V, p. 377.

74. Patterson, *Portsmouth: A History*, pp. 33–4.

75. Camden, *Britannia*, p. 170.

76. E.S. Washington, 'Hampshire and the Catholic Revival of the Fifteen-Eighties', *Hampshire Studies*, pp. 59–62, 64–70; A.J.C. Reger, *A Short History of Emsworth and Warblington*, Portsmouth, 1967, pp. 18–19, 22.

77. E.S. Washington, *Portsmouth in the Age of the Armada*, Portsmouth Museums Society Publication, no. 3, 1972, pp. 17–20.

78. Oppenheim, *Administration of the Royal Navy*, pp. 209–10.

79. D. Dymond, *Captain John Mason and the Duke of Buckingham*, P.P. 17, Portsmouth, 1972.

80. *V.C.H. Hampshire*, III, p. 179.

81. Ibid. p. 189; East, *Portsmouth Records*, pp. 422–34.

82. Dymond, P.P. 17, pp. 6, 12, 13; *V.C.H. Hampshire*, V, p. 377; H.T. Lilley and A.T. Everitt, *Portsmouth Parish Church*, Portsmouth, 1921, pp. 65, 68.

83. C. Oman, 'The Civic Plate and Insignia of the City of Portsmouth', *The Connoisseur*, 1965.

84. East, *Portsmouth Records*, pp. 645–6.

85. Stone, *Family and Fortune*, pp. 218, 223, 226–8; *V.C.H. Hampshire*, III, pp. 220–1.

86. Stone, *Family and Fortune*, p. 233; Reger, *History of Emsworth and Warblington*, p. 22.

87. J. Webb, *The Siege of Portsmouth in the Civil War*, P.P. 7, Portsmouth, 1969.

CHAPTER 5 – FROM CIVIL WAR TO WATERLOO

1. For helpful comments on this essay I am grateful to Suzanne Thomas, Sarah Quail and to my co-editor Barry Stapleton.

2. John Missing to the Earl of Sandwich, 19 Nov. 1781: Sandwich MSS. 105/399. I am obliged to the Hon. Victor Montagu for permission to cite from this collection.

3. *C.S.P.D. 1663–4*, pp. 200, 235, 263; P.R.O. Chancery Proceedings, Six Clerks' Series, C10/153/105, Neale v. Hoppar, 1669. Neale's main residence was at Warnford; his estates included land at Widley.

4. John Fielder, Sir William Lewis and Richard Norton to John Pym, 7 Sept. 1642: Hist. Mss. Comm, *Portland MSS.*, I, p. 61. For further details see J. Webb, *The Siege of Portsmouth in the Civil War*, P.P. VII, 1969.

5. Bodleian Library, Oxford, MS, Rawlinson Poet 79, ff. 64, 63v.; P.R.O. Lay Subsidy Rolls, E179/176/554.

6. T.F. Kirby, *Winchester Scholars*, 1888, p. 169; B.L. Add. MSS. 39972, f. 82; P.C.R.O. CHU15/3, folder of miscellaneous notes on Widley.

7. J. Walker, *An Attempt towards Recovering an Account of the Numbers and Sufferings of the Clergy*, II, 1714, , p. 93; *C.S.P.D. 1668–9*, pp. 93–4, 98, 113; ibid, 1670, p. 143.

8. E. Calamy, *The Nonconformists' Memorial*, 2 vols., 1702–13, II, *passim*.

9. *L.G.*, 2008, 12–16 Feb. 1684; J.H. Thomas, 'Learned in the Laws of England: Recorders of Portsmouth, 1658–1685', *Portsmouth Archives Review*, VII, 1984, pp. 1–22.

10. P.C.R.O. CE1/8, Book of Elections and Sessions 1662–1674, f. 110v; CE1/10, Book of Elections and Sessions 1684–1700, f. 9v; G.W. Keeton, *Lord Chancellor Jeffreys and the Stuart Cause*, 1965, *passim*; J.P. Kenyon, *The Stuarts*, 1967 edition, p. 148.

11. James II to Dartmouth, 5 Dec. 1688; Sir Richard Beach to same, 5 Dec. 1688: Hist. Mss. Comm. *MSS. of Earl of Dartmouth*, p. 224.

12. M. Ashley, *James II*, 1977, pp. 255–6.

13. Dartmouth to Samuel Pepys, 14 Dec. 1688: (ed.) J. Smith, *The Life, Journals, and Correspondence of Samuel Pepys*, 2 vols., 1841, II, p. 197; ? to John Ellis, 20 Dec. 1688:(ed.) G.A. Ellis, *The Ellis Correspondence*, 2 vols., 1829, II, p. 374.

14. P.C.R.O. CE1/10, n.f. I am obliged to Sarah Quail for drawing this to my attention.

15. James Vernon to the Duke of Shrewsbury, 22 Oct. 1698: (ed.) G.P.R. James, *Letters Illustrative of the Reign of William III*, 3 vols., 1841, II, p. 204; ? to the Earl of Oxford, 27 Nov. 1708: P.R.O. State Papers Domestic, S.P. 34/10/154; P.C.R.O. Miscellaneous Sessions Papers, 11A/16/53,57.

16. Sir C. Petrie, *The Jacobite Movement*, 1932, p. 130; G. Marcus, *A Naval History of England*, I, 1961, p. 259, n.2; London Customhouse to Portsmouth officers, 20 Sept. 1715: P.C.R.O. 11A/10/54; P.C.R.O. 11A/16/295,302,304.

17. P.C.R.O. S1/31, Oath Roll; S2/20, Sacrament Certificates for Dec. 1715.

18. H.R.O. Q.R. Sessions Rolls, Indictments, Midsummer 1716.

19. Southampton Civic Records Office, Miscellaneous Papers.

20. P.C.R.O. S2/25, Sacrament certificates for May 1744 and Dec. 1745; Office of Ordnance to Portsmouth, 20 Dec. 1745: P.C.R.O. 380A (Xerox copy).

21. *L.G.*, 374, 14–17 June 1669; *Calendar of Treasury Books and Papers 1731–4*, pp. 528–9; *Calendar of Home Office Papers 1773–5*, p. 301; (ed.) W. Westergaard, *The First Triple Alliance: The Letters of Christopher Lindenov, Danish Envoy to London 1668–72*, Copenhagen, 1947, pp. 392, 396–7, 423, 429, 435; L. von Ranke, *A History of England Principally in the Seventeenth Century*, 6 vols., 1875, VI, p. 168.

22. *Calendar of State Papers Venetian 1661–4*, pp. 124, 132–3, 137, 143, 146.

23. I. Grey, *Peter the Great: Emperor of All Russia*, 1962, chapter XIII; *G.M.*, XXVII, 1757, p. 381; *Annual Register for 1768*, 6th edition, 1800, p. 106.; P.C.R.O. CE1/15, Elections and Sessions Book 1776–1816, pp. 133–4. The Prince of Wurtemburg was in England for his marriage to the Princess Royal. An ardent bibliomaniac, he owned, amongst other items, 9,000 bibles of different editions.

24. N. Luttrell, *A Brief Historical Relation of State Affairs*, 6 vols., 1857, VI, pp. 53, 66.

25. *C.H.O.P. 1766–9*, p. 589; Haslar Hospital, Minutes of Physician & Council 1767–1772, *passim*; 1772–1772, *passim*; Letter Book of Council 1764–1772; Sandwich MSS, item 380, List of Portsmouth Voters, 1775; (ed.) J. Simmons, *Journeys in England,* 1969 edition, p. 194.

26. *C.S.P.D. 1666–7*, p. 398; F.C. Abell, *Prisoners of War in Britain 1756–1815,* 1914, pp. 166, 168.

27. P.R.O. Admiralty Minutes, Adm. 3/58, Sept. 1747–Feb. 1748, *passim*; ibid, Adm. 3/59, Feb.–Aug. 1748, *passim*.

28. *G.M.*, XXVII, 1757, p. 186; *A.R. for 1758*, 9th edition, 1795, p. 81. Confined at Portchester, he made a second, but unsuccessful, escape attempt: ibid, p. 81.

29. *A.R. for 1778*, 4th edition, 1800, p. 200; *A.R. for 1793*, 1794, p. 17. Three French prisoners escaping from Forton in 1807 returned to France, taking a Portsmouth boatman with them. He was later released and repatriated: *A.R. for 1807*, 1809, p. 494.

30. Sir Charles Hedges to the Duke of Somerset, 26 Jan. 1704: *C.S.P.D. 1703–4*, p. 510; Luttrell, VI, p. 355.

31. H.R.O. Probate Records, Bishops' series, inventory of John Earwaker, dated 8 Aug. 1686; (ed.) A.J. Willis and M. Hoad, *Borough Sessions Papers 1653–1688*, 1971, P.R.S., 1, *passim*; P.C.R.O. Borough Sessions Papers, S3/25, deposition dated 5 March 1695; S3/102, deposition dated 9 Jan. 1735; S3/127, deposition dated 17 March 1748.

32. Mr Potter, *The Traveller's Pocket-Book*, 1775, pp. 154–5; P.C.R.O. S3/106, deposition dated 13 July 1737; S3/98, deposition dated 14 July 1732; B.L. Add. MSS 33652, Journal of Revd John Skinner for 1818, f. 11. Portsmouth recruiting sergeants are known to have attended Weyhill fair.

33. P.R.O. C8/297/125, Worlidge v. Warre, 1682; James Crosse to Sir Robert Walpole, 11 May 1733: Cambridge University Library, Cholmondeley Houghton Collection, Correspondence, 1978. I am obliged to the Dowager Marchioness of Cholmondeley for permission to quote from the collection.

34. P.R.O. Chancery Masters' Exhibits, C108/286, Gosport Yard Paybook 1745–50, n.p.

35. *C.S.P.D. 1672–3*, p. 503; *C.S.P.D. 1656–7*, p. 458.

36. J. Sadler, *The Hampshire Directory*, Winchester, 1784, pp. 85, 74; P.R.O. C7/247/19, Newland v. Jaques, 1682.

37. P.R.O. Port Books E190/830/3, Portsmouth Port Book (Coastal, Inwards), Dec. 1678–Dec. 1679, *passim*.

38. T.S. Willan, *The English Coasting Trade 1600–1750*, 1967 reprint, p. 211. A Newcastle chaldron weighed 53 cwt.; a London chaldron weighed 26 cwt. Haslar Hospital, Minutes of Physician and Council 1772–1777, *passim*. G.L., MS.11936 Sun Fire Insurance Policy no. 31015, dated 7 May 1724.

39. (eds.) N.W. Surry and J.H. Thomas, *Book of Original Entries 1731–1751*, P.R.S., 3, 1976, p. 1v, n.10; *C.T.B.P. 1735–8*, p. 218. In Sept. 1813 a whale stranded off the Isle of Wight was cut up by a South Sea whaler at the Mother Bank for oil, valued at £500. It was noted that 'A similar occurrence never happened before within the isle of Wight': *A.R. for 1813*, 1814, pp. 79–80.

40. *C.S.P.D. 1664–5*, pp. 135–6; ibid, 1677–8, p. 469; Hist. Mss. Comm. *House of Lords MSS. 1708–1710*, p. 322. In Jan. 1712 a Swedish ship was repaired at crown expense in Portsmouth yard: *Calendar of Treasury Books 1712*, p. 110.

41. P.C.R.O. S3/144, deposition dated 16 Apr. 1757. In May 1743 a crewman from a Portuguese vessel 'now in the harbour' attacked a local Jewish boy: ibid, S3/118/151, deposition dated 17 May 1743.

42. (ed.) E.B. Sainsbury, *A Calendar of the Court Minutes of the East India Company 1677–9*, 1938, pp. 65, 169; P.R.O. State Papers Foreign S.P. 105/153, Levant Company Court Book 1669–1676, ff. 104, 269, 351; *Despatches from England to Fort St George 1744–7*, 1931, *passim*.

43. Richard Norton to Secretary Coventry, 20 Sept. 1679: *C.T.B. 1679–1680*, p. 239.

44. C.U.L. C(H) Papers 41/23, 24; William ? to ?, 15 Feb. 1673: B.L. Add. MSS. 33278, f. 40.

45. *The Inhuman Murder of Galley and Chater*, 1748. For further details of local smuggling see E. Carson, *Smuggling and Revenue Officers in the Portsmouth Area in the Eighteenth Century*, P.P., no. 22, 1974.

46. Arnold to Richard Norton, 8 March 1723: H.R.O. Daly MSS. 5M50/843. Such were Arnold's shortcomings that in 1725 the Treasury held a full-scale enquiry into his conduct: C.U.L. C(H), Papers 44/20/1–4. For further details of both smuggling and trade see J.H. Thomas, *The Seaborne Trade of Portsmouth 1650–1800* P.P. no. 40, 1984.

47. Sadler, *passim*.

48. *L.G.*, 4939, 13–15 Dec. 1711. The hostelry is known today as The Ship and Bell Hotel.

49. *Admissions to Lincoln's Inn 1420–1799*, 1896, *passim*; Sir H.F. Macgeagh and H.A.C. Sturgess, *Register of Admissions to the . . . Middle Temple*, 3 vols., 1949, I, p. 285.

50. G.L., MS. 5266/1–3, Barber-Surgeons Company Apprenticeship Bindings 1658–1725, *passim*; (ed.) D.F. McKenzie, *Stationers Company Apprentices 1671–1700*, 1974, *passim*; (ed.) McKenzie, *Stationers Company Apprentices 1701–1800*, 1978, *passim*.

51. For Jaggard's activities see J.H. Thomas, 'A Seventeenth-Century Merchant's Account Book', in (eds.)Webb et al., *Hampshire Studies*, Portsmouth, 1981, pp. 141–67; C.R.B. Barrett, *The History of the Society of Apothecaries of London*, 1905, p. 144.

52. Goldsmiths' Company, London, Court Books, XI, p. 448.

53. (ed.) E.B. Sainsbury, *Calendar of the Court Minutes of the East India Company 1674–6*, 1935, pp. 398, 406; India Office Library, East India Company Court Minutes, B/37, Apr. 1682–Apr. 1684, f. 96a; B/38, Apr. 1684–Apr. 1687, f. 147a; *G.M.*, LVIII 1788, p. 1129; Customs and Excise Records 58/1.

54. Surry and Thomas, *Book of Original Entries*, p. xliv; H.R.O. Probate Records, Admons, administration of Chamberlain Atkins 1750.

55. Williams and Glyns Ltd., Birchin Lane, London, Ledgers of Edward Backwell, Ledger R., 1669–70, f. 458. I am indebted to the bank for permission to cite from their records.

56. Sandwich MSS., item 380.

57. P.R.O. E179/176/559.

58. *G.M.*, XXIII, 1753, p. 97.

59. *L.G.*, 3964, 4–8 Nov. 1703; Sadler, pp. 115, 131, 86. Baker was appointed agent for Portsmouth and the Isle of Wight, 25 March 1783, in penalty of £1,000: G.L., MS. 14386, Agents Bond Book 1786–1841, f. 91.

60. Mrs Bramston to Mrs Hicks Beach, 23 June 1794: HRO 20M64/15. For the royal visit see M. Lewis, *Spithead: An Informal History*, 1972, pp. 164–5.

61. *A.R. for 1804*, 1806, p. 441; (ed.) L. Wolf, *Essays in Jewish History*, 1934, pp. 251–2.

62. P.C.R.O. S3/95, certificate dated 28 Oct. 1730; *Salisbury Journal and Devizes Mercury*, 26 July 1762; R. Fourneaux, *Tobias Furneaux, Circumnavigator*, 1960, pp. 154–62.

63. James Wolfe to mother, 11 Feb. 1758: D. Ford, *Admiral Vernon and the Navy*, 1907, p. 191; R. Wilkins, *The Borough: Being a Faithful, tho' Humorous Description, of one of the strongest Garrisons, Sea-Port Towns, in Great Britain*, 1748, p.2.

64. (ed.) J.J. Cartwright, *The Travels through England of Dr Richard Pococke*, 2 vols., Camden Soc. 1888–9, II, p. 117.

65. P.C.R.O. CHU27/2A/4, Portchester Mixed Register 1694–1803, n.p; *A.R. for 1802*, 1803, p. 399.

66. See J.H. Thomas, *Portsmouth and the First Fleet 1786–1787*, P.P. no. 50, 1987, *passim*.

CHAPTER 6 – THE NINETEENTH CENTURY

1. Cromford was established by Richard Arkwright to provide dwellings for workers in his cotton-spinning mill in 1771.

2. Samuel Bentham's role in the expansion of the dockyard is developed in Chapter III.

3. For comment on Grant's work at the Royal Clarence Yard where he was storekeeper 1831–51, see Chapter III.

4. *Census Report 1801*.

5. A. Temple Patterson, *'Palmerston's Folly' The Portsdown and Spithead Forts*, P.P. no. 3, Portsmouth, 1967. Construction of the five forts of the Elson–Gomer line west of Gosport had commenced in 1852, for which see A.D. Saunders, 'Hampshire Coastal Defence since the Introduction of Artillery', *The Archaeological Journal*, CXXIII, 1967, p. 50.

6. R.C. Riley, *The Evolution of the Docks and Industrial Buildings in Portsmouth Royal Dockyard 1698–1914*, P.P. no. 44, Portsmouth, 1985, p. 22.

7. R.C. Riley, *The Industries of Portsmouth in the Nineteenth Century*, P.P. no. 25, Portsmouth, 1976, p. 9.

8. Benjamin Bramble, who resided in Southsea, received a number of contracts from the Admiralty for the construction of building slips and docks in the 1840s and 1880s. However, most contractors were London firms. See Riley (1985) *op. cit.*

9. J. Cramer, 'William Treadgold Iron Merchants, Bishop Street, Portsea', unpublished dissertation for English Local History Diploma, Portsmouth Polytechnic, 1982, p. 80.

10. L.G. Carr Laughton, 'Maritime History', in *V.C.H. Hampshire and the Isle of Wight*, V, 1912, p. 398.

11. W.G. Gates, *Portsmouth Through the Centuries*, Portsmouth, 1931, p. 78.

12. Robert R. Dolling, *Ten Years in a Portsmouth Slum*, 6th edition, 1903, pp. 108–9.

13. R.C. Riley, 'The Portsmouth Corset Industry in the Nineteenth Century', in (eds.) Webb et al.,*Hampshire Studies* Portsmouth, 1981, pp. 241–64.

14. R. Dixon and S. Muthesius, *Victorian Architecture*, 1978, p. 87. See also R.C. Riley and Philip Eley, *Public Houses and Beerhouses in Nineteenth Century Portsmouth*, P.P. no. 38, Portsmouth, 1983, pp. 25–7.

15. M.J. Freeman, 'Turnpikes and their traffic: the example of southern Hampshire', *Institute of British Geographers Transactions*, NS 4(3), 1979, pp. 411–34.

16. Gosport and Fareham were linked with Southampton, and therefore with London, in 1841. Portsmouth, Havant and Emsworth were linked with Brighton in 1847, and the Fareham–Portsmouth line was opened in 1848. The Portsmouth 'direct' route to London via Rowlands Castle was completed in 1859.

17. Branch lines were opened to Stokes Bay in 1863, Hayling in 1867, East Southsea in 1885 and Lee-on-the-Solent in 1894.

18. *Census Abstracts, 1861, Houses and Population in Counties.*

19. M. Hallett, *Portsmouth's Water Supply 1800–60*, P.P. no. 12, Portsmouth, 1971, p. 22.

20. R. Rawlinson, *Report to the General Board of Health on the Sewage, Drainage and Water Supply of Portsmouth,* 1850.

21. R.C. Riley, *The Houses and Inhabitants of Thomas Ellis Owen's Southsea*, P.P. no. 32, Portsmouth, 1980, p. 16.

22. M. Lewis, *Spithead: An Informal History*, 1972, pp. 154–77; G.R. Wade, *The Wind of Change: Naval Reviews at Spithead 1842–56*, P.P. no. 49, Portsmouth, 1987.

23. Dolling, *Ten Years, passim.*

24. British Association, *Handbook and Guide to Portsmouth*, Portsmouth, 1911, p. 94.

25. J. Chapman, 'The Geographical Evolution of Portsmouth', in (ed.) J.B. Bradbeer, *Portsmouth Geographical Essays*, 1, Portsmouth, 1974, p. 13.

26. C.W. Chalklin, *The Provincial Towns of Georgian England*, 1974, p. 123.

27. J. Chapman, *The Common Lands of Portsea Island*, P.P. no. 29, Portsmouth, 1978, p. 9.

28. Ibid, p. 11.

29. Ibid.

30. Fareham (1805), Portchester (1808), Forest of Bere (1810), Eastney and Milton Commons (1810), Warblington (1810), Wymering (1812) and Chalton (1812). Beeston and Pitcroft Fields (1817) and a further part of Warblington (1819) followed.

31. J. Chapman, 'The parliamentary enclosures of West Sussex', *Southern History*, 2, 1980, p. 77.

32. *Hampshire Telegraph*, 15 Oct. 1810.

33. W. Cobbett, *Rural Rides*, 1950, p. 120.

34. Hayling (3 under the 1836 Act; 2 under that of 1840), Droxford (1851), Hambledon (2 in 1852; 2 in 1865), East Meon (1845 and 1856), Meonstoke (1856), Soberton (1858), Titchfield (4 in 1859) and Havant (1864).

CHAPTER 7 – THE POPULATION OF THE PORTSMOUTH REGION

1. I am most grateful to my co-editor James H. Thomas for helpful comments on this chapter.

2. See Chapter I, p. 2 for map of known sites of prehistoric man's habitation.

3. See Chapter II, p. 16.

4. See Chapter II, pp. 16–17.

5. See Chapter IV, p. 49.

6. See Chapter I, p. 12 and Chapter II, p. 18.

7. For the size of medieval households and the appropriate multiplier to convert individuals into numbers in each household see J.C. Russell, *British Medieval Population*, Albuquerque, 1948, pp. 22–32, and J.T. Krause, 'The Medieval Household: Large or Small?' *Ec.H.R.*, IX, 1956, pp. 420–32.

8. Total calculated from acreages returned in 1831 census pp. 562, 576 and 580. This assumes that acreage changes were minimal between 1086 and 1831.

9. See Chapter IV, p. 46.

10. Russell, *Medieval Population*, pp. 34–54, 118–146.

11. (ed.) M.M. Postan, *The Cambridge Economic History of Europe*, Vol. 1, 1966, pp. 561–5. Such wide variations have depended largely on whether the average medieval household was considered to have contained from as few as 3.5 or as many as 5 people.

12. Krause, op cit., pp. 420–32; M.M. Postan, *The Medieval Economy and Society*, 1975, pp. 30–38; J.Z. Titow, *English Rural Society 1200–1350*, 1969, pp. 66–71. Historians generally have shown greater support for a larger household and certainly for one averaging 4.5 people.

13. Russell, *Medieval Population*, pp. 246–73; *Econ. Hist. of Europe*, 1, p. 562.

14. D.G. Watts, 'A Model for the Early Fourteenth Century', *Ec.H.R.*, XX, no. 3, 1967, pp. 543–4 and Chapter IV, p. 51.

15. Titow, *Rural Society*, pp. 45–46, 169–72.

16. Ibid. pp. 80–90.

17. Ibid. pp. 78–9.

18. *Econ. Hist. of Europe*, 1, p. 564.

19. Ibid; H.S. Lucas, 'The Great European Famine of 1315, 1316 and 1317', *Speculum*, V., (1930), reprinted in (ed.) E.M. Carus-Wilson, *Essays in Economic History*, Vol. 2, 1962, pp. 49–72.

20. M.M. Postan and J.Z. Titow, 'Heriots and Prices on Winchester Manors', *Ec.H.R.*, XI, no. 2, 1958, pp. 392–410; Postan, *Medieval Economy*, p. 38.

21. *Econ. Hist. of Europe*, 1, p. 566; and Postan, *Medieval Economy*, p. 40.

22. W. Beveridge, 'Wages in the Winchester Manors', *Ec.H.R.*, VII, 1936, pp. 26–43; W. Beveridge, 'Westminster Wages in the Manorial Era', *Ec.H.R.*, VIII, 1955, pp. 18–35; *Econ. Hist of Europe*, pp. 566–7.

23. Postan, *Medieval Economy*, p. 41.

24. J. Hatcher, *Plague, Population and the English Economy 1348–1530*, 1977, pp. 21–6.

25. J.F.D. Shrewsbury, *A History of Bubonic Plague in the British Isles*, Cambridge, 1971, pp. 90–1.

26. Titow, *Rural Society*, pp. 69–70.

27. (ed.) D.G. Watts, *Titchfield, a History*, Titchfield, 1982, p. 39, percentage estimated mainly from analysis of Court Book, B.L. Loan 29/59, f291 sq. ex. info. D.G. Watts.

28. *Cal. Close R.* Edward III, IX 432, membrane 19 quoted in Shrewsbury, *Bubonic Plague*, p. 89.

29. *Originalia Roll* 29 Ed. III m.8. cited in P. Ziegler, *The Black Death*, 1970, p. 150.

30. Titow, *Rural Society*, p. 70.

31. (ed.) V.H. Galbraith, *Anonimalle Chronicle 1333 to 1381*, Manchester, 1927, p. 77.

32. T.H. Hollingsworth, *Historical Demography*, 1969, pp. 385–6.

33. *V.C.H. Hants.*, V, pp. 421–2.

34. Hollingsworth, *Historical Demography*, p. 358; C. Creighton, *A History of Epidemics in Britain*, Cambridge, 1891–4, reprinted 1964, I; Hatcher, *Plague, Population*, pp. 57–61.

35. Hollingsworth, *Historical Demography*, pp. 378–87; Hatcher, *Plague, Population*, pp. 26–8, 68–9.

36. Beveridge, 'Wages in Winchester Manors', pp. 38–43.

37. P.R.O. E179/181 and 182.

38. B.L. Harleian 495 ff237–39.

39. William Salt Library, Stafford, MS Salt 33.

40. H.R.O. B/2/A 1725 Visitation Return 2 vols.; B/2/A/2 1788 Visitation Return, this latter has a number of damaged entries and many returns do not appear to have survived, hence for many communities information does not exist.

41. D. Hodson, *Maps of Portsmouth before 1801*, P.R.S., 4, 1978, pp. 31–2 and frontispiece; B.L. Cotton MS Augustus I.i.81.

42. See P. Laslett and R. Wall, *Household and Family in Past Time*, 1972, pp. 125–58 for household size from the sixteenth to the nineteenth century.

43. (ed.) L. Toulmin Smith, *The Itinerary of John Leland*, 1964, I, pp. 279–85.

44. P.C.R.O. 906A.

45. P.R.O. C179/173/181.

46. (ed.) D.G. Watts, *Titchfield, a History*, pp. 34–5.

47. *C.S.P.D. 1665–1666*, p. 32.

48. The 1676 total excludes Southwick, Boarhunt, Widley and Wymering for which no figures were returned in 1725.

49. D. Defoe, *A Tour Through the Whole Island of Great Britain*, 2 vols., 1962 edition, Vol. I, pp. 137–8.

50. For estimates of the national population and London's contribution see E.A. Wrigley and R.S. Schofield, *The Population History of England 1541–1871, a Reconstruction*, 1981, pp. 208–9 and 531–5.

51. P.R.O. E179/176/565. A multiplier of 4.5 is used to convert the number of houses into occupants of households.

52. In 1697 the number of parishes increased to 27 with the creation of Gosport out of Alverstoke parish.

53. See Wrigley and Schofield, *Population History, passim*.

54. See J.C. Cox, *Parish Registers of England*, Ottawa, New Jersey reprint, 1974, pp. 1–3.

55. The parish registers of the Portsmouth region are all deposited in record offices. They are listed chronologically along with their commencement dates as follows P.C.R.O. CHU 39/1A/1–4 Chalton, 1538, CHU 14/1A/1–5 Farlington, 1539; CHU 39/1A/6–7 Clanfield, 1565 bap., 1548 bur.; CHU 43/1A/1–5 Fareham, 1558; CHU 42/1A/1–4 Alverstoke, 1560; CHU 29/1A/1–4 North Hayling 1571; CHU 40/1A/1–3 Blendworth, 1586; CHU 46/1A/1–2 Rowner, 1590; CHU 41/1A/1–7 Catherington, 1601; CHU 27/2A/1–5 CHU 27/2B/1–2 CHU 27/2D/1–3 Portchester, 1619; CHU 19/1A/1–5 Warblington, 1647 bap., 1656 bur.; CHU 38/1A/1–2 Havant, 1653; CHU 15/1A/1–6 Widley and Wymering, 1653; CHU 3/1A/1–14 Portsea, 1654; CHU 2/1A/1–9 Portsmouth, 1654; CHU 28/1A/1 South Hayling 1673 bap., 1675 bur.; CHU 26/1A/1–4 Bedhampton, 1688 bap., 1686 bur.; CHU 23/1A/1–6 Gosport 1697. H.R.O. 50M73A PR 1–5 Soberton, 1546 bap., 1539 bur.; 87M70A PR 1–3 Wickham, 1557; 68M81A PR 1-3 Southwick, 1588; 37M73A PR 1–4 Titchfield, 1590; 80M76A PR 1 Meonstoke, 1599; 46M69 PR 1–3,5,6 Hambledon, 1601 bap., 1603 bur.; 66M76A PR 1–3 Droxford, 1635 bap., 1633 bur.; 69M81A PR 1 Boarhunt, 1654.

56. Nonconformist registers used at P.C.R.O. are CHU 91/2 1785–1812 Orange Street Chapel, Congregationalist, births and baps; CHU 71/1A/1 1794–1812 Roman Catholic bap; CHU 81/W13/1 1798–1812 St Peter's Chapel, Methodist, bap.; Canon R.E. Scantlebury, *Hampshire Registers* Vol. IV, *The Registers of Gosport 1759–1812*, publications of the Catholic Record Society Vol. XLIX, 1955.

57. Chapter V, p. 63.

58. Between 1701 and 1710 Portsmouth parish registers indicate that average annual burials numbered over 278, while baptisms were under 234.

59. B.L. Add, MSS. 33278, ff. 69-70. I am grateful to Dr James H. Thomas for this reference.

60. The Dockyard employment statistics are derived from National Maritime Museum ADM/B and ADM/BP 1687–1711. National Maritime Museum Ser/131, B.L. Add. Mss. 9324, 1756–1832. I am greatly indebted to my former colleague Dr Trevor Harris for allowing me the use of his collected data.

61. (ed.) W.G. Gates, *Records of the Corporation 1835–1927*, 1928, p. 63.

62. Censuses of Great Britain 1801–1901. An exception to population growth could be Southwick. Unfortunately boundary changes make the position unclear.

63. R.C. Riley, *The Industries of Portsmouth in the Nineteenth Century*, P.P., no. 25, 1976, p. 9. Weekly dockyard wages fell from £6,000 to £3,000 and those still employed had their wages reduced; W.G. Gates, *Illustrated History of Portsmouth*, 1900, p. 606.

64. F.N.G. Thomas, 'Portsmouth and Gosport: A Study of the Historical Geography of a Naval Port', unpublished M.Sc. thesis, London University, 1961, pp. 52–4.

65. R.C. Riley, *The Evolution of the Docks and Industrial Buildings in Portsmouth Royal Dockyard 1698–1914*, P.P. no. 44, 1985, pp. 15–21.

66. R.C. Riley, *The Growth of Southsea as a Naval Satellite and Victorian Resort*, P.P. no. 16, 1972, pp. 3–9.

67. Ibid. p. 11.

68. Census of Great Britain 1871, Vol. II, p. 77. This latter comment was essentially a repetition of a similar one made in the previous census in 1861, when the increase in population on Portsea Island was 'attributed mainly to the government works in progress; the number of labourers and artizans employed in HM Dockyard, as well as the military force in the garrison, is much larger than in 1851', Census of Great Britain 1861, Vol. II, p. 254.

69. Carpenters have been excluded from the number of building workers since it is not known what proportion of them worked in the dockyard. There were 517 enumerated in 1841 and 704 in 1851.

70. Census of Great Britain 1881, Vol. III, p. 67.

71. Census of Great Britian 1851, Vol. I, pp. 48–9.

72. A.J. Holland, *Ships of British Oak. The Rise and Decline of Wooden Shipbuilding in Hampshire*, 1971, pp. 56–7.

73. *Hampshire Telegraph and Sussex Chronicle*, 18 July 1846, quoted in R.C. Riley, *Industries in Portsmouth*, p. 15.

74. Plymouth, also a town with dockyard employees and sailors' wives, similarly had a concentration of corset manufacture suggesting comparable factors in the availability of cheap female labour influenced development there.

75. P. Christie, 'Occupations in Portsmouth 1550–1850', unpublished M.Phil. thesis, Portsmouth Polytechnic, 1976, p. 17.

76. R.C. Riley, 'The Portsmouth Corset Industry in the Nineteenth Century', in (eds.) Webb et al., *Hampshire Studies*, 1981, pp. 241–8.

77. G. Pinckard, quoted in W.G. Gates, *History of Portsmouth*, 1900, pp. 487–8.

78. P.D. Hopgood, 'The Workings of the Contagious Diseases Act in Portsmouth', in *The Portsmouth Times and Hampshire Telegraph*, 30 March 1872, quoted in P. Christie, op.cit., p. 210. See also H. Tudge, 'Women and Crime in Eighteenth Century Portsmouth', unpublished dissertation for Diploma in English Local History, Portsmouth Polytechnic, 1986, pp. 35–57.

79. Twenty-fourth, thirty-fourth, forty-fourth, fifty-fourth and sixty-fourth *Annual Reports of the Registrar General of Births, Deaths and Marriages in England*, 1861, 1871, 1881, 1891, 1901.

80. B. Stapleton, 'Migration in Southern England', *Southern History*, Vol. X, 1988, pp. 47–93.

81. E.A. Wrigley and R.S. Schofield, *Population History*, 1981, p. 529.

82. Ibid.

83. Robert Rawlinson, *Report to the General Board of Health on the Sewage, Drainage and Water Supply of Portsmouth*, 1850, and Jean Stanford and A. Temple Patterson, *The Condition of the Children of the Poor in Mid-Victorian Portsmouth*, P.P. no. 21, 1974, p. 3.

84. PCRO 11A/22/13 Henry Slight's report, *Intramural Interments, Medical Statistical and Historical Evidence . . . on the Cemeteries of Portsmouth, 1850*, quoted in Rosemary Phillips, 'Burial Administration in Portsmouth and Portsea 1820–1900' unpublished dissertation for Diploma in English Local History, Portsmouth Polytechnic, 1979, p. 7.

85. For the cholera outbreak and Rawlinson's Report see Mary Hallett, *Portsmouth's Water Supply 1800–1860*, P.P. no. 12, 1971, and J. Noon, *King Cholera comes to Portsmouth*, Portsmouth, 1972.

86. P.C.R.O. P3 30 November 1844, Plans and Sections of Spithead and Langstone Docks and Ship Canal. I am grateful to Dr Patricia Haskell for this reference.

87. White's *History, Gazetteer and Directory of the County of Hampshire*, Sheffield, 1878, p. 387.

THE NATURAL ENVIRONMENT

CHAPTER 8 – GEOLOGY AND PHYSICAL LANDSCAPE

1. W. Whitaker, 'List of works on the Geology, Mineralogy and Palaeontology of the Hampshire

Basin', *Journal of Proceedings of the Winchester and Hampshire Scientific Literary Society*, 1873, pp. 108–127.

2. Geological Survey of Great Britain (England and Wales), Portsmouth (Sheet 331) (1893, first colour printing 1903, reprinted with minor amendments 1964); Fareham (Sheet 316) (1900, first colour printing, 1905, latest version 1958); Southampton (Sheet 315) (1899, reprinted 1964, 1979).

3. C.J.A. Meyer, 'On the Lower Tertiary deposits recently exposed at Portsmouth', *Quarterly Journal of the Geological Society*, XXVII, 1871, pp. 74–89.

4. O. Fisher, 'On the Bracklesham Beds of the Isle of Wight Basin', *Proceedings of the Geological Society*, 1862, pp. 65–94.

5. C. Reid, *The Geology of the Country around Southampton*, Memoir of the Geological Survey (UK), 1902; H.J.O. White, *The Geology of the Country near Fareham and Havant*, Memoir of the Geological Survey (UK), 1913; *idem, The Geology of the Country near Lymington and Portsmouth*, Memoir of the Geological Survey (UK), 1915; W. Whitaker, *The Water Supply of Hampshire*, Memoir of the Geological Survey (UK), 1910; C. Griffin and R.M. Brydone, *The Zones of the Chalk in Hants.*, 1911; R.M. Brydone, *Stratigraphy of the Chalk of Hants.*, 1912.

6. A.H. Taitt and P.E. Kent, *Deep Boreholes at Portsdown (Hants.) and Henfield (Sussex)*, 1958.

7. Institute of Geological Sciences, Wight (Sheet 50°N – 02°W), 1977; Geological Survey of Great Britain (England and Wales), Gravity Survey Overlay Map (Sheets 19 and 23), 1968; Geological Survey, Aeromagnetic Map of Great Britain, England and Wales south of National Grid Line 500 Kms N., (Sheet 2), 1965.

8. D. Curry and C. King, 'The Eocene succession at Lower Swanwick Brickyard, Hampshire', *Proceedings of the Geologists' Association*, LXXVI, 1965, pp. 29–35; D. Curry, F. Hodson and I.M. West, 'The Eocence succession in the Fawley Transmission Tunnel', *Proceedings of the Geologists' Association*, LXXIX, 1968, pp. 179–206; C. King, *The Stratigraphy of the London Clay and associated deposits*, Tertiary Research Special Paper no. 6., Rotterdam, 1981.

9. C.P. Chatwin, *The Hampshire Basin and Adjoining Areas*, 3rd edition, 1960; R.V. Melville and E.C. Freshney, *The Hampshire Basin and Adjoining Areas*, 4th edition, 1982; I.M. West, 'The Geology of the Solent Estuarine System', in *The Solent Estuarine System: An Assessment of Present Knowledge*, N.E.R.C. Publication Series C, no. 22, 1980.

10. Taitt and Kent, op cit., *passim*; W.G. Burgess, A.J. Burley, R.A. Downing, W.M. Edmonds and M. Price, *The Marchwood Geothermal Borehole – a preliminary assessment of the resource*, 1981.

11. A.S. Gale, 'Penecontemporaneous folding, sedimentation and erosion in Campanian Chalk near Portsmouth, England', *Sedimentology*, XXVII, 1980, pp. 137–151.

12. J.M. Hancock, 'The petrology of the Chalk', *Proceedings of the Geologists' Association*, LXXXVI, 1975, pp. 499–536.

13. E. Irving, 'Palaeomagnetic evidence for shear along the Tethys', in (eds.) C.G. Adams and D.V. Ager, *Aspects of Tethyan Biogeography*, 1967, pp. 59–76.

14. B. Daley, 'Some problems concerning the Early Tertiary climate of Southern Britain', *Palaeogeography, Palaeoclimatology and Palaeoecology*, XI, 1972, pp. 177–190.

15. White, *Lymington and Portsmouth*, p. 10.

16. C. Evans, 'On the Geology of the neighbourhood of Portsmouth and Ryde', *Proceedings of the Geologists' Association*, II, 1873, pp. 61–76, 149–174; Whitaker, *The Water Supply*, p. 199.

17. P. Burman, 'Palaeosols in the Reading Beds (Palaeocene) of Alum Bay, Isle of Wight, U.K.', *Sedimentology*, XXVII, 1980, pp. 593–606.

18. Meyer, loc.cit., *passim*.

19. Whitaker, *The Water Supply, passim*; King, op cit., p. 78.

20. J.W. Elwes, 'Sections opened on the new Railway from Fareham to Netley', *Papers and Proceedings of the Hampshire Field Club*, II, 1888, pp. 31–9.

21. Curry and King, loc.cit., *passim*; J.P. James,'Report of Field Meeting to Lower Swanwick, Hampshire', *Tertiary Times*, II, 1974, pp. 23–8; King, op cit., pp. 80–3.

22. C. King and D.J. Kemp, 'Exposures in the London Clay Formation of the Gosport Area (Hants)', *Tertiary Research*, III, 1980, pp. 71–81.

23. King, op cit., pp. 78–80.

24. King, ibid., pp. 31, 91.

25. White, *Lymington and Portsmouth*, p. 25.

26. Fisher, loc.cit., pp. 77–9.

27. D.J. Kemp, A.D. King, C. King and W.J. Quayle, 'Stratigraphy and Biota of the Elmore Formation (Huntingbridge division, Bracklesham Group) at Lee-on-the-Solent, Gosport, Hampshire', *Tertiary Research*, II, 1980, pp. 93–103; D. Curry, A.D. King, C. King and F.C. Stinton, 'The Bracklesham Beds (Eocene) of Bracklesham Bay and Selsey, Sussex', *Proceedings of the Geologists' Association*, LXXXVIII, 1977, pp. 243–54; D.J. Kemp, 'The Selsey Division (Bracklesham Group) at Lee-on-the-Solent, Gosport, Hants.', *Tertiary Research*, VII, 1985, pp. 35–44.

28. W.J. Quayle and J.S.J. Collins, 'New Eocene crabs from the Hampshire Basin', *Palaeontology*, XXIV, 1981, pp. 733–58; M.D. Crane and W.J. Quayle, 'Two new hexapod crabs of the genus *Goniocypoda*, Woodward (Crustacea, Decapoda) from the Hampshire Basin', *Tertiary Research*, VII, 1986, pp. 101–105; D.J. Kemp, 'Report of Field Meeting to Lee-on-the-Solent, Hants.', *Tertiary Times*, II, 1975, pp. 173–4; 'Account of excavations into the Campanile Bed (Eocene), Selsey Formation at Stubbington, Hants.', *Tertiary Research*, I, 1976, pp. 41–5; 'Fossil Sharks, Rays and Chimaeroids of the English Tertiary Period', *Gosport Museum Special Paper*, 1982, and *The Selsey Division*, pp. 39–43; D.J. Ward, 'A New Species of Chimaeroid Fish from the Upper Bracklesham Beds (M. Eocene) of Lee-on-the-Solent, Hampshire', *Tertiary Research*, I, 1977, pp. 101–104; 'Additions to the fish fauna of the English Palaeogene; 1. Two new species of Alopias (Thresher Shark) from the English Eocene', *Tertiary Research*, II, 1978, pp. 23–8; C.J.O. Harrison and C.A. Walker, *Birds of the British Middle Eocene*, Tertiary Research Special Paper, no. 5, 1979, pp. 19–29.

29. A.D. King and D.J. Kemp, 'Stratigraphy of the Bracklesham Group in recent exposures near Gosport, (Hants)', *Tertiary Research*, III, 1982, pp. 171–187; Curry, Hodson and West, loc.cit., *passim*; White, *Lymington and Portsmouth*, pp. 20–29.

30. H.W. Bristow, C. Reid and A. Strahan, *The Geology of the Isle of Wight*, Memoir of the Geological Survey (UK), 1889; Fisher, loc. cit., pp. 91–2; E. Tillotson, 'Earthquakes, explosions and the deep underground structures of the United Kingdom', *Journal of Earth Science*, VIII, 1974, pp. 353–364.

31. (ed.) D.K.C. Jones, *The Shaping of Southern England*, 1980, pp. 28–33, 50–2; D.K.C. Jones, *Geomorphology of the British Isles: Southeast and Southern England*, 1981, pp. 6–133.

32. D.J. Carter, 'The Historical Geography of the Forest of Bere, Hampshire', *South Hampshire Geographer*, I, 1968, pp. 74–100.

33. D.K.C. Jones, 'The influence of the Calabrian transgression on the drainage evolution of south-east England', in (eds.) E.H. Brown and R.S. Waters, *Progress in Geomorphology*, Institute of British Geographers, Special Publications no. 7, 1974, pp. 139–158; Jones, *The Shaping*, pp. 22–37.

34. R.J. Small, 'Geomorphology', in (ed.) F.J. Monkhouse, *A Survey of Southampton and its Region*, Southampton, 1964, pp. 37–50; R.J. Small, 'The Tertiary geomorphological evolution of south-east England: an alternative interpretation', in Jones, *The Shaping*, pp. 49–70; H.N. Hutchinson, 'Is the drainage of the Isle of Wight antecedent?', *Transactions of the Institute of British Geographers*, N.S., VII, 1982, pp. 217–226; P. Pinchemel, *Les plaines de craie du nord-ouest de bassin Parisien et du sud-est du bassin de Londres et leurs bordures; étude de géomorphologie*, Paris, 1954.

35. S.W. Wooldridge and D.L. Linton, *Structure, Surface and Drainage in South-East England*, 1955, originally published by Institute of British Geographers, Publication no. 10, 1939.

36. D.T. John, 'The soils and superficial deposits on the North Downs of Surrey', in Jones, *The Shaping*, pp. 101–130.

37. Jones, in Brown and Waters, pp. 145–154, and Jones, *Geomorphology*, pp. 104–33; Small, in Jones, *The Shaping*, pp. 59–67.

38. J.M. Hodgson, et al., 'The geomorphological significance of Clay-with-Flints on the South Downs', *Transactions of the Institute of British Geographers*, LXI, 1974, pp. 119–31; P. Marten, 'Palaeogene mineralogy in the south-eastern Hampshire Basin', unpublished report, Department of Soil Science and Geology, University of Wageningen, 1980.

39. D.N. Mottershead, 'The Quaternary History of the Portsmouth Region', in (eds.) D.N. Mottershead and R.C. Riley, *Portsmouth Geographical Essays*, II, Portsmouth, 1976, pp. 1–21.

40. L.S. Palmer and J.H. Cooke, 'The Pleistocene deposits of the Portsmouth district and their relation to early man', *Proceedings of the Geologists' Association*, XXXIV, 1923, pp. 253–82.

41. C.E. Everard, 'The Solent River: a geomorphological study', *Transactions of the Institute of British Geographers*, XX, 1954, pp. 41–53; 'Erosion platforms on the borders of the Hampshire Basin', *Transactions of the Institute of British Geographers*, XXII, 1956, pp. 33–46.

42. C.E. Everard, 'Submerged gravel and peat in Southampton Water', *Proc. H.F.C.*, XVIII, 1954, pp. 263–85; K.R. Dyer, 'The buried channels of the 'Solent River', southern England', *Proceedings of the Geologists' Association*, LXXXVI, 1975, pp. 239–45.

43. A.M. ApSimon, C. Gable and M.L. Shackley, 'Pleistocene Raised Beaches on Ports Down, Hampshire', *Proc. H.F.C.*, 31, 1977, pp. 17–32.

44. J.M. Hodgson, 'The low-level Pleistocene marine sands and gravels of the West Sussex Coastal Plain', *Proceedings of the Geologists' Association*, LXXV, 1964, pp. 547–62; R.G. West and B.W. Sparks, 'Coastal Interglacial Deposits of the English Channel', *Philosophical Transactions of the Royal Society, Series B*, CCXLIII, 1960, pp. 95–133; F. Shephard-Thorn and G.A. Kellaway, 'Quaternary Deposits at Eartham, West Sussex', *Brighton Polytechnic Geographical Society Magazine*, IV, 1978, pp. 1–8.

45. G.A. Kellaway, J.H. Redding, E.R. Shephard Thorn, and J.P Destombes, 'The Quaternary history of the English Channel', *Philosophical Transactions of the Royal Society, Series A*, CCLXXIX, 1975, pp. 189–218.

46. West and Sparks, loc. cit., *passim*; R.C. Brown, D.D. Gilbertson,C.P. Green and D.H. Keen, 'Stratigraphy and environmental significance of Pleistocene deposits at Stone, Hampshire', *Proceedings of the Geologists' Association*, LXXXVI, 1975, pp. 349–63.

47. C. Reid, 'The Pleistocene deposits of the Sussex coast and their equivalents in other districts', *Quarterly Journal of the Geological Society*, XLVIII, 1892, pp. 344–64.

48. T. Codrington, 'On the superficial deposits of the south of Hampshire and the Isle of Wight', *Quarterly Journal of the Geological Society*, XXVI, 1870, pp. 528–51; J. Prestwich, 'The raised beaches and 'Head' or 'Rubble Drift' of the South of England', *Quarterly Journal of the Geological Society*, XLVIII, 1892, pp. 263–343.

49. D.H. Keen, 'Some aspects of the Pleistocene Succession in Areas Adjoining the English Channel', unpublished PhD thesis, University of London, 1975, pp. 83–132; D.H. Keen, 'The Environment of Deposition of South Hampshire Plateau Gravels', *Proc. H.F.C.*, 36, 1980, pp. 15–24.

50. M.L. Shackley, 'Preliminary Note on Handaxes Found in Gravel Deposits at Warsash, Hampshire', *Proc. H.F.C.*, 27, 1970, pp. 5–7; J.C. Draper, 'Mesolithic Distribution in South-East Hampshire', *Proc. H.F.C.*, 23, 1964, pp. 110–19; M.L. Shackley, 'Stream Abrasion of Flint Implements', *Nature*, CCXLV, 5 May 1974, pp. 501–2.

51. R.B.G. Williams, 'Some estimates of periglacial erosion in southern and eastern England', *Biuletyn Peryglacjalny*, XVII, 1968, pp. 311–335; 'The weathering and erosion of Chalk under periglacial conditions', in Jones, *The Shaping*, pp. 225–48.

52. C. Reid, 'On the origin of dry Chalk valleys and of Coombe rock', *Quarterly Journal of the Geological Society*, XXXIII, 1887, pp. 364–73; A.J. Bull, 'Cold conditions and landforms in the South Downs', *Proceedings of the Geologists' Association*, LI, 1940, pp. 63–71; R.J. Small, 'The role of spring sapping in the formation of Chalk escarpment valleys', *Southampton Research Series in Geography*, I, 1965, pp. 3–29; 'The origin of Rake Bottom, Butser Hill', *Proc. H.F.C.*, XXI, 1958, pp. 22–30; P. Gordon and R.A. Shakesby, 'Study of the Valley Infill, Rake Bottom, Butser Hill', *South Hampshire Geographer*, VI, 1973, pp. 10–20; C.A. Evans, 'Post-glacial environmental change, Gravelhill Bottom, Butser Hill', unpublished B.A. dissertation, Portsmouth Polytechnic, 1974.

53. H. Godwin, 'A submerged peat bed in Portmsouth Harbour. Data for the study of postglacial history', *New Phytologist*, XLIV, 1945, pp. 152–5; Mottershead, loc. cit., pp. 13–16.

54. D.D. Brumhead, 'The coast between Titchfield Haven and Lee-on-the-Solent', *Wessex Geographer*, IV, 1963, pp. 35–42.

55. D. Hodson, *Maps of Portsmouth before 1801*, Portfolio 1, *P.R.S.*, 4, Portsmouth, 1978, Maps Nos. 1, 6, 8 and 11.

56. D. Harlow, 'The littoral sediment budget between Selsey Bill and Gilkicker Point, and its relevance to coast protection works on Hayling Island', *Quarterly Journal of Engineering Geology*, XII, 1979, pp. 257–65; Anon, *West Winner Reclamation Feasibility Study*, 3 vols., Report to City of Portsmouth, Portsmouth, 1973; N.B. Webber and J.R. Davies, 'Research on Exceptional Sea-Levels in the Solent', *Dock and Harbour Authority*, LVII, 1976, pp. 232–3; B.J. Lonsdale, 'A sedimentary study of the eastern Solent', unpublished M.Sc. thesis, University of Southampton, 1970, pp. 20–2.

57. W.C.F. White, 'A gazetteer of brick and tile works in Hampshire', *Proc. H.F.C.*, 28, 1971, pp. 81–97. White, *Lymington and Portsmouth*, p. 10.

58. White, *Lymington and Portsmouth*, pp. 70–73.

59. W.C. Engledue, quoted in A. Temple Patterson, *Portsmouth: A History*, Bradford-on-Avon, 1976, pp. 114–15.

60. D. Halton Thomson, *The Hydrology of the Portsmouth District*, British Water-works Association Official Circular no. 81, 1929; 'Streams and Wells in the Portsmouth District', *Transactions of the Southeastern Union of Scientific Societies*, 1930, pp. 102–11.; *A History of the Portsmouth and Gosport Water Supply*, Portsmouth and Gosport Water Company, 1957; M.J. Hallett, *Portsmouth's*

Water Supply, 1800–1860, P.P. no. 12, Portsmouth, 1971; Anonymous, *A History of Portsmouth Drainage, 1865–1965*, Portsmouth, 1965.

61. J.B.W. Day, 'Infiltration into a groundwater catchment and the derivation of evaporation', *Water Supply Papers of the Geological Survey of Great Britain*, Research Report no. 2, D.S.I.R., 1964; D.N. Mottershead and G.E. Spraggs, 'An Introduction to the Hydrology of the Portsmouth Region', in (eds.) Mottershead and Riley, *Portsmouth Geographical Essays*, II, 1976, pp. 76–93.

62. T.C. Atkinson and D. Ingle Smith, 'Rapid groundwater flow in fissures within the Chalk: an example from south Hampshire', *Quarterly Journal of Engineering Geology*, VII, 1974, pp. 197–205.

63. Whitaker, *The Water Supply, passim*; D. Halton Thompson, 'A Further 20 Years Record of Rainfall and Water Levels in the Chalk at Chilgrove, West Sussex', *Journal of the Institution of Water Engineers*, XII, 1951, pp. 193–201.

64. A.T. Macdonald and W.J. Kenyon, 'Run-off of Chalk streams', *Proceedings of the Institute of Civil Engineers*, XIX, 1961, pp. 23–8.

65. Mottershead and Spraggs, in Mottershead and Riley, pp. 83–7.

66. Taitt and Kent, *Deep Boreholes, passim*; N.L. Falcon and P.E. Kent, 'Geological Results of Petroleum Exploration in Great Britain, 1945–1957', *Geological Society of London*, Memoir no. 2, 1960, pp. 8–9; Anonymous, 'Oil in Dorset', British Gas, 1980; Anonymous, *Prospectus of Marinex Petroleum Ltd.*, 1980.

67. Burgess et al., *The Marchwood Borehole, passim*; I.M. West, 'Geology of Hampshire in Relation to Petroleum Exploration', in *Offshore Oil Exploration and Development in Hampshire*, Proceedings of a Seminar held at Winchester on 3 October 1980, Winchester, 1980, pp. 17–20; D.J. Carter, 'The Search for Oil and Gas in Hampshire', *H.F.C. Newsletter of Geology Section*, no. 3, 1981, pp. 2–5.

CHAPTER 9 – CLIMATE, SOILS AND THE TERRESTRIAL FLORA AND FAUNA

1. For a more detailed account of climate and weather see R.G. Barry, 'Weather and Climate', in (ed.) F.J. Monkhouse, *A Survey of Southampton and Its Region*, Southampton 1964, pp. 73–92; S.J. Harrison, 'Local Climate of the Portsmouth Area', in (eds.) D.N. Mottershead and R.C. Riley, *Portsmouth Geographical Essays*, II, Portsmouth, 1976, pp. 51–65; (ed.) M. Batemen, *Atlas of Portsmouth*, Portsmouth, 1975, Section 2.1.

2. D.N. Mottershead, 'The Quaternary History of the Portsmouth Region', in (eds.) Mottershead and Riley, *Portsmouth Geographical Essays, II, Portsmouth*, 1976, pp. 1–21.

3. There is no detailed account of the soils of the Portsmouth region, but a full description of the similar soils of the West Sussex plain is contained in J.M. Hodgson, *Soils of the West Sussex Coastal Plain*, 1967.

4. D. Appleton, R. Dickson and G. Else, *The Insects of the Forest of Bere*, 1975.

5. S. Woodward, 'An investigation of small mammal populations in an area of woodland', unpublished undergraduate project, Portsmouth Polytechnic, 1982.

6. G. Ryle, *Forest Service*, 1969.

7. D.I. Morgan-Huws and F.R. Stranack, 'The Southwick Estate Woodlands – their present status and conservation potential', *Journal of the Portsmouth & District Natural History Society*, 3, no. 3, 1982, pp. 104–11.

8. J. Buchanan, *Ancient Woodland Survey Stage 2*, Nature Conservancy Council, South Region, 1978.

9. A.P.N. House, *Identification of woodlands of importance to nature conservation in South England. Stage 3. Field Surveys in Hampshire*, Nature Conservancy Council, South Region, 1979.

10. Appleton, Dickson and Else, *The Insects*, 1975.

11. W. Cobbett, *Rural Rides*, 1830.

12. F.R. Stranack, 'Wildlife conservation in the Agricultural environment', unpublished project report, University of Southampton, 1977.

13. A.G. Tansley, *The British Islands and their Vegetation*, Cambridge, 1949.

14. J.E. Chamberlain, *A natural history of the area*, Portsmouth City Museum, 1974.

CHAPTER 10 – THE AQUATIC FLORA AND FAUNA

1. D.J. Nicholls, C.R. Tubbs, and F.N. Haynes, 'The effect of green algal mats on intertidal macrobenthic communities and their predators,' *Kieler Meeresforschungen Sonderheft*, V, 1981, pp. 511–20.

2. (eds.) F.N. and B.D. Haynes, *Langstone Harbour Study: The effect of Sewage Effluent on the Ecology of the Harbour*, Portsmouth Polytechnic, 1976; S.L. Wright, 'The pollution load entering Southampton Water and the Solent' in *The Solent Estuarine System*, Natural Environment Research Council Publication, Series C, no. xxii, 1980, pp. 62–3; A.J. Phillips, 'Distribution of Chemical species' in ibid, pp. 44–61; N.B. Webber, 'Hydrography and Water Circulation in the Solent', in ibid, pp. 25–35.

3. P.J. Reay, and M.B. Culley, 'Fish and Fisheries in the Solent', in *The Solent Estuarine System*, 1980, pp. 86–91;*Langstone Harbour Study, passim.*

4. C.H. Thorp, 'The Benthos of the Solent', in *The Solent Estuarine System*, pp. 76–85.

5. Ibid; M.M. Foolad, 'Biology of certain macrofaunal invertebrates of aerobic and anaerobic muds in Langstone Harbour', unpublished PhD thesis, Portsmouth Polytechnic, 1983; P.S. Smith, and F.N. Haynes, *Macrofauna of Haslar Lake*, Portsmouth Polytechnic, 1985; Smith, Haynes and N.S. Thomas, *Macrofauna and their use as a food source by birds in Langstone Harbour*, Portsmouth Polytechnic, 1986; Haynes and A. Joyner, *Macrofauna of Tipner Lake*, Portsmouth Polytechnic, 1983; *Langstone Harbour Study, passim*; Nicholls, Tubbs and Haynes, *Kieler Meeresforsch.*, V, pp. 511–20.

6. *Langstone Harbour Study, passim*; E.G.B. Jones, 'Marine micro-organism and seaweed in the Solent', in *The Solent Estuarine System*, pp. 64–72.

7. C.R. Tubbs, and J.M. Tubbs, 'The distribution of Zostera and its exploitation by wildfowl in the Solent, Southern England', *Aquatic Botany*, 15, 1983, pp. 223–48.

8. (eds.) F.R. Stranack and J. Coughlan, *Spartina in the Solent.*

9. F.N. Haynes, 'Spartina in Langstone Harbour, Hampshire', in *Spartina anglica in Great Britain*, Focus on Nature Conservation no. 5, Nature Conservancy, Shrewsbury, 1983, pp. 5–10; F.N. Haynes, and M.G. Coulson, 'The decline of Spartina in Langstone Harbour, Hampshire', *Proc. H.C.F.*, 38, 1981, pp. 5–18.

10. I. Hepburn, *Flowers of the Coast*, 1952, *passim.*

11. M. Bryant, 'The flora of Langstone Harbour and Farlington Marshes', *Proc. H.F.C.*, 24, 1967.

12. C.R. Tubbs, 'Wildfowl and waders in Langstone Harbour', *British Birds*, 20, 1977, pp. 177–99; Tubbs, 'Processes and Impacts in the Solent' in *The Solent Estuarine System*, pp. 1–5; Tubbs, 'Bird populations in the Solent 1951– 1977', ibid, pp. 92–100; Tubbs, and J.M. Tubbs, 'Wader and Shelduck Feeding distribution in Langstone Harbour, Hampshire', *Bird Study*, 27, 1980, pp. 239–48.

13. A.J. Prater, 'Distribution of coastal waders in Europe and North Africa', *Proc., International Conference on Conservation of Wetland Wildfowl*, Hertigenhaten, 1974.

14. R. Seymour, *River management and keepering*, 1970.

TWENTIETH-CENTURY PORTSMOUTH

CHAPTER 11 – THE TWENTIETH-CENTURY ECONOMY

1. This dominance was no new phenomenon as can be seen from the discussion in the chapter on the nineteenth century.

2. Extensive references to the changes taking place in the dockyard are to be found in I.E. King, *Forty Years of Change at Portsmouth Dockyard*, paper read to the Institution of Naval Architects April 1955, copies of which are in the Portsmouth and Gosport branches of Hants County Library.

3. Details of the wartime activity can be found in W.G. Gates, *Portsmouth and the Great War*, Portsmouth, 1919.

4. F. Groves, 'The British Navy of Today', in *National Union of Teachers Conference Souvenir*, 1926, p. 81.

5. A wealth of factual detail on shipbuilding and employment levels is contained in F.N.G. Thomas, Portsmouth and Gosport: A Study in the Historical Geography of a Naval Port, unpublished M.Sc. thesis, London University, 1961.

6. King, op cit., p. 6.

7. Gosport Public Library, 'The Gosport Aircraft Company', (typescript notes), undated.

8. *Portsmouth Evening News*, 16 Jan. 1922.

9. R. Venables, 'OEC Lees Lane', *Gosport Records*, No. 6, 1973.

10. L.F.W. White, *The Story of Gosport*, undated. See also Lesley Burton, 'Gosport's Yachting Heyday', *Gosport Records*, No. 7, 1973, pp. 23–27.

11. J. Palmer, *John Palmer Ltd.*, undated.

12. Portsmouth Central Library, D.H. Middleton, 'Ashes to Ashes', cyclostyled MS.

13. For details of the City of Portsmouth expansion policies see G.J. Ashworth, 'Planning, the Economy and the Environment', in (ed.) R. Windle, *Records of the Corporation 1966–74*, Portsmouth, undated.

14. F.H.W. Green, *Hampshire*, (Part 89 of 'The Land of Britain) 1940, p. 139. See also L.G. Troup, 'Chalkland Farming in Hampshire', *Journal of the Royal Agricultural Society*, 92, 1931, pp. 183–200.

15. C.J. Gleed, 'The Strawberry Industry of South Hampshire', ibid, pp. 201–13.

16. F.H.W. Green, op cit., p. 348.

17. For the early history of the Society see J.H. Mihell, *A Record of the Formation, Progress and Present Position of the Portsea Island Mutual Co-operative Society*, Portsmouth, undated.

18. *National Union of Teachers Conference Souvenir*, 1937; See also (eds.) J.E. Nichol and A.H. Summers, *British Association Handbook to Portsmouth*, 1911.

19. L.F.W. White, op cit., p. 168.

20. A.F. Milton and L.T.A. Bern, *Portsmouth City Transport 1840–1977*, Leigh Park, 1977.

21. M. Lock, *Outline Plan for the Portsmouth District*, 1949.

22. Gosport Public Library, Anonymous, *The Development of Lee-on-the-Solent (Lee Brittain)*.

23. British Medical Association, *The Book of Portsmouth*, Portsmouth, 1923.

24. A.M. Fraser, 'Municipal Health Services', in ibid, p. 163.

25. *The South-East Study*, 1964.

CHAPTER 12 – LEISURE AND CULTURE

1. (ed.) H.T. Lilley, *Guide to Portsmouth, Southsea and Neighbourhood*, Portsmouth, 1899.

2. (ed.) W.P. Watkins, *Southsea and Portsmouth at a Glance – Official Guide 1908*, Portsmouth, 1908.

3. For Matcham's connections with the Portsmouth theatres, see B. Walker, *Frank Matcham, Theatre Architect*, Belfast, 1980.

4. (ed.) W.G. Gates, *City of Portsmouth Records of the Corporation 1835–1927*, Portsmouth, 1928.

5. F.W. Lipscomb, *Heritage of Sea Power*, 1967, p. 210.

6. The rôle and constitutions of the various committees are described in S. Peacock, *Borough Government in Portsmouth 1835–1974*, P.P. no. 23, Portsmouth, 1975.

7. H. Sargeant, *A History of Portsmouth Theatres*, P.P. no. 13, Portsmouth, 1971.

8. R. Barker et al., *Cinemas of Portsmouth*, Horndean, 1981.

9. R. Esmond, *Portsmouth Not So Old*, Portsmouth, 1961, p. 58.

10. S.E. Harrison, *The Tramways of Portsmouth*, 1963; for a description of an Easter fair on Portsdown, see Esmond, *Portsmouth Not So Old*, pp. 78–82.

11. *Portsmouth Evening News*, 12 May 1891; 14 Dec. 1962.

12. W. Curtis, *Southsea, its story*, Alresford, 1978, pp. 37, 40.

13. Esmond, *Portsmouth Not So Old*, p. 87.

14. See Esmond, above, Chapter 10, for a description of Saturday evenings in Charlotte Street, and pp. 5–9, 16–18 for street games in Queen Street, Portsea. See also F.J. Proctor, *Reminiscences of Old Portsmouth*, Portsmouth, 1931, for children's pastimes.

15. Portsmouth Football Club *Golden Jubilee 1898–1948 Official Handbook*.

16. W.G. Gates, *Portsmouth and the Great War*, Portsmouth, 1919, pp. 37–8; A. Temple-Patterson, *Portsmouth, a history*, Bradford-on-Avon, 1976, pp. 136–7. Lipscomb, *Heritage of Sea Power*, pp. 211–13.

17. Only one Zeppelin ventured over the town, on the night of 25 Sept. 1916. It dropped four bombs, harmlessly, into the harbour.

18. Curtis, *Southsea*, p. 49; Lipscomb, *Heritage of Sea Power*, p. 215; Temple-Patterson, *Portsmouth*, pp. 137–8.

19. *Hampshire Telegraph*, 13 April 1928; *Evening News*, 27 Aug. 1971, 18 July 1973.

20. The Princes Theatre was converted into a cinema in 1924.

21. The Southsea Light Orchestra consisted entirely of unemployed musicians whose first concert took place on the South Parade Pier in a dreadful storm and with practically no audience. *Evening News*, 24 Nov. 1938.

22. For a description of popular leisure activities in Portsmouth between the wars see the many small booklets published by the W.E.A. Local History Group including: *Going to Work in Portsmouth*, Portsmouth, 1981; F. Ford, *Childhood Memories*, Portsmouth, 1980; *Memories of Arundel Street*, Portsmouth, 1980; and also G.H. Dunbar, *As I saw it*, Portsmouth, 1980.

23. See R. Barker, *The Schneider Trophy Races*, 1971, and D. James, *Schneider Trophy Aircraft*, 1981.

24. *The Book of Portsmouth*, Portsmouth, 1923, has an excellent chapter on Portsmouth sports by the Revd Bruce Cornford, vicar of St Matthew's, Southsea.

25. *Portsmouth Airport Opening Pageant Souvenir Programme*, 1932.

26. For a description of children's pastimes see W. Greer, *A Pompey Boy in the 30s and 40s*, Portsmouth, 1981.

27. The Royal Counties Agricultural Show came to Portsmouth in 1871, 1880, 1891, 1906, 1914, 1925, 1931, 1939, 1953 and 1959. The first and third shows were at the future Victoria Park site and North End Recreation Ground respectively, but all others were on Southsea Common.

28. See *Smitten City – the story of Portsmouth in the air raids 1940–44*, Portsmouth, 1944.

29. The Municipal Concerts were organised for the Libraries, Museums and Arts Committee and the Council for the Encouragement of Music and the Arts (CEMA) principally by two city officers – the City Librarian & Curator, Harry Sargeant, and the South Parade Pier Box Office Manager, Alex Kinnear. Harry Sargeant was also a founder in 1945 of the Little Theatre, later Arts Theatre, and during his term as Librarian until 1967 he was instrumental in providing much encouragement and support to the arts in the city, using the Central Library as a headquarters, booking office and property store.

30. City of Portsmouth *Council Minutes*, 13 July 1943.

31. The Southsea Shakespeare Actors set a unique record in 1966 when they became the only amateur company under an amateur director (K. Edmonds Gateley) to have performed the entire Shakespeare canon.

32. E. Fraser, *The Story of the Portsmouth Museums Society*, Portsmouth, 1977. The post of City Archivist was made full-time in 1960.

33. *Duisburg-Portsmouth Friendship 20th Anniversary Booklet*, 1970, Portsmouth P.L.

34. (ed.) V. Blanchard, *Records of the Corporation 1956–65*, Portsmouth, 1971.

35. Blanchard, *Records of the Corporation 1956–65*.

36. These included: B. Masters, *Portsmouth Through the Centuries*, 1964; A. Corney, *Fortifications in Old Portsmouth*, 1965, and *Southsea Castle*, 1967; and *Portsmouth, a Guide to Places of Historic Interest*, 1968.

37. The major local musical, dramatic, literary and historical societies, with dates of inception, functioning in 1987 are: Drama: Arts Theatre (1945), Phoenix Players (1953), Portsmouth Players (1926), Polytechnic Dramatic & Musical Society (1921), Southsea Shakespeare Actors (1947), Hornpipe Arts Centre (1984). Music: Portsmouth Choral Union (1880), Milton Glee Club (1948), Portsmouth Glee Club (1930), Portsmouth Music Club (1942), Portsmouth Baroque choir (ex-Drayton Choral Society, 1952). Other: Dickens Fellowship (1906), Museums Society (1952), Film

Society (1936), Portsmouth Society (1973), Poetry Society (1971), Friends of City Records Office (1975), Historical Association (. . . .).

CHAPTER 13 – POST-WAR DEVELOPMENTS

1. Census 1961 and 1971.

2. Social Science Research and Intelligence Unit (SSRIU) Population Mobility in Portsmouth, 23 Jan. 1974.

3. This figure excludes Bournemouth which was part of Hampshire in 1971, and had a density of 13.4 persons per acre.

4. SSRIU Households: Portsmouth and Neighbouring Areas, October 1973. Overcrowding is measured in terms of persons per room without taking room size into account: one to one and a half persons per room is considered as overcrowding and more than one and a half persons per room is severe overcrowding. It is, however, a crude indicator only.

5. Portsmouth City Council Minutes 312; 360/1969; 196/1970; see (ed.) R. Windle, *Records of Portsmouth Corporation 1966–1974*, no date, pp. 28 and 142.

6. Portsmouth City Council Minutes 337/1966; 1213/1966; Booklet – Objectives and Proposals of the City Council, July 1973.

7. Portsmouth Housing Committee Minutes 1974 and Housing Department Records.

8. Notes on Portsmouth Main Drainage, 1965, 1975, City Engineers Department.

9. Portsmouth City Council Minutes 1317/1966.

10. Portsmouth City Council Minutes 84, 756 and 997/1969; 487–632/1970; 567/1973.

11. It is interesting to note that by 1971 the coefficient of industrial specialisation (used in the census) for Portsmouth was 31.4. The coefficient varies from a maximum of 100, which indicates maximum specialisation, to a lower limit, which depends on the number of categories used and a figure of 31.4 indicated substantial diversification of the city's economy. (The lower limit, for the 1971 census, of the Standard Industrial Classification for the 27 classes used was 19.2.)

12. (ed.) R. Windle, *Records of Portsmouth Corporation 1966–1974*, pp. 64–7 provides an outline of the development of the Polytechnic.

13. Registrar General's Statistical Review for England and Wales 1961–1972 and Hampshire County Council Medical Department 1973.

14. Solent Sailing Conference papers, Winchester 1972.

15. City of Portsmouth Secretariat paper – 'Vandalism', 1975.

16. Portsmouth City Council Minute 974/1970: see *Records of Portsmouth Corporation 1966–1974*, p. 76.

17. City Council Minutes 536/1972; 379/1973; 10 and 80/1974.

18. City of Portsmouth, Report of Working Party on Development of Portsmouth and Southsea as a Holiday Resort and Centre of Recreation, 1973.

19. *Records of Portsmouth Corporation 1966–1974*. The chapters, 'The Reorganisation of Local Government' and 'Politics and Administration' contain detailed analyses of the composition, function and role of the City Council before and after April 1974.

CHAPTER 14 – PORTSMOUTH – RETROSPECT AND PROSPECT

1. See Chapter I, p. 11.

2. Ibid, pp. 5–6.

3. See Chapter 4, p. 50.

4. B.L. Harleian, MS. 595 ff. 237–9.

5. A.T. Patterson, *'Palmerston's Folly': The Portsdown and Spithead Forts*, P.P. no. 3, Portsmouth, 1968.

6. C.R. Tubbs, *Langstone Harbour: A Review of its Ecology and Conservation Objectives*, 1975.

7. P.E. Lloyd and C.M. Mason, 'Spatial Variations in New Firm Formation in the UK. Comparative Evidence from Merseyside, Greater Manchester and South Hampshire', *Regional Studies*, 18, 1984, pp. 207–20.

8. S. Brettell and D. Robinson, 'Local Economic Outlook', *Portsmouth Local Economy Bulletin*, Portsmouth, 1986, p. 8.

9. C. Mason, 'New Firms and Economic Development: A Case of Excessive Expectations', *Portsmouth Local Economy Bulletin*, 3, Portsmouth, 1987, p. 5.

10. For projected output and employment prospects to 1990 see *Portsmouth Local Economy Bulletin*, 1, 1986, pp. 8–9; 2, 1986, p. 9; 3, 1987, pp. 3–4; 4,1987, pp. 4–5. Banking and finance includes insurance and real estate services; distribution includes hotels, catering and public houses; miscellaneous services include public administration and domestic service.

INDEX

259